Ethnographic Encounters in
Southern Mesoamerica

Studies on Culture and Society
Edited by Richard M. Leventhal and J. Jorge Klor de Alva

ETHNOGRAPHIC ENCOUNTERS IN SOUTHERN MESOAMERICA: ESSAYS IN HONOR OF EVON ZARTMAN VOGT, JR.

Edited by
Victoria R. Bricker and *Gary H. Gossen*

Studies on Culture and Society
Volume 3

Institute for Mesoamerican Studies
The University at Albany
State University of New York

Distributed by
University of Texas Press

For submission of manuscripts address the publisher:
Institute for Mesoamerican Studies
The University at Albany
State University of New York
Albany, New York 12222

For copies address the distributor:
University of Texas Press
Post Office Box 7819
Austin, Texas 78713-7819

Cover: *Expulsion of the Protestant Converts from San Juan Chamula*. Original drawing by Marian López Calixto of San Juan Chamula, Chiapas. Commissioned by Gary H. Gossen as an illustration for a text on the subject of the Chamula Protestant movement. (See related article by Gary H. Gossen in this volume.)

Library of Congress Catalog Card Number: 89-80221
ISBN: 0-942041-12-7
Printed in the United States of America

Evon Zartman Vogt, Jr.

TABLE OF CONTENTS

PREFACE

The importance of offering a volume of essays in honor of Evon Z. Vogt has been latent in the consciousness of many of us over the past few years. Our intellectual and personal debts to him are not easily forgotten. With Vogtie's retirement in sight, and the retirement dinner scheduled, it seemed that the optimal moment for a gesture of appreciation and celebration was upon us. With this in mind, a group of us—Frank Cancian, George and Jane Collier, John Haviland, Robert Laughlin, Frank Miller, Victoria Bricker, and Gary Gossen— consulted in the fall of 1987. We were able, with the willing complicity of Nan Vogt, who agreed to keep these plans a secret from Vogtie, to contact a large network of Vogtie's students, colleagues, and friends. Those who are represented in this volume committed themselves to contributing previously unpublished essays that would in some way (anecdotal, ethnographic, comparative, or historical) bear witness to Vogtie's eclectic intellect and lifelong concern for the ethnographic documentation of cultural change and continuity in the United States Southwest and, primarily, in Southern Mesoamerica.

We wish to express our thanks to Nan Vogt and to Gordon Willey, who served as willing intermediaries in securing and checking necessary biographical and bibliographical data for this project. Finally, we express our deep gratitude to Richard Leventhal and Jorge Klor de Alva, officers of the University at Albany's Institute for Mesoamerican Studies, for their splendid cooperation in facilitating the timely publication of this volume.

Gary H. Gossen
University at Albany, SUNY
Victoria R. Bricker
Tulane University

INTRODUCTION

Gary H. Gossen
University at Albany, SUNY

Victoria R. Bricker
Tulane University

This volume celebrates the extraordinary contribution of Evon Zartman Vogt, Jr.—known to all of us as Vogtie—to social science in the twentieth century. It would be a mistake to limit these introductory remarks to Vogtie's contribution to anthropology, for eclecticism and interdisciplinary dialogue have been hallmarks of his career. Indeed, the Harvard Chiapas Project—in its remarkable thirty-year life history that spans two generations—has provided first-hand field experience in traditional societies for literally hundreds of individuals of diverse backgrounds. It is also the case that the Harvard project has provided substantial glimpses of United States life and culture for a number of Zinacantecos and Chamulas who have had the opportunity to visit this country. Therefore, in considering the careers that have been formed and enriched through Vogtie's inspiration and generosity, we find that anthropologists are but some of the individuals whose lives Vogtie has touched. These include Zinacanteco and Chamula politicians and corn farmers, Mexican mestizo professionals and business people, physicians and psychologists, linguists and sociologists, journalists and novelists, as well as to a surprising mosaic of anthropologists. All of us have known him as a warm and supportive friend, and through him, our lives and work have changed in ways both small and great.

With regard to Vogtie's engagement with anthropology and anthropologists, the patterns of eclecticism and pragmatism emerge as dominant themes in his personal and intellectual style. We recall a favorite phrase that Vogtie would often use in helping students and colleagues to sort out some enigma in the interpretation of data or to pick up the pieces after some setback, missed appointment, or large-scale disaster in the field. He would invariably produce a *refresco* or a beer and speak of the importance of "rolling flexibility." Roughly interpreted, this means "there are lots of ways to achieve the same end." This was intended, of course, as a pragmatic philosophy of problem-solving in the field. However, this key phrase may also offer a microcosmic "encapsulation" of Vogtie's own worldview. What does "rolling flexibility" mean as a leitmotif in a long, influential, and productive career?

A glimpse at the table of contents of this volume—a cross section of the scholarship that Vogtie has inspired—will show that he was never, and is not today, a dogmatic advocate of any particular paradigm or approach. Indeed, he has responded with imagination and data-rich analyses to several of the major

1

paradigms and approaches in the history of twentieth-century British, American, and French anthropology. Throughout the thirty years of the Harvard Chiapas Project and even before, in the period when Vogtie worked on the Ramah Project of comparative ethnography of the United States Southwest, he has been an eclectic, providing New World data sets for some of the great ideas of our time. From the Chicago years, Vogtie worked within the framework of controlled comparison (Eggan 1954), producing significant works in the context of the Ramah Project, the goal of which was to assess the role of culture in establishing various adaptations (Pueblo Indian, Navajo, Mormon, Hispanic, and Anglo-Texan) to a relatively homogeneous southwestern physical ecology (Vogt 1955a; Vogt and Albert 1966). From the Harvard project years come major responses to some of the great issues and paradigms of the mid-twentieth century; notably, the theoretical and methodological issues of continuity and change (Vogt n.d., 1964d, 1965a); community studies, to which Vogtie contributed his *magnum opus* on Zinacanteco ethnography (1969b); structural analysis (Vogt and Vogt 1970); and symbolic analysis (1976). Other consistent and pervading themes of his work have been ritual and religion. He has written dozens of papers and several books on these topics, beginning with *Water Witching U.S.A.* (Vogt and Hyman 1959). His *Reader in Comparative Religion: An Anthropological Approach*, co-edited with William Lessa (Lessa and Vogt 1958; now in its fourth edition), has, for more than a quarter of a century, provided a cross-cultural perspective, both classic and contemporary, of the variety of religious beliefs and experiences. It is truly noteworthy that his insights on the subject have been drawn from both United States data and popular culture (his new manuscript "Saints and Superstars: Ritual and Modern Life") and from his better known studies that are based on highland Chiapas data.

While Vogtie's own topical and theoretical inclinations have been apparent to each new cohort of graduate students who have worked with him, he has never expected us to follow a particular methodology or theoretical persuasion as a condition for his help and support. Indeed, he has consistently urged us to reconsider theoretical orientations that don't seem to be working as first premises. He makes a practice of this very reassessment process in his own intellectual style. With such a substantial respect for pragmatism, Vogtie has always been extraordinarily willing to listen to and to learn from others. The Harvard Chiapas Project, from its beginning in 1957 to the present, has been just such a dialogue. Disciplinary labels, professions, and epistemological premises have never limited Vogtie's listening and reading. In fact, intellectual diversity is the very essence of Vogtie's style; it guides not only his thinking, but also the company he keeps.

Consider the lot of us who are gathered here to celebrate Vogtie as scholar, mentor, and colleague. Among us are practitioners of a broad spectrum of approaches in the humanities and social sciences. If one were to analyze this group to locate a common denominator that would identify Vogtie's "school," the results would undoubtedly be inconclusive. What truly emerges as a continuing theme in his own work and that of his students is the primacy of the ethnographic archive itself, of field data set down with such fidelity, quantity, and detail that they provide in themselves the source for corroboration or disconfirmation of the analysis proffered. In this sense, theory per se has never held primacy in Vogtie's worldview. He has, rather, been concerned with overseeing the compilation of an ethnographic archive of the Tzotzil peoples of the Chiapas highlands that is, by our reckoning, without parallel in the social anthropology of twentieth-century Latin America. From linguistics to domestic architecture, from metaphysics to kinship terminology, from ethnohistory to the technology of weaving, from archaeological applications of ethnographic analogy to stimulating dialogue with epigraphers, the Tzotzil region of Mexico represents, in the world ethnographic archive, a comprehensive data base comparable to that of the Pacific Northwest of North America, or the southern Nilotic region of Africa, or the Trobriand Islands.

By direct extension, this suggests that Evon Z. Vogt has created the infrastructure, trained the personnel, and provided the comprehensive published record of research that place him in the league with Franz Boas, E.E. Evans-Pritchard, and Bronislaw Malinowski. Indeed, Zinacantán has become a standard world benchmark in cross-cultural studies, and Evon Z. Vogt is indelibly attached to the place, as surely as Boas is attached to the Kwakiutl, Evans-Pritchard to the Nuer, or Malinowski to the Trobriand Islands. Of this select circle of ethnographic luminaries, we believe that Vogtie is perhaps most similar to Franz Boas in that the goals of the Harvard Chiapas Project parallel in striking ways Boas's ambitious research agenda in the Pacific Northwest. Vogtie's goal in founding the Harvard Chiapas Project, inspired by his vision of a basic macro-Maya cultural persistence within Greater Mesoamerica, was to create an ongoing ethnographic archive of culture change in the Chiapas highlands. This phenomenon of continuing cultural integrity that is nevertheless able to adapt to rapidly changing regional political and economic realities is to be understood through what he now calls a "phylogenetic model" (1964d and n.d.). Franz Boas had a similar agenda in mind as he organized the Jesup North Pacific Expedition, seeking primarily the history and relationships of the cultures of the Greater Pacific Northwest, including the Siberian Coast (Freed et al. 1988:9). In concept and scope, as well as in the large-scale funding and international cooperation necessary for its realization, there are even more similarities between Boas's role as the linchpin in the Jesup Expedition and Vogtie's founding and sustaining role in the Harvard Chiapas Project. Along with the similarities in grandeur of conception and the vast production of ethnographic and linguistic archival material must be added the recruitment of "an extraordinarily diverse and fascinating staff" (Freed et al. 1988:9). It is awkward and presumptuous to attach such flattering language to ourselves and the present collaborators who have shared the Chiapas experience, but surely we are "extraordinarily diverse."

The Harvard project, like the Jesup Expedition, required many talents and substantial international cooperation. It was never a party-line endeavor, neither in theory, style of ethnography, nor mode of reporting. All of us were welcome to bring our own intellectual predispositions and skills to bear on the problems of continuity and change in Tzotzil and Tzeltal communities as these groups have dealt with the forces of accelerating change in the latter half of the twentieth century. We were asked only to work hard, preferably in the native languages, homes, and fields, and to make our field notes available to the general archive of the Harvard project.

Vogtie's own catholic vision of anthropology, together with the extraordinary warmth and hospitality that he and Nan provided at the Harvard Ranch, brought an odd lot of us—with extraordinarily diverse styles and backgrounds—together as a community. Many Tzotzils, Tzeltals, and *ladinos* belong to this community, just as we belong, in various manners and degrees, to their communities. The binding agent has always been dialogue and ethnographic encounter. Even away from Chiapas, we belong to a dispersed community of cooperative scholarship and common interests. Nevertheless, we remain a heterogeneous lot. There are among us novelists and poets, ethnohistorians and folklorists, linguists and statisticians, philosophers and psychologists, ecologists and economists, photographers and painters, materialists and idealists. Vogtie has given to all of us, generously. Yet his own respect for intellectual integrity and autonomy has never bound any of us to a particular point of view. Again, we come to eclecticism, and again, the similarity of certain of Vogtie's characteristics to those of Franz Boas comes to mind. Boas never sought a group of students and colleagues who were clones of himself. We know, rather, that his students became advocates of diverse strains of what was to become the heterogeneous texture of American anthropology in the mid-twentieth century. In a similar manner, Vogtie's students have come to occupy intellectual positions that span a broad spectrum of American anthropology in the late twentieth century.

The Harvard Chiapas Project has also enjoyed a number of cooperative institutional links with Mexican federal and state agencies with regard to *indigenista* research. Indeed, the Instituto Nacional Indigenista provided some of the earliest infrastructure for the project (a small house in a hamlet of Zinacantán) when it first began in the early 1960s. Vogtie's works and those of many of his students have in fact appeared in Spanish translation in various monograph series and journals that are supported by the Mexican government. These cooperative links were recognized in the great honor that Vogtie received in 1978, when he was decorated Knight Commander, Order of the Aztec Eagle, Republic of Mexico, for distinguished service to Mexican *indigenista* research.

It is surely worth noting that the Harvard Chiapas Project has made a major contribution to the lives and careers of many of the individuals of San Lorenzo Zinacantán and San Juan Chamula who have been associated with it. As the autobiographical accounts of three Zinacantecos (translated by Robert Laughlin) and one Chamula (translated by John Haviland) in this volume testify, Vogtie's project taught them the value of literacy in Tzotzil and Spanish and provided them with skills in language instruction, ethnographic description, tape-recording and transcription, and typing. Not mentioned by them, but probably equally valuable, were the heightened self-esteem and the skills they developed in dealing with outsiders, which several of them have put to good use on behalf of their native communities. The project counts among its Tzotzil associates two men who later became chief magistrates (*presidente municipal*), one in Chamula and the other in Zinacantán. They and others among the Tzotzil contributors to this volume have been involved in local literacy programs and efforts to bring roads and cooperatives to their townships. What is striking about the careers of these men is that the project provided the skills, but not the agenda. Each man had his own unstated objectives for availing himself of the opportunities presented by Vogtie and his students in such a way as to better his own life and brighten the future of his community.

The photo essay by Frank Cancian honors two Zinacantecos who freely gave of their time in support of the project. Juan Vásquez was the elder statesman and shaman to whom many anthropologists turned for insights on the political history and religious customs of Zinacantán. For many anthropologists, an interview with Domingo de la Torre or a brief sojourn in his home was their first introduction to life in Zinacantán.

In the next essay, Susan Tax Freeman shares with us her field notes from the summer of 1959 and gives us some personal glimpses of what it was like to be a student of Vogtie's in the field during the early years of the Chiapas Project. Frank Miller's essay rounds out that picture further, noting that Vogtie's skills as a horseman, acquired from his early life in the Southwest (Nan Vogt, this volume), served him in good stead in the rugged mountains of central Chiapas.

Miller's essay and the essays by George Collier and the Prices share a theme of generational transformations, namely the very different political, economic, and intellectual adaptations that have been made by two generations of Huistecos, Zinacantecos, and Harvard anthropologists. They represent the fulfillment of one of Vogtie's long-term goals for the Harvard Chiapas Project—the controlled study of cultural continuity and change in a single region. From this perspective we learn that neither the Tzotzils nor the anthropologists who have studied them have been unresponsive to the great political and economic forces that have engulfed highland Chiapas during the past ten years. The historical perspective taken by these five students of Vogtie's has changed our understanding of the time depth of "traditional" economic and political behavior in the Tzotzil sector of Chiapas.

The next essay, by Thomas Crump, examines the relationship between fiscal systems and local political autonomy in several Tzotzil and Tzeltal communities. It exemplifies the principle of controlled cross-cultural comparison (Eggan 1954) that Vogtie envisioned as one of the goals of the Harvard Chiapas Project.

Two members of the Harvard project, Jane Collier and Carol Greenhouse, made studies of Zinacanteco law before going on to investigate legal systems in other parts of the world. In her contribution to this volume, Collier compares and contrasts American and Zinacanteco stories of conflict and shows that the differences can be summarized as a contrast between "whodunits" and "whydunits." Greenhouse's essay, which is also about the American legal system, uses Vogtie's (1955a) analysis of the value system of the "Home-steaders" of New Mexico as the point of departure for her essay on cultural and legal pluralism in the United States.

The Harvard Chiapas Project counts among its members several students who went on to become professional psychologists. They include Carolyn Pope Edwards, Patricia Greenfield, and Carla Childs, who are represented by the next two essays. Edwards looks back at her undergraduate field experiences in Zinacantán and wrestles with a problem that she was unprepared to deal with at the time, namely how to explain the difficult transition from infancy to early childhood that she recorded in her field notes in 1968 and 1969. The other two psychologists have teamed up with noted pediatrician, Berry Brazelton, to produce a remarkable synthesis of more than two decades of research on infant and child motor and cognitive development in Zinacantán.

The issues of Tzotzil life history and concepts of self are cast against a backdrop of accelerating social change in the essay by Gary Gossen. This paper presents the biography of a recently assassinated Tzotzil Protestant leader, whose life brought him into fatal conflict with both the traditional and modern worlds of Chiapas.

Vogtie has always had a special interest in ritual and concepts of the soul, and the next four essays address these concerns. In the first, Victoria Bricker teases out the pre-Columbian meanings that underlie Carnival rituals in modern Chamula. The relationships between and among souls, selves, and social iden-tity are explored for Chamula by Priscilla Rachun Linn in the second essay and for Zinacantán and Santiago Chimaltenango (in the western highlands of Guatemala) by John Watanabe in the third. The fourth, and last, essay on religion, by Nicholas Colby, is concerned with divination, comparing the cognitive aspects of this practice among the Ixils of northwestern Guatemala and the ancient Greeks and Chinese.

Linnéa Holmer Wren, an art historian, was associated with the Harvard Chiapas Project during her undergraduate years at Radcliffe. Her contribution to this volume is an essay on representations of the Maya ballgame in the art of Chichén Itzá.

Jerome Levi, one of Vogtie's most recent students, has conducted fieldwork in both the highlands of Chiapas and the Sierra Tarahumara of northern Mexico. He offers an essay comparing the social ecology of these two regions.

Finally, this volume honors Vogtie, not just as a scholar and a teacher, but also as a person. The essays by Nan Vogt, Fred Eggan, and Gordon Willey tell us about the formative experiences in New Mexico and at the University of Chicago and Harvard that led to his decision to undertake research in highland Chiapas, the objectives he chose for the project, and his belief that ethnographic training was more effective when it took place in the field, rather than in the classroom. All of us who have worked with Vogtie as students and colleagues have benefited from his vision and wisdom. These essays are expressions of our appreciation for the many ways he has enriched our personal and professional lives.

EVON ZARTMAN VOGT, JR.

Nan Vogt

Evon Zartman Vogt, Jr. was born on August 20, 1918, in St. Mary's Hospital, Gallup, New Mexico, the oldest living child and only son of Evon Zartman Vogt, sheep rancher, and his wife, Shirley Bergman Vogt. A daughter, Shirley Ann, had died at the age of eighteen months from spinal meningitis a few months before. Vogtie and his three younger sisters, Barbara, Jo Ann, and Patti, were reared in the family ranch house near Ramah, New Mexico, and attended the town school with mainly Mormon schoolmates. Their nearest neighbors were Navajos and the sheep herders, who were what we then called Spanish-Americans, who lived in small settlements nearby and were employed by Vogtie's father, manager of a large sheep company. Zuni Indians lived six miles west in one of their farming villages—the pueblo itself was twenty miles beyond—and interspersed in the area at various distances were Anglo ranchers and bean farmers. It was a richly diverse community of cultures that surrounded the family ranch.

Evon Z. Vogt, Sr. was born and grew up in Dayton, Ohio, and attended the University of Chicago. He contracted tuberculosis in his senior year and traveled west to New Mexico to recover in 1905. He engaged in various enterprises in and around Albuquerque and Santa Fe, saved money, and traveled to Europe in 1914. He was in Paris when the war broke out and had difficulties getting out of France because of his German name. On his way back to New Mexico he stopped in Chicago to visit his older brother, Charles, who had married a widow with two grown daughters. Katherine Martin Bergman Vogt's daughters were Dorothy and Shirley, and young Shirley caught Evon's eye. They were married July 17, 1915, in Chicago and honeymooned in the Pecos Mountains near Santa Fe, New Mexico. They took the train to Gallup and went by horse and wagon to the ranch house Evon had built with rocks from Indian ruins on property he had homesteaded near Ramah. An upright piano was among the trunks and household articles that accompanied them from Chicago!

Daddy Vogt was a jolly, gregarious man who spoke French, German, and Spanish, as well as some Zuni and Navajo. He enjoyed having visitors at the ranch, whether nearby Indians or other neighbors stopping for a few minutes or hours, or his University of Chicago Delta Upsilon fraternity brothers and their families for a week or more. Shirley Vogt was a meticulous housekeeper, excellent cook, and accomplished seamstress with a fine sense of style. She made most of her own wardrobe, as well as those of her three daughters, and was a good hostess who made her guests feel welcome, comfortable, and entertained.

Among the many people who spent time at the ranch was Clyde Kay Maben

Kluckhohn, who came to the Southwest to recover from rheumatic fever in the mid-1920s. His adoptive mother, Mrs. George Kluckhohn, had arranged for him to spend time with her cousin, Shirley Vogt, and family in the sunshine and fresh air of the pinyon, juniper, and pine covered mesa country. It was then that Vogtie first met Clyde, and Clyde became interested in the area and its many cultural groups, which were to become his research focus later.

Shirley had taken to western ranch life amazingly well, despite her city rearing in Chicago. She learned to ride horseback on the honeymoon pack trip in the Pecos Mountains and continued to ride until the age of eighty. The family enjoyed picnics, pack trips, and hikes in the surrounding mesa country, and swimming in the summer and ice skating in the winter on the Ramah reservoir.

Until the age of fourteen, Vogtie had been expected to take over management of the sheep ranch and spent much time during school vacations helping with lambing, dipping, shearing, and herding. He has often said he found the herding boring, but it gave him contact with the Spanish-American herders and practice in Spanish—and time to read, if no one was watching!

In November, 1931, a heavy snow storm (six feet over a four-day period) killed most of the sheep, despite heroic efforts by Daddy Vogt and his herders to try to reach the flocks, stamp down the snow, and haul feed to them. Vogtie spent each day cutting down a tree and splitting it into lengths for the fireplace and kitchen stove. Overnight the supply would be depleted, and Vogtie had to repeat the tasks for several days following. He describes the experience as the time when he truly grew up.

Vogtie finished nine grades in the village school—as far as the Ramah school went. His father sent him to Santa Fe for his sophomore year and to the Gallup High School for his junior and senior years. He lived with family acquaintances and helped with household chores in return for room and board. He graduated first in his class from Gallup High School and was also president and valedictorian and had the lead in the class play.

His father encouraged him to apply to the University of Chicago, and he received a full tuition scholarship, but delayed a year to work in the mines of Nevada and save money for college. His work in the placer mine meant long, hard days with rough, tough men, one of whom repeated often, as a warning to Vogtie, the story of an acquaintance who had come to the mines after high school to make and save money for college but who had always drunk and gambled his pay and remained a miner all his days.

Vogtie entered the University of Chicago in the autumn of 1937 and worked during his freshman year for his room and board for Nathaniel Plimpton, the university comptroller, who primarily required chauffeuring and company at meals. His freshman advisor, Mr. Trevino, suggested he major in anthropology on the basis of his background, but Vogtie chose geography instead. He pledged Delta Upsilon in the spring and moved into the fraternity house for the following three years, becoming steward and ordering supplies for the house from Charles Percy (later the senator from Illinois), who had the wholesale food concession for the fraternities.

In his senior year, Vogtie learned to fly, was president of Chapel Union (an ecumenical student group), and was a student marshall of his class. He graduated in the spring of 1941 with an A.B. in geography and received a Charles R. Walgreen Fellowship for graduate work in anthropology. He had decided by that time that geography was, at least for him, an intellectually sterile field and that his freshman advisor had been foresighted as to the direction his studies should take him.

The summer of 1941 he worked as a ranger at Montezuma Castle National Monument in Arizona. He had previous experience as a ranger—two summers at El Morro National Monument and one summer at Bandelier National Monument—due in part to his father's having been custodian at El Morro some years before and having friends in the Park Service.

Vogtie and I were introduced in December, 1939, by his former girlfriend and found we both enjoyed dancing and music. On September 4, 1941, we were married in Salina, Kansas, and honeymooned for three weeks in the Southwest. Highlights were the wedding dance in Ramah and camping at Grand Canyon and Canyon de Chelley after a week at Montezuma Castle, Arizona, where he finished his ranger job. We returned to Chicago and Vogtie began graduate studies. He had three part-time jobs: assistant head usher at Rockefeller Chapel, leader of a play group of nine-year-old boys, and research assistant in the anthropology department. The professors under whom he studied and whom he admired were Fred Eggan, Robert R. Redfield, and William Lloyd Warner. He enjoyed his studies and would have continued without interruption, but Pearl Harbor intervened.

Vogtie made application to join the navy in the spring, and we spent the summer at the Vogt Ranch, where he began a study with Zunis at nearby Pescado, riding horseback to and from the village five miles distant. We were working at an army camp near Salina in September when his navy orders came through. Vogtie reported to officers' training at Dartmouth to become a sixty-day wonder: two months to become an ensign. He was assigned in November to the Naval Air Technical Training Command in Memphis, Tennessee. Daddy Vogt died in January, 1943, and we joined the rest of the family for the funeral in Gallup. Vogtie returned to his navy duty of being in charge of three barracks of men until May, when he was assigned to be executive officer of the train that took the 450 men to California for duty in the Pacific. He tells of the feeling of power he enjoyed in being able to order the train halted when the men needed a rest or calisthenic break.

A few weeks later he was assigned to duty in Brazil for a year as administrative officer of a PBY air squadron and then went to air combat intelligence school at Quonset Point, Rhode Island, from May, 1944, to February, 1945. He served as air combat intelligence officer at the rank of lieutenant senior grade on the carrier *Bon Homme Richard* in the Pacific from March to September, 1945. He returned to graduate study at the University of Chicago in January, 1946, to do fieldwork and write his master's thesis on the Norwegian farmers of Grundy County, Illinois, under the direction of Professor William Lloyd

Warner. Clyde Kluckhohn came to give a lecture at the university, and Vogtie had a chance to discuss his Ph.D. dissertation topic with him. The two of them agreed that a study of the Ramah Navajo veterans was of mutual excitement and interest.

In the summer of 1947 Vogtie began fieldwork with the Navajo veterans and returned to Chicago in March, 1948, to write his dissertation, *Navaho Veterans: A Study of Acculturation.* Clyde had consulted his colleagues in the Department of Anthropology at Harvard and had Vogtie come east for a talk and interviews with the departmental faculty. He was offered an instructorship and began teaching in September, receiving his Ph.D. in absentia in December of that year.

By this time we had three children: Shirley Naneen, born March 6, 1945, in Salina, Kansas; Evon Zartman Vogt III (Terry), born August 29, 1946, in Chicago, Illinois; and Eric Edwards Vogt, born October 22, 1948, in Ayer, Massachusetts—just a month after our arriving at Harvard. We lived in Harvardevens, the former hospital area of Ft. Devens where the prefab buildings had been made into small apartments that Harvard leased to then rent to young faculty and graduate students. Vogtie had a car pool with graduate students for the one hour trip via old Route 2 to his office on the fourth floor of Emerson Hall. He also had a study a half block from the apartment to use evenings and weekends. Social life in the prefabs was pleasant, and we entertained anthropology faculty and students from Cambridge in our small quarters on many an evening.

We moved into a prefab on the Charles River in Cambridge before Vogtie began to teach summer school. It was a hot, muggy summer, and Vogtie vowed never again to teach summer session; nor did he until 1984. After a visit in Salina in August, we drove to the Vogt Ranch to live for the year Vogtie was in the field as deputy coordinator of the "Comparative Study of Values in Five Cultures" or the Ramah Project, as it was more familiarly known. Clyde Kluckhohn was the director of the five-year research endeavor. John M. Roberts and Vogtie shared the coordinator position and took turns being in the field and back at Harvard. Jack Roberts had been in the field the previous year, the first year of the project. Our time was interesting in research for Vogtie and nice for our children, who had their cousins again as built-in playmates, while I enjoyed the company and help of Mother Shirley and Jo Ann in sharing child care and housework. They made it possible for Vogtie and me to fly to Mexico City for ten days, a visit that planted the seed in his mind for possible research in Mexico.

Vogtie was back teaching at Harvard during 1950-1951. The following summer we were once again at the Vogt Ranch as headquarters for his supervising the research. In October we moved to Fence Lake, where Vogtie began his own research with the bean farmers there. We drove to Guadalajara with the children and Mother Shirley Vogt in February and found a house to rent for the coming fall. Vogtie returned to continue with interviews in Fence Lake and found the pattern of water witching interesting, a subject that became a book a few years after the community study itself was published.

September, 1952, found us in Chapala, Jalisco, Mexico, for the autumn term in order for Vogtie to write up his year's research. The Kluckhohns joined us there in October, after their trip to Australia, and stayed at the hotel around the corner from our rented home. We shared many excursions, conversations, meals, and bridge games, and an occasional fiesta or short boat trip on Lake Chapala.

The spring term of 1953 Vogtie again taught at Harvard, and in June we made our way across the country to Palo Alto, California, for a summer seminar on "Acculturation," in which Vogtie participated, and where our fourth child, Charles Anthony Vogt, was born on July 27, in which we both participated. We returned to Cambridge in time for fall term lectures for Vogtie. The next three years followed the pattern of school terms at Harvard and summers in New Mexico, as Vogtie finished his obligations as coordinator of the Ramah Project.

His skills as an administrator were evident to us in his plans for the family, as well as in academic areas. He was always, and still is, planning ahead in every part of his life, whether family schedules and events, research designs, courses, departmental plans, or travel. He mentioned to me shortly after Eric's birth that we would have to plan for having three children in college in 1966. What he did not foresee was that we would also have a fourth child in prep school. He made reservations for twenty family members at Phantom Ranch at the bottom of Grand Canyon a year and a half in advance successfully, but had trouble reserving rooms at Spanish *paradores* that far ahead. They wrote back to say they accepted reservations no more than a year in advance.

His views that there is always room for improvement and that everything should get better with time and effort came partly from his family and partly from his early years with Mormon teachers and classmates. His promptness and attention to details are assets that can also be liabilities, as those of us less prompt and careful can attest. Under his tutelage, his family and a number of students have learned to wash windows and mop floors until they gleam. A good teacher, in or out of the classroom, he has always delighted in helping beginners in skills in which he has some expertise: tennis, bridge, poker, horseshoes, darts, dancing, and horseback riding. It made for a nurturant, instructive father and grandfather.

The summer of 1954 Vogtie made a short reconnaissance of the Huichol area in Jalisco, Mexico, but small, deadly scorpions persuaded him it was no place for his children. He did meet Dr. Alfonso Caso, Director of the Instituto Nacional Indigenista (INI), on that trip and indicated his interest in finding a field site in Mexico. The following year Caso invited him to a meeting in Mexico City of the directors of the several INI field centers, and Vogtie was given a ten-day visit by car to INI centers in Chiapas, Oaxaca, and Veracruz. The Chiapas highlands captured his interest, and he began thinking and making plans for research there.

During the summer of 1956 Vogtie participated in a Social Science Research Council Inter-University Seminar on "American Indian Culture Change" held at the University of New Mexico in Albuquerque, and we rented a house there. In September we went to California for his year at the Center for Advanced Studies in the Behavioral Sciences in Palo Alto. Other anthropologists there that year were E. E. Evans-Prichard, A. Kimball Romney, John M. Roberts, John W. M. Whiting (as well as others). Ray Hyman came for a month or two to work with Vogtie on *Water Witching U.S.A.*, and Duane Metzger was there to work with Kim Romney. We all thoroughly enjoyed our time there.

In December we drove to Chiapas and back in three weeks to see whether the family would also be captivated by the valley of San Cristóbal de las Casas and the surrounding area. Vogtie's enthusiasm was contagious, and we gave unanimous consent to his proceeding with plans for research in Chiapas. I was touched by his wanting us to be with him and his desire to have us feel comfortable with the fieldwork situation.

Our headquarters in San Cristóbal de las Casas, Chiapas, came to be known as the Harvard Ranch and is to this day, even after its sale in 1981. The walled property enclosed four buildings and a garden and was rented from Calixta Guiteras Holmes, a Cuban anthropologist friend. The buildings housed our family, two or three graduate student couples, and had large rooms used for mid-summer seminars and marimba parties. The fourth building held four studies and a storage room. Students came back from days or weeks out in the villages to report their adventures to Vogtie and often to have their first shower, salad, or peanut butter sandwich. Volley ball, ping-pong, darts, and horseshoes were available for free hours. Late afternoons we gathered around the fire, where the students and Vogtie could discuss their varied field research, exchange ideas, and debate the merits of recent anthropological articles and ideas. We had occasional suppers and picnics for all the field party and planned card games and dances in the evenings, because, except for two movie theaters, there was little in the way of night life in San Cristóbal. We also celebrated all the birthdays with early morning *mañanitas* or noon time lunches at the ranch, complete with *mariachis*. None of us, in particular the cake baker, will forget the summer we had ten birthdays to celebrate.

Once in a while we visited the students in the villages where they lived with Zinacantecan families, and we also visited the Zinacantecan men who had come to Cambridge to live with us for a month or six weeks to help teach the students the Tzotzil language before their summer research in Chiapas. The Zinacanteco friends and informants often came to the ranch to be interviewed, to borrow money, or for social visits, meals, and parties.

Vogtie describes in some detail the history of the Harvard Chiapas Project from 1957 to 1977 in his introduction to the *Bibliography of the Harvard Chiapas Project: The First Twenty Years 1957-1977* (1978). The past eleven years have added a few more undergraduates to the 114 he listed and a few more to the 39 graduate students who did research under his guidance. It also brought the honor of being decorated as Knight Commander, Order of the Aztec Eagle, Republic of Mexico, on January 6, 1978, in Mexico City, an honor he appreciates greatly.

What both of us appreciate but can never express adequately is our gratitude to the students and colleagues with us in Chiapas. We have many wonderful memories of those years and of the fine and delightful people with whom we enjoyed adventures and good times. We are deeply indebted to them all for adding dimensions to our emotional and intellectual lives in so many and varied ways. We feel privileged to have had the encouragement, support, help, and hospitality of many Mexican friends, especially the family of Ignacio Bernal and Alfonso Villa Rojas and his wife, Dolores, in Mexico City; and Frans and Gertrude Duby Blom and the families of Leopoldo Velasco Robles and Gustavo Armendariz in San Cristóbal de las Casas.

The years that Vogtie has been at Harvard have provided colleagues with whom he has shared ideas, research data, and teaching, and from whom he has derived guidance and inspiration. Foremost among them has been Gordon R. Willey, Middle American archaeologist, with whom he taught seminars on the Maya. His influence has been considerable, and his friendship has meant much to Vogtie. We have also been enriched by the friendship of the many other colleagues and their spouses in the Department of Anthropology through the years.

Finally, and with deep gratitude, I wish to thank the editors and contributors to this Festschrift volume. That his former students initiated the endeavor and that other valued friends and colleagues participated in bringing the volume to fruition will, I know, bring heartfelt pleasure to Vogtie at its presentation.

EVON Z. VOGT, JR.—THE MAKING OF AN ANTHROPOLOGIST

Fred Eggan
University of Chicago

I first met Vogtie in the spring of 1941 when he was graduating from the University of Chicago. He had been born and brought up on a ranch near Ramah, New Mexico, surrounded by Navajos, Zuni, Mormons, Spanish-Americans, and Anglo-Americans (an environment ideal for the development of a prospective anthropologist). His father was a sheep rancher, but was also the founder and editor of the Gallup *Independent*. He had attended the University of Chicago around the turn of the century, before coming to New Mexico for his health, so it was natural for him to steer his oldest son in that direction. A distant cousin, Clyde Kluckhohn, had spent time on the ranch in the 1920s recovering from rheumatic fever and at this time began an interest in the Navajos that became central to his later career as an anthropologist.

When Vogtie arrived at the University of Chicago in 1937, his freshman counselor advised him to major in anthropology, but for some reason he rejected that advice and chose geography instead. The Department of Geography was a distinguished one in the 1930s, and his later interest in settlement patterns and aerial photography in field research must stem from his geographical training as an undergraduate. For graduate work, he decided to transfer to the Department of Anthropology. A decade earlier I had made a similar decision as an undergraduate at Chicago with a major in psychology and a minor in geography—transferring to the newly established Department of Anthropology after teaching for a couple of years to save money for graduate work.

In the 1930s Chicago was an exciting university, with Robert M. Hutchins as president and Robert Redfield as dean of social sciences. Fay-Cooper Cole had started a graduate program in anthropology and had added Edward Sapir and Redfield to the staff. When Sapir went to Yale in 1931, A.R. Radcliffe-Brown came as a visiting professor from Australia and remained until 1937, when he was called to Oxford. In 1935 William Lloyd Warner, a student of Robert Lowie whom Radcliffe-Brown had brought to Australia in 1926, came from Harvard with a joint appointment in anthropology and sociology. I was appointed as an instructor that same year on returning from a period in the Philippines. I had been a member of the Laboratory of Anthropology Summer Field Party on the Hopi Reservation in 1932, and I had written a thesis in 1933 on the social organization of the western pueblos, as well as making brief field studies of the Choctaw, Cheyenne, and Arapaho.

During the 1930s social anthropology was established at Chicago as a

15

comparative discipline concerned with both society and culture and emphasizing structure and function as well as history, though it was not widely accepted
in the United States until after World War II. What we were doing is exemplified
in *Social Anthropology of North American Tribes* (Eggan 1955), presented to
A.R. Radcliffe-Brown upon the occasion of his accepting the chair of social
anthropology at Oxford University.

After being admitted to graduate studies in the Department of Anthropology,
Vogtie married Nan Vogt and began work that fall. Redfield had just completed
a ten-year study of the folk culture of Yucatán under the auspices of the Carnegie
Institution in Washington, D.C., and his associate, Sol Tax, was finishing an
extensive survey of Maya communities in Guatemala under the same auspices
and was soon to join the department. These were models that influenced Vogtie
when he started the Harvard Chiapas Project in the 1950s. But he was initially
attracted to William Lloyd Warner, who had interrupted writing his thesis at
Harvard on the Murngin to begin a study of Newburyport, Massachusetts, and
Natchez, Mississippi—projects that involved numbers of graduate students and
resulted in two series of works entitled the Yankee City Series and Deep South.
The initial volume of this undertaking was *The Social Life of a Modern
Community* (Warner and Lunt 1941).

Vogtie's graduate work was soon interrupted by Pearl Harbor, but he had a
full year before he went into the navy in the fall of 1942. After graduating from
officer's training school he had a year's assignment in Brazil with a PBY air
squadron, and he later served on a carrier in the Pacific as an air combat
intelligence officer—activities that broadened his experience and increased his
competence. He returned to graduate work in January, 1946, along with a large
number of GI's who were anxious to make up for lost time and put their wartime
experience to good use. Warner had begun a study of a Midwest community,
Morris, Illinois, and Vogtie was put to work studying the Norwegian farmers in
the surrounding regions. Here I could help him since I had spent a period in a
Norwegian community in southern Minnesota as a boy, and I supervised his
master's thesis informally. His first published papers were concerned with the
structure of rural life in the Midwest.

For his doctoral dissertation, Vogtie turned to Clyde Kluckhohn for advice.
Kluckhohn had continued his interest in the Navajo begun at Ramah in the
1920s. After graduating from Wisconsin in 1928 with a degree in the classics,
he had studied at Vienna and then at Oxford as a Rhodes scholar, where he read
anthropology with Robert R. Marett. He taught at the University of New Mexico
before going to Harvard in 1935, where he remained until his early death from
a heart attack in 1960.

After receiving his Ph.D. in 1936, Kluckhohn started the Ramah Project, a
long-range, intensive study of Navajo culture and the processes of culture
change, with particular reference to Navajo children. This project was expanded
in 1949 into the "Comparative Study of Values in Five Cultures," which
encompassed all the major groups in the Ramah area.

Clyde Kluckhohn recommended that Vogtie write a dissertation on the experiences of Navajo veterans in adjusting to life on their return from the war. In the summer of 1947 Vogtie began research on the veterans in the Ramah area. The next year he wrote a thesis later published as *Navajo Veterans: A Study of Changing Values* (1951). While it was being considered, Harvard offered him a job as instructor in social anthropology in the newly established Department of Social Relations. John Adair had been writing a parallel thesis on Zuni veterans, and they later wrote a joint comparative study of Navajo and Zuni adjustments to their return.

After his first year of teaching, Vogtie and Jack Roberts were made coordinators of fieldwork for the Values Project, alternating in the field and teaching at the university. Vogtie also began field research on the Fence Lake community, which was made up of Texas homesteaders who were growing beans by dry farming for the commercial market, an activity that was ultimately the victim of the drought. In the meantime, Kluckhohn had helped to establish the Department of Social Relations at Harvard, had become director of the Russian Research Center, where he served from 1947-1954, and had served as president of the American Anthropological Association during 1947. More and more responsibility for the Values Project was assumed by Vogtie, along with Florence Kluckhohn who had a major role from the beginning. In addition to a number of important articles, Vogtie published *Modern Homesteaders: Life in a Twentieth Century Frontier Community* (1955a) and participated in a summer seminar on "Acculturation" held at Stanford University, and a Social Science Research Council Inter-University Seminar on "American Indian Culture Change," where he presented an important paper on the Navajo. His final contribution to the Values Project came a decade later when he edited (with Ethel Albert) the *People of Rimrock: A Study of Values in Five Cultures* (1966).

In the mid-1950s Vogtie began to look towards Mexico and to plan for a project of his own. He had been in Mexico for brief periods, including field reconnaissance in the Huichol country, but in 1954 he met Alfonso Caso, the director of the Instituto Nacional Indigenista (INI), who invited him to a meeting of their field directors and took him on a tour of the Mexican field stations the following year. The Chiapas region, occupied by Tzotzil and Tzeltal Maya-speaking Indians who inhabited some thirty-seven distinct communities, centered around the *ladino* town of San Cristóbal de las Casas, founded by the Spanish conquerors in 1528. The Chiapas highland Maya were largely monolingual in the 1950s and, except for a few surveys, were largely unstudied and unknown. The following year, 1956-1957, Vogtie was a fellow at the Center for Advanced Study in the Behavioral Sciences at Stanford and began to design his project and to apply for the requisite grants. While at the center he was able to visit Chiapas, where Alfonso Villa Rojas was the INI director for the Tzotzil-Tzeltal area. Alfonso Villa Rojas had been Redfield's associate in the Yucatán study and had been brought to the University of Chicago, where he studied with Sol Tax and helped Redfield write *Chan Kom, A Maya Village* (Redfield and Villa Rojas 1934). Later Dorothy Eggan and I spent several months with Alfonso and his wife in Mexico City. By the mid-1950s he was an excellent social anthropologist and provided Vogtie with initial support in getting started.

Vogtie himself has provided an excellent account of the history of the project in his introduction to the *Bibliography of the Harvard Chiapas Project: The First Twenty Years 1957-1977* (1978), and Nan Vogt (see essay in this volume) has provided supplementary materials on the more informal aspects of life in Chiapas. Over one hundred undergraduates spent summers in the field, and some forty or more graduate students (mostly from Harvard) wrote doctoral theses on various aspects of Maya life, a concentration of talent probably unparalleled in recent times. Graduate students were attracted to the Maya project from several foreign countries, and various American universities participated in a more limited way. Chicago, building on Redfield's previous studies of the Maya in Yucatán and Tax's surveys and intensive studies in Guatemala and Chiapas, had developed a "Man-in-Nature Project" in the mid-1950s. This project focused upon the social, cultural, and linguistic change in the Chiapas highlands and was directed by Norman McQuown, Robert McC. Adams, and Julian Pitt-Rivers. Here, McQuown and his students concentrated on linguistic surveys of Tzeltal and Tzotzil communities for lexical reconstruction and sociolinguistic problems. Adams conducted area-wide surveys and selected excavations. Pitt-Rivers conducted community studies, with emphasis on special topics. I kept up with the Chiapas projects by listening to my colleagues and reading their reports.

Reading Vogtie's introduction to the *Bibliography of the Harvard Chiapas Project: The First Twenty Years 1957-1977* (1978), we are impressed by the rational development of the various phases of the Chiapas Project and the archives of ethnographic information that have resulted. The integration of the teaching program with field research through freshman seminars on the Maya not only recruited students for the graduate program, but widened the range of topics investigated. The graduate seminars on Middle America and the Maya offered knowledge and critical discussion of work in progress. Systematic training in Tzotzil was important in order to bypass Spanish and the need for interpreters. This training resulted in major contributions such as Robert Laughlin's *Great Tzotzil Dictionary of San Lorenzo Zinacantán* (1975), which provides a model for future work and may ultimately allow linguists to reconstruct proto-Maya in detail and add history to the comparative dimension. Here the work of Norman McQuown in systematically studying and archiving Maya languages and putting them on computers will be of great assistance. The current work of linguists such as Floyd Lounsbury and others in cracking the Maya code with reference to the glyphs and finding a language beyond the dates will soon provide a historical dimension based on documents that will illuminate the Classic period of the Maya in a way that the archaeologists have only been able to suggest.

Just as the comparison of Zinacantán and Chamula widens our perspectives, so will the detailed study of other communities add new and unexpected ramifications to our knowledge of Maya life and culture. Air photo mosaics have been put to use in studies of demography and settlement patterns, but will ultimately provide a new view of the landscape and its changing role in the development of Maya culture.

The Chiapas Maya Project is thus an end in itself—a *katun* in the study of the Maya—and the prelude to a new phase in our understanding of the Maya and their culture. Vogtie's experience with the Harvard Chiapas Project suggests that a new organization needs to be developed. We have seen that he built on selected principles from social anthropology and the early projects developed by Kluckhohn and others with regard to the Navajo, and Redfield and Tax with regard to the Maya of Yucatán and Guatemala, as well as with the seminal contributions of Tozzer in earlier years. Future developments will need more than individual universities and scholars, and cooperative inter-university institutions will need to be developed and financed. Whatever happens, the Harvard Chiapas Project is assured of an important place in future developments, and Professor Evon Z. Vogt can look forward to a well-earned "retirement" in which he will probably be busier than he is at present. We all salute him with a "well done!"

ACKNOWLEDGMENTS. This contribution is written as an expansion of portions of Nan Vogt's account of their life together and covering almost a half century. I am grateful to Nan for furnishing me with a copy of her paper and other documents, as well as encouragement.

VOGT AT HARVARD

Gordon R. Willey
Harvard University

Vogtie—or Evon Zartman Vogt, Jr., to be formal about it, as he never is—first came to Harvard University in 1948, so he was already here, and a member of the faculty in the Department of Anthropology, when I joined that body in 1950. Thus, he has always outranked me as the doyen of the department, even though he is five years younger. In those days, the early 1950s, we were surrounded by a number of distinguished seniors, long in residence. My great predecessor in Maya archaeology, Alfred Marston Tozzer, although just retired, still maintained an office in the Peabody Museum. Vogtie's mentor, Clyde Kluckhohn, with whom he had worked in the Southwestern United States, was the leading ethnologist-social anthropologist of our department, and Earnest Albert Hooton, the renowned physical anthropologist, was its chairman. These were all remote and Olympian figures, or so they seemed in those first years. Closer to us were J.O. Brew, the Southwestern archaeologist, who was also director of the Peabody Museum, Hallam Movius, the coming star of Old World paleolithic studies, and Douglas Oliver, an ethnologist with Melanesian and Polynesian interests. These three, however, were "old Harvard hands." That is, they had been undergraduates or graduates here before becoming faculty members. So, they knew their way around the Harvard community. Vogtie and I, coming in as we did from elsewhere, were the only clearly "new ones."

This initial "outsider" status that Vogtie and I shared was probably one of the reasons he and I became friends early on. Another reason may have been that we were both Westerners or Middle Westerners. Vogtie, born and raised in New Mexico, was a true Westerner, who had gone to college in the Middle West, at the University of Chicago, while I was Middle-Western born, then transplanted to California, after which I went to the University of Arizona. In our undergraduate college milieus we had both lived in fraternity houses. I think this gives those who experience it something in common. In addition to these circumstances, when we came to Harvard, we were in no way rivals. Vogtie was committed to ethnology and social anthropology and I to archaeology. While we had mutual interests in Americanist culture-historical problems, we came up on these from different perspectives, ending as collaborators rather than competitors. Finally, and over and beyond all of these reasons, I think that the main reason we became close friends was simply that Vogtie was a very congenial fellow. You liked him almost immediately and were drawn to him.

Vogtie's wife, Catherine—better known as Nan—has presented the detailed biographical facts about him in a preceding memoir. As she tells us, he was born on a ranch in New Mexico in 1918. After high school in Gallup, New Mexico,

VOGT AT HARVARD

he went to the University of Chicago, his father's old alma mater. There, as had his father before him, he pledged Delta Upsilon. After graduation, with an undergraduate degree in geography, he decided to continue at Chicago with graduate work in anthropology. Before he did this, however, he and Nan were married, and then World War II interrupted his graduate plans for a while. He served in the United States Navy, both in Brazilian and Pacific waters. Returning to Chicago after the war, he completed his Ph.D. in anthropology and came to Harvard in 1948. This was his first teaching post, and, as it has turned out, Harvard has remained his only place of regular academic employment throughout his career. He was an instructor for two years, from 1948 until 1950, advancing to assistant professor in the latter year. He became associate professor in 1955, and he was made a full professor in 1959.

While I do not know all the reasons that led Vogtie to choose anthropology as a profession, I have always assumed that the idea must have evolved rather naturally with him in the Southwestern setting of his boyhood. On the Vogt Ranch, near Ramah, New Mexico, he grew up in colorful surroundings. For instance, he had an early familiarity with Southwestern archaeological ruins. He was surrounded by Pueblo and Navajo Indians and Spanish-speaking Americans. With his father an educated man of intellectual interests, Evon Jr. was raised in an atmosphere of racial and cultural tolerance. Early on, Vogtie was influenced by the young Clyde Kluckhohn, a relative on his mother's side of the family, who, for health reasons, had come out to New Mexico and who lived at the Vogt Ranch for an extended period. Clyde, although not formally an anthropologist at that time, was vitally interested in the Southwest, its land and its people. Later, in his summer vacations from college, Vogtie worked as a temporary park ranger with the National Park Service, being assigned to a number of the Park Service archaeological ruins. This background and these experiences, taken altogether, undoubtedly led him into courses in geography and anthropology, first as an undergraduate and then later as a graduate. The University of Chicago had a renowned Department of Anthropology, headed by Fay-Cooper Cole and staffed by such people as W. Lloyd Warner, Robert Redfield, and Fred Eggan. Nan has told me that Warner, perhaps more than any other of his professors, influenced Vogtie in his early graduate years, turning him toward studies of social class structure. She recalls a seminar or term paper that Vogtie produced on the social structure of Salina, Kansas, her own old hometown, for which she served as the key informant.

From Warner's guidance, Vogtie went on to work under Fred Eggan, especially in Navajo acculturation studies. The particular subject was that of Navajo veterans who had returned from World War II to their old homes and communities in New Mexico. This work was to result in his doctoral dissertation and was later to be published at Harvard (Vogt 1951).

Vogtie's other major work deriving from this Southwestern setting was based on his field research with Texas bean farmers, people who had moved to New Mexico as recent immigrants (Vogt 1955a). In both of these Southwestern studies, Vogtie pursued a very definite comparative or cross-cultural interest, examining the contrasts between the ways that such diverse groups as the Navajos, Spanish-Americans, Zuni, Mormons, or Texas homesteaders adapted within the Ramah environmental region (Vogt 1955b; Vogt and O'Dea 1953; Vogt and Roberts 1956). This was the essence of the "Comparative Study of Values in Five Cultures" research, headed at Harvard by Clyde and Florence Kluckhohn during the 1950s. Vogtie served as deputy coordinator of the project, later succeeding to the position of coordinator. He was always very much alert to and concerned with the ecological interface between culture and society and the environmental setting, but he was then, and has always been, convinced of the determinative importance of the values or ideology with which any human group addresses its environment. We used to argue about this. I was inclined then, and still am, to look for ecological explanations of social and cultural forms and traits. Clearly, in the New Mexican Values Studies, the Mormons or the Texas bean farmers, or "Homesteaders," both seemed to have traits that appeared nonadaptive to their environmental settings. These obviously were ideological "carry-overs" from their past history and experience; but, I asked, were not these ideologies, these values created by what went on in some ancient ecological interface, prior to the arrival of these peoples to the Ramah region? Vogtie would concede the logic of this, but this search for origins was not where his interest lay. What held his attention was the way in which ideas and values, no matter what their primary formation may have been, were the guiding forces by which people lived and arranged their lives. I began to realize that this was a difference between an ethnological point of view (his) and an archaeological one (mine). I suppose both concerns are of legitimate interest, but I think I learned from Vogtie the importance of the latter, and, in so doing, I began to realize that the search for ultimate origins may be somewhat sterile or even impossible, that man in society is always confronting his circumambient natural and social world with the ideas that he brings with him from the antecedent past. Also, in this confrontation, ideas are constantly in process of change.

At Harvard one of Vogtie's favorite courses reflected this fascination for ideology. This was the one on primitive religion. The course, open to both undergraduates and graduates, was a popular one. A byproduct of it was the book, *Reader in Comparative Religion: An Anthropological Approach,* which he published with William A. Lessa (Lessa and Vogt 1958). In addition, Vogtie offered seminars or pro-seminars in "Introductory Social Anthropology" and on "Method and Theory in Social Anthropology." He also gave instruction in Middle American ethnography and ethnology. This was at the time I was giving my first seminars in Middle American archaeology. In those days graduate students in social anthropology were required to take at least one course or seminar in archaeology, and archaeologists were similarly obliged to cross over. As a consequence, he and I worked together in the supervision of students, especially those who wanted to specialize in the Middle American area. From our frequent informal consultations about such student training, we had the opportunity to discuss a good many matters of mutual interest to both archaeology and ethnology, and we decided to offer a joint survey course on New World archaeology-ethnology. As I recall, we did this for seven years, from 1954 until 1961. We would move rapidly over the two American continents, area by area, with me laying down the archaeological beginnings and Vogtie taking up the story from the time of the European conquests to the present. Ethnographic analogy was, of course, crucial to much of the archaeological interpretation, and, in turn, the archaeological past was offered as some explanation of what was found on the ethnohistoric horizon. This was before numerous critiques were issued about the dangers of assuming smooth and unbroken continuity between prehistoric past and historic present, of relying overmuch on a steady adherence between form and function. Vogtie and I were certainly aware of these limitations, but we both thought then, and still do, that such an ordering of the data has more in its favor than against it, especially in the construction of a beginning frame of reference for culture-historical research. Later, during the 1960s, we collaborated again, this time on a Maya seminar that examined various problems from joint ethnohistoric and archaeological perspectives. This latter collaboration grew very directly from Vogt's own fieldwork in the Maya country of Chiapas, Mexico. As his Maya researches compose the main body of his research during his career at Harvard, I will consider these at some length, but will lead into the subject in the context of a narrative of Vogtie's activities here at Harvard and elsewhere.

Vogtie's first Mesoamerican ethnological fieldwork—indeed, the first fieldwork he had done outside of the Southwestern United States—was with the Huichol and Cora tribes of western Mexico, specifically in the states of Nayarit and Jalisco. This was carried out in the summer of 1954. He was, at that time, primarily interested in a comparative examination of acculturation in the two tribes. He published an article on the Mexican work in the following year (Vogt 1955c). But in 1955, Vogtie visited the Chiapas highlands, in southern Mexico. This was at the invitation of Alfonso Caso and others of the Mexican Instituto Nacional Indigenista. On this trip he had the opportunity to review the ethnographic surveys that the Mexican ethnologists had been carrying out there among the Tzotzil and Tzeltal Maya. On his return to the United States, he talked about his recent fieldwork. While he had enjoyed and profited from the Huichol-Cora project, it was clear that it was the Maya of Chiapas who had captured his imagination.

At that time, I had been working in the Maya lowlands of British Honduras, doing an archaeological settlement pattern study—a new departure for Maya archaeology—at Barton Ramie, in the Belize Valley of that country. Vogtie was especially interested in what I was doing. He began to ask me questions about the probable social structure that lay behind these settlement arrangements that I had been recording. How did individual residential remains or house platforms relate to families and family groups? What were the probable social correlates of larger clusterings of "house mounds"? How did these settlement data, and the social inferences derived therefrom, relate to the larger Maya ruins, that is the "cities" or "ceremonial centers"? My data were all prehistoric, largely of the Preclassic and Classic periods, but Vogtie was even then asking questions that would link archaeology and ethnology, questions that arose from some of the things he had seen in his visit to the Chiapan Tzotzil groups.

As we participated in our joint archaeology-ethnology course, and I continued to tell him about my Barton Ramie findings, he was the one who suggested that I write a paper on my field observations and on how these might relate to the structure of ancient Maya society (Willey 1956). Indeed, Vogtie was extremely supportive of settlement pattern archaeology early on. It was also his idea that I organize a symposium on the theme of prehistoric settlement patterns in the New World for the December meetings of the American Anthropological Association in 1954. I did this, and the proceedings of the symposium were published shortly thereafter (Willey 1956), with Vogtie writing "An Appraisal of Prehistoric Settlement Patterns in the New World" for the volume (Vogt 1956).

Vogtie had begun to make preparations for what was to turn out to be his long-term fieldwork in Chiapas, but before he really got going on this he spent the 1956-1957 academic year as a fellow at the Center for Advanced Study in Palo Alto, California. This gave him the opportunity to finish up some research and writing projects. One of these was a study of the good old American trait of "water dowsing" or "water witching." For those who might not know just what this is, it is the magical location of subsoil water, preparatory to well digging. One interesting aspect of his findings was the tenacity of the faith in the water-dowsing procedure here in New England—no matter what the economic, social, or even educational bracket of the convinced dowser. Vogtie published a book about it with Ray Hyman (Vogt and Hyman 1959). But besides this and other writing chores, he especially enjoyed his interactions with a variety of social science colleagues at the center. Vogtie had, and has, a "collegial" touch. He is not reticent about speaking of his own work, but he is no monologuist. When he tells you about what he is doing, he does it in a way that engages your interest and that usually draws you out into talking about your own researches and experiences.

While he was in Palo Alto, I remember Vogtie made one trip back East in the fall to join me in New York for a National Research Council committee meeting that had been called to plan for a *Handbook of Middle American Indians*. He and I were both on that committee, and he was a tower of strength at that meeting and in the subsequent ones that led eventually to the production of such a handbook under Robert Wauchope's general editorship (Wauchope 1964-1975). Vogtie served as volume editor for volumes 7 and 8 of the series (Wauchope and Vogt 1969). This is a good time to mention that Vogtie has always been a reliable "team player," as he was in the *Handbook of Middle American Indians* enterprise. Anthropology has its share of prima donna personalities, but Vogtie is not one of them. While never hesitant to speak his mind, and in strong disagreement if he feels it, he seeks consensus rather than division, especially when it is necessary to get an important job done. This quality has served him and others well. In this connection, I think of him as our Department of Anthropology chairman (1969-1973). I should also note that he served the university as a member of the Administrative Board of the Faculty of Arts and Sciences for a five-year period (1951-1956). Later, he was master of Kirkland House for an eight-year stint (1974-1982). All such jobs demand the patience and skills that it takes to work successfully with others, in these instances both colleagues and students. Vogtie enjoyed these assignments. He has told me that the administrative board membership and the housemastership were posts in which to learn about Harvard University, but he also classed them as "heavy duty" insofar as time and energy were concerned.

But to get back to Chiapas, Vogtie's field studies there were to result in major contributions to Mesoamerican and American anthropology. They are centered on the ethnography and ethnology of the Tzotzil community of Zinacantán. In the course of these studies he has given us the most thoroughgoing analysis of modern Maya settlement extant. It is also an analysis that links settlement to basic economy and to religious and sociopolitical structure. While essentially ethnologic and ethnographic, it is research of inestimable value to Maya archaeology. It is to be emphasized that at the same time that Vogtie studied Zinacantán settlement, he also continued to follow his long-abiding interests in religion and symbolism. In doing this, he has revealed the role of ideology in the structuring of the lives of the Zinacantecos. Many of his results and ideas were presented in a series of preliminary papers (Vogt 1961, 1964a, b, c), but his two major monographs, the basic ethnographic one, *Zinacantán: A Maya Community in the Highlands of Chiapas* (Vogt 1969b), and the other on religion and ideology, *Tortillas for the Gods: A Symbolic Analysis of Zinacanteco Rituals* (Vogt 1976), have consolidated his position in the very forefront of modern ethnographers, ethnologists, and social anthropologists working in Mesoamerica. For the Zinacantán community study, Vogtie was awarded the 1969 Harvard University Faculty Prize for the best work of scholarship written by a faculty member, and this same work also received the Sahagún Prize that same year from the Mexican Instituto Nacional de Antropología e Historia.

Over and beyond these direct contributions, Vogtie's role as director and leader of the Chiapas investigations is reflected in the work and writings of a host of students, many of whom are represented in this present volume dedicated to him. He has been a firm believer in the doctrine that the field was the place for the most effective training of an ethnologist, and he followed up this belief with both graduates and undergraduates.

But I want to return to Vogtie's settlement pattern findings at Zinacantán. They command attention, especially archaeological attention. To begin with, the territory of the *municipio* of Zinacantán measures about 14 km in diameter, totaling an area of 177 km^2. Archaeologists familiar with Maya settlement studies will note that this is a land area size consistent with many of our territorial estimates for the ancient Maya polities of the lowlands. Like these lowland polities, Zinacantán has its "ceremonial center." In this case, the Zinacantán ceremonial center is marked by the Catholic church, by the local offices of the supervising Mexican governmental bureaucracy, and by a few modest *ladino*-owned stores or shops, which serve the community as outlets for goods brought in from the *ladino* world. The total population of this center is only 394 persons, including the few *ladinos* who live there. The great majority of the population of the *municipio* (totaling 7611 persons in all) does not live in or near the ceremonial center but, instead, resides in hamlets, or *parajes,* which are scattered throughout the 177 km² territory. Such *parajes* vary in population from as few as 50 to over 1200 persons. Some of them, especially the larger ones, might be considered as "minor ceremonial centers" within the overall Zinacantán settlement pattern, inasmuch as they are marked by small "shrines." The parallel to ancient Maya lowland settlement is, thus, obvious: (1) a major or principal ceremonial center, which incorporates religious or public buildings, dominates a small territory; (2) within this territory, and presumably within the orbit of the control of the major ceremonial center, are a number of hamlets where most of the people of the territory reside; and (3) some of these hamlets have features or structures which indicate that they functioned as minor ceremonial centers.

Vogt chose one such Zinacantán hamlet or *paraje*—one by the name of Paste'—for intensive ethnological study. Paste' had a population of 1276 persons. These Paste' inhabitants conceived of their *paraje* living space as covering about 5 km². Within this space, actual residential settlement was divided into five clusters of houses, each centered around a natural water hole. Each cluster, in turn, consisted of several patrilocal, extended family households. The individual households were marked by two to five separate buildings, usually facing onto a little open space or patio. Such buildings served as the living and sleeping houses and/or storage facilities for the members of the one or more biological families who made up the extended family household. Again, in this breakdown of hamlets into house clusters, and house clusters into individual houses or patio house arrangements, we note similarities to the archaeologically observed settlement record, especially that of the southern Maya lowlands (see Willey 1981).

How did the Zinacantán system operate economically, socially, religiously, and politically? Vogt has described the economy as basically agricultural, supported by the labors of the hamlet or *paraje* populations. There were some differences in wealth within these populations. Some families controlled more land and were more productive, but any large inequities in wealth tended to be leveled out by the relatively costly religious duties that were carried out by the priestly hierarchy of the community. A consideration of these duties and this hierarchy leads us directly into the social, religious, and political structure of the *municipio.*

As indicated, priestly duties generally fell heaviest on the wealthier individuals and families because they were the ones who could afford such religious *cargos.* There were over fifty *cargo* positions in the Zinacantán religious hierarchy, and these were ranked in four ascending levels. The positions were filled on a rotating basis. A young individual entered into *cargo* service on the lowest level of the priestly hierarchy. For a year this *cargo* holder was required to reside in the main Zinacantán ceremonial center in order to perform properly his various duties. By so doing, he must withdraw from economically productive work as a farmer in his *paraje*. Thus, he and his family must have sufficient economic resources to enable him to do this and also to bear other expenses incurred in the course of his priestly activities. After his year's duty is completed, he returns to his usual agricultural duties in his *paraje*, and someone else takes his place at the ceremonial center. After a few years, this first young man may go back into religious service—assuming he and his family are still able to afford it—and this time he goes back in on the next highest level of the priestly hierarchy. Again, after a year, he rotates back to his farm. He may, in the period of his life, do duty on all four levels of the hierarchy, advancing by seniority and experience to the top echelon, and finally emerging as a *pasado*, or retired "elder statesman." Although individual and extended family wealth does have a role in community leadership and governance, the system is essentially an egalitarian one, one which does not allow for great accumulation of wealth and one in which prestige and power is distributed among a relatively large number of individuals through rotated office and achieved seniority of service.

The big question about the Chiapas highlands Zinacantán system, especially for those of us in Maya archaeology, is how closely does it replicate what happened in the old Classic Maya communities of the adjacent Maya lowlands? Vogtie has argued for its continuity from ancient times to the present day. While he has been willing to concede that the ancient Maya may have made accommodation for certain professionals in ritual, iconography, calendrics, and hieroglyphic writing to have been in ceremonial center residence full time, it is his opinion that real authority in the Classic period was maintained through a rotating *cargo* system of office similar to that seen in Zinacantán. A point in his argument is the "integrative" power of the *cargo* system. It helps explain how a society dependent upon a dispersed agricultural population, which resided in small hamlet groups scattered over relatively large territorial plots, held itself together for concerted religious and political activities. The body politic was literally "laced" together by the constant rotation of hamlet farmers into positions of control in the major centers. The idea has appeal, but most archaeologists do not think that the great Classic Maya centers of the first millennium A.D. were built and maintained in this way. For one thing, we know that many of them are more properly viewed as "urban," rather than "vacant," centers. For another, recent advances in hieroglyphic translations place great emphasis on the prestige and power of a hereditary elite and on what are, in effect, numerous "royal families." It is, of course, possible that the Zinacantán *cargo* rotation system approximates an ancient Maya pattern of shared or distributed power—one, perhaps, in operation back in Middle Preclassic times. This system was then superceded by one of more centralized hereditary authority in the Late Preclassic and Classic periods. After this, with the breakdown of Maya civilization following the Spanish Conquest, the *cargo* system, as seen in Zinacantán, came back into existence on the ethnohistoric level, or so one line of argument goes. Arguments and debate about Vogtie's interpretations still go on, but the most important thing in all of this is that Vogtie opened up a dialogue with Maya archaeologists in a way that no ethnologist had done before. One thinks of the late Robert Redfield and his work in connection with A.V. Kidder's Carnegie Institution Maya program. What Redfield and Villa Rojas (1934) did in their Yucatecan *Chan Kom, a Maya Village* study was a brilliant tour de force in ethnology and social anthropology, but it was not historically oriented in the way that Vogt's Zinacanteco research has been. *Chan Kom, a Maya Village* did not, at that time at least, have the relevance to archaeology that Kidder was seeking. *Zinacantán: A Maya Community in the Highlands of Chiapas* (Vogt 1969b) has that relevance. It has forced archaeologists to think about certain dimensions of their data—particularly their settlement and social organizational dimensions—in a way that they have not done before, and this is so whether they agree with the specifics of Vogt's arguments or not.

On his side, Vogtie has not been indifferent to archaeological criticism in this interchange. In a recent review of his work and its reception, he has gone down the list of what he considers to be his principal findings and hypotheses of twenty years before and appraised these in the light of what we have since learned (Vogt 1983). In this listing, he begins with the observation that the Zinacantán settlement pattern of ceremonial center, hamlets, house clusters, and individual households, and the spatial relations of all of these remains as a highly workable model, for both Maya highlands and lowlands and for the archaeological past as well as for the ethnographic present. In his opinion, the few exceptions to this model can be explained away, historically and topographically.

Secondly, he states that the subsistence model of maize and beans and swidden-type cultivation still appears to be the most successful generalization about Maya agricultural economics. He accepts the importance of raised field and terrace cultivation—new archaeological discoveries for the lowlands—but counters with the assertion that these did not lead to settlement nucleation. I would agree here if we define this "nucleation" to be of a "central Mexican type." I think, however, that these intensive cultivation techniques may have helped make possible a lowland Maya form of urbanism at certain ceremonial centers. Tikal is the Classic example, and there are a good many others. What we are talking about is a concentration of 70,000 people within a zone of 120 km^2 (the approximate Tikal estimate). This is in contrast to the central Mexican highland urbanism of Teotihuacan, with its 200,000 people within an area of only 20 km^2.

Vogtie's third point is that he sees nothing to dispute a patrilocal, patrilineal, and patriclan model of Maya kinship. The evidence here is essentially a projection of ethnographic or ethnohistoric data backwards in time. I see nothing to dispute this very seriously. We know, of course, that the female line was very important in royal inheritance in ancient Classic times; there is glyphic textual information telling us this, but this seems insufficient to set aside the high probability that historic and modern kin organization has ancient Maya beginnings.

Vogt's fourth point or conclusion deals with the highly controversial matter of *cargo* rotation of offices. He still favors the idea that the old Maya priests and nobles rotated in and out of religious and political office in much the same way that the modern Zinacantecos do. He concedes, without question, the presence of a hereditary elite in Classic times, including rulers and dynasties; but he still raises the question of how permanent was their residence in the center and wonders if different lineages, or perhaps branches within lineages, may not have alternated in rulership duties and "palace residence." I still remain doubtful of this interpretation.

But I have learned from Vogtie and from ethnology in this debate. It seems highly likely that the ancient Maya had devised strong integrative mechanisms to bind society together. These would have been needed in linking center to hamlet, as well as in establishing ties between elite and commoner. One such mechanism, or set of mechanisms, would have been the constant movement of peoples from outlying farms and hamlets to the ceremonial centers and vice versa. The carrying of foodstuffs and goods would have been one purpose in these movements, the issuance of governmental directives or orders another. Ritual processions also probably took place along such routes, as is the case today in Zinacantán. In visualizing all of this, Vogt (1983) has outlined what he calls his "periphery-to-center-pulsation model" for hamlet-center interaction.

This is an ethnologist's vision or model. It arises out of Vogtie's empathy with, and sympathy for, the people he is studying. I remember visiting Zinacantán with him. It was the only time I was ever there—in 1960, I believe. I was fascinated with the way he moved around in "his" community of Paste', dressed in the colorful costume of the Zinacantecos, exchanging the time of day with the householders and farmers. In the ceremonial center he conversed with the then-current *cargo* holders with ease and enjoyment. He introduced me as his "compadre," which, indeed, I am, insofar as that term and concept can be translated into English and Anglo-Saxon social behavior: I am godfather to his youngest son, Charles. I recall being rather ill at ease, though, as the Zinacantecos critically (I thought) regarded this rather improbable-looking compadre. I would have made a poor ethnologist. I have often thought archaeologists and ethnologists have gone on their different career ways because of their different temperaments. Nevertheless, as I hope I have made clear, in talking about Vogtie and the Maya, ethnologists and archaeologists can learn from each other.

This theme of shared learning and investigation in Maya studies was particularly featured in a symposium that Vogt thought up and organized. It was held at the Burg Wartenstein under the auspices of the Wenner-Gren Foundation in the summer of 1962. He cochaired it with the distinguished Mexican archaeologist, the late Alberto Ruz Lhuillier. Participants included a wide range of Maya scholars: linguists, ethnologists, and archaeologists, including in the latter group some hieroglyphic experts. It was Vogtie's attempt to view all of the Maya-speaking peoples of southern Mesoamerica in time and in space, in accordance with what he called his "genetic" or "phylogenetic" model of the Maya. It marked a major stock taking and review in Maya research, the results being published shortly after the conference as *Desarrollo cultural de los Mayas*

(Vogt and Ruz 1964) and then brought out again, seven years later, with some revisions (Vogt and Ruz 1971). It is an outstanding achievement of which Vogtie can be proud.

In 1978 Evon Z. Vogt, Jr. was made Knight Commander, Order of the Aztec Eagle, Republic of Mexico, in recognition for his services to the people of that republic. Already a member of the American Academy of Arts and Sciences (since 1960), Vogt was elected to the United States National Academy of Sciences in 1979. He is clearly one of the nation's outstanding ethnologists and social anthropologists today. Vogtie's successful career in anthropology has been made possible and has been marked by certain basic qualities. I would say that the first of these qualities is his ability and willingness to work cooperatively with others. This quality is undoubtedly tied to another, which is his fundamental and pervasive optimism. He can convince his colleagues, collaborators, and students that they can achieve things beyond the original limited goals they had set for themselves. And, thirdly, there is Vogtie's great persistence, his ability to follow through. His work, especially that of the Harvard Chiapas Project, is a testament to this persistence.

And so, after thirty-nine years of association, I salute an old friend. He is still going strong. I wish him all the best.

THEY HAD A VERY GREAT MANY PHOTOGRAPHS[1]

John B. Haviland
Reed College

José Hernández was known at the time as Bik'it Chep—Little José—although now, more than twenty years later, he is normally referred to simply as Chep Apas, after his home hamlet in the *municipio* of Zinacantán, where he is one of the most important men. His career has had its ups and downs: distinguished early service in the ritual hierarchy, a flirtation with politics, a corn mill, a truck, cattle in a land reform colony, and, of course, several anthropologist compadres. He visited the United States on several occasions. In the early spring of 1968 he stayed with the Vogts in Weston, Massachusetts, and made the daily trip to William James Hall, at Harvard, to work with Chiapas Project students. He is a handsome man, with an unforgettable voice. This voice graced the Tzotzil dialogue tapes several generations of fledgling anthropologists used to learn such classic phrases as *ak'o pertonal batz'i jset' tajmek kunen sikil a'al che'e*, "give pardon for just a bit of my little cold water, then"—an elaborately polite formula for presenting cane liquor as a prelude to a request. When Chep stayed with the Vogts, in February and March of 1968, the Chiapas Project was in full swing, and his was the *batz'i* voice behind the *batz'i* language that several of us tried both to learn and to teach at the same time. Chep seemed to most of us sophisticated, relaxed, and reasonably at home in Cambridge. He moved easily between groups of undergraduate students (whose questions he patiently fielded no matter how odd), people he had known in previous years in Chiapas who could speak to him in a smattering of Tzotzil, and groups of *mol profesoretik*—senior professors to whom his hosts introduced him. Yet few, if any, of us, knew what he thought about the strange life of the project that he observed in his daily routine.

Partly out of a sense of archival responsibility, but mostly to give him something to occupy his time between Tzotzil classes and the sporadic visits of inquisitive undergraduates, we had asked Chep to keep a diary of what he did and saw during his stay. Now, more than twenty years later, I have run across this otherwise forgotten journal, still incomplete as he left it, some sixty-odd typewritten pages in a dusty folder in my basement. I present here fragments of Chep Apas's 1968 Cambridge diary as a Zinacanteco tribute both to Vogtie and to the Chiapas Project of the time.

In this day and age, when Zinacantecos fertilize their cornfields with petrochemicals, drive weekly cargo trucks to Mexico City, feud over Mexican party politics, and pick strawberries in Oregon, Chep's naive Zinacanteco vision of the United States in 1968 is a reminder of a forgotten age. His words capture both our anthropological practices of the time (reflected in Chep's reports of how he was asked to spend his days) and one Zinacanteco's view of our personal customs and habits (reflected in his observations out of working hours).

There are several notable features in the original Tzotzil text, carefully typed and corrected by hand in the simplified practical orthography we used at the time. Perhaps the most interesting has to do with the voice and perspective Chep adopts. There is a delicate switching between the inclusive and the exclusive, in the first person plural, which clearly shows that Chep's intended audience is a group of his Zinacanteco peers; his inclusive "we" includes the universe of all those who know what a Zinacanteco knows. His exclusive "we" includes only Chep himself and the mob of gringos with whom he hobnobs. In a parallel way, Chep's use of Tzotzil directional expressions (both deictically anchored verbs like *bat* and *tal,* "set out from here" and "set out towards here," or *yul* and *k'ot,* "arrive here" and "arrive there," and in directional clitics following main verbs) shows that, although he was physically present in Cambridge as he wrote, he was conceptually anchored at home in Zinacantán. In this practice he anticipates the usage of present-day Zinacantecos who must grapple with the same perspective issues as they write letters or telephone (!) home from afar.

People familiar with the Chiapas Project of the time will recognize most of the protagonists here. The most prominent are Nan and Vogtie themselves: Mother Catherine and Father John, or Me'tik Katal and Totik Xun as Chep normally calls them. The Tzotzil teachers who worked with Chep are Victoria (Bricker) and Xun Jvabajom, John "Musician" Haviland. Of the students that Chep refers to, several are likely still to be reading these notes: Palas from Italy (Francesco Pellizzi), Telex (Rick) and Candy Shweder, Bik'it Xun John Miyamoto, and Markux Mark Rosenberg. Doctor Thomas is Berry Brazelton. All of us, as Chep reminds us—politely stifling a yawn behind his Tzotzil words—had lots and *lots* of photographs, and always served liquor.

This short translation is dedicated to the memory of Chep Vaskes skrem mol Petul Vaskes, of Nabenchauk, who died in the United States twenty years and three months after Chep Apas wrote these diary entries about his American visit.

11 FEBRUARY, 1968

This is a text about how I got to Boston. I arrived at 9 P.M. at the airport in Boston. There Father John was waiting for me with John Musician, and his wife, and one of John Musician's friends, and his wife, too. John Musician, being a very good friend of mine, gave me a gift, a scarf, but it was very beautiful, made of wool—a very warm scarf. Well, when we had finished talking with each other, I went with Father John, and we went as far as his house, in Weston. When we got to his house, he gave me a beer in a can. We drank the beer. Father John also drank it.

Well, after we had finished drinking the beer, we went to the school of his son—Carlito is his name—because they had gone to ski in some place far from where Father John's house was. But we waited just there at the school where he studied. After we had waited for a little while, he came; he came on an autobus. When he came, we went back to Father John's house.

Well, when we got there we drank a different kind of liquor, and we conversed. I showed him my new pants, which we had bought in New York. I had bought them with Telex, and his wife Paxku'. But it was Father John who paid for the pants, which were for wearing in the snow, because it was very cold. . . .

We went to where a Mexican was going to school. His name was also Carlito, but his father and mother were in Mexico. . . . (Later when) he arrived at Father John's house, he went to visit me in the room that Father John gave me. Well, when Carlito got there, he spoke very well; he conversed very well.

"Well, how are you, Chep? Have you come here to the United States?" he asked me.

"Well, I have come, Carlito. How are you? Have you also come here to the United States?" I said to him.

"Well, I have come, because here is where I have come to study," he told me.

"Well, that's fine," I told him.

"Well, it seems fine—the people have such good hearts," said the boy.

"Well, you know how to speak English well," I told the boy.

"Well, now I do know, but when I arrived here at first, I didn't know how to speak English, either," said the boy.

I had a good talk with that Carlito.

. . . Well, when we finished eating, then they played cards—*baraja* it is called in Spanish. But only Mother Catherine played, with the two Carlitos: one American boy and one Mexican, but they both were named Carlito. Well, when they finished playing cards, then we went to watch television. It's just like a movie: one can see everything that the people do. . . . It is very nice to watch. . . . Well, when we had satisfied ourselves watching television, I went to my room, because my eyes were tired out from watching television.

12 FEBRUARY, 1968

Well, early on Monday, Father John went to see me in my room.

"Well, how was it, Chep? Did you sleep well? Were you too cold?" he asked me.

"No, Father John, I slept very well, because my bed is very warm," I told him.

"Ah, well, that's good then," said Father John to me.

"That's good," I told him.

But the bed he gave me was very good, indeed: it was electric. It was connected to the electric current.

. . . Well, when we had finished eating, we went to the university where all the students gather. But we went by car. Well, I arrived at the building. I was shown where I could work every day. That's when I spoke to all the boys and girls, the students. All the people who wanted to learn Tzotzil were there. . . . But they were very happy, indeed, to see that I had arrived at the university where all the boys and girls would learn.

. . . Well, when we had finished eating, we started to work again, and they asked how one should talk in Tzotzil. John Musician was making a primer in Tzotzil, and they wanted to learn to be very good professors of Tzotzil. They knew how to talk a little, but there were still words they didn't understand in Tzotzil; there were some whose meanings in Spanish they didn't know, and that's why they wanted to learn.

. . . Well, when we arrived at a different office, Father John took in some photographs, along with a small machine. But that little machine gave a strong light, which was for the photographs, so that we could see well the photographs of all the people that the students had met. That small machine was just like a movie the way it projected the pictures.

But one could really see well what the people were doing. There were some of people curing on the sacred mountains around Zinacantán Center. There were some where people were sick, and the curers were just killing the chickens. And you could see all of San Cristóbal and Teopisca—you could see them perfectly. And you could see Zinacantán, and Nabenchauk, and Apas, and you could see some of Atz'am during the festival of the Rosary. The steward-royals were there, with the musicians, with the elders—the large *alcalde* and the small *alcalde*— and the *regidores* with the scribes, and all the stewards, with their musicians and their sacristans. Everything could be seen on that small movie.

. . . They had a party to celebrate my arrival in the United States. It was a very good party that Father John put on, with all the students. All the people who had been in Chiapas gathered together: the boys and the girls, together with the new students—all gathered together. We drank two or three kinds of liquor, for the party. There I talked with all the boys and with the girls. All of them talked to me. They asked me how long I would be in the United States.

"Well, Chep, how are you? Did you arrive well in Cambridge? Did you have no problems on the airplane?" the boys and girls asked me.

"I arrived well. I had no problems on the airplane, because I am accustomed to airplanes. . . . But it's only that I was just like some kind of dumb person, because I don't know how to speak English. I couldn't speak, and I couldn't understand what people were saying, I was just very stupid," I told the students.

"Ah, but why, wasn't there anyone who spoke Spanish among the people who came with you on the airplane?" they asked me.

"No, there was no one who spoke Spanish," I told them.

"Ah, that's bad, then," said the boys and the girls.

"It is somewhat bad. But I did arrive, finally, even dumb," I told them.

"Well, did you pass through New York? How did you like it, good or bad?" they also asked.

"Ah, it was very good, indeed. I saw the big stores. I ascended a building, supposedly the tallest one of all," I told them.

"Well, weren't you afraid on such a tall building? Could you see all of New York?" they said.

"I saw a bit, but you couldn't see everything because there was too much smoke—smoke from the machines, from the factories," I told them.

"Ah, so you didn't see everything then," they said.

"No, but I did see a lot, all the same. It's just that you couldn't see everything. We traveled on a train, and I saw the animals," I told them.

. . . Later we watched television. You can see everything that the people do. Even if it's far away, you can still see it on television: the way they play on the surface of ice, for the boys and girls have learned all kinds of games. They play with a different kind of ball, but that ball travels very fast, because the ice is extremely slippery. But since they have learned well how to move on the surface of the ice, they like to play. But nonetheless, they still fall down sometimes, because the ice is very slippery.

13 FEBRUARY

Well, when we got to the big building, there wasn't anyone there yet. We were all alone, because we arrived early. Well, as for me, since I knew already what work I was to do, I began to work. I wrote on a typewriter; I made a great text, about what I was doing every day.

Well, later on, John Musician arrived, with Victoria. They went to ask about still more words, ones they still didn't understand properly. I had a conversation with them.

Well, later on, John Musician took along another machine, called a tape recorder, because he had recorded all the music for the *cargo* holders. The music for the steward-royal was there, and for the stewards, and for the *alféreces,* and for the senior *alcalde* when they decorate their altars. And there also was the music for the entertainers at the festival of St. Sebastian the Martyr. He had recorded all of the pieces there on the tape. . . .

Later, a woman came. Her name was Candy. She came, but she came to teach me their language, called English. She had brought another tape recorder with her, because she had recorded there on the tape how one speaks in the morning, as when one says "Good morning" in Spanish. And she had recorded how one ought to ask what a boy's or a girl's name is, and also how one asks where they come from. She had recorded all of that. Well, on the first day that she taught me, I learned only three or four words.

Later in the day, we went to still another office, which was where the students learned Tzotzil. They gathered together, and we three taught them: myself, with John Musician, and with Victoria. We taught them Tzotzil: how to speak properly in Tzotzil. We recorded the Tzotzil on a tape recorder, so that the boys and girls could hear it. Well, when the boys and girls could pronounce the Tzotzil well, John Musician asked them what it meant in English, because he wanted to see if they knew what it meant in their own language. Of the boys, some knew, some didn't know what it meant in their language.

That is how I spent one day, the thirteenth of February.

14 FEBRUARY

When we had finished watching television, I went to my own room, because I wanted to study my English, because I really want to learn how they speak. I studied English for perhaps one hour, but in that one hour that I studied English, I only learned a very little. Well, when I had studied a few words of English, I went to sleep, because it was already late at night.

15 FEBRUARY

Well, when we had finished eating, we went to watch television, because the boys and the girls were playing every night, trying to see who had learned the best how to play on the surface of the ice. They raced, and they danced, and they played with a ball—but it was a different sort of ball, a square piece of rubber, but just thin, not thick. They tried to insert it in a goal. But they didn't put it in with their hands; instead they had specially made sticks they hit it with. Well, whoever put the most into the goal would win. That's what they did every night.

16 FEBRUARY

Well, when I got to my office, Father John said to me: "Well, Chep, you're going to fix these papers; you're going to fasten them together in groups of two sheets," he told me.

"Well, fine, I'll fasten them," I told him. I began to fasten the papers. He gave me a stapler in order to fasten the papers.

Well, when I had finished stapling the papers, I went to my office. When I arrived in my office, just then the person who taught me English arrived. She went to see whether I had learned a bit, because she had put the words on a paper for me.

"Are you here, Chep?" said the woman named Candy.

"I'm here," I told her.

She taught me how to pronounce each letter.

Well, when she had finished teaching me, a student of Tzotzil arrived. It was a girl named Rosa. I taught her some Tzotzil. When I had finished teaching the girl, another student, a boy, arrived as well. He was called Francesco, a boy from Italy. I taught him for an hour, too. I finished teaching him. Then another boy arrived, called Paul. I also taught him for an hour, and I finished with him. Well, when I had finished teaching each one separately, then all four of them gathered together, and they asked me if I wanted to write down on paper how they should ask for food in Tzotzil when they finally got to Chiapas.

"Well, okay, why not," I told them. So I wrote down on paper how one should talk in Tzotzil.

Well, when I had finished writing on paper, we began to converse in Tzotzil, because I wanted to see which one knew best how to talk in Tzotzil. There were four of them gathered there in my office, two boys and two girls. Well, the boys—they knew less Tzotzil, but the two girls could speak better. One of the girls was called Rosa and the other Catherine. The boys were called Francesco and Paul. But they couldn't pronounce Tzotzil. The girls could pronounce it better.

Well, when I had finished talking with them in Tzotzil, they asked what the name in Tzotzil was for head, hair, eyeball, eyebrow, eyelash, nose, mouth, lips, teeth, the whole face, the ears. They asked about everything. When I told them the name for each kind of thing, they wrote it down on paper. However much I told them, they wrote it all down.

Well, when the time came for me to return to Father John's house, we hadn't finished, but I had to return home. Well, the students wanted to continue learning more, but when the time came, I went home. I left the boys and girls there, because they went on studying the words, and writing them down.

. . . When we were eating, Father John said, "Well, today, Chep, all of my children are together. It's just like a big festival, what we're doing today," said Old John.

"Yes, it's like a big curing ceremony, what we're doing, it seems," I told him.

"That's right," said Father John.

Well, when we had finished eating, they taught me a game with cards, but I really wasn't familiar with the game. Because there is a different kind of money, but it is plastic money. The one who wins is the one who gets the number twenty-one. But if someone gets more than twenty-one, he loses. He has to pay more. But if someone doesn't get as much as twenty, he loses less. That's how we played for a while. Well, later on we went to another room to watch television. Once we had satisfied ourselves watching television, I went to sleep, because it was already late at night.

17 FEBRUARY

A friend of mine arrived, named Mark. He came to pick me up where I was working, because I was going out sightseeing with him. We got on a train inside the earth. We went across the river, because we were going to look at a large building in Boston, a very tall building. It has perhaps fifty-two stories, and that's why we went to become acquainted with it, since I hadn't been there on my previous trip to the United States. When we arrived, we went up. When we were on the highest floor, we looked at all the other big buildings. On the other hand, the little ones couldn't all be seen, because Boston is very big. That's why we didn't see everything.

Well, when we had finished looking, we went to a store where they sell liquor. Markux went in to buy a bottle. He took it with him back to where his room was, but first we passed by where he was studying how to work as a doctor. We looked at all the photographs of the first doctors, because all their photos were there. Well, when we'd finished looking at the photographs, we went to look at the bones: the bones of dead people. But all the bones were there: head bones, face bones, the nose, the bones of the mouth, the bones of the neck, of the shoulder blades, and the ribs, the teeth bones—all the bones. That's what Mark studied, because he was learning to be a doctor. Well, when we had finished looking, we went to another room. We went to look at pictures of people's blood.

But the pictures were very small, too small to see with just the eyes. We can only see them if we look at them with an apparatus. There is such an apparatus, especially made to look at them with. With that one can easily see the blood. It looks very large in the apparatus, and you can see the blood as little round things, that look something like pills, except that there are also ones that look blue green. But some are smaller and some are bigger, as well. Well, Mark said that our blood has its little animals, too, but I wasn't able to see the animals that he said were there. Perhaps I am too stupid, and that's why I couldn't see them. Well, when we had finished looking at other people's blood, he asked if he could look at my blood.

"Well, you can," I told him.

"Well, good, then. Let's see how it is, but I'll have to take a bit of your blood out," he said to me.

"Well, that's all right," I told him.

"Well, okay, I'll take it out of your fingertip," he said.

"Well, that's all right," I told him.

He pricked one of my fingers with a needle, and he took out some blood from my fingertip. When he had finished taking it out, he put it on a small piece of glass, but it was a special piece of glass made for that purpose. There were two little pieces of glass, and he smeared both of them with blood. When he had finished smearing them, we looked through the apparatus, and I saw all of how my blood looks. . . .

Then we went to a dining room for all the doctors who are learning how to operate on people. They say that they store dead people there. They say that that is how they learn how to open up people who are especially sick. But we didn't go in to look at the dead people, because I myself didn't want to look; we just looked at their photographs instead.

18 FEBRUARY

We went to watch television, because it was Sunday. This was the end of the games in France, with the boys and girls playing. They had a very good large festival in France for the end of the games. They were only going to play again in four years, but in a different country, and there would be different boys playing as well. The ones who won were given gifts. The ones who didn't win didn't receive gifts; they just played for free. That's what I saw on the television. Well, when the festival was over, all the boys and girls sang.

19 FEBRUARY

Well, Mother Catherine and I went to a clinic, because they were going to look at my teeth, since they were hurting quite a bit. That's why I went to have them looked at. Well, when we got there,

"Wait a little while because the doctor hasn't come yet," said the women or the girls that worked there at the clinic.

"Okay," Mother Catherine told them.

Well, when the doctor arrived, he looked at the list of the people who wanted to have their teeth treated. Well, I waited a little while, while he finished looking at the mouths of the other people who had arrived first, when I hadn't yet arrived. Then the doctor called me, since my name was already on the list, since his secretary had written down on paper the names of the people as they arrived.

Well, when I was called, I went where the doctor was. He looked at my teeth. Well, before he rinsed my teeth, first he asked me whether I ever went to the dentist when I was in Chiapas.

"Well, how many times a year do you go to the doctor for your teeth?" one nurse asked me, a boy, because he was the only one who knew Spanish, and that's why he asked me if I ever went to the doctor.

"Well, as for me, since I am an Indian, I don't go much to the doctor, only if my teeth get sick," I told him.

"Well, when did you first go to the doctor about your teeth?" he asked me.

"I went to the doctor the first time perhaps four or five years ago," I told him.

"Well, when was the last time you went?" he also asked.

"I went to the doctor in September, but he just gave me some medicine to get rid of the pain in my teeth," I told him.

"Well, did it work?" he asked.

"No, it didn't get better, it hurt later on," I told him.

"Well, what do you use to rinse your mouth?" he asked me.

"Well, since I am an Indian, I rinse my mouth just with water," I told him.

"Well, when do you rinse your teeth?" he asked me.

"I rinse them when I finish eating," I told him.

"All right, how old are you, do you know?" he asked me.

"I know. I am thirty-three," I told him.

"Well, what month were you born," he said as well.

"I was born on December fifteenth," I told him.

"Well, what work are you doing here?" he asked me.

"Well, I have come as an informant for the anthropologists, because they want to learn what our customs are like," I told him.

"Well, what is your address and what is your telephone number?" he asked me.

"Ah, I don't know, but the wife of the professor has come, and she knows," I told him.

"Okay," he said to me. He went to ask Mother Catherine, because she had stayed in the other room. When he had finished asking me these things, a doctor looked at my mouth. But he just looked with his eyes. Well, when he had finished looking, then he went to take some pictures of my teeth with X-rays, because that is the tool for looking at our teeth. Well, when this woman had finished looking at my teeth with X-rays, "You should come at four o'clock," she said.

. . . Well, when the classes were finished, I went another time to the clinic with Mother Catherine. Well, when we got there we waited a little while for the doctor. Well, when the doctor arrived, he rinsed out my teeth with a machine. He really rinsed them all well, but while he was rinsing them, I really felt a lot of pain, because blood came out of all my teeth. Well, when he had finished rinsing them, I returned home with Mother Catherine. But the doctor told the girl to tell us "You should come another time," she said, or so Mother Catherine told me, because she was the one who was told this, since I don't understand English myself.

20 FEBRUARY

Well, I awoke early on the twentieth of February, and I went to the bathroom and washed. I rinsed my mouth, but my teeth really hurt. Well, Mother Catherine knew that I couldn't eat any meat, so she gave me chicken eggs, since they are softer to eat. Well, when I had finished eating, we went to the building where we worked every day.

21 FEBRUARY

The woman named Candy arrived, to teach me English. Later, Victoria arrived, and I worked with her. She had a text about jokes, and we looked at it to see if the spelling was right or wrong. Well, later John Musician arrived, and I worked with him, too. He had a list of Tzotzil words. Later, Little John arrived, and I worked with him, too, since he had a text about how the jaguar entertainers arrive at the house of old man Xun Chiku' in Elan Vo', the one who guards the *t'ent'en* drum that is used for the fiesta of St. Sebastian. We looked that over to see whether it was properly written. Well, when I finished working with him, a girl arrived, named Pascuala. I also worked with her, since she wanted to learn how to count in Tzotzil.

Well, when I finished working with her, John Musician arrived again, because he took me off to his house to eat supper with him. Well, when we finished eating, we went out, and we went to a bar where there were musicians, and we went to enjoy ourselves. But it was eight o'clock at night when we arrived at the bar. And there were very many people, so we had to wait for a long time. Well, when we entered, the musicians hadn't arrived yet. After a little while, the musicians arrived and they began to play their instruments, but their tunes were very good indeed. Well, when the first group of musicians had finished playing five songs, they left. Another group of musicians came. There were five men and one girl. Well, the men were the ones who played the music. The girl sang, but she really knew how to sing, that girl. They also played about five sets of songs. Well, when they had finished their five sets, a man came, and he said that all the people who had come in first could go out now, because there were still more people waiting around outside. Well, when he said that everybody should go out, we also left, and all those who were waiting outside went inside. We didn't see what happened after that.

Well, on our way back, John passed by to buy ice cream. He and one of his friends, named David, got together the money between the two of them. Well, when they had bought it, we went to the friend's house, because that's where we were going to eat the ice cream. When we had finished the ice cream, we went to Father John's house. John Musician was going to take me there, but it was already eleven o'clock at night when we arrived at the friend's house. Well, when we set out for Father John's house, it must have been almost midnight, and John Musician got lost, since he didn't know the way. Well, when we got to Father John's house, we drank a bit of liquor and we also ate a little. Well, when we had finished drinking and eating some bread, John Musician returned to his house. Well, as for me, I went to sleep.

21 FEBRUARY

Well, when we finished eating, we went to the building where we work every day. When we arrived, there wasn't a single person there, because at that time there was no work in all the offices, because that was a day on which all the people took a rest. That was the day that George Washington either was born or died. But as for me, I worked, since I'm not an American, and that's why I worked anyway.

22 FEBRUARY

Well, when I had finished eating, Father John said to me that it was the day on which the machine that was for washing clothes worked.

"Well, Chep, you can change your clothes, because it's the day that the machine works; Mother Catherine will wash them for you," said Father John.

"Well, okay," I told him.

... Well, we got to the office, and we went down below, to a room underneath the ground. We went to watch a film about how the people who live farther north live. They don't see the sun the entire year, because they say that there are four months when they don't see the sun. They don't see it during the shortness of the sun; they only see it during its longer path.

But these people do not have good houses. Their houses are nothing but ice. Their clothes are just animal skins. When they eat, they eat animal flesh, but raw, since they don't have proper fires. They just have tiny fires, just animal oil. But that is only to warm the insides of their houses: they don't use it to cook their food. For there are no forests, just pure ice.

As for the animals, they kill them in the sea, but they use arrows to kill them. They have no rifles, no machetes, no knives. The knives they do have are just like axes, but they use them to skin the animals. But the women are the ones who skin the animals, but they are very used to skinning animals, since they can finish skinning one in just a moment. Well, once they have skinned it, they immediately eat the animal raw. But they are really big animals that they kill out on the ocean, so big that one man can't carry one animal. In order to carry the animals home, they have a kind of canoe, but their canoes can travel on the surface of the ice. But they just have dogs working for them to drag their canoes along—six dogs that they have tied with a rope. I saw that the canoe moves along because they pull it, but the dogs travel very fast. It's just like a wagon that they use to haul the animals, and the dogs can also carry two or three people.

But who knows how it is that they don't die of the cold, because they travel on pure ice.

That is how all the people in the north live.

Well, when they are in their houses, the men and the women, the boys and the girls, work. But they have a different sort of work: they make gods, but they carve them from rock. That's their work after they finish eating. Their gods are very beautiful, but they are pure stone.

Well, there was one man who had a son. The son went to sea, because he wanted to kill an animal in the sea. Well, he got one animal, and when he was about to reach his house, his mother and his other relatives came to meet him, because supposedly it was the first time he had killed an animal. Well, when they ate the animal, the boy's father didn't eat it, because they say that's the custom: a man doesn't eat the meat of the first animal his son kills. That's what I saw.

Father John said to me, "Well, Chep, we're going to work a little. We'll put into a book all the photographs for the year 1967," said Father John.

"Well, alright," I told him.

"Well, for all the photographs, you can pick out which ones belong with each other," said Father John.

"Okay," I told him.

I began to select the photographs. There was one of the president, with the *alcaldes,* with the senior *alcalde* and the junior *alcalde,* with the *regidores,* and the scribes. There were photos of all of them. There was a photograph of Domingo de la Torres, and Mariano Anselmo. And there was a picture of Domingo's wife, with his children. There were many photographs. And there were photographs of people from other hamlets as well. There was a photo of old Chep Nuj, with his wife and all his daughters. There were photographs of old Yermo's family. And there was a photograph of old Xun Vaskes from Nabenchauk, with his children. And there were also photographs of people from Apas. There was a photograph of the curers, when the students were there, when the curers gave candles for the mid-year ceremony. So there were lots of pictures. There were pictures of the musicians, and I selected them first. When I had finished sorting them, I put them in a book. The book was especially made for storing photographs.

24 FEBRUARY

When we got to Old John's house, I went to wash, because there was going to be a party at the house of a student, named Rick, with his wife Candy. Well, when I finished washing, I went to the dining room and we ate. When we finished eating, I changed my clothes. Once Father John and Mother Catherine had changed their clothes, we went to the house of the person who was having the party. Well, when we got there, there were already other men and women, boys and girls, there. Lots of people had gathered together at Rick and Candy's house. When we arrived, they offered us liquor. We drank it: Father John and Mother

Catherine drank, also John Musician and his wife, and Little John, and Victoria and her husband, and Nora and also her husband. And other men and women drank, too, but I didn't know them.

One man arrived who had come from Cuba with his wife, because he had run away from his own country. He said he had run away from a man who didn't know God in church. The man was an evangelist, named Fidel Castro. The man who came to the United States was a Catholic, who did know the saints in church, and he didn't like Fidel Castro's way of thinking. That's why he had come to the United States. That's what he told me when we talked together. But he knew how to speak English very well, since it had been four or five years since he left Cuba, and that's why he had learned English.

But the party that Rick and his wife gave had no musicians. There was just a machine, a tape recorder, that played the music. But it played the music very well. Well, while the tape recorder was playing the music, all the people conversed and drank liquor. Well, when it began to get late, some of the people went home. But Father John and Mother Catherine and I stayed longer, and it was three o'clock in the morning when we left. We went to Father John's house, but we were a bit drunk. When we got home it must have been 3 A.M. Well, I went to sleep right away, since I was very sleepy, and I had also gotten a bit drunk myself.

25 FEBRUARY

Well, I woke up early on the twenty-fifth of February, and I went to the bathroom to wash. But I was very ill with a hangover from the liquor we had drunk at the fiesta. When I woke up on the morning of the twenty-fifth, the sun was already high. It was already eight o'clock, because it was near dawn when we went to sleep. Well, when I got up, Father John was already awake, since he must be resistant to sleepiness. . . .

We went to try a game, called darts. But that was a game I didn't know. First Old John gave numbers, 301 points he wrote on a paper. Well, he handed out three darts each to all four of us. When he had passed them out, we began to play, because the idea was to see who would first get down to 0 from the 301 points written on the paper. But the first one to win was Father John's son, Carlito. Well, later the next one to win was Father John. Next I won. Well, the other Carlito, the Mexican, didn't win at all.

. . . Later we went to three different churches, which were near the museum. Well, first we went to a church for Catholics, and there I saw Our Holy Father Christ in the Catholic church. Then we went to a church for Protestants. It was called a church, but it had no saints: it just had a cross inside the church. Well, later, we went to another church for Judas. But we didn't go in, since someone was learning to play the organ. That's why we didn't go in. But I could see enough to see that there were no saints.

26 FEBRUARY

. . . Father John arrived, but it was already past 6 P.M. It was already dark.

"Well, Chep, we're going to the house of Doctor Thomas. But first we have to pass by another building to drink a little liquor," said Old John.

"Okay," I told him.

We went to another building where the old professors can drink liquor. Well, when we had drunk liquor, we went to the house of the man called Doctor Thomas, since we were going to have dinner there. When we arrived, first he gave us liquor. We all drank together, because lots of people had gathered together. There was Father John and his wife. One of his sons was there with his sweetheart. Mark was there. I was there. Rick and his wife were there. Another boy arrived, the nephew of Doctor Thomas's wife. Well, when we had finished drinking liquor, we ate dinner. We ate chicken. Old Doctor Thomas offered us very good food.

When we had finished eating, Doctor Thomas showed a movie. He had a little machine that was for looking at photographs, since he had stored away a great many photographs. There was one of the president in Zinacantán Center. There was a picture of Domingo with his wife. There were pictures of all the students of anthropology. There was a picture of all of Doctor Thomas's children, and photographs of people from Na Chij. There were pictures of people from Nabenchauk, and from Apas, when Doctor Thomas was examining them. We looked at all the photographs, but Doctor Thomas had a very great many photographs stored away. Well, when we had finished looking at the photographs, we returned to Father John's house, but it was already late at night when we left. When we got to Father John's house, I went to sleep.

29 FEBRUARY

Well, there was a Professor González, and two other friends of his—both younger—had also been invited. Both of them came from Argentina. They talked a great deal, the whole time they were there at his house. They began talking about the troubles in Argentina. They mentioned the war in Viet Nam, and they talked about how the government had changed in Argentina. They had very many things to talk about, but I couldn't understand everything they said, because they didn't talk Spanish the way Mexicans do. They speak differently.

1 MARCH

. . . Father John arrived.

"Well, Chep, let's go to the hamlet, but who knows if we'll get there, because my car is somewhat ill," said Father John.

"Okay, let's go," I told him.

We went to where he had left his car; we got in, and we set out. But Father John's car broke on the road. When it broke, he stopped it, and got out.

"Well, Chep, wait for me here. I'll go to search for a mechanic to see what's wrong with my car. Let's see if perhaps it can be fixed," said Father John.

"Okay, I'll wait for you here," I told him.

Father John left. I waited there a while. Shortly he arrived with a mechanic, but in the mechanic's car.

"Well, let's go in this man's car, because he's going to take my car to his workshop," said Father John.

"Okay, let's go."

I got out of Father John's car, and we got into the mechanic's car. Father John's car was towed away. We got to the workshop, and Father John had a talk with the senior mechanic. He asked him whether they would fix it right away.

"I can't, it's too late. I'll fix it tomorrow," said the master mechanic.

"Okay," said Father John. His car stayed there.

2 March

Victoria arrived.

"Well, Chep, let's go to the first floor to see a movie," she told me.

"Okay, that's fine, let's go," I told her.

We went down and watched a movie about all the people at the festival of St. Lawrence. There were pictures of all the *alféreces*, the *mayordomos*, the captains. There were pictures from the time they go to greet the visiting saints from Ixtapa and from Salinas. There were pictures of people in cantinas, drinking liquor, and there was a picture of a mariache in Doña Elisea's house. There were pictures of the horse race, and pictures of the gringo students who were there watching the festival. There was a picture of the ritual advisor at Yermo Nuj's house, and of his ritual helpers. . . . There were pictures of how they made the gunpowder for the cannons for old Chep Nuj. There were pictures of his daughters carrying firewood, and pictures of how they went to the well for water or to wash clothes and blankets. There was everything.

There were pictures of old Chep Nuj with his son-in-law, his daughter's husband. They were playing music in Chep Nuj's house. There was a picture of old Chep Nuj with another son-in-law, while they were eating, with his wife and daughters patting tortillas.

3 March

We got up very early in the morning, because Father John, Mother Catherine, and Carlito were all going to ski. As for me, I stayed in Father John's house, because he told me that John Musician would come to pick me up, since I was going to accompany him on a visit to the Museum of Science in Boston, near Cambridge.

Father John said to me as he left: "Well, Chep, you can wait for John Musician because he's coming to pick you up," said Father John.

"Well, what time will John Musician come?" I asked Father John.

"He'll come at ten o'clock," said Father John.

"Okay," I told him.

I waited for John Musician, but he arrived at 10:30. When he arrived,

"Are you here Chep, do you want to go out for a trip?" he asked me.

"Well, let's go, then," I told him.

"Well, Chep, what do you prefer to see? Do you want to see the museum or would you prefer to go see the ocean?" John Musician asked me.

"Well, perhaps it would be best if we went to see the museum, because the ocean is very cold," I told him. Because there was lots of snow at that time. . . .

We went to the Museum of Science. We went to see what they had in that museum. There were all kinds of animals, and there were photographs of the world, the earth, the oceans, where each country was—they had everything in that museum. There were pictures of how children are born inside women's bellies. There were pictures of how it looks after one month in its mother's belly, and of when it is two months old, and three months . . . and in its eight month and in its ninth month, up until the time the baby is born. When women have a hard time giving birth, the way the doctors cut the umbilical cord—you could see everything.

You could also see how doctors do operations, when they remove diseases from people who have them in their stomachs. Everything is in that museum.

Well, later on we went to see a man with electricity. He would get a bit of light out of his hand, and he would give it to other people, but the light was very strong. You could feel it in your bones. I tried it. Well, later we went to see a man with two snakes, one a large female snake, the other a small female snake. They wrapped themselves around his hand, because they were very tame snakes. Well, when we finished watching all this, we went to see some different birds, because there they had all different kinds of birds.

4 March

Well, at four o'clock in the afternoon, I went to the doctor with Mother Catherine again. They were going to rinse my teeth another time. We got to the building where the doctor works, and we waited awhile. Well, when the doctor arrived, he looked at my teeth right away. He rinsed them very well, but it took him a long time to do it. Well, once my teeth were clean, Mother Catherine and I returned, but we passed by to pick up Father John in his office, because his car was still broken.

. . . When we had finished eating, we looked at papers and books. But a little later, I went to sleep, since my teeth were hurting me a bit.

7 March

Later on, another boy arrived, Mariano, a student of Tzotzil. I worked with him as well, and he asked me about when a Zinacanteco woman married a Chamula, or when a man married a Chamula, did they change their clothes, or if a Chamula or a Zinacanteco or someone from another Indian community changed his clothes to *ladino* clothes, could they change themselves into *ladinos*. That's what he wanted to find out. He asked how one could recognize a Chamula or a Zinacanteco, or some other Indian, if they dressed like a *ladino*. That's what he wanted to know. Well, I told him that you could recognize them if they didn't have the same sort of face as a real *ladino*. Well, when I had told him that, he asked whether you could tell a Zinacanteco from a Chamula, or someone from another place, if they had nice clothes like a *ladino*.

"Well, you can recognize them, because the Zinacantecos don't walk around in groups; they prefer to walk one by one, when they dress like *ladinos*," I told him.

"Well, how about Chamulas, how do you recognize if they're Chamulas or from some other place?" said the person called Mariano.

"Well, you can recognize Chamulas because they only walk around in twos, or sometimes one by one like Zinacantecos," I told Mariano. "Well, other Indians don't walk around singly, but instead in groups of four or five," I told him.

"Well, so that's how you can tell them apart then," said Mariano. But he had a very hard time understanding the truth about how one can recognize people who have changed their clothing.

8 March

Later on, Mariano came another time. He wanted to ask how Chamulas speak when they meet a Zinacanteco on the path. I told him that Chamulas say *ulo'* to Zinacantecos. Well, when he had asked about Chamulas, he asked how Zinacantecos talk to people from San Andrés. I told him that they say *amikó*. When he had asked that, he asked about Tenejapa. I told him how the Tenejapas speak with Zinacantecos.

"They say *ta*," I told him.

Later he asked about Cancuc. I told him that it was just the same, *ta*.

He asked about Guaquitepec, about Sitalá, about Ocosingo, about Chilón, about Yajalón—about everything. I told him that all the faraway people spoke the same way. They say *tat*. Later, he asked about Huistán, and I told him that they say *tot*. Later he asked about San Felipe, and I told him that they say *to*. Later he asked about Ixtapa, and I told him they also say *amiko*.

9 March

I stayed at John Musician's house, because I had dinner there with John Musician and his wife and another four of his friends: two men and two women who had arrived at John Musician's house. We ate together. Well, when we had finished eating, one of John Musician's friends had us watch photographs, because he had been in Japan, and so they were pictures of Japanese people that he let us look at. There is a machine that makes the pictures appear larger. But John Musician's friend had brought a very great many pictures with him. Well, when we finished looking at all the pictures, it was already late at night. But they kept on talking even after John Musician's friend had finished showing us the pictures. Well, later, John Musician's friends went home. When his friends had gone, we went to the house of another of John Musician's friends, because the students were having a party that we went to watch. But it was already one o'clock. We stayed there about one hour. Well, later, we went to Father John's house, but it was already 2:20 A.M. I went right to sleep because I was feeling very sleepy.

END NOTE
[1] The editors regret that it was impossible to publish the Tzotzil for this set of ethnographic observations.

AS FOR ME AND
THE HARVARD CHIAPAS PROJECT

Robert M. Laughlin
Smithsonian Institution

Well, as for me, I have rendered these Mayan historical records of the Harvard Chiapas Project as they were written. The first three are reminiscent of Mayan glyph texts, less genealogy and the supernatural. They are catalogs of events, carefully dated, with the place of action and the protagonists' names scrupulously recorded. Except for deliberately humorous references to gringo cannibalism and Indian witchcraft, the actors appear as unsmiling as in a formal photograph. They seem to have responded with confidence to the challenge presented to them by their employers, and, indeed, each has become a prominent figure in later years. Despite the hardships, many unmentioned, there is a hint of nostalgia for the days of the Harvard Chiapas Project, appreciation for the opportunity to travel abroad, and remembrance of strong bonds of friendship made with the foreigners who came to study their culture with a persistence difficult to comprehend. Under the direction of *Mol Xun* this project became a community of fellow workers.

SLO'IL MARYAN LOPIS MENTES

Ja' no'ox jna'oj ta 1968 ta 8 de enero, kojtikin li mol profesor Evon Vogt. "Mol Xun" sbi ta batz'i k'ope. Ja' bankilal jpas mantal ta skotol jchan vunetik ta Universidad de Harvard, Massachusetts. Lek yamiko sbaik xchi'uk ti anima jtote.

A ti mol Xune, oy snaik li' ta Jobele, "Rancho de Harvard" sbi. Ja' te ta xk'ot skotol li jchan vun prinkoetike.

Veno ti anima jtote te xa ono'ox ta x'abtej ti ta 1968 une. A ti och ta abtel tajmek ti anima jtote ta 1966. Jal xa ono'ox te ch-abtej.

Ava'un; ti mol Xun une, oy ep chtalanuk ti yajchan vuntake. Ta sk'an ta xchanik ya'ik ti slo'il ya'yejik ti moletike. Ja' ta sjak' ya'ik k'u s'elanil ech' li antivo k'ope, li kventoe, li ochel ta nae. Skotol ta sk'an ta xchanik yajchan vuntak li mol Xun une, yu'un toj lek ta xa'iik ti namal krisanoetike.

Veno komo k'alal vulanuk tal ta yosilal Chiapa li jchan vunetike ta sk'anik yajchol k'op o informante sventa batz'i k'op schi'uk ta xa ono'ox ta xchanel talel li vune. Oyun xa ta kinto anyo xchanel ti ta 1968 une. Ja' o te xich' talel mantal ti anima jtote ti ta sk'an jun chib yajtz'ibajom ti jtotik Xun une. Ja' ti oy ep ti jchan vunetike; komo ep ta tos ta sk'an ta xch'an ya'ik ti lo'iletike. Oy ta sjak' xchan ya'ik sventa abtel ta chobtik, sventa otol k'ak'al, sventa ilolal, sventa ak' chamel; ti k'u yelanil ta xak'be sbaik chamel li kavron inyoetike; sventa antivo k'op, kvento, sventa pas abtel yu'un martomaetik ta k'in, sventa meltzanel chapanel ta kavilto. Skotol k'usi sk'an xchanik ti jchan vunetike.

Veno li vo'on Maryanune, te liyak'bik kabtel. Ja' li'abtej xchi'uk li profesor Jpetule, lek vinik. Jun a'vil li'abtej xchi'uk. Batz'i bij tajmek. Lek xchanbe sk'op li Chamulae. Laj slapbe sk'u'. Xchan ti k'u yelan kuxul ti Chamulae. Batz'i lek bat yajchan vun ti mol profesor mol Xune. Meltzaj jlik vun ku'un kutik—"El Sol del Mundo"—sbi ti vune.

Veno ta 1970 ta vakib marso tal mantal ta nom, ti stak' xibat ta xanobal ta slumalik ti jtotik Xune, yu'un oy te mas jchan vunetik tzk'an ta xojtikinikun, ti k'u yelanil li'abtejkutik jun a'vil xchi'uk ti Jpetule.

Veno solel lik jmeltzan skotol ti jvunaltake. Meltzaj jlik jvunal sventa permiso yu'un jtot jme' ja' ti mu to bu ep ka'vilale. Jk'oponkutik jun jlisensaro te ta Jobel ja' li mol Daniel Sarmiento Roja li sekretaryo sventa kovyerno ta orae.

Veno te meltzaj skotol ti jvunaltake. Libat k'alal ta nom, ja' to te ta Universidad de Harvard ta 15 de marso 1970. Jun u te lipaj, ja' spasbun pavor li mol Xun xchi'uk li mol Petule.

Pves kol yalik ti chib moletike, laj stzakikun ta muk', oy kojtikinbe ti slumalike. Jech o ta ora ta to xvul ta ko'onton ti buch'u ech' jchi'in ta abtele, batz'i chabanuk xk'otik ta skotolik ti amikoetike, yu'un li namal krisanoetike, batz'i lek tajmek yo'ontonik.

K'alal lisut talel ta nome liyak'bi to kabtel chanib a'vil ta Rancho.

Veno laj ti kabtele, libat jsa' yan kabtel ta yan opisina, pere mas kich' tal jvokol xa.

Veno ta k'unk'un te laj sa' talel yan ti kabtele.

Ta milnovesyento ochenta li'abtej xchi'uk ti mol jlisensaryo Jaime Sabines yitz'in ti anima mol Juan Sabinese, laj yak'bun kabtel jun a'vil xchi'uk o'lol a'vil.

Laj un, bat jsa' yan kabtel no'oxtok. Te li'abtej to ox chanib a'vil xchi'uk li Robert M. Laughlin li sventa Sna Jtz'ibajom tey jmeltzan jayibuk livroetik, ta ora te oyun ta jpas mantal ta jlumal. Vo'on peserente un. Te pasik pertonal mu masuk ep laj jtzak ta vun li jlo'ile, yu'un ch'abal mas ep syempo ku'un. Batz'i vokol ta xokob jlikeluk ti jk'ak'ale. Te jk'opon jbatik k'usi ora antzetik viniketik li' ta Norte Amerika! Chabanoxuk ta akotolik!

MARYAN LOPIS MENTES

I just remember that on January 8, 1968, I met Professor Evon Vogt. "Mr. John" is his name in Tzotzil. He was the senior director of all the students from Harvard University, Massachusetts. He was a good friend of my late father.

Mr. John had houses here in San Cristóbal called "The Harvard Ranch." All the American students arrived there.

Well, my late father had been working there in 1968. My late father began working in 1966. He worked a long time there.

Many of (Mr. John's) students came there. They wanted to learn the traditions of the elders. They asked about the history, the tales, and weddings.

Mr. John's students wanted to learn everything, for these foreigners were very interested.

Well, when the students came to Chiapas they wanted a translator or inform- ant (to teach them) Tzotzil and Spanish. I was learning to read and write. In 1968 I was in fifth grade. It was then that my late father was told that Mr. John wanted one or two writers. Since there were a lot of students they wanted to study many things. Some studied corn farming, or calendars, or curing, or witchcraft; how the damned Indians made each other sick, or history, tales, stewardship, court cases. The students wanted to learn everything.

Well, they gave me, Maryan, work. I worked with Professor Peter,[1] a good man. I worked with him for a year. He was very smart. He learned the Chamulas' language well. He wore their clothes. He learned how the Chamulas lived. Professor Mr. John's student did very well. We wrote a book called *El sol del mundo*.[2]

Well, on March 6, 1970, word came from far away that I could take a trip to Mr. John's land, because there were more students who wanted to know me, and how I worked for a year with Peter.

Well, I just began to set in order all my papers. Since I wasn't very old, a letter of permission from my father and mother was prepared. We spoke to a lawyer in San Cristóbal, Mr. Daniel Sarmiento Rojas, who is the governor's attorney general now.

Well, all my papers were prepared. I went abroad to Harvard University on March 15, 1970. I stayed there one month. Mr. John and Mr. Peter did me the favor.

Well, thanks to these two gentlemen, they respected me and I came to know their country. So I still think of those whom I worked with, and send greetings to all my foreign friends who were so kind.

When I came back I worked four more years at the ranch.

Well, when my job ended I looked for another job in another office, but it was harder.

Well, after a while I found another job.

In 1980 I worked with the lawyer Jaime Sabines, younger brother of the late Mr. Juan Sabines.[3] He gave me a job for a year and a half.

After that I looked for another job, too. I worked four years with Robert M. Laughlin for Sna Jtz'ibajom (the writer's cooperative). We prepared several books there. Now I am in charge in my town. I am the mayor. Please forgive me for not writing down more of my conversation, but I have very little time. It is very hard to get a free day. We'll talk together again sometime, you men and women of America! Greetings to you all!

SLO'IL ROMIN PERES PERES

Ta oxib abril ta 1988. A li'e ja' jun teksto skventa ti k'usi ora italik ti krinkoetik vo'nee. Ja' ox ta 1959 k'alal iyulik ta Jobele. Ja' me ba'yi iyul tal ti mol Evon Z. Vogt xchi'uk ti mol Nicholas Colby ja' ta 1959 i sa' yaj'informante un. Ja' ti

AS FOR ME AND THE HARVARD CHIAPAS PROJECT

anima mol Sarate une xchi'uk li mol Antun Lopis Peres ta Vo'ch'oj Vo'e xchi'uk ti me'el Tonik Nibak une. Ja' ba'yi i'abtejik ta tz'ibajel ta batz'i k'op un. A ti mol Saratee yu'un ja' o maxtro ta Paste' k'alal i'abtej xchi'uk li mol Evon Z. Vogt. A ti mol Evone ismeltzan jun sna tey ta Paste'. Ta tz'akal iskomes skventa chanob vun.

Bveno ta tz'akal ja' o ital ti mol Dr. Robert M. Laughlin. Istambe ti abtel ta batz'i k'op une. Isa' la yamiko Jteklum un. Ja' la ba'yi ispas ta yamiko ti mol Chep Xantis Peres une. Ixch'amunbe la sna. Yu'un la oy to ox jp'ej smol chukal na pero Jobel la un. Ja' la tey inaki ti mol Dr. Robert M. Laughlin une.

Va'i un isa' ti much'u sna' x'abtej ta tz'ibajel ta batz'i k'op une. Ja' ispas ta amiko ti anima Romin Teratol une. Ja' me jal i'abtej xchi'uk li mol Dr. Robert M. Laughlin. Ispas epal tekstoetik yu'un batz'i vokol ixchanik li batz'i k'op ti krinkoetik une. Ta mas to tz'akal un ti Romin Teratol une ibat k'alal slumal krinkoetik un. Tey ibat ta chanubtasvanej un. Ja' xa ibat xchi'uk li Maryan Alelino Peres. Ja' o xa ital li mol Dr. Frank Cancian une xchi'uk li mol Dr. George Collier une. Mas xa ep'ol un. Oy ep li yajchanubtasvanejik une. Tey xa ta x'abtej li mol Chep Ernantis Peres ta Apas. Ja' me ep i'abtej ta chanubtasvanej ta batz'i k'op un. Ja' me jal i'abtej xchi'uk li mol Dr. George Collier yu'un ispasik ep tekstoetik skventa vo'ne k'opetik xchi'uk yantik kventoetik un. Li mol Chepe ibat k'alal slumal ti krinkoetike ta Boston tey ta Universidad Jarvar ta Kembrich. Ja' ixchanubtas jutuk ta batz'i k'op ti jchan vunetik tey ta universidad ti much'u italik ta abtel li' ta alto yu'un Chiapae.

Pero oy ep ti much'u iskolta sba ta abtel skventa ti batz'i k'ope. Oy yan moletik ja' k'u cha'al ti anima mol Chep Ernantis Peres Nuj i mol Giyermo Ernantis Peres Nuj xchi'uk ti anima mol Xun Vaskis Xul Jol xchi'uk ti anima mol Petul Peres Tzu. Ja' ispasik informar ti vo'ne k'opetike ti k'usi x'elan spasojik ti vo'ne moletike.

Bveno ital yan ti krinkoetik une. Ja' ti Dr. Victoria Bricker xchi'uk li Dr. John Haviland ital xchanik batz'i k'op une, pero yu'un batz'i vokol iya'iik ta chanel ti batz'i k'op une. A li vo'one ijkolta xa jba ta abtel un. Ijpas tekstoetik un pero yu' nox ja' ta sfavor ti mol maxtro Evon Z. Vogt, yu'un ja' yajchan vuntak skotol ti yantik krinkoetike. Oy to me ep yantik jchan vunetik talemik ta slumal krinkoetik o me ta yan o lum ta mas nom balamiletik ja' k'u cha'al ta Italia ta Japon i oy to nan yantik pais talemik ti jchan vunetike komo mu xa jna' lek skotol.

Bveno ta 1964 li'abtej xa ta chanubtasvanej jchi'uk ti mol profesoretik une asta ta 1969 ta 26 marso libat k'alal slumal ti mol profesor Evon Z. Vogt tey ta jun muk' ta jteklum Boston ta jun Universidad Jarvar ta Kembrich. Ja' tey li kom sjunal u ta avril. Ijchanubtas ta batz'i k'op ti jchan vunetik une, pero batz'i vokol ta xa'iik ta chanel un komo ja' ti oy mu sna'ik lek li kastilya une. Pero ixchanik onox jutuk ti batz'i k'op une. K'alal italik ta Jobele sna'ik xa k'usi xi ta xk'opojik un. A ti mol profesor Evon Z. Vogt ja' ta spas mantal skventa ti jchan vunetik une. A li vo'one ja' tey likom ta sna sjunul ti u k'alal teyon une.

Bveno ta 1973 ta marso libat otro jun bvelta noxtok. li'ech' ta estado New Orleans ta University Tulane yu'un ja' tey ti Dr. Victoria Bricker. Ta tz'akal libat k'alal Boston ti buy mol profesor Evon Z. Vogt tey ta Universidad Jarvar i tey likom ta sna otra bvelta.

Bveno k'el avil totik Lol ja' nox yech li jlo'ile kol iyal li jtotik mol Xune.

ROMIN PERES PERES

April 3, 1988. This is the story of when the gringos came long ago. It was in 1959 when they arrived in San Cristóbal. The first to come was Mr. Evon Z. Vogt and Mr. Nicholas Colby. It was in 1959, and they looked for informants. It was the late Mr. Sarate and Mr. Antun Lopis Peres from Vo'-ch'oj Vo', and Mrs. Tonik Nibak. They were the first who worked, writing in Tzotzil. Mr. Sarate was a teacher in Paste' when he worked with Mr. Evon Z. Vogt. Mr. Evon built a house in Paste'. Later he left it to be used as a schoolhouse.

Well, later Dr. Robert M. Laughlin came. He began work in Tzotzil. He looked for a friend in Zinacantán Center. First they say he made friends with Mr. Chep Xantis Peres. He borrowed his house. He borrowed (Mr. Chep's) house. (Mr. Chep) once had an old thatch-roofed house. That's where Dr. Robert M. Laughlin lived.

Well, he looked for someone who knew how to write Tzotzil. He made friends with the late Romin Teratol, who worked for a long time with Dr. Robert M. Laughlin. He wrote many texts because the gringos had a very hard time learning Tzotzil. Later Romin Teratol went to Gringoland. He went to teach there. He went with Maryan Alelino Peres.[4] Then Dr. Frank Cancian came with Dr. George Collier. Now there were more people. There were many of their teachers. Now Mr. Chep Ernantis Peres from Apas worked a lot teaching Tzotzil. He worked a long time with Dr. George Collier, for they prepared many texts having to do with history, and other texts. Mr. Chep went to the American's country, to Boston. It was there at Harvard University in Cambridge that he taught the students, those who came to work, here in the mountains of Chiapas.

But there were many who helped in doing the work in Tzotzil. There were other gentlemen, such as the late Mr. Chep Ernantis Peres Nuj and Mr. Giyermo Ernantis Nuj, and the late Mr. Xun Vaskis Xul Jol and the late Mr. Petul Peres Tzu. They were the ones who provided the history about how the old time people lived.

Well, more gringos came. Dr. Victoria Bricker came with Dr. John Haviland to learn Tzotzil, but they found Tzotzil to be very hard to learn. As for me, I helped now in the work. I prepared texts, but it was for Professor Evon Z. Vogt, because all the other gringos were his students who came from America, or they came from other countries further away, such as Italy, Japan, and maybe other countries, because I can't remember them all now.

Well, in 1964 I worked as a teacher with the professors. On March 26, 1969, I went to Professor Evon Z. Vogt's country, there in the city of Boston, at Harvard University in Cambridge. I stayed there all of April. I taught the students Tzotzil, but they thought it hard to learn since some didn't know Spanish well. But still they learned a little Tzotzil. When they came to San Cristóbal they already knew how to talk. It was Professor Evon Z. Vogt who directed the students. I stayed in his house the whole month when I was there.

Well, in March, 1973, I went another time. I went to New Orleans to Tulane University where Dr. Victoria Bricker was. Later I went to Boston where Professor Evon Z. Vogt was, at Harvard University. And there I stayed another time at his house.

Well, see here, Mr. Bob,[5] that's all my talk. Send thanks to Mr. John.

SLO'IL ANTZELMO PERES PERES

Beno lo'ilajkotik ava'i jp'el cha'p'eluk ta xkalbe ava'i smelol k'uxi lik kojtikin ti brinkoetik vo'nee. Ta melel ti vo'nee mu jna' k'u x'elan ti brinkoe mu xkojtikin.

Va'i un ja' k'ot sk'oponon ti anima jkumpare Romin Teratole. Ik'ot ta slikeb oktuvre ta 1963. Yu'un lisk'anbe vokol ti ak'o la ba jchi'in ta slumal brinkoe, yu'un la ta x'ik'e ech'el. K'usi un mu la sk'an xbat stuk yu'un la ya'yoj lo'il ti ta xti'vanik li brinkoetike, yech'o la ti ta sa' ech'el xchi'il une.

Va'i un k'alal ijch'un une liyak'be jun limete pox. "Beno mu k'usi un, sk'an me chachan jutukuk tz'ibajel ta jk'optik un mu jna' mi xu' van avu'un," xiyut un.

"Beno yu' nan ta jk'el kik mi jchan," xkut.

"Mu k'usi che'e Antzelmo yu'un chibat ti ta Jobel cha'ej, ba jk'opontik jkumpare Lol, ba kalbetik ya'i ti cha'abulaj chba achi'none. Te xa cha'abtej o un ja' chachan ti tz'ibe," xiyut un.

"Beno stak' xibatik ba jk'el k'u x'elan taj akumpare. Ja' mu jna' mi mu van teuk sti' un," xkut un.

Va'i un ta xcha'ejal libatotikotik un. Ja' to yech ikojtikin o ti sakil krix-chanoetik une. Ja' yech ijchan o ti tz'ib ta batz'i k'ope. Le'e ta vo'lajuneb k'ak'al ijchan o lek. Sk'an ti kajvaltike muk' bu ch'ayem xka'i k'alal tana, ja' to chi'abtej o.

Va'i un ti k'alal ista sk'ak'al ti chibatotikotik ta namal balamil, lilok'otikotik ech'el ta jtob oktuvre. Vaxakib k'ak'al yo' lik'ototikotik oe. Ta karo libatotikotik. Te lik'ototikotik ta jun jteklum, "Santa Fe Noevo Mejiko" sbi. Tey likomotikotik chib u, yu'un ay jtuk'ibtastikotik k'opetik ta jun muk'ta vun, yu'un ta xmeltzaj jun muk'ta liksyonaryo ja' ay yich' tuk'ibtasel lek ti k'opetik une.

Beno ta yual pevrero ta 1964, li'abtej jchi'uk jun mol botaniko, mol "Maltil Te'tikil Chitom" la sbi. Ta tz'akal li'abtej ta Rancho Jarvart. Te li'abtej jchi'uk mol profesor Xun. Ta tz'akal li'abtej jchi'uk Palas Kansyan, te li'abtej jchi'uk jun Jorje sbi.

Laje li'abtej jchi'uk Biktorya sbi jun antz. Te li'abtej jchi'uk jun Mikulax sbi noxtok. Ta slajeb xae li'abtej xchi'uk jun Palas J'ak' Chamel xalbeik yu'un ja' ta sjak'be smelol k'usitik x'elan ti j'ak' chameletike, yech'o ti ja' isbiin o j'ak' chamel yu'unik une. Ja' to te ikojtinik o ti brinkoetik chalik une.

Va'i un tz'akal libatotikotik to j'ech'el noxtok ta slumal ti brinkoetike noxtok ta 1967. Tey xa lik'ototikotik ta batz'i yutil xa slumalik tajmek un. Ja' Vaxinton sbi li yo' bu lik'ototikotik. Tey likomotikotik chib u noxtok, yu'un ay jtuk'ibtastikotik slok'oltak bik'it beetik skventa li' ta Sotz'lebe. Yu'un ja' tey i'och tal ta muk'ta vun meltzajem yu'un ti labal k'opetike. Yech'o ti ja' ayich' tuk'ibtasel xchi'uk sbitak une.

Beno ta tz'akal un listak ta ik'el jun kamiko, "Xun Tontik" sbi likem tal ta nom, li' tal abtejuk ta Jobele.

Va'i un tal ka'i k'usi chiyalbe, ti listak ta ik'ele. Te liyalbe ti ak'o abtejkon jchi'uke.

"Beno stak'," xkut. Te li'abtej jchi'uk. Ijpaktikotik vunetik yu'un oy smeltzanojik ta vun skventa ta x'ayan Ninyo ta Sotz'leb xchi'uk ta Chamu.

Va'i un te li'abtej jchi'uk vo'lajuneb k'ak'al. K'alal ilaj ti abtel te yo'e liyalbe mi jk'an xi'abtej jal.

"Beno ti mi oy ti abtele chi'abtej," xkut.

"Beno mu k'usi che'e ba jk'opontik li mol Telexe," xiyut un.

Va'i un tey libat ta abtel ta jun opisina "Inaremak" sbi un. Tey k'ot jta "Manvel Nuj" xchi'uk jun ulo' "Maryan Kalixto" sbi. Ja' te ikojtikin o jbatikotik lek jchi'uk teye.

Va'i un ta tz'akal iyu' jun tzobojel yu'un skotol antropolokoetik li' ta Jobele. Litake ta ik'el uk un. Tey libat ba ka'i k'usitik ta xalik. Ti k'alal lik'ot une ja' to ika'i, "Ta me xak'opoj uk un, ja' chaval ti k'usitik x'elan avil ti krixchanoetike, ti balamil ta nom ti k'alal la'ay ta paxyale," xiyut un.

Taj x'elan li'albate lixi' jutuk ja' ti mi mu xa xul ta jol k'usitik x'elane.

Va'i un te lik'opoj uk un. Ja' ikal ti sjaylok'elal k'otikon ta nome, xchi'uk k'usuk k'usitik x'elan ikil ti balamiletike, ti krixchanoetik mi lek yo'onik o mi chopol. Ikal noxtok ti oy abtejemotikotik xchi'uk ti antropolokoetike, ch'abal k'usi oy komem ku'untikotik jtz'ujuk une. Te ijk'an koltael ti ak'o sutuk tal jutukuk ti kabteltikotike.

Va'i un ta tz'akal ijk'antikotik koltael ta kovyerno ta Tuxta, ja' ti "Xun Sabines" sbie te liyak'botikotik jayib u koltael.

Beno ta 1983 ja' o xa ital koltael ta nom ta skventa Survival. Ja' yech te chi'abtejotikotik o k'alal tana jchi'uk ti jchi'iltak ta abtele. Oy oxib jteklum chi'abtejotikotik, jchop ulo', jmolol, xchi'uk li sotz'leb une. Chi'abtejotikotik skventa vo'ne k'opetik jujun jteklum; xchi'uk teatro kinyol chba kak'tikotik iluk jujun parajel.

Ja' no'ox yepal ti jlo'ile.

ANTZELMO PERES PERES

Well, let's exchange a word or two. I'll tell you how I got to know the gringos long ago. It's true I didn't use to know what the gringos were like.

Well, my late compadre, Romin Teratol, arrived to talk to me. He arrived at the beginning of October, 1963, to ask me the favor of accompanying him on a trip to Gringoland, because he was going to be taken there. But he didn't want to go alone, because he had heard the talk about how gringos ate people, so he wanted a companion.

Well, when I accepted he gave me a bottle of cane liquor. "Well, you need to learn to write in our language. I don't know if you can do it," he told me.

"Well, I guess I'll see if I can," I said.

"Alright then, Antzelmo, I'm going to San Cristóbal the day after tomorrow. We'll go talk to my compadre Bob. We'll let him know that you will do the favor of joining me. That's where you will work, you'll learn to write," he told me.

"Well, we can go. I'll see what that compadre of yours is like. Who knows if he won't eat me there!"

Well, we went two days later, and so I met the white people. That's how I learned to write Tzotzil. I learned it well in two weeks. Thanks to Our Lord, I haven't forgotten it, and I work with it now.

Well, when the day came for us to go abroad, we left on October 20. It took us a week going by car. We arrived in a town called Santa Fe, New Mexico. There we stayed two months, because we went to correct the words in a large book, because a big dictionary was being prepared and the words had to be corrected properly.

Well, in the month of February, 1964, I worked with a botanist called Martin Peccary.[6] Afterwards I worked at the Harvard Ranch. I worked there with Professor John. Later I worked with Frank Cancian, and I worked with someone called George. When that was over I worked with a woman named Victoria, and I worked there, too, with someone called Nicholas.[7] Finally I worked with a guy called Francesco the Witch Doctor, because he was asking all about witchcraft, and that's why they called him the Witch Doctor.[8] By then I had gotten to know the gringos, as they say.

Well, afterwards we went another time to Gringoland in 1967. We reached the very interior of their country. The place we arrived at was called Washington. We stayed there two months, too, because we went to correct the photographs of the trails here in Zinacantán. With a lot of discussion they were put on large sheets of paper. So they were set in order, together with their names.

Well, later a friend from far away, called John Stony Place, sent for me.[9] He came here to San Cristóbal to work.

Well, I came to hear what he had to say to me, since he had sent for me. He asked me to work with him.

"Well, okay," I said. We worked together folding pages because they had prepared a book about Christmas in Zinacantán and Chamula.

Well, I worked two weeks there. When that work was finished he asked me if I wanted to work for a long time.

"Well, if there's work, I'll work," I said.

"Well, alright, we'll go talk to Mr. Andrew," he told me.[10]

Well, I went to work at an office called Inaremac.[11] Then I met Manvel Nuj and a Chamula called Maryan Kalixto.[12] We got to know each other very well there.

Afterwards there was a meeting of all the anthropologists in San Cristóbal.[13] I was sent for, too. I went to hear what they had to say. When I arrived, I heard,

"You will speak, too. You're to say what you thought of the people and the country far away when you took your trip," I was told.

Being told that, I felt a little scared that I wouldn't remember how it was.

Well, I spoke, too. I told how many times I had gone abroad, and what I thought of the country, whether the people were good or bad. I also said that we had worked with the anthropologists, but that nothing had been left with us. I asked for help so that a little of our work would come back.

Well, later we asked for help from the governor in Tuxtla, Juan Sabines. He helped us a few months.[14]

Well, in 1983 help came from abroad from Survival.[15] So we have been working together since then. We work in three towns. (There is) a Chamula, a Tenejapan, and Zinacantecos. We work on the history of each town and we give puppet shows in each of the hamlets.

That's all my talk.

SLO'IL CHEP ERNANTIS PERES

Jun informe ta ta sjabilal 1961.

Ital jun profesor skventa Universidad ta Jarvard. Ja' sbi jtotik Xun Evon Voti. Ja' yik'oj tal yajchan vuntak tal yojtikinik k'u x'elan ti slumal Tzinakanta ti k'u x'elan kuxulik, k'u x'elan chk'opoj, k'u x'elan tzpasik abtel skventa kajvaltik, k'u cha'al martomoetik, alperesetik, rejiroletik, muk'ta alkalteetik xchu'uk skotol jpas k'opetik.

Bveno a li vo'one ja' to ox chi'abtej ta skventa chonolajel k'u cha'al sbi komersiante. A li vo'one ja' o oy yabtel ti anima jni' mol Antun Xulub Te' sbie. Ja' o muk'ta alkalte ta Jteklum. Ja' primero te ik'ot yo' o bu xch'amunoj jp'ej sna ta Jteklume. Ja' primero te ik'otik xchu'uk yajchan vun ti jtotik Xun une. Ilo'ilajik. Ijak'bat ti mol Antun Xulub Te' mi sna' vun, mi sna' kastilya, mi sk'an x'abtej xchu'uk ti antropoloketike ta skventa Universidad de Jarvard ti te oy ta Boston ta estado de Masachuset sbie.

"Bveno a li vo'one mu xu' xi'abtej yu'un mu jna' vun. Ja' nox jna' jutuk li kastilyae," xi ti anima mol Antun Xulub Te'e. "Pero ti mi yu'un chak'anike oy jun jni' Chep Apas sbi. Ja' sna' vun. Sna' kastilya. Pero ja' nox ti sk'an jak'el k'usi ora tzut tal ta chonolajele yu'un chk'ot ta chonolajel ta Viya Flores. Ti mi xak'anike chibat jk'el junuk k'ak'al. Chkalbe li jtzebe ak'u yalbe smalaotik junuk k'ak'al lavi chtal lunex martexe," xi la ti mol Antun Xulub Te'e. Ja' yech isk'opon sbaik xchu'uk ti jtotik Xun Voti sbie.

"Bveno mol Antun abulajan che'e batan ba albo latzebe, ak'u yalbe ti Chepe ak'u smalaotik lavi chtal lunex martex k'alal vo'ob vakib k'ak'ale yu'un ta jk'an ta jk'opontikotik ta ora chka'i mi sk'an mi mu sk'an x'abtej xchu'uk li vo'otikotike yu'un chitalotikotik yech. Te ch-ech' kik'ot li vo'ot une," xi la ti mol Xun Voti une.

Ja' yech ikom sk'oplal yu'unik un.

Bveno ti mol Antun Xulub Te'e ital sk'elon ta jna ta Apas un. Iyal la komel ti ak'u jmala yech ti ta lunex martex une.

AS FOR ME AND THE HARVARD CHIAPAS PROJECT

Bveno k'alal lik'ot ta jna une liyalbe ti kajnile.

"Bveno lavi layul tale li' i'ay li jtote. Chamala li ok'obe li cha'eje yu'un la chtal sk'oponot xchu'uk li alemanetike," xi ti kajnil une.

"Bveno ta jmala. Chka'i k'usi li abtele, chka'i mi xlok'kventa ti k'usi abtelal tzk'ane. Jna'tik k'usi sjalil tzk'an. Jna'tik mi xnop xka'i k'usuk yu'un ja' li ja' mas nopem xka'i li chonolajele," xkut ti kajnile. Ijmala ti k'usi k'ak'alil yaloj komel une. Ik'otik xchu'uk jtotik Xun ti jni' mole.

"Mi li'ote, Chep? Mi xu' xilo'ilajotik jlikeluk yu'un li' italik alemanetike yu'un la tzk'an cha'abtej achu'uk chibuk u. Ta la xastoj. Ja' la tzk'an chaval k'u cha'al chapas kanal ta k'ak'al. Xu' xalo'ilaj achu'uk li mol profesore jtotik Xun sbi. Ja' jepe tzkotolik. A li yane ja' yajchan vuntak yu'un la tzk'an chchanik li batz'i k'ope, li jk'optik skventa Tzinakantae. Xchu'uk k'usuk tzk'an la cha'i k'usi la tzpas li martomoetike, li alperesetike, li moletike, li mol alkaltee, li rejiroletike. Ja' chavalbe skotol ta batz'i k'op i chavalbe ta kastilya. A li yich'ojik tal pox presko une. Ak'o la pertonal jset'uk yu'un la tzk'an chchan k'u cha'al jkostumpretik li' ta jlumaltik," xiyut ti jni' mol Antun Xulub Te'e.

"Bveno k'uxi jtotik Xun? K'usi tal avalik? K'usi la chak'anik? Xu' xilo'ilajotik jlikeluk. Albon k'usi li abtel chak'anike. Chka'i mi xu' mi mu xu' yu'un ja' li mu jna' xixokobe yu'un ja' nopem xka'i li chonolajele yu'un ja' mas chik'ot skotol k'ak'al te yo' oe," xkutik un.

"Bveno Chep ak'o pertonal jset'uk pox xchu'uk presko yu'un li' lital jchu'uk li mol Antun Xulub Te'e, li muk'ta alkaltee, yu'un tey ikojtikin jbatikotik ta Jteklum. Ijak'be much'u mas sna' vun, sna' kastilya li' ta Apase yu'un ta jk'an chi'abtejotik chib oxibuk u k'u cha'al jun informante. Jna'tik mi xak'an," xiyut ti jtotik Xun Voti.

"Bveno a li vo'one ta jpas proval mi xu' mi mu xu' ku'un pero ja' to k'alal vaxakib k'ak'al yu'un oy to te jkomesoj jun tanto li turasnue, li mantzanae, li perae, li jol itaje, yu'un ta jk'an to ta jlajes ta jmoj skotol," xkut ti jtotik Xun Votie.

"Bveno Chep pero yu'un ta jk'antikotik chapas proval junuk k'ak'al o chibuk k'ak'al ok'ob cha'ej yo' o ta jk'eltik mi lek mi mu lekuk chava'i ti abtele. Xchu'uk k'usuk ja' nox ti mu xana' k'usi x'elan li talemotikotike. Yu'un mu xu' xjelav mas ti k'usi ora chisut ta Estados Unidos yu'un ja' ti oy jun vun pasaporte sbie. Yech'o ja' ta jk'antikotik o ta ora lavabtele ti mi xa'abulaj une, Chep," xiyut ti jtotik Xun Voti.

"Bveno xu' ta jpas proval junuk k'ak'al li ok'obe pero ti cha'eje chibat ta pversa, chba jlajesbe xchonel skotol li jp'olmale yu'un oy jun kompromiso ku'un xchu'uk ti much'u ch- abtejik ta skventa spasik kurtir ti tzeik to turasnue. Yu'un chich'cha'mil oxmil turasnu yech'o mu jk'an jch'ay ti kompromiso une," xkutik ti jtotik Xun xchu'uk ti yajchan vuntake.

"Bveno Chep ja' nox ti mu xak'an xach'ay lakompromisoe, pero lakanale kreoke mu'yuk chch'ay ti k'usi yepal chapas kanal ta k'ak'ale, yu'un xu' xajtojtikotik. Ti mi yu'un xak'an xabat ti ok'obe ja' mas lek. Primero batan ba k'elo lanegosyoe porke repente sok xk'a' li turasnue. Bveno ti mi lasut tal ti ta Viya Flores une jmoj xa ta jtamtik li abtele asta agosto," xiyut ti jotik Xun Evon

Voti.

"A li vo'one mu xu' jch'ay li kompromisoe porke yu'un ta jk'an ti skotol k'ak'al oy jkliente yech'o ta jpas kumplir ti jk'ope yu'un ja' yech ko'on li vo'one. Ja' nox yech ti mi lek ikil ti abtel xchu'uk vo'oxuke ta jpas kumplir uk un. Yech'o ti mi yu'un xu' chava'iik ti ja' primero chibat jk'el ti jnegosyo chibat ok'ob pero ja' to chisut tal cha'ej ta melkulex. Xu' xi'abtej ta jveves ta vyernex pero li ta savaroe ta rominko ta pversa chibat yu'un ja' sk'ak'alil lek xch'am skotol ti k'usitik stak' chonele. Ta lunex un ta jtambe otro j'ech'el asta vyernex un. Ja' yech skotol xemana. Ta jujun savaro rominko ja' chibat k'alal Viya Flores. Yu'un ja' yech chkom trate ti mi lek chava'i li vo'oxuke. A li vo'one ja' yech xu' chka'i," xkut ti jtotik Xun Voti.

"Bveno Chep xu' ti mi xak'an xakoltaotikotik xchu'uk jchan vunetike. Chchanubtas ta batz'i k'op."

"Bveno stak' che'e, ta jpas proval mi jna' k'u x'elan ti abtel chak'anike. Kol aval li poxe li preskoe. Kuch'tik che'e!" xkutik ti jotik Xune. Ikuch'tikotik ta komon un. Ilaj kuch'tikotik un ikom ti akverto chak taj une. Ja' yech ijtambe o ti abtel xchu'uk ti jtotik Xun profesor skventa Universidad Jarvard sbie. K'unk'un inop xka'i ti abtele. Ja' yech inel ti jun vcrano ta primcro jabile.

Bveno ta otro jun o jabil italik xa mas ep ti yajchan vune. K'alal mas xa ep to jchan vunetike mu xa stak' xibat ti ta Viya Flores une. Mas xa segido li'abtej xchu'uk ti jchan veuntik une. Ibatik xa ta jna xchanik k'usi x'elan chve' ti kampesinoetike.

Bveno ti viniketike ja' yabtel ti tz'un chobtike, a li antzetik ja' yabtel ti tzmeltzan vaj, tzkuch si', chchuk' k'u'ule. Ja' yech ixchanik abtel ta chobtik ti kremotike, ixchanik k'u x'elan ta tz'unel, k'u x'elan ta ak'intael, k'u x'elan ta pakel, k'u x'elan ta k'ajel, k'u x'elan ta skuchik tal ta xchobtik chxul o k'alal snaik ti yiximik jujun ti viniketik. Ti k'alal ch'abal to ox ti be karoetik ta xchabajebik ta xchu'uk ta jujun parajel ti butik nakajtik ti viniketike. Skotol to ox krixchano naka to ox ta ka'etik tzkuchik ti yiximike, ti xchenek'ike. Pero ti jchan vunetike ja' yech ixchanik i'abtejik. Skotol ti kremotike ixchanik k'u x'elan ch-abtej viniketik. Ti tzebetike ja' yech ixchanik ti k'u x'elan ch-abtejik ti antzetik tzinakantekoetike.

Bveno chkaltik ava'iik k'usi li yabtel ti viniketike i k'usitik yabtel ti antzetik yajchan vun ti jtotik Xun Voti.

Primero yabtel vinik: (1) boj osil, (2) boj k'ajben, (3) ovol chobtik, (4) ak'in chobtik, (5) cha'lom ak'in chobtik, (6) jos yav chenek', (7) pak chobtik, (8) k'ajoj, (9) maj ixim, (10) jik'aaej ixim, (11) ch'ol ixim ta koxtal, (12) tz'is koxtal, (13) ovol chenek', (14) ak'in chenek', (15) bul chenek', (16) maj chenek', (17) jik'aej chenek', (18) ch'ol chenek' ta koxtal, (19) tz'is skoxtalil chenek', (20) skuchel ta ka' ixim chenek'. Ja' yabtel skotol ti viniketik li' une.

A li yabtel ti antzetike ja' xa la li' chtale: (1) kuch si', (2) lakanej panin, (3) sapel panin, (4) sjuch'el panin, (5) pak'anel vaj, (6) stukesel uch'imo', (7) spasel k'oxox, (8) sjalel k'u'uletik, (9) stz'isel k'u'uletik, (10) xchuk'el k'u'uletik, (11) skuchel spetel yolik, (12) smesel xch'ubael na, (13) sk'elel smak'lanel kaxlan chitom. Ja' yech yabtel skotol ti antzetike. Ja' yech ixchanik skotol ti jchan vunetik talemik ta Estados Unidos, stakoj tal ti jtotik Xun Voti. Ja' yech ti kostumbre k'u cha'al kuxul skotol krixchano tzinakanteko.

Bveno a li vo'on une, ja' kabtel ti xchanubtasel ta batz'i k'ope. Vo'on xa chisjak'beik mi xu' mi mu xu' xkoltavanik ta spasel ti k'usi tzpas ti jun vinike ti jun antze yu'un tzk'an chchanik spasel skotol ti k'usitik abtelal oy skventa viniketik skventa antzetik kampesinoetik.

Ja' yech li'abtej. Ja' yech i'ech' ti otro jun veranoe. Ta otro jun o jabil liyalbeik xa ti ma'uk nox ti oxib u jujun jabile.

"Bveno Chep lavie ta jk'antikotik chi'abtejotik mas yu'un ta jk'antikotik cha'abtej mas. Chatz'ibaj xa ta vun xchu'uk k'usuk chachan spasel manejar li gravadorae, yu'un ep xa k'opetik tey tzakal yu'un mu xka'itikotik lek k'usi k'opal chal ti krixchanoetik. Tey pasbil gravar une, yech'o un abtejkotik mas un! Chapas ta batz'i k'op chapas ta kastilya," xiyutik un.

"Bveno mu jna' k'u xachiik li vo'oxuke. A li vo'one ikojtikin xa jutuk ti abtele pero vo'oxuk chavalik mi lek o mi chopol ti kabtele. Ti mi yu'un lek chavilike ta jch'un k'u x'elan chavalike k'u x'elan chak'anike," xkutik profesoretik une. Oy xa oxvo'ik, jun ti jtotik Xun Votie, otro jun ti mol Palas Kansyan i otro jun ti jkumpare George A. Kolyer sbie.

"Bveno ti mi yu'un chtun ep ixim skventa avabtele pero xu' xapas lachobe. Yu'un xka'itikotik ep chtun avu'un ixim chenek' pero ja' lek mi xu' ja' xa nox li skventa chobtike, mi mu'yuk xa chabat skventa chobtike, mi mu'yuk xa chabat skventa li komersyantee. K'alal xa'och ta avabtele jna'tik mi xu' xbat sk'el k'u x'elan ti skventa pas abtel, skventa martomo rey itz'inale, chbat sk'elik k'usi li pas abtele k'u x'elan tzpasik," xiyutik ti profesoretike.

"Bveno a li vo'one xu' nan. Mu xu' xakutik. Mu jna'. K'usi xi ti jvabojometike xchu'uk ti moletike. A li vo'one che'e mu xu' xkal ta jtuk yu'un mu to jna' k'u x'elan ti pas abtele yu'un ja' to primero kabtel pero stak' ja' to te xkaltik ta yorail," xkutik un.

A li vo'on une ijtambe ti abtele skotol k'ak'al. Ja' xa nox ijk'an permiso ti k'alal ta yora ak'intik asta k'u cha'al li'och o ti ta martomo rey itz'inale.

Bveno ti k'alal vo'on xa martomo reyone ibatik svula'anikon ti profesoretike xchu'uk jchan vunetike. Tey ikom jlom ti tzebetike ti kremotike. Isk'elik ixchanik ti k'usi tzpas ti martomo reyetik ta jujun savaro ta jujun rominko. Ispasik gravar ti sonetik skotol ti jaykoj ti son martomo rey une. Isk'elik k'u x'elan chlok' yual ti ta jujun rominkoe.

Bveno ti k'alal xlaj ti jujun savaro rominkoe ja' o chisjak'be k'usi skventa ti uch' poxe ti chich' tzanel kantelae ti chich' nitel ual yu'un ti jtotik Iskipulae.

Bveno a li vo'one ja' xa chkalbe ta jtz'iba ta vun ti k'usitik xi chal ti k'usitik xi k'evujin ti jvabajometike xchu'uk ti martomo reyetik ti mexonetike. Ja' xa chka'i k'uxi ti tzakal ta gravadorae. Ja' yech inel o ti jabile. Ja' yech ixchanik o ti batz'i k'ope. Ixchan spak'anel vaj ti tzebetike. Oy jun Viktorya sbi. Ti tzebe. Ja' tey o skotol ti savaro rominkoe. Ta mas xa tz'akal ik'otik xa yan ti kremotike ti tzebetike. Toj ep i'ayik yojtikinik ti k'usi x'elan ti pas abtele. Te ixchanik spasel ti k'usi sk'an pasele. Li tzebetike ixchanik jutuk spasel vaj. Li kremotike ixchanik stijel vob biolin arpa kitara. Yu'un oy jun Xun Jvabajom sbi pero batz'i toj lek sna' yoxibal ti vobe. Ja' jlikel chchanik o ti oy sgravadorae xchu'uk k'usuk yu'un toj p'ijik skotolik. Ma'uk yech k'u cha'al krixchano mejikanoe. Ja' yech li'abtej jchu'uk vaxakib balunebuk jabil.

Bveno ti k'alal lilok' ta martomo rey itz'inale ilaj jpas komel ti k'in Xanchavaxchan une, libat k'alal Estados Unidos. Ispasik imbitar ti profesoretike.

Bveno primero ijchap skotol ti vunetike; primero ti akta nasimyento, karta rekomentasyon bvena kondukta xchu'uk akta no antesedentes penales xchu'uk tarjeta de vakunasyon. Ta slajeb un ja' xa ay jlok'es ti pasaporte provisyonal sbie.

Bveno a ti vunetik skotol une ja' liskolta ta xchapel ti jun kamiko Lol Bik'it Nab sbi une, yu'un ja' stuk mas ba'yi ixchan ti batz'i k'ope. A le'e ko'ol xa xchu'uk jun batz'i k'ope. A le'e ko'ol xa xchu'uk jun batz'i tzinakanteko k'u cha'al tey ayanem ta Jteklum.

Bveno yech'o un ja' ispas pavor lixchapbe skotol ti k'usitik vunal sk'an yo' o xu' xijelav o ti ta advana ta mikrasyon ta embajada ta visa. Pero k'alal lik'ot ta Mejiko une ik'ele skotol ti jvuntake.

Bveno skotol ti jvuntak kich'oj ech'ele lek skotol pero k'alal lisk'anbeik jkartiyae ja' o chopol ika'i yu'un jna'oj ti ch'abal ku'une, pero ti ta jpasaporte une tey batem ti smatrikulail une. Ja' toj tzotz chopol ibat o un yu'un ta ora isa'ik tey ta Mejiko une.

"Bveno a li matrikula li' tzakal ta pasaportee ch'abal yech matrikula yech'o un mu xu' xajelav. A li much'utik xu' xjelave yu'un lek skartiya. Aora lavi ch'abal lakartiyae li' chasut ta anae! Mu xu' xajelav ta jun o pais yu'un ma'uk nox ti matrikula chtune yu'un tzk'an chavak' iluk lakartiyae. Yech'o un mas lek batan ba ich'o tal k'alal ana. Ta jk'eltik mi melel ti oy lakartiya liberado. Ok'ob xatal xchu'uk lakartiyae. Lavi ta orae sutan ech'el ta ora!" xiyutik ti ta Mejikoe.

"Bveno pero li vo'one yu'un ch'abal jtak'in. Mu xu' xisut yu'un ana'ojik ti nom xa komem ti Chiapae. A li vo'one naka nox ta jk'an chibat ta paxyal chba kojtikin k'u x'elan ti Estados Unidos une," xkut li vo'one pero komo talem ti jun jkumpare George sbie tal yik'on ech'el. Ital k'alal Jobel. Ti k'alal chapal xa ox skotol ti jvuntake ikalbetikotik ta cha'vo' ti naka nox paxyal chibate kojtikin ti slumal grinkoetike, ti ja' nox yu'un ti jkumpare George sbie yu'un yech nox chispas invitar ech'el ta slumal. Mu'yuk xkalbetikotik mi yu'un abtel chibate yu'un ja' ti ch'abal jkartiyae.

"Bveno a li vo'one ma'uk ta jak' mi abtel o mi ma'uk abtel chabat. La kosa ke yu'un prinsipalmente lakartiya. Ti mi oye xu' xajelav, ti mi yu'un tey komem ta anae ok'ob ba ich'o tal! Cha'ej xu' xatal apas presentar un ch'abal problema," xiyutikotik ta advana ta yaleb avyon ta Mejiko une.

"Bveno sinyor a li vo'one ak'on ta pertonal mu xisut ech'el. Yu'un ch'abal jtak'in a ti yu'un jk'ulejikone k'u cha'al vo'oxuke xu' xisut lavi ta orae pero komo toj me'onone ch'abal jtak'in. Mu k'usi xisut o ech'el pero ti mi chavak'ikon ta pertonale ta jk'an chka'i mi xu' xkak' jutukuk jmulta yu'un ana'ojik intiyo kampesinoone. Mu jna' k'usitik vunal sk'an chtun skventa ti nom byajee yu'un ja' ti batz'i jutuk ti estudio ku'une. Pero li vo'one yu'un ta jk'an chkojtikin k'u x'elan ti Estados Unidos une," xkut ti ta advanae.

"Bveno ti mi yu'un mu xak'an xasut ech'el avich' tal takartiyae, mi yu'un chak'an chabat avojtikin ti Estados Unidos, chavak' vaxakib syen. Ta jk'el k'uxi stak' pasel ti vunetike. Ti mi yu'un xak'ane. Ti mi mu xak'ane mu'yuk pversa mas lek ti mi chasut ta jmoje. Ja' vo'ot chanop lek k'usi mas lek yu'un toj tzotz stunel ti kartiyae yu'un chak'anbat jujun advana asta k'u cha'al xak'ot o ti bu k'alal chak'an chabate."

"Bveno a li vo'one ti yu'un oyuk jtak'ine lek xu' xkak' ti k'u yepal chak'anbekone, pero li vo'one yu'un lakalbeik xa ti yu'un toj me'onone, pero ti mi yu'un chapasbekon jun pavore chkak' chanibuk syen che'e," xkut un.

"Bveno a li vo'one mu jch'un ti toj povreote yu'un li vo'one mu xkojtikin k'u x'elan li Estados Unidos yu'un ja' nox chk'otik ti much'utik jk'ulejetike much'utik oy stak'ine, pero mi xak'an xavak', sutan li' toe!" xiyutik ta Mejikoe.

Ijnop ti ja' mas lek k'usi k'op ta mas nom un. "Bveno stak' che'e, ta jtoj ti kinyentoe pero mi mu'yuk xa me k'usi k'op ta mas nom un," xkut un.

"Bveno mi atoj ti kinyentoe ch'abal xa k'op asta k'u cha'al xak'ot k'alal syudad de Boston estado de Masachuset pero ja' nox ti oxib u k'u cha'al yaloj lapasaporte. Ti mi xijelav mas une oy xa smultail noxtok un."

"Bveno a li vo'one ja' nox ti oxib ue chibate. Chisut tal yech yu'un oy kajnil oy jch'amaltak komem," xkut un.

"Bveno lek che'e, chakalbe yech yu'un ep xa yech te komemik o ti mejikanoetike ja' ti much'utik batemik ta chik' ak'ale, pero li vo'ote ta jk'an chavalbon k'usi li abtel chabat oe. Mas lek jamal xavalbon. Ja' yech ta jmeltzan o ech'el lavune," xiyutik un.

Bveno li vo'one komo kaloj xa ox ba'yi ti paxyal nox chibat une. Ja' xa yech ikal un ti yu'un ja' nox chispas invitar ti jkumpare Jorjee. Mu'yuk xkalbe k'usi chba jpas ti ta Estados Unidos une.

Bveno ja' yech lijelav o ti ta Mejikoe. Ikak' ti vo'ob syen pexu une. Tey lipaj jun k'ak'al ta Mejiko skventa ti jvuntak un. Ta jun o k'ak'al lilok' ech'el un. K'alal ijta jujun ti advana une jutuk xa k'opetik. Lik'ot k'alal Nveva Orleans. Tey lipaj jtobuk k'ak'al. Li'abtej jchu'uk ti jkumpare Jorjee. Ta tz'akal libat ta k'alal Vaxinton. Libat ti yo' o bu sna ti mol Lol Bik'it Nab sbie. Te li'abtej chib xemana jchu'uk ti Lol Bik'it Nab une. Ta tz'akal un libat k'alal Nveva York. Likom jun xemana. Li'abtej jchu'uk ti jun Telex sbi. Liyak'beik kojtikin k'usitik oy ti jujun estado xchu'uk ti batz'i mero kapital Vaxinton une. Ta mas tz'akal un libat k'alal syudad de Boston estado de Masachuset. Lik'ot une ispasik jun muk'ta k'in skotol li muk'tik profesoretik xchu'uk skotol jchan vunetike. Ja' istzoban ti jtotik Xun Voti. Live'otikotik ikuch'otikotik pox servesa. Ta jun o k'ak'al ijtambe abtel jchu'uk skotol jchan vunetik profesoretik ja' to k'u cha'al inel o ti oxib u. Pero ti jujun rominkoe chiyik'ik ech'el ta paxyal. Li'ay k'alal mar Atlantiko yo' o bu toj muk'tik ola chak' ti mar une.

Ta mas tz'akal un li'ech' ta Chikago pero ech'el be xa nox, mu'yuk xa li'abtej. Ja' yech ikojtikin ti Estados Unidos une. Ikil toj mas chyal ti yeloe ti nyevee. Ja' yech inel ti primero byajee.

Libat ta xchibal byaje ja' nox yech te li'ech' ti ta 1967. Ta yoxibal byaje un mas xa ep ikojtikin. Libat xa k'alal San Fransisko Kalifornya yo' o Palo Alto sbie, ja' xa ti Universidad de Stamford sbie. Ja' xa ta 1971. Ja' slajeb byaje li'ay un. Pero ja' toj mas lek ikil un yu'un ja' ch'abal chyal yelo. Lek k'ixin. Ja' yech ikojtikin k'u x'elan chve'ik te yo' oe. Mu'yuk vaj ja' nox naka pan Bimbo skventa vaje.

Bveno ja' yech ilaj o ti oxib byajee. Kol iyal ti jtotik Xun Voti xchu'uk skotol yantik profesoretik xchu'uk skotol jchan vunetik ti liyak'beik kojtikin ti slumalike! Pero lavie ta jna' to ta jk'an to. Kiluk to ko'on batikon otro j'ech'eluk ya'el yu'un skotolik toj lek yo'onik. Pero lastima ti mu'yak xa ti abtel yu'unike. Lavie mu'yuk xa k'usi k'op yu'un oy xa lek jvuntak. Oy xa jkartiya skotol.

Bveno a li vo'one k'alal ta jyules ta jole lek xa ya'el ti teyon xae, pero mu xa k'u xkutik un, ja' ti ilaj ti abtele.

Bveno jtotik Xun, jme'tik Katal xchu'uk skotol ach'amaltakik, xchu'uk jkumpare Jorje, jkumale Xunka', mol Palas Kansyan, xchu'uk yajnil Palas, mol Lol Bik'it Nab xchu'uk yajnil, Viktorya xchu'uk smalal, kumpare Xun Jvabajom li' tzotz chakalbeik ti chabankoxuk ta akotolik. Kol avalik ti avik'ikon ech'el ta alumalike.

CHEP ERNANTIS PERES

A report about the events in the year 1961.

A professor from Harvard University came. His name was Mr. John Evon Vogtie.[16] He brought his students so they would get to know about Zinacantán country, how (the people) lived, how they talked, how they held religious office, such as stewards, ensign bearers, prefects, grand *alcaldes,* and all the civil officials.

Well, I had worked in marketing as a merchant. It was when my late father-in-law, Antun Xulub Te', held office. He was the grand *alcalde* in Zinacantán Center. (Mr. John) arrived first at the house (that my father-in-law) had borrowed in the Center. Mr. John arrived first with his students. They conversed. Mr. Antun Xulub Te' was asked if he could read and write, if he knew Spanish, if he wanted to work with the anthropologists of Harvard University there in Boston, in the state of Massachusetts.

"Well, as for me, I can't work, because I'm not literate. I just speak a little Spanish," said the late Mr. Antun Xulub Te'. "But if you like, I have a son-in-law, named Chep Apas. He is literate. He speaks Spanish. But we have to ask when he is coming back from marketing, because he trades in Villa Flores. If you want, I'll go see him some day. I'll tell my daughter to tell him to wait for us on Monday or Tuesday," said Mr. Antun Xulub Te'. That's how he and Mr. John Vogtie talked together.

"Well, Mr. Antun, please ask your daughter to tell Chep to wait for us on Monday or Tuesday, in four or five days, because I'd like to talk to him right away to learn if he wants to work with us or not. We'll come to pick you up," said Mr. John Vogtie.

That's what they agreed to.

Well, Mr. Antun Xulub Te' came to see me at my house in Apas. He left word that I should wait on Monday or Tuesday.

Well, when I arrived home my wife told me.

"Well, now that you have returned, my father came here. You're to wait tomorrow or the day after, because the Americans are coming to talk to you, because the Americans want you to work with them," said my wife.[17]

"Well, I'll wait. I'll hear what the work is, if the kind of work they want will be profitable. Who knows for how long. Who knows, too, if I'll get used to it, because I'm used to marketing," I told my wife. I waited for the day they had said. My father came with Mr. John.

"Are you there, Chep? Can we chat for a minute, because the Americans have come, because they want you to work for two months with them. They'll pay you. They want you to say how much you earn a day. You can talk with Professor John. He is the boss of them all. The others are his students. They say they want to learn Tzotzil, the way we talk in Zinacantán. And they want to hear what the stewards, the ensign bearers, the elders, the grand *alcalde,* and the prefects do. You will tell them everything in Tzotzil, and you'll tell them in Spanish. They have brought some cane liquor and soft drinks. Grant a little pardon, they say, because they want to learn the customs in our town," my father- in-law, Antun Xulub Te', told me.

"Well, what is it about, Mr. John? What did you come to say? What do you want? We can chat a little. Tell me what kind of work you want. I'll think it over, whether I can or not, since I don't have any free time, as I'm used to trading and I go there (to Villa Flores) every day," I said.

"Well, Chep, grant pardon for a little cane liquor and soft drinks, for I've come with Mr. Antun Xulub Te', the grand *alcalde,* for we got to know each other in the Center. I asked him who was most literate and spoke Spanish best in Apas, for we want to work two or three months with an informant. Who knows if you want to," said Mr. John Vogtie.

"Well, I'll see if I can or not, but a week from now, because I left a load of peaches, apples, pears, and cabbages there, and I want to finish it all up," I told Mr. John Vogtie.

"Well, Chep, we'd like you to try it out one or two days, so we can see whether you like the work or not. Besides, you don't know how we came. We can't let the deadline pass for returning to the United States, as there is a paper called a passport. So we want your work right away if you'll do the favor, Chep," Mr. John Vogtie said to me.

"Well, I can try it out for a day tomorrow, but the next day I have to go and finish selling all my merchandise, as I have a deal with the people who ripen peaches when they're still green. They're receiving two to three thousand peaches, so I don't want to lose the deal," I told Mr. John and his students.

"Well, Chep, I understand that you don't want to lose the deal, but as for your wages, I think you won't lose out on your daily pay, for we can pay you. If you want to go tomorrow, that's better. First, go and see about your business, so the peaches won't go bad and rot. When you return from Villa Flores we'll start working till August for sure," Mr. John Evon Vogtie told me.

"As for me, I can't lose the deal, because I want clients every day, so I'm true to my word, that's how I feel. The same way, if I like working with you, I'll be true to my word, too. So if it's alright with you that I go first to see about my business, I'll go tomorrow, but I'll come back the day after tomorrow, on Wednesday. I can work Thursday and Friday, but on Saturday and Sunday I have to go, because those are the days when everything for sale is snatched up. On Monday I'll start again (and work) until Friday. Every week like that. Every Saturday and Sunday I'll go to Villa Flores. That's how the deal is if you agree. As for me, I can do that," I told Mr. John Vogtie.

"Well, Chep, that's fine if you want to help us with the students. You'll teach in Tzotzil."

"Well, alright then, I'll see if I know how to do the kind of work you want. Thanks for the cane liquor and soft drinks. Let's drink then!" I told Mr. John. We drank together. When we finished drinking the deal was settled like that. That's how I started working with Professor John of Harvard University. Gradually I got used to the work. That's how the summer ended the first year.

Well, the next year more of his students came. When there were more students I couldn't go anymore to Villa Flores. I worked more frequently with the students. Now they went to my house to learn what the customs were, what the farmers ate.

Well, the men's work is planting corn, while the women's work is making tortillas, carrying firewood, washing clothes. So the boys learned about planting, weeding, doubling, harvesting, how every man carries his corn from his cornfield so that it arrives at his house. When there used to be no roads the men grew corn in each of the hamlets where they lived. Then all the people carried their corn and beans on mules. That's how all the boys learned, how they worked. They learned how the men worked. The girls learned how the Zinacanteco women worked.

Well, I'll tell you what the men's work was and what the women's work was—of Mr. John Vogtie's students.

First the men's work: (1) felling, (2) clearing stubble, (3) planting corn, (4) weeding corn, (5) second weeding, (6) preparing milpa for bean planting, (7) doubling, (8) harvest, (9) flailing, (10) winnowing, (11) pouring corn into bags, (12) sewing bags, (13) planting beans, (14) weeding beans, (15) bean harvest, (16) bean flailing, (17) bean winnowing, (18) pouring beans into bags, (19) sewing bean bags, (20) carrying corn and beans on muleback. That's the work of all the men.

Now the women's work comes here: (1) carrying firewood, (2) boiling corn, (3) rinsing corn, (4) grinding corn, (5) patting tortillas, (6) making posole, (7) making toasted tortillas, (8) weaving clothes, (9) sewing clothes, (10) washing clothes, (11) carrying their children, (12) sweeping and cleaning up house, (13) watching after and feeding chickens and pigs. That's the work of all the women. That's what all the students learned who came from the United States, sent by Mr. John Vogtie. That's what the customs are, how all the Zinacanteco people live.

Well, as for me, it was my work to teach in Tzotzil. They asked me what the men and women did, if they could help a man or woman do what they were doing, because they wanted to learn to do all kinds of work that men and women farmers do.

That's how I worked. That's how the next summer passed. The following year they told me it wasn't just for three months each year.

"Well, Chep, now we want to work more. Now you will write, and in addition you will learn to use a tape recorder, because now there are a lot of words recorded, and we don't understand very well what words the people are saying. They are recorded, so let's work harder! Do it in Tzotzil and do it in Spanish," they told me.

"Well, I don't know what you think. As for me, I've gotten to know the work a bit, but you should say whether my work is good or not. If you think it's good, I'll agree to what you say, to what you want," I told the professors. There were three now: one was Mr. John Vogtie, another was Mr. Frank Cancian, and the other, my compadre, George A. Collier.

"Well, Chep, we've seen that you have learned to work the way we want. You have learned now a bit how to write in Tzotzil, so who knows what you think, whether you'd rather work in the cornfield, or work as a merchant. Who knows if you just want to look at our work every day. If you can, if you'd like to, then it won't be just for the summer, but for every month. You'll have to work in the winter, because more students want to come, so you'd make a living if you didn't grow corn anymore or go trading. There's work with us every day."

"Well, as for me, I could probably work every day, but I can't stop growing corn, for I need a lot of corn, because I'll have a religious position. I'll be junior steward-royal in 1964. My name is written down for that in the grand *alcalde*'s book. So I can't do without my cornfield. As for trading, I don't have to go. But if you have more work I can pay for more laborers," I told Mr. John, Mr. Frank Cancian, and compadre George.

"Well, if you need a lot of corn for your office you can grow corn. We understand you'll need a lot of corn and beans, but it would be good if it was just corn, if you didn't go marketing. When you enter office who knows if (the students) can go and see what office holding is like, junior steward-royal, go see how they do religious offices," the professors told me.

"Well, as for me maybe they can. I can't tell you. I don't know. It's whatever the musicians and the elders say. As for me, I can't say by myself, because I don't know yet about office holding, since this is my first position, but we can find out when the time comes," I told them.

As for me, I began working every day. I just asked for leave at weeding time until I entered the office of steward-royal.

Well, when I was a steward-royal the professors went to visit me with their students. Some of the girls and boys stayed there. They learned what the stewards-royal did every Saturday and Sunday. They recorded songs, all the songs of the stewards-royal. They saw how the flowers of Our Lord Esquipulas were changed and how the chaplets were brought out each Sunday.

Well, when each Saturday and Sunday were over they asked me why cane liquor was drunk, why candles were lit, why the chaplets of Our Lord Esquipulas were counted.

Well, as for me, I listened to them there. I wrote down on paper what the stewards-royal and the publicans said when they sang. I listened to what was recorded by the tape recorder. That's how the year ended. That's how they learned Tzotzil. The girls learned to make tortillas. There was a girl named Victoria. She was there every Saturday and Sunday. Later other boys and girls came. So many came to learn about office holding. They learned to do what they wanted to do. The girls learned a bit how to make tortillas. The boys learned to play musical instruments: fiddle, harp, guitar. There was a fellow named John Musician, but he knew so well how to play all three of the instruments.[18] They learned very quickly because they had tape recorders and besides they were all so smart. They weren't like Mexican people. So I worked with them eight or nine years.

Well, when I left the position of junior steward-royal and celebrated the fiesta of St. Sebastian, I went to the United States. The professors invited me.

Well, first I got all the papers ready; first the birth certificate, the letter of recommendation of good conduct and no penal record, and the vaccination card. Finally I got a temporary passport.

Well, a friend, Bob Little Lake, helped me get all the papers, because he was the first to learn Tzotzil.[19] He was like a real Zinacanteco born in the Center.

Well, so he did me the favor, he got all the papers ready so I could pass through customs and immigration, (and get) the visa at the embassy. But when I arrived in Mexico City all the papers were looked at.

Well, all the papers I took were fine, but when they asked for my military card I was upset because I knew I hadn't one, but the record for it went with the passport. But it was terrible as they demanded it in Mexico City.

"Well, the record written here on the passport isn't right, so you can't pass over. The people who can cross over have good military cards. Now since you haven't your military card, go home! You can't go to another country, because it isn't just the record that's needed, because you have to show your military card. So it's better if you go home and bring it. We'll see if it's true that you have an authorized card. Tomorrow come with your card. Go home right now!" they told me in Mexico City.

"Well, as for me, I haven't any money. I can't return as you know Chiapas is far away. I just want to go on a trip to know the United States," I said, since my compadre had come to take me. He had come to San Cristóbal. When all my papers were ready we told them that two of us were just going on a trip to get to know Gringoland, because my compadre George had invited me to his country. We didn't tell them that I was going to work, since I didn't have my military card.

"Well, as for me, I'm not asking if you are going to work or not. The important thing is the military card. If you have one you can cross over, if you left it at home, tomorrow go get it! You can come the next day to present it and there'll be no problem," they told us at the immigration office at the airport in Mexico City.

"Well sir, forgive me, I can't return. I haven't the money. If I were rich like you I could return right away, but I am very poor and have no money. I have no way to return, but if you forgive me, I would like to pay a small fine, because you know that I am an Indian farmer. I don't know what papers are needed for a trip abroad, because I haven't studied much. But I want to know what the United States is like," I told the immigration officer.

"Well, if you don't want to return home to bring your military card, if you want to get to know the United States, hand over 800 pesos. I'll see if something can be done to the papers. That's if you want to. If you don't want to, you don't have to, it's better if you just go home. You decide what's best, for the military card is very important, because every immigration officer will ask for it until you get to where you want to go."

"Well, as for me, if I had the money, I could give you as much as you ask, but I told you already that I am poor, but if you'll do me the favor, I'll give you 400," I told him.

"Well, as for me, I don't believe you're so poor, because I don't know what the United States is like. The only ones who get there are the rich, the ones who have money, but if you want to give 500 pesos you can cross over, but if you don't want to, you don't have to, go home!" they told me in Mexico City.

I decided it would be better to give the 500 pesos. "Well, alright then, I'll pay the 500, but so long as there won't be trouble further along," I said.

"Well, if you pay the 500 there's no problem getting to the city of Boston, in the state of Massachusetts, but only for the three months stated in the passport. If the deadline passes there's another fine."

"Well, as for me, I'm only going for three months. I'll return then, because I've left my wife and children behind," I said.

"Well, fine then, I tell you that because there are many Mexicans who have stayed for good, those who've gone to make charcoal, but I want you to tell me what work you're going to do. It's better if you tell me openly. Then I'll prepare your paper," they told me.

Well, as for me, I already said from the start I was just going for a vacation. I already said that my compadre George had invited me. I didn't tell them what I was going to do in the United States.

Well, that's how I crossed over from Mexico. I gave them the 500 pesos. I stayed one day in Mexico City for my papers. I left the next day. When I came to each of the immigration officers there was hardly any trouble. I reached New Orleans. I stayed there twenty days working with my compadre George. Afterwards I went as far as Washington. I went to Bob Little Lake's house. I worked there two weeks with Bob Little Lake. Afterwards I went to New York. I stayed a week. I worked with a fellow named Andrew.[20] They showed me things in each state and in the capital, Washington.

Afterwards I went to the city of Boston, in the state of Massachussets. I arrived at the big university of Harvard. When I arrived, all the important professors and all the students gave a big party. Mr. John Vogtie assembled them. We ate, we drank liquor and beer. The next day I began working with all the professors and students until the three months ended. But every Sunday they took me on trips. I went to the Atlantic Ocean, where the sea made very big waves.

Later I went to Chicago, but just passed through. I didn't work anymore. That's how I got to know the United States. I saw how much ice there was and how much snow fell. That's how the first trip ended.

I made the second trip in 1967. On the third trip I got to know much more. I went to San Francisco, California, to Palo Alto, to Stanford University. That was in 1971. That was the last trip I took. But I thought it was the best, since there wasn't snow. It was good and warm. That's how I got to know how they eat there. No tortillas, just Bimbo bread in place of tortillas.

Well, that's how the three trips ended. Thanks to Mr. John Vogtie, and all the students who let me get to know their country! But now I still remember, I want to go. I'd like to go another time, because they were all good people. But it's a shame they no longer have work. Now there's no problem, because I have the proper papers. Now I have my military card, everything.

Well, as for me, when I think of it, it would be good if I were there, but there's nothing we can do, since the work is finished.

Well, Mr. John, Mrs. Catherine, and all your children, and compadre George, comadre Jane, Mr. Frank Cancian, and his wife, Francesca, Mr. Bob Little Lake and his wife, Victoria and her husband, compadre John Musician, I send the warmest greetings to you all.[21] Thank you for taking me to your country.

ACKNOWLEDGMENTS. I am indebted to Ted Slupesky for entering this material into the computer.

END NOTES

[1] Jpetul—Gary Gossen.

[2] *Los Chamulas en el mundo del sol: tiempo y espacio en una tradición oral maya.* (Gossen 1979).

[3] Jaime Sabines, prominent Mexican poet, is a brother of the late ex-governor of Chiapas, Juan Sabines.

[4] Maryan Antzelmo Peres Peres.

[5] Totik Lol—Robert Laughlin.

[6] Maltil Te'tikil Chitom—Dennis Breedlove.

[7] Mikulax—B. N. Colby.

[8] Palas J'ak' Chamel—Francesco Pellizi.

[9] Xun Tontik—John Burstein.

[10] Mol Telex—Andrés Aubrey.

[11] Instituto de Asesoría Antropológica para la Region Maya, A.C.

[12] Maryan Kalixto—Maryan Lopis Mentes.

[13] "Cuarenta Años de Investigaciones Antropológicas en Chiapas," held in 1982.

[14] Antzelmo's chronology is incorrect here, for it was when this job lost funding that aid was requested at the meeting of anthropologists.

[15] Cultural Survival, Inc.

[16] Jtotik Xun Evon Voti.

AS FOR ME AND THE HARVARD CHIAPAS PROJECT

[17] I have translated *alemanetik* as "Americans." This term, referring to fair-complexioned people, was the most common in 1961.
[18] Xun Jvabajom—John Haviland.
[19] Lol Bik'it Nab—Robert Laughlin.
[20] Telex—Richard Price.
[21] Jme'tik Katal—Catherine C. Vogt; Jkumale Xunka'—Jane Collier.

IN MEMORY OF JUAN VASQUEZ
(c. 1890-1981)
AND
DOMINGO DE LA TORRE
(1934-1976)

Frank Cancian

University of California, Irvine

L ike many anthropologists sent to Zinacantán by Evon Vogt, I met Juan Vásquez and Domingo de la Torre soon after I arrived.

Juan, a man of many talents and great verve, had a large family and a full career in public life. By the time members of the Harvard Chiapas Project first knew him in the late 1950s and early 1960s, he had been mayor of Zinacantán many times, he had passed through all four levels of the religious hierarchy, and he was established as a shaman. We were a small part of his life, but he gave us many personal experiences and memories, as well as tales and stories like those published by Robert Laughlin.

Domingo de la Torre came from a small, poor family. He began to work with Harvard Chiapas Project anthropologists while he was in his early twenties, and continued for most of his life after that. A patient and intelligent man, sometimes a moody man, he introduced many students to Zinacantán and did work of great subtlety with veteran anthropologists. When he died in 1976, he was survived by his wife Matal (Magdalena) and five children. The photos presented here follow Matal and his eldest son, Juan, to the present.

Robert Laughlin (1977) has written more about each of these men in his *Of Cabbages and Kings: Tales from Zinacantán.*

JUAN VASQUEZ AND DOMINGO DE LA TORRE

Figure 2. Waiting to take his corn to market, 1971.

Figure 1. Juan Vásquez during a curing ceremony, 1961.

JUAN VASQUEZ AND DOMINGO DE LA TORRE

Figure 3. 1971

Figure 4. 1981

JUAN VASQUEZ AND DOMINGO DE LA TORRE

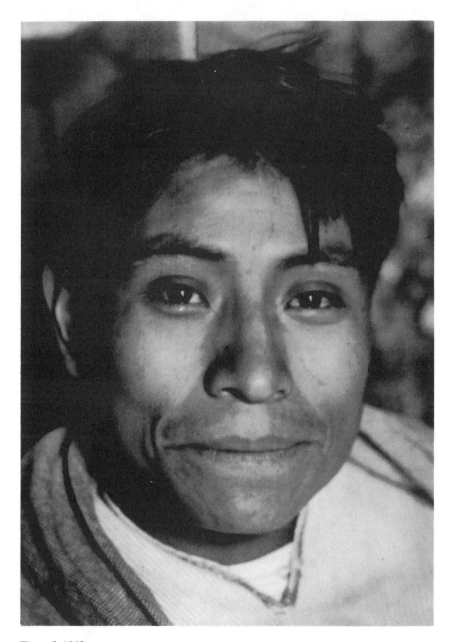

Figure 5. 1962

Figure 6. Domingo de la Torre in his cornfield, 1961.

JUAN VASQUEZ AND DOMINGO DE LA TORRE

Figure 7. Matal with Juan, 1961.

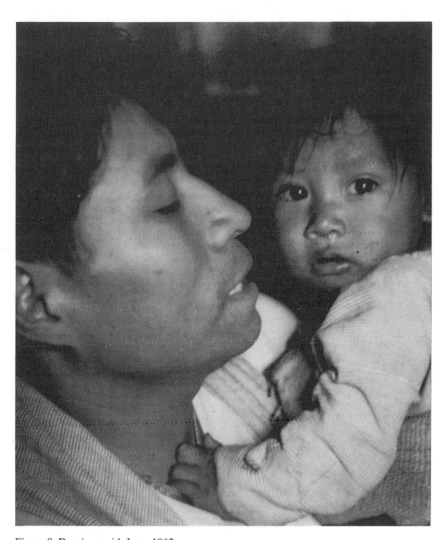

Figure 8. Domingo with Juan, 1962.

JUAN VASQUEZ AND DOMINGO DE LA TORRE

Figure 9. Juan with his brother José, 1971.

Figure 10. 1971

JUAN VASQUEZ AND DOMINGO DE LA TORRE

Figure 11. Juan's wedding dinner, 1984.

Figure 12. Juan at his wedding ceremony, 1984.

JUAN VASQUEZ AND DOMINGO DE LA TORRE

Figure 13. Matal with her granddaughter, 1988.

Figure 14. Juan with his daughter, 1988.

NOTES FROM THE CHIAPAS PROJECT: ZINACANTAN, SUMMER 1959

Susan Tax Freeman
University of Illinois, Chicago

During my first year of graduate study in the Department of Anthropology at Harvard, Vogtie invited me to do fieldwork in Zinacantán on the Chiapas Project, then in its beginning years. I had once visited Chiapas (in 1957) and watched from the sidelines as members of the University of Chicago's Chiapas Project and others compared notes at an informal conference in San Cristóbal. Vogtie and Frank Miller, who was beginning his work in Huistán, were also in San Cristóbal at the time; I had occasion to visit Indian communities in the area as well. Now I applied for, and received, a research grant and fellowship from the Anthropology Program of the National Institute of Mental Health, and I went to Chiapas in June of 1959, while Nick and Lore Colby were ending their year's fieldwork in Zinacantán. As a junior graduate student with course work still to complete, I was assigned a workable topic for a summer's research: the technology and social context of weaving (and thereby costume production) in Zinacantán. I had time enough to prepare by reading the published material on Maya back-strap weaving (principally Lila O'Neale's [1945] monograph on Guatemala) and, for more general purposes, to peruse the microfilmed notes of Alfonso Villa Rojas's work in Oxchuc in the 1930s and some of the notes of the expedition to Chiapas by Mexican anthropologists from the Escuela de Antropología e Historia in Mexico City led in the winter of 1942-1943 by Sol Tax. This work complemented my spring term course work on Mesoamerican ethnology under Vogtie. I arrived in Chiapas on June 18, 1959. As I arrived two weeks prior to the Vogt family, it was the Colbys who lodged me in San Cristóbal and introduced me to the Zinacantecos in both Zinacantán Center and the *paraje* of Paste'.

As the project's most junior member to date, and perhaps also as a single female, I was probably the object of special tutelage but also the beneficiary—as so many others were to become—of the special qualities of sharing that a team project provides. Vogtie, Frank Miller, and the Colbys had all forged their own ways at that time; my way was laid in part by them. For a variety of reasons, I did not pursue my doctoral research in Zinacantán, did not return to Chiapas after a brief second visit in December to January, 1959-1960, and have never since then worked on a team field project. Separated, thus, from the peculiar constraints as well as the special benefits of the joint research project, and by thirty years from my Chiapas fieldwork and my juniority of that time, I offer here some reflections on the project's importance—and Vogtie's as field director—for my extraordinarily rich and affecting first experience in anthropological fieldwork. As documents of the drama of that experience, I offer excerpts from my unpublished field diary.

On July 22, I became the first anthropologist (or so I was told) to move into an Indian house in Chiapas. This would not have been possible without the Colby's help. On my first days in Chiapas, I accompanied Nick on his final or near-final visits to Zinacantecos with whom he had worked closely. I began my study of weaving in this context and with the Colbys' guidance. I began systematic observation with two families in Paste'. Then in the home of Antonio Montejo Cruz and his wife Maruch, in Zinacantán Center, I was invited to take up the loom myself. "You are so slow," observed Maruch, "that even your fleas are dancing with boredom." That every human provides the residence for a number of fleas was to come true for me in that same house. At our first meeting, Maruch invited me to move in. The invitation was, I know, a product of the affection the couple felt for the Colbys; it was not likely to have been proffered otherwise, to a stranger. Even the Colbys, being two, had lived on their own. But Nick Colby gave me more of value on that visit. When a neighbor, Domingo de la Torre Peres (later a steady employee of the project), stood in Maruch's doorway, watching me weave and translating Maruch's comments for me, Nick said to me quietly: "Watch the eye contact between the two of them—it shows they're good friends. Otherwise people avoid looking directly at each other." Shared intelligence of this sort, in the few days we had together, along with the insightful field report Nick had written that drew in part on his acquaintance with Antonio and Maruch, offered me keys for understanding the world I was entering. His hard-won insights, along with my residence in a native home, helped me in one short summer to experience Zinacanteco social life at a level of intimacy I would have been pleased to attain after a much longer time.

During that summer, I had five brief sojourns in Antonio and Maruch's home (interspersed with work in Paste', where I lodged in the project's house with the Vogts). The first of these began on July 22. The second of two closely contiguous periods of residence in early August covered the patronal fiesta of San Lorenzo. For this occasion, Vogtie moved into the house inhabited by Domingo de la Torre, his wife, mother, and aunt, next to the home in which I had been staying. Thus was begun the tradition of intensive observation from the vantage point of Zinacanteco domestic life that Vogtie followed with later students, lodging them with willing hosts (Vogt 1979:285). Thanks to Nick Colby's guidance, I was sensitized to Zinacantecos' senses of social distance and proximity and was able to discern, at times like the August fiesta, patterns like the following, recorded afterwards:

> I counted [on August 8] eighteen people in the house for lunch. This calls for a word about the procedure in the house when there are guests. I am writing this actually after the fiesta and have had by this time, as I will describe, a great deal of experience with guests.
>
> All guests appear to bring their own food with them—tortillas,

dried meat, a couple of pots, beans. In the case of a family of visitors, the women will use the fire to cook their meals, and they will eat in their part of the house—the same part where they keep their things and spread their sleeping mats at night. The eating is in family groups. Maruch only grinds and cooks for those who are in "her" group—Antonio and me—and we eat at any time we please, from the table, whereas the others do not have a table. If Maruch has the fire well occupied when another couple or family has mealtime, they just wait until she has finished. However, they may also fix their meal before we eat. In the case of single man—two Ixtapa sacristans and one of the musicians—Maruch does a little more for them, and on occasion they joined Antonio and me at the table and got some soup to supplement their dry food. Maruch also on occasion presented each family with a pot of vegetables and—quite often—with coffee.

Occasions like this—indeed most normal days, short as my time was—were so rich in new events that every few days of residence required as many days of note-taking in San Cristóbal. Vogtie monitored the periodicity of my visits in Zinacantán; left to my own devices and mesmerized as I was by my life there, I might never have torn myself away from San Cristóbal. As it was, I filled memo pads with reminders and sequences of events and employed the insufficient mnemonic devices at my command to help me retain not only events but also impressions of them. I did not impose furniture or machinery on the household—hence no typewriter or table—and in any case could not depend on any inactive daylight hours to permit consistent recording. I took notes on substantive exchanges in odd moments as soon as I could do so, so as to retain their true content and sequences.

Antonio involved me in a rather trying conversation in the later afternoon [of July 22]. I can't remember how it began, but I believe we were talking about the fact that a Zinacanteco is taken to the cemetery with all his possessions when he dies, and people in "my country" are not.

"Why, *why* is it, Susana, that we all are going to die?"

I said that it was the way Diós wanted it, I don't know why, but it happens to everyone in the world.

"Yes, everyone, everybody." But the fact did not console him. "I have no sons, nobody, *nobody*. There will be no one to take care of my things when I die, no one to remember me, no one to do what is necessary with my belongings."

I replied, inadequately, that he will not die for forty or fifty years yet.

"Yes, but then I will be old. I will not be able to walk. I will not be able to do anything. Maruch will be old, and she won't be able to do anything. She will be left all alone when I die, and who will there be to do things for her?"

I said something about friends.

"*Friends*!" He scoffed. They are apparently not to be counted upon. "We have no *sons*." He touched his arm: "Flesh. This will be all in the grave." He pointed at me."Your flesh will all be in the grave too. They will carry it to the cemetery."

I said yes, I know that.

He referred once more to himself. "All this will be in the grave. *Chin* will be in the grave [he was learning English words from me], *cheek* will be in the grave, everything, everything."

I commented that at least as long he is alive he appears to be learning very well, and we continued in a lighter tone. His attitude was serious and very truly questioning, but along with it there was an undertone of self-indulgence, as if to say: "I can ask you all these questions and you can't answer them any better than I. You know, Zinacantecan men are not supposed to waste their time doing this; they should be busy weaving hats instead. But just one minute more. . . ."

Much of my writing capacity in daytime was consumed with the recording of technical material on weaving and elements of the costume. Conversations like the above were frankly more difficult to record openly, for there was no apparent reason to do so. However, the written word and the tape-recorded word (about which this couple had learned from the Colbys) became very important, particularly to Antonio, as steps toward the preservation of himself for posterity, especially because he was childless. Ultimately, I was asked to record for his keeping memories, such as the words to some songs I sang, or, for posterity, things that he dictated to me, such as his (or sometimes Maruch's) dreams, which he would call to me in the night, advising that I should be prepared to write them out as soon as the morning fire was lit.

Antonio dreamed [on July 23] that he went to the cantina and met a friend there. "Do you want a beer?" asked the friend. "Why not?" said Antonio. The two drank beer. Salud! Salud! and bottles clinked. The friend then took out a piece of bull meat that was raw and they both began to eat it with the beer, but it was very tough. They finished the beer and the friend ordered a small bottle of *trago*. The meat had blood in it. Antonio took out a handkerchief to wipe off the blood from his face. The beer was finished, and they began the *trago*. They left the cantina. In a matter of a minute Antonio found himself in Chamula, all alone. He didn't know where his friend had gone. He went to a house. He felt very dizzy, and his head was whirling from the *trago*. A girl came out and she was fat and very pretty, had nice clothes, and she asked him if he wanted *trago*.

"Yes." "Here is your *trago*"—she brought him a cup. He asked the girl what her heart said. She lifted her skirt and showed her genitals and said, "Look, look how I am." Antonio wanted to kill that girl and her family. Instead, he ran, to the river, and he jumped in under the water with all his clothes on. When he came out he met another friend in the road. "What happened?" said the friend. "Oh, I want to kill a Chamula." "But why?" the friend asked. "I want to drink; let's look for *trago*," said Antonio.

N. B. This morning when Antonio woke from his dream, he said he was sick and went outside to spit and cough volubly. Later, when he had told the dream to me, he said that he had been sick in the morning from the raw meat he had eaten in the night. He said that when he went outside to spit, a little bit of the blood from the meat came out.

Antonio Montejo suffered from alcoholism and had been helped by Nick and Lore Colby to abstain from drinking, which he had successfully done for months before I met him and Maruch. The only way in which the culture can be said to treat the abstainer kindly is the convention that he may participate in ritual drinking by funneling his share into a bottle. This Antonio usually did, and he took an occasional tranquilizer he had been given. The advent of the patronal fiesta was already weighing on him when I met him, and the pressure to drink may be reflected in this dream.

Antonio was a powerful curer in the community (thereby also a suspected witch), and so I was also witness to his diagnosis and treatment of clients who came to see him, and, on fewer occasions, I accompanied him out to cure in a patient's home, although I never witnessed a major curing ceremony. Some amount of this activity was nocturnal. Some of Antonio's dictations to me were both curing and hexing chants that he wanted recorded for posterity. The latter were given me principally in the relative privacy of San Cristóbal.

As the fiesta of the patron saint approached, people from outlying settlements and other towns began to arrive to stay in Zinacantán Center. Antonio and Maruch were called upon to lodge their friends, allies, and compadres in their spacious house (though it was a traditional one-room structure). Given Antonio's prominence, lodgers were numerous. The eighteen-person lunch of August 8 was followed by the nights of the fiesta proper, on which a total of twenty-seven people slept under our roof. On August 10, Antonio began to drink. I surely recognized then, for it is reflected in my notes, the degree of terror that Antonio's drinking represented for the neighborhood, particularly its women; but I am now again struck by it as I reread the diary. It was a relief to me—and, as the diary shows, of some utility to Antonio—that Vogtie was lodged nearby. Vogtie kept a close watch on the events in our household and was within shouting distance of us, as were so many other people. If either Vogtie or I had felt that I was in physical danger, I should have moved elsewhere. It was certainly Vogtie the field director and not my embroiled self who brought me, on schedule, out of the domestic tempest and into San Cristóbal to gain perspective and write my notes.

[B., T., and M., friends of mine from San Cristóbal who knew Antonio, were at the fiesta on August 10 and visited his house briefly in the afternoon.]

When T. asked Antonio how his heart was, he said that he did not know where it was, whether in heaven or on earth. . . . Then he explained that it was hard when his friends came and brought *trago,* that he would much rather they didn't but brought anything else instead—like cigarettes or cookies [which these three had brought]. . . . Then he wanted T. and M. to take his picture. He asked me and B. to pose with him. While we were standing by the cross [in the house-yard] he turned to me and said very quietly that he had hit Maruch. I said, "But Antonio that's very bad. Why?" and he said, "I just hit her—I don't know why. I said I had another girl in Navenchauk (it's a lie!), and she got angry, and I hit her. Now I'm sad." Then he didn't say any more, and after the three had left we went into the house. Maruch did not speak to him but went about making tortillas. In a few minutes a family came (a compadre—Antonio has eighty), and without ado Antonio began to pulse the small daughter. He rendered his diagnosis, which I did not catch and never had a chance to ask. Then Maruch fed the family. . . . While the family was eating, Maruch, still at the metate, began to cry and tell them the story of how Antonio hit her. She was weeping really bitterly, as much as I have ever seen anyone cry. Antonio was sitting rather sullenly on the bed. Finally he and the compadre got up and left (about 11:00 A.M.). After this Maruch came to sit by me and began to cry again—just as hard—and showed me her black eye. She talked a bit, but I couldn't understand. I said all sorts of useless things to her in Spanish, and eventually she stopped crying and went to work sewing. Soon the two Ixtapa women [guests in the house] came back from the fiesta, and Maruch told them. They translated for me: Antonio was drinking. Antonio had been drinking in the morning with that compadre, and Antonio was drinking now. He had even come back once for money, and he was already quite drunk. (I had been out for a while at that time, it seems.)

I was horrified. This explained his behavior in the morning. I suddenly realized also what a really horrible strain he must have been under for the last days—and the last time I had seen him, sulking in the house, was at that time when the decision to drink was very close, and he was still completely aware of the consequences it would bring. He really did not know where his heart was.

For the rest of the afternoon, the Ixtapa women and I stayed in the house with Maruch—also one comadre who is sleeping there.

Maruch worked all the time, but once in a while burst into uncontrollable tears. Vogtie came by and heard what had happened. Then he left. All afternoon the women just stayed there, but the tension built: how soon was Antonio going to come home, and what would he be like? Maruch said he was going to come to beat her. I could see that they were all in mortal terror.

At 5:00 he came. The children in the yard sent in an electrified warning, and immediately everyone in the house [all women] had melted against the walls. I have never seen such terror. I was sitting in front of the fire: I remained there. He came with the compadre. He stopped in front of the yard cross and said something to it. Then he came into the house with the compadre, and no one in the house was breathing. He was teetering, and he was gruff, but superficially no different from all the hundreds of drunk men around; but there was something that could be *felt* that said that this was no ordinary drunk man but one who knows that he could kill people and himself, doesn't want to do it, but has to. It was terribly, terribly sad, and I began to shake. Antonio and the compadre sat down. They greeted everyone gruffly. There were some half-hearted replies from the walls. Maruch didn't say a word. She was sitting in a corner of the bed. Antonio greeted me, said my name, shook hands. He and the compadre drank some *trago*. One thing became rather evident to me: the men were in a very structured and subordinate relationship to him; the women were afraid, were expected to be afraid, and he *knew* they were afraid. The only person whose reaction he could not predict (and neither could I) was mine. I had a feeling I was going to be called on pretty soon in one way or another, and yes, after a few minutes, he got up and asked me to help him put away his things—his shoulder-bag and his new hat. We went over to the trunk and put them in. Then he sat down again and in a minute asked me to get cigarettes. I did. A few minutes later he asked me to go down to the store to get three beers. I told him that he would have to give me money. He did, with effort at counting, and I left. I went by way of Vogtie's house just to tell Vogtie that Antonio was back. Vogtie said he'd come over in the evening, and we would go to the fiesta, and we would gauge the situation with Antonio then. As I emerged into the road to go to the store, the neighbors were all at their gates, also in terror, and they said things like "be careful" as I went by. I ran through the church yard to Domingo's store [a cooperative organized for the fiesta]. Domingo stood up and greeted me cordially. He looked at me blankly as I told him Antonio was drunk. "Sick," I added. "There is a special price for friends," said Domingo. "I am taking the beer back to Antonio," I said, as Domingo wanted to open the bottles. He looked at me. "I'll open them for you," said Domingo cordially. "*I will open them myself*," I said. I was too upset to see how funny it was. Poor Domingo hadn't been able to stand it with two sleepless nights and lots of compulsory *trago*. He had trouble counting the money. Then he held out his hand and said, "*Que le vaya bien.*" This was the last straw: I took the beer and fled.

I opened the bottles for Antonio and the other man, and they began to drink. When the beer was finished, Antonio asked Maruch for coffee. She produced it immediately. Antonio was joking and laughing, but only the compadre was with him. Then he asked me to sit next to him for coffee, and I spent the next half hour dunking cookies into his coffee for him, and he counted the cookies each time, looked impressed, and exclaimed. . . . Then he said that he and I were going to take a walk, and he explained to everyone that I am his daughter. I said of course I am his daughter, but I told Vogtie that I would wait for him to go to the fiesta too, and that we would all do it together. Antonio agreed to wait. A few minutes later Vogtie came, and we left, with Juan, the Ixtapa sacristan. They started by ordering beer (and Antonio insisted on a bowl of shrimp) at the store where we once bought candles before going to church, an uncomfortable memory I had while we were there . . . church. . . . During their first beer I left and went back to the house, told Maruch that Vogtie was taking care of Antonio and would bring him back when it was possible. Maruch gave me a bowl full of supper, which I couldn't eat very much of, and gradually we began going to bed.

At 11:00 Vogtie carried Antonio in and put him on the floor. Maruch motioned him to leave, and then she just sat looking at Antonio. I was awake, and one of the Ixtapa women next to me was awake. Antonio was completely helpless on the floor. Maruch said nothing. He groaned and muttered monosyllables. She still said nothing. It was a terrible sight. He reached out his hand for her help to get him up, and she didn't move. By this time I had my head buried in the covers and was begging her to help him, completely unconscious of what I was doing, in English. Finally Maruch told him to get up and get into bed. She was still sitting in a corner of the bed. Antonio was rolling on top of the sleeping Ixtapanecos. Somehow he got to his feet and picked up a chair, holding it over his head, over Maruch: he was not even swaying. The Ixtapa woman and I were both praying out loud. Antonio let the chair drop to the floor, and he himself fell into a sitting position. Now Maruch moved and took two more chairs away from him to the other side of the room, and Juan from Ixtapa got out of bed. He took Antonio outside to relieve himself and left him there: all we could see was Antonio's arm as he tried to get off the ground and back into the house. Finally he did come back in, and Juan sat down with him at the fire and talked to him very quietly for several minutes. Then he and Maruch got him into bed.

Antonio was the first person up [on August 11]. He swayed from the bed to the doorway and asked pardon of everyone he stepped on. He came back and sat down. He and the compadre [who slept here] began to drink *trago*. It was 5:00 A.M.

When I sat up in bed, Antonio said, "Susana, you're crying." I told him I wasn't crying, and I got up. Gradually people began to leave the house. The compadres from Navenchauk left without ceremony. The Ixtapanecos went to their fiesta duties, and their wives went with them. Soon Antonio and I were sitting together at the table while Maruch set out frijoles. Antonio would not eat them. I ate them to have something to do. A Chamula came: Antonio asked me to pour out a bottle of *trago* for them. They drank it. Then another compadre came, and they finished another bottle. Finally the man left, and some of the Ixtapanecos came back. Antonio said he was going to buy *trago*. He picked up the cash box from the *trago* sales: Maruch had locked it. He started to throw it at her, then at me. I told him I was going to get some beer and that he should put the box down. I got three bottles from Vogtie, and when I came back I found him not particularly asking for them so I put them away. Soon he did ask. We were alone again. He began to drink beer and was very quiet. Then he wanted shrimp. Then he wanted lime on the shrimp.

Vogtie had stopped by earlier and told Antonio that he hoped he would not drink like this for more than once a year. That he could get very sick from it. Now as Antonio was drinking his beer I asked him if he would listen to me for a minute. He told me he would. I told him that in Mexico and in my country and in Zinacantán and all over the world there are some people who have a certain sickness. Those people cannot drink because when there do the *trago* stays in their blood. The doctors do not know anything to do about it. But after the *trago* has been in their blood for awhile, they die. Antonio looked up and told me he did not want to listen to me any more. He said I didn't understand that he *wanted* to die. He wanted to go to the *panteón*. Then I would cry. I mentioned that I didn't want him to die. Then he told me, "after all I am only drinking for these two days—yesterday and today—for the fiesta, for the Lord, my patron." I said, "Sure?" He said "Absolutely." Then he told me that tomorrow, like other days, he was going to Tuxtla to sell things. What is he going to sell? A watermelon [the one Nan sent him as a present], a pair of shoes [some sneakers left by Manuel Zabala], and, and . . . peaches! I asked where the peaches were to come from. He stood up: "I am going to cut them right now." He strode into the yard. "Let's go pick peaches," he shouted, and a minute later he had forgotten that and was on his way to see Vogtie. He got ten pesos from Vogtie and then went down to the river to wash. Vogtie told me we would leave later in the morning. I went back to the house. Maruch had broken down again, and the Ixtapanecos were back. Soon Antonio came back again and asked for the last of the three beers. At this one I motioned that I was going to put an Equanil into it—there was one left from a bunch Nick had given Antonio [and no counter-indications for use with alcohol]. One thing that no one told me, however, is that whatever other qualities Equanil may have, it does not dissolve in beer. Maruch was watching me. The pill began bouncing up and down in the bottle. I had no way of getting it back to mash it, and Antonio was beginning to ask loudly for his beer. Finally I got the pill to sit in the foam and handed the bottle to him, hoping that it would go down in the first gulp. It did not. The next thing I knew Antonio was holding the pill in one hand, and the bottle in the other, and staring at it in sheer amazement. Then he dropped the pill into the fire and began drinking again. I was ready to explain that beer is made out of yeast pills, and one of them must not have dissolved. There was no need for that: he just dropped it unceremoniously into the fire and my heart sank. Soon he had put on his high-backed sandals and was off again to the cantina. Maruch was still crying. At this point Vogtie came up with the Landrover to pack things, and I said goodbye to everyone. I told Maruch that if things got really bad she should find me at Casa Na Bolom in San Cristóbal, and I would find some pills that might help. She said that if it went on much longer she would move into her family's house, and she promised to find me if they needed pills. Her eye still hurt. I told her "aspirin." She said she would remember it. When I went down to meet Vogtie [who had gone ahead with the car to watch the *alféreces* parade to one of the four houses they will visit today] I got some aspirins from him and took them back to Maruch. She was very grateful and gave me a purple ribbon, which is connected with the Virgen de la Asunción. It is the kind of ribbon which the women always wear around their necks along with the beads. Then I said goodbye again, and we left.

On August 15, Domingo reported to us (in San Cristóbal) that Antonio had stopped drinking on the very day we last saw him, but that Maruch had left him and gone to her family's house. Ten days later, when I visited with the intention of staying with Domingo's family next door, I found Antonio and Maruch together and ended up staying with them, for this time there was tension [exacerbated by drinking] in Domingo's family. In fact, I stayed in both houses before that visit ended, and it was extended when Antonio and Maruch came into San Cristóbal and stayed with me at the Casa Na Bolom. From there, I was bid goodbye when, a few days later, I left for the United States.

I was mistaken about Antonio's longevity. He was to die at the hands of rival villagers in an encounter at a mountain shrine during a curing expedition only a few years later (see the account in Vogt 1969b:413-415). I did not see him or Maruch again after the first days of January, 1960.

The margins of my notes are filled with jottings and questions from Vogtie, who read them all and guided my pursuit of particular questions and the structure of my time. The summer's work resulted in two very different pieces of writing. A file manuscript on weaving and its social context grew out of my formal inquiries. An article on "displacement" activity grew from my experiences at the fireside and in the daily company of my hosts in all their varied activities; it addressed the qualities of personal interaction between Zinacantecos (Tax 1964). My diary shows the tension between focused inquiry and the absorption of more varied facts, objects of general curiosity about the cultural system. The focused inquiry helped to keep me on track for a summer's work and out of subject matter assigned principally to other present or future investigators who were my seniors in graduate study. This was frustrating to my explorers' sense, especially because Zinacantán was still so relatively little understood, and when I eventually began field research in Spain, I worked alone. But I carry Zinacantán and the summer of 1959 with me in important ways.

The intensity of my summer, both in the density of events and in the fact that I was privileged to experience them so deeply, came to me because I was (as were Vogtie and everyone yet to come) the beneficiary of sharing in a team effort. Whatever the topical constraints of such a project on one not ready to be committed to a major part in it, they are far outweighed by the privileges, in this case, of sharing friendships of confidence forged by carefully trained, sensitive, and wise senior members. The summer of 1959 is for me a standard of cultural learning and exchange to be striven for everywhere and replicated wherever possible. Since then, I have never lived alone when doing fieldwork nor kept house for myself, but always lodged with native hosts and cherished the gleanings from around the fireside, the kitchen table, and the family circle, searching out their substantive connections with the topics of more formal study and using them to advance that study. For these reasons, the days in Paste' living among colleagues were for me paler; but they did, on the other hand, place me in sight and hearing of Vogtie's painstaking, exemplary formal interviews, for which he used the place heavily.

Vogtie's genial and casual exterior conceals an organized (and very caring) disciplinarian whose concerns made of my relatively undisciplined self a better anthropologist—especially for the study of social structure and ceremonial organization—than I would have made of myself, unguided. The research-topic assignment, the marginal notes and queries, as well as the model Vogtie showed me in the field itself—in interview situations but also more generally—are things for which I am deeply grateful, professionally their beneficiary forever.

One day in the summer of 1959, a Zinacanteco man came to the Harvard project's rented apartment in San Cristóbal so that Vogtie could review his prospects for a job with some aspect of the project. I was in the room at the time. The man cited among his credentials that he had already worked with a North American student of Zinacantán, Sol Tax, in 1942-1943. Vogtie introduced me as Sol Tax's daughter. Later in the interview, the man expressed curiosity about how the daughter of Sol Tax should come to be in Chiapas with Evon Vogt. Vogtie explained this way: "When I was a student, Sol Tax was my teacher. Now I am a teacher and his daughter is a student, so I am able to teach her in return." The idea, understood and welcomed by the visitor, was to reciprocate things of value.

Vogtie did.

THE COLLAPSE OF COMPLIANCE: NATIONAL IMPLICATIONS OF LOCAL CHANGES

Frank C. Miller
University of Minnesota

Thirty years ago, on the last day of Ph.D. fieldwork in the *municipio* of Huistán in the highlands of Chiapas, I took a final trip to the town center to observe the voting in the presidential election held on the first Sunday of July in 1958. Although I had read about the fabled efficiency of the Partido Revolucionario Institucional (PRI) in conducting elections that would give a landslide to its candidates, I nevertheless was impressed by the care with which election officials showed the Huistecos how to vote by pointing to various names on the ballot that carried the proper party designation. Every PRI candidate was clearly marked with the party's distinctive symbol, yet the officials were taking pains to ensure that no one voted accidentally for the wrong person.

Adolfo López Mateos was elected president of the republic by the expected landslide. I was not able to stay in Huistán to hear the results there, but I am sure that all of the PRI candidates received virtually a unanimous vote.

As I began to write this essay in July of 1988, another PRI candidate, Carlos Salinas de Gortari, was elected president, but this time there was no landslide; on the contrary, there was even widespread skepticism that he had actually won the popular vote. The official results, delayed by "computer problems" and "atmospheric conditions" and announced eight days after the voting, gave 50.4 percent to Salinas, 31.1 percent to Cuauhtémoc Cárdenas, son of a revered former president and candidate of the leftist coalition, and 17.1 percent to Manuel Clouthier of the Partido de Acción Nacional (PAN), a right-of-center party.

The results of the recent election are widely interpreted as evidence of a dramatic shift in the Mexican political landscape, and there will no doubt be a long debate among politicians, pundits, and professors about the reasons for the results and their implications for the future of Mexico. An opening salvo was rapidly fired by Jorge Castañeda, a professor of political science at the Universidad Nacional Autónoma de México and a frequent contributor to the Op-Ed page of the *New York Times*. He argued that Salinas would carry a burden into office because the party's credibility and legitimacy would "suffer dearly" (Castañeda 1988). He detailed how well both of the opposition candidates had run in Mexico City and most other large cities throughout the northern region of the country, where PAN has been building strength for many years, and in the state of Michoacán, where Cárdenas had served as governor. He then suggested that the election was a "mosaic of paradoxes" because the man who campaigned on a platform of political modernization owed his victory to "two of the most backward and conservative sectors of Mexican society—the peasants and caciques" (Castañeda 1988). (For the first time that I can remember in the *New York Times,* "cacique" was neither placed in quotation marks nor explained, perhaps indicating that this handy Mexican term for "political boss" has become a loan word in English.)

Professor Castañeda (1988) asserts that the new president "is indebted to the votes tallied, though not necessarily cast, in the poorest, most isolated and ignorant parts of rural Mexico. . . . a slice of the nation that gave Mexico its soul in the past but does not belong to its future." After summarily condemning twelve million people, one-third of the electorate, to oblivion, he insists that "Mexico is living its most important democratic experience in many decades. . . . and could well emerge a happier, prouder and more stable nation" (Castañeda 1988).

I fervently join in the hope that Mexico emerges as a more stable nation, but I wonder what, in Castañeda's vision of the future, the poor, ignorant peasants are going to be doing amid the happiness, pride, and stability. If they are expelled from the future, they might take some action that would disturb the happiness and stability that their compatriots will be enjoying.

This essay will present some impressionistic evidence for a more hopeful vision of the role of the peasantry in Mexico's future. Since the evidence comes from my personal experience with a tiny sample of the peasantry, I make no claims that it can be generalized to prove an argument. Instead, I hope that this account might serve as a wedge to open a crack in the wall that seems too often to separate urban intellectuals from the common people in the countryside. This essay is an exploration in the kingdom of possibility, not a documentation of a well-charted domain.

The Mexican and North American social scientists who chart the peasant territory have increasingly come to agree about the means by which the national state has incorporated and controlled the peasantry. Hewitt de Alcántara (1984) offers an admirably comprehensive account. "Historical structuralism" is the label that has been adopted for the consensus that emerged during the 1970s after five decades of research. Some of the most influential works contributing to the consensus are by Warman (1976, 1980), and a variant of the approach has been applied to Chiapas by Wasserstrom (1983).

Influenced by these analyses, George Collier has recently interpreted peasant politics in Chiapas within the same general framework. He applies Warman's analysis of Morelos to Chiapas: "land reform initiated sustained market exploitation of the peasantry, enabling dependent industrial capitalism to develop on the basis of cheaply fed and cheaply paid labor in a country no longer troubled by peasant revolution" (Collier 1987:95). The land reform in Morelos began in the 1930s, but was not implemented in Chiapas until the presidency of Lázaro Cárdenas in 1934-1940, the high point of the land reform. He then considers the political consequences of the development program operated by the Instituto

Nacional Indigenista (INI), focusing on the role of the *promotores,* the Indians who were hired and trained to be agents of change in agriculture, education, and health. These posts created new opportunities for brokerage and filled a vacuum that had existed since the decline of the land reform and of the Union of Native Workers that also has been established during the Cárdenas administration.

Collier asserts that the INI program engendered fragmentation and factionalism by revising priorities and thereby undercutting one group of brokers and supporting another and by turning its functions over to other agencies. For example, health programs were turned over to the Secretaría de Salubridad y Asistencia, and the innovative educational effort was shifted to the Secretaría de Educación Pública. The overall conclusion is that, by means of "land reform and Indianist development, the State forged a quintessentially mid-20th century compliance among the indigenous municipios of highland Chiapas" (Collier 1988:95).

Many questions could be raised about the empirical foundations of historical structural analyses such as Collier's, but there is a deeper issue concerning the relationship between human agency and social structure (Giddens 1979). I do not wish to caricature the views of the historical structuralists, but it is difficult not to notice the underlying message that the state pulls the strings and the hapless peasant puppets dance. Perhaps compliance was not engendered primarily by the ingenuity of national agencies playing off groups of brokers against each other; perhaps the peasants made a political choice to cooperate in order to maintain the flow of benefits—the land granted in the land reform, the health services where none existed before, the vastly improved education in the INI schools. Now that land is not being redistributed, health services are restricted because of cuts in funding, and the schools have been entrusted to the lethargy of the Secretaría de Educación Pública, the quintessentially mid-twentieth century compliance may collapse with surprising speed.

I return now to the story of my personal encounter with some Huistecos, who have taught me much about the issue of agency and structure. I am grateful to them and to Evon Vogt, whose friendship, leadership, and wise counsel helped to sustain me.

Vogtie and I arrived in Chiapas at the beginning of the "dog days" of August in 1957. The expected break in the rainy season fortunately came to pass, for our first task was to do a reconnaissance of the Tzeltal and Tzotzil zones in order to select sites for research. Vogt's (1978:15) own account of this period reports accurately that we traveled by Landrover, on horseback, and on foot, but neglects to mention that he grew up on a sheep ranch in New Mexico and was an expert horseman, whereas I grew up in Illinois and had ridden a pony for about ten minutes when I was nine years old. When we arrived in Oxchuc after a long day on wooden saddles, I began to realize that Vogtie was not going to coddle me.

But I was going to respect age and rank. A local shopkeeper offered to accommodate us and showed us a tiny room that had a single cot with a thin mattress, so I insisted that my advisor take the cot. While I slept numbly but blissfully on the concrete floor, he fought a valiant but hopeless battle against the fleas.

During that month I learned in the best possible way how to do fieldwork—by watching a master do it. Whether he was explaining the purpose of the research to Monseñor Flores, principal assistant to the bishop in San Cristóbal, deflecting the attentions of drunks on fiesta days, or interviewing municipal presidents, Vogtie was able to connect on a direct and personal level with people, to engage their interest, and to enlist their cooperation.

Meeting with the Monseñor was critically important because there was growing Catholic-Protestant conflict in the region. North American linguistic missionaries associated with the Summer Institute of Linguistics were having an impact on some Indian communities. A few years before, an entire village (a large one of about 1000 people) converted to Protestantism. As a counter to this perceived threat, the Catholic church mounted an effort for religious renewal in Indian communities. As anthropologists interested in learning Indian languages, we were vulnerable to misperceptions of our role. The Monseñor assured us that he would tell the priests that we were legitimate anthropologists and ask them to pass the word around when they traveled their circuits to Indian communities.

My plan for research was to study the impact of the INI development program, especially the diffusion of modern medicine. Since I wanted to observe the process as it was actually happening, I hoped to do fieldwork in a village that was changing rapidly. We sought the advice of Alfonso Villa Rojas, the distinguished anthropologist who was director of the INI Coordinating Center for the Tzeltal-Tzotzil zone. He suggested Huajam, a village in the *municipio* of Huistán, where an INI medical post was about to open. (The names of the village and villagers have been changed to preserve privacy.) He and Dr. Francisco Alarcón, head of the medical program, took us there to ask permission for the research. It was readily granted, and they arranged for my food and lodging. In this and other ways, they offered many personal kindnesses and professional advice and assistance.

I began fieldwork with special advantages: an exceptional mentor at Harvard, who read my field notes and wrote detailed comments; institutional and personal support from the INI director and other staff; the secular blessing of the bishop; ample funding from a Doherty Fellowship; and the use of the Harvard Landrover, which became my principal tool for reciprocity, as I quickly assumed the role of chauffeur in weekly trips to San Cristóbal for mail. Perhaps the most important advantage was the receptive attitude of Artemio Bolom, leader of the village, and Miguel Moshán, a young resident hired and trained by INI as a *promotor de salud* to staff the new medical post.

I set up residence in Huajam on September 13 and spent two uneventful days going around introducing myself and chatting with people. One of my main concerns was whether or not to take photographs at the Independence Day celebration to be held on September 15 in the school. I had been warned about photography; some Indian people might think that cameras steal their souls, and using a flash would be particularly obtrusive. The *ladino* teacher made the decision for me, once he learned that I had a camera, by insisting that I use it.

I had never worked with a film director before, and I was not sure that I met his demanding standard of speed and efficiency. He was obviously in charge, so I assumed that he would get the blame if any souls were lost. Apparently none were, for the reaction to the flash was amusement, not fear.

That night I slept the serene sleep of a child who survived the first day at school. While walking to the school early in the morning, I watched the smoke from breakfast fires filtering through the hand-split pine-shingle roofs; it seemed to welcome me into a tranquil domesticity.

The reverie was rudely interrupted at the school when a distinguished-looking man with steel-gray hair and white beard berated me in Tzotzil. The teacher told me that he was the grandfather of the health promoter and that he had said, "Many of us don't want you here." A few weeks later the promoter, Miguel, informed me that his grandfather and many others were suspicious that I was a Protestant missionary. "After all," he laughed, "you look more like a missionary than a Huisteco."

I launched into a long discourse on the religious situation in the United States, explaining that there were many kinds of Protestants, that most Protestants and Catholics got along well together, that my parents were Protestant but I did not belong to any religious group.

Miguel seemed to be satisfied with this excessively elaborate explanation, but other people kept raising the issue, usually when they were drunk. I quickly learned not to try to persuade drunks with rational arguments, but I did not know how to handle the issue, other than to hope it would wither away.

Professor Vogt had told me that one of the best ways to build rapport is to leave for a while and promise to return. People are likely to be skeptical and then reassured when the promise is kept. So I had an anthropological rationale for doing what I planned to do anyway: visit my wife and children back home in the United States.

The circumstances of my departure in late November reassured me about the future. I had arranged for ethnomusicologist Sam Eskin to record some of the musicians in Huajam. Most of the villagers turned out to watch the proceedings, and many of the men bade me a surprisingly fond farewell. Then everybody—men, women, and children—lined the road as we drove away, and they smiled and waved until we disappeared around a distant bend.

After this send-off, I was not surprised when Vogtie's prediction about rapport came true. When I returned, those who had been cordial the first time were clearly glad to see me, and the reluctant ones were friendlier. As I steadily gained trust and confidence, the suspicions about missionaries withered away after all.

The main goal of my research was to study change as it was taking place and to seek to understand how the response to innovation was shaped by social dynamics and community values. This interest led me naturally to an increasing focus on decision-making by individuals, families, and the village assembly (Miller 1965). In those days we were taught to control our subjectivity as much as possible, so my written works create the impression that the focus on decision-making was entirely a scholarly choice of analytical strategy. The truth of the matter is that I was fascinated by local politics and by the role of the leadership in shaping but not controlling the process. For the first time in my life, I witnessed a full-scale consensus-building system in action. In countless hours of meetings, the will of the majority was never imposed on the minority. If dissenters could not be persuaded to acquiesce, the proposal was abandoned. When I lectured to classes about community dynamics in the development process, I was not so cautious as I was in print, and I cited Huajam as an example of consensus creating a capacity for effective action.

No one would deny that the village occupied an environment that imposed many ecological, economic, and political constraints that were impervious to any amount of participatory decision-making and effective action. The recognition of limits produced, not a sense of defeat and despair, but rather, a determination to explore the possibilities that were available. The citizens debated alternatives vigorously and actively attempted to shape the direction of change by selecting innovations perceived as strengthening the community. They would be outraged if anyone were to label this process "compliance with the national state."

For a year after I left the field, I sent letters, photographs, and Mexican stamps, but heard nothing in return. I felt a strong nostalgia for Chiapas and intended to go back some day, but other projects took priority. Then one day, after twenty years, an unexpected telephone call from the World Bank led to a small grant for a restudy that would be part of a twenty-six-nation study of appropriate technology for water supply and sanitation.

My return to Huajam was heartwarming. This time I was accompanied by my wife, Cynthia Cone, an anthropologist who was eager to share the experience, and our youngest child, Emily, age five. Emily surprised us by her industry and enthusiasm in helping people dry corn and quickly made her reputation as a hard-working peasant girl. We spent the first evening drinking with Don Artemio and his family, talking about old times, and looking at all the photographs that I had sent.

The next morning I went to visit the parents of Miguel Moshán, the former health promoter who had moved up in the INI system and was now living in San Cristóbal. A young woman in the patio responded to my greeting and then said brusquely, "Who are you, and where do you come from?"

Assuming she was a member of the family, I told her about my earlier research, mentioning various Moshán names. She persisted, "Why have you come back?"

I explained about the World Bank's interest in a follow-up study, so that villages elsewhere in the world could learn to improve their water supplies and sanitation.

"What is this World Bank? I've been to the state capital, and I haven't seen any branches."

As I tried to answer that question, she interrupted: "What good is your study going to do our community? What right do you have to come here and take information back to some bank we never heard of? How is that going to benefit us?"

I could not believe what was happening. Assuming she was one of Miguel's sisters, twenty years before her grandfather had challenged me, and now she was doing the same thing, only more effectively. During my earlier time there, women lived rather secluded lives, so I had never had a conversation with any of them. Fortunately, her father came out of the house and welcomed me as warmly as I had hoped. He assured my inquisitor that I was a friend of the family, and she excused herself. She was indeed Miguel's sister, the first woman from Huajam to go to high school in San Cristóbal and now a teacher in a distant Indian town. She was able to attend high school because she could live with Miguel's family. One of her brothers was also a teacher, as were two cousins. More than a dozen young people from Huajam were attending secondary school in the city. About a third were women, most of whom worked as maids so that they would have a place to live and money for clothes and books, plus a little to send home to parents.

A few days later I asked Don Artemio about the condition of the INI development program. "The rich get money and we get priorities," he replied.

"You get priorities?" I asked.

"Nothing but priorities. The government is spending most of the money from oil on building big factories. All we get is fine words about the goals of the Revolution."

"INI isn't helping the Indians any more?"

"Well, INI has done lots of good things. The most important is education. The schools are much better, and now girls can go to high school and become teachers. Also INI brought us modern medicine and better breeds of pigs and fruit trees. But the fields do not produce as much corn as they used to. Many years ago, before you were here the first time, the agronomists wanted us to plant what they said was a better variety of corn. Some of us tried it in part of our fields. It hardly made food for the pigs. Later we learned that you need fertilizer for that kind of corn, and all we had was a little manure from the oxen. Now you can buy fertilizer in San Cristóbal, but it is too expensive for us, and we can't get loans."

INI cannot deliver what does not exist. Agricultural research in Mexico has shifted away from an emphasis on commercial monoculture and toward an effort to improve peasant agriculture. For hilly regions above 1500 m the traditional farming systems are still the most productive, and the altitude in Huajam is about 2500 m.

I asked Don Artemio about prospects for the future. He replied, "We'll have to work harder and survive as best we can."

Our next trip to Huajam was in February of 1980. Don Artemio told me that, if I wanted to do any research, I would have to talk to the new headman, a young man who had been two years old in 1957. The new headman told me that I would have to present a petition to the town assembly. In the meeting all of my old friends—Artemio, his son-in-law, Miguel Moshán's father, and others—spoke in favor. Two young men, including Miguel's brother Pedro, were emphatically against any research.

After a long discussion, the headman turned to me and said: "Don Francisco, we are not agreed. You understand how we operate here. If we are not agreed, permission is not given." Once again, the majority would not impose its will on a determined minority, and I was defeated by the very system that I had praised so often. For the third time, a member of the Moshán family challenged my presence. The challenge prevailed for reasons that I learned from Miguel two months later: there was a serious conflict over land use, and no one really wanted me to witness it.

In January, 1987, Cynthia and I traveled once again to Chiapas. The first person we went to see was Miguel, who was sitting in his living room with two large books in his lap. After welcoming us, the first thing he said was, "Now we are Christians."

"Oh, you're a Christian," I replied.

"Yes, I'm a Christian, I'm not a Catholic anymore."

"The Catholics aren't Christians?"

"They're not true Christians, they're Romanists."

"What do you think is the difference?"

"Romanists take orders from the Pope in Rome. We belong to the Mexican Presbyterian church, which is not under foreign control."

Miguel explained that he was studying the Bible with the help of a biblical dictionary, because he was in training to be a lay minister. Every Saturday he went to classes in theology and church history. Already he was helping to organize congregations in Indian villages. The one in Huajam was meeting on Sunday, and he would be happy to take us along.

On the way to the village we listened to Miguel's sophisticated exegesis of the Bible and discussed the role of religion in the community. For him, Protestantism seems to be as much an intellectual as a spiritual odyssey. Reading the Bible is enormously important to him. He reads the old familiar stories and ponders their significance for his own life and for the historical moment in which he lives. Although he is not learning liberation theology in class, he tends to read the Bible as the liberation theologians do: from the point of view of the poor and the powerless. In the folk Catholicism that he formerly embraced, God and Jesus are remote figures; the potent characters are the patron saints of the community and the Virgin Mary, especially in her apparition as the Virgin of Guadalupe, the patron saint of Mexico. In the New Testament the potent figure is Jesus, acting vigorously in the world, driving the moneylenders out of the temple and challenging the authority of the Roman rulers. By contrast, the statue of the patron saint in the local church may be close physically, but to Miguel it appears psychologically remote and politically passive.

The leaders of the congregation in Huajam were none other than the headman and my two adversaries of 1980. Miguel introduced us to his brother Pedro by saying, "Don Francisco is one of us now." We were warmly welcomed and addressed as "Brother" and "Sister."

What was I supposed to do now? Repeat my explanation of thirty years ago that my parents were Protestants but I did not belong to any religious group?

The meeting adjourned and we departed. Pedro said, "Come back any time, Don Francisco, you are welcome here."

This essay began with a question about the future of the peasantry in Mexico. The spread of Protestantism is frequently seen as a source of conflict that will make the future more problematic. It can also be interpreted as a sign of vitality, just as the recent election is a sign of vitality. If Mexico can manage a transition to greater pluralism in politics and religion, then Casteñada's hope for a happier, prouder, and more stable nation might well come to pass.

CHANGING INEQUALITY IN ZINACANTAN: THE GENERATIONS OF 1918 AND 1942

George A. Collier
Stanford University

Major trends of Mexican development have transformed Zinacanteco stratification twice during the twentieth century. Agrarian reform in the late 1930s enabled an older generation of Zinacantecos to farm corn on seemingly equal terms within which they forged new productive relations based on rank by mid-century. Younger Zinacantecos, drawn increasingly by the 1970s oil-led boom into semiproletarian wagework and commerce in the 1970s and 1980s, are experiencing an opposite trajectory of rank on the decline and class stratification on the rise. This is an examination of trends in Zinacanteco stratification from the perspective of two generations of Zinacantecos of the hamlet of Apas, those born in and just after 1918, and those born around 1942—Evon Vogt's age-mates and my own.

Zinacantán is one of several Maya peasant communities in the ethnic hinterland of San Cristóbal de las Casas. Zinacantán had a 1980 population of 13,006 living primarily in hamlets dispersed in municipal territory traversed by the Pan-American highway. During the 1960s, Zinacantecos specialized in milpa cultivation of corn, on highland communal and *ejidal* lands (from Mexican agrarian reform) in part, but particularly on marginal lands rented from ranchers in the lowland Grijalva River valley adjacent to them to the south (Cancian 1965, 1972). Recent developments have drawn poor and youthful Zinacantecos into wagework and wealthier individuals into commerce. Apas is the Zinacanteco hamlet I have studied, beginning in 1963 and from time to time over a twenty-five year period (G. Collier 1975, 1985, 1987; Collier and Mountjoy 1987).

My analysis concerns regional and national impacts on stratification in Zinacantán, especially between generations within households and among community members in relations of production and sociocultural processes. Mid-century agrarian reform favored labor-intensive production in Zinacantán. Bride-wealth-based marriage emerged in the 1950s as household heads strove to retain the labor of offspring by indebting them through costly courtships. At the same time, Zinacantecos began to clamor for civil-religious *cargo* positions, which flourished as a system validating and enforcing stratification based on the rights in the productive labor of others. The Zinacantán described on the basis of ethnographic work of the Harvard Chiapas Project in the 1960s (cf. Vogt 1978) epitomized these developments, which Zinacantecos of the generation of 1918 experienced as their coming to maturity.

Subsequent trends have effected yet another change in Zinacanteco productive relations and stratification. Oil-based development during the late 1970s drew Zinacantecos out of labor-intensive agriculture and into semiproletarian wagework in construction outside the community. Youths found it possible to escape the indebting burdens of courtship by eloping and then settling familial accounts with cash earned on the job rather than through work in parents' cornfields. Meanwhile, the *cargo* system became increasingly hamlet-based for most first-level participants. Although the economic crisis since 1982 has returned many Zinacantecos from wagework to agriculture, milpa cultivation has irreversibly changed from labor intensive to chemical intensive inputs, while agrarian stratification in Zinacantán increasingly reflects regional class relations. The generation of my Zinacanteco age-mates has thus come to maturity in a changed world.

THE GENERATION OF 1918

Let us consider Zinacantán of the 1960s in terms of the generation of Zinacantecos born around 1918 to families from the hamlet of Apas. At the outset, considerable variations in class-based wealth differentiated the prospects of this generation of Zinacantecos. Some were of fortunate, landholding families; most were among the landless who had returned to the highlands after being freed from indentured labor on lowland ranches by the Carrancistas in the Mexican Revolution. As adolescents in the 1930s, many worked as laborers for Apas landowners; others helped their families cultivate borrowed land. But as this generation married in the closing years of the Lázaro Cárdenas presidency, land reform, definitively granted to Zinacantán in 1940, substantially ameliorated differences among them based on property (Figure 1). The generation of 1918 thus entered adulthood as rough equals in terms of land held as a productive asset, leaving behind the class-stratified world of their elders' experience.

The granting of *ejido* linked beneficiaries of Mexican land reform in Apas to those in other Zinacanteco hamlets through leadership in the administrative and ceremonial center, *jteklum,* and probably served to reconsolidate municipally-based ethnic identity among the generation of 1918 and their seniors. The integrity of Zinacantán had been eroded over the previous century by the encroachment of *ladino* haciendas into communal lands and former national lands (*terrenos baldíos*). The *ejido* reconstituted Zinacanteco control of land in two homogeneous tracts corresponding to the grants to Zinacantán and Jokch'enom, its western *parajes.* Administration of the grants oriented hamlets sharing in the principal grant to *ejidal* leaders in *jteklum* and in an important way to the newly forged PRI (Cárdenas's Partido Revolucionario Institucional) as the guarantor of the new order.

The beneficiaries of land reform all took up milpa in the *ejido* as rough equals, but with the passage of time they elaborated productive relations that engendered inequality on new terms. Families matured and population grew, but the land base did not keep pace (despite *ejidal* increments granted in the 1950s),

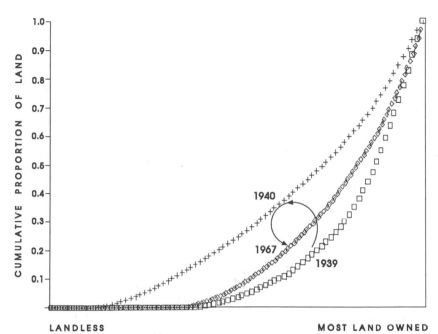

Figure 1. The distribution of property in Apas, Zinacantán. The cumulative distributions of land held by married men in Apas are shown for 1939, just before the distribution of *ejido* under Mexican land reform; for 1940, just after the distribution of *ejido*; and for 1967. In the graphs, individuals are ranked from left to right in terms of amount of land owned, and the curves show the total proportion of all property owned by a given individual and all those with less land. Equal ownership in a given year would have resulted in a plot along the diagonal of the graph of cumulative distribution for that year. Disparities in property ownership were evened out by the distribution of *ejido* in 1940 to most, but not all, married men. By 1967 many maturing younger men lacked land and disparities in ownership had reappeared.

and Zinacantecos from Apas and elsewhere began to cultivate marginal lands for milpa rented from ranches in the nearby Grijalva Valley. To build up labor for production, Zinacantecos accumulated rights in other people in two ways. Elder farmers subordinated youth of their own households by elaborating bride wealth. They also took advantage of newly emerging inequalities in land tenure (Figure 1), resulting from demographic growth on lands of fixed extent, by employing poorer Zinacantecos in farming and building them into political followings. Within a framework of ostensible equality, rank emerged as a dominant idiom for differentiating followers from leaders, juniors from seniors, low status *cargo* holders from more prestigious ones, and so forth.

Beginning in the 1950s, Zinacanteco marriage shifted from earlier bride service to a pattern of bride wealth with extended and costly courtships. In the bride-wealth system, a young man had to petition a girl's parents for her hand in ritual—*jak' olajel*—which involved considerable expenses of liquor and the assistance of kinsmen as petitioners. After the petition, the prospective groom had to visit his betrothed's house regularly—*k' ubanel*—for one or two years, bringing gifts of food to compensate her household for the cost of raising her. The next step involved a "house entering" ceremony—*och' el ta na*—in which the groom's family formally introduced him into the household of the bride. The marriage ceremony—*nupunel*—was the last step in this costly progression that left bride and groom indebted to the groom's family, with whom they generally lived for a period of years after marriage, working off their debt in productive labor. Rarely in the 1960s, youth would elope—*jatav lok' el*—to attempt to avoid these costs, offering a smaller sum to request pardon—*lajes mul*—of the bride's family after the fact.

This marriage system subordinated youths to elders through debt in relations of production. Juniors could afford to marry only by borrowing from elders, at the price of laboring for them during a period of extended virilocal residence after marriage (Collier 1968). Bride wealth thus underpinned rank in relations of production reminiscent of those that have been described for Africa (Meillassoux 1972; Terray 1972).

Simultaneously, Zinacantecos elaborated rank by expanding service in ritual *cargos* in the *municipio*'s ceremonial and administrative center, *jteklum*. As described by Cancian (1965), the *cargos*, a system of voluntary service of ritual posts graded in cost, functioned in the 1960s as a prestige system celebrating the reputation and followings of those who had been particularly successful in orchestrating household-based milpa production (Cancian 1965). This ritual system especially burdened young adults with debt, because all adults were expected to take up an entry-level *cargo* position (the most costly). In this latter respect, *cargos* indebted juniors to elders just as much as did bride wealth in marriage. At the same time, the entire system of debt and lending put successful elders in a position to make loans, differentiating them from other mature men and enabling them to accumulate followings of less successful men, both senior and junior. By accumulating rights in others' production, the generation of Zinacanteco elders born in the decade of the Mexican Revolution built the bases for power wielded over kin in localized lineages and over followers in the arenas of hamlet and municipal politics.

Elaboration of the marriage and *cargo* systems are both apparent in the lives of those of the generation of 1918 I have studied in Apas since 1963. The first offspring of this generation attained marriageable age in the 1960s, along with youngsters of other somewhat older generations that had contributed to new Zinacanteco stratification. Mol Maryan Ahte' (a pseudonym), for example, was just over forty-five when his son Chep, the eldest of ten children, married in 1964 after a courtship of three years culminating in a house-entering ceremony and marriage. Not long after, Maryan's daughter Loxa was asked for in marriage, courted for two and a half years, and married formally after a house entering. As Loxa married virilocally, she and her husband did not continue to contribute to the production of her father's household, but Chep and his wife did, coresiding with Mol Maryan until three years after the birth of their own first child in 1966. During the 1960s, Mol Maryan farmed on rented lands in the lowlands, planting four *almuds* of seed in 1967 in a fairly sizeable family operation aided by six working-aged daughters and sons.

As they passed through their forties, Mol Maryan Ahte' and others of his generation took up first *cargo* service almost exclusively in *jteklum,* the ceremonial center, even though a chapel and four entry-level *cargos* had been set up in Apas. Maryan served as *mayordomo* of San Sebastián. Others served as junior and senior *mayordomo rey,* as *pasionero,* as *mesonero,* and as *mayol.* Many have subsequently taken second and third *cargos* in *jteklum;* indeed of eleven men born in Apas between 1918 and 1922 and still alive in 1988, four have taken at least two *cargos,* and three have completed three. In modern-day Zinacanteco factional politics, eight of the eleven have retained affiliation through *jteklum* to the PRI. It would not be accurate to think of *jteklum cargo* service and PRI affiliation as exclusively the experience of this generation, for other older Zinacantecos, whose identities also had been underpinned by the granting of *ejido* in 1940, shared in that experience. Rather, this generation participated with particular vigor in the system of productive relations that matured during the 1960s as they themselves passed through middle age.

THE GENERATION OF 1942

Zinacantecos of my own generation are becoming middle aged in the 1980s in a world much changed from the one we described in the 1960s. The oil-related boom of the López Portillo years transformed the regional economy of southeastern Mexico. It drew Zinacantecos and other Indians into construction jobs in large numbers. In the process, labor-intensive agriculture dwindled, and new labor proletarianization and commerce undercut the relations of production inhering in Zinacanteco agriculture in the 1960s. Even as Zinacantecos returned to agriculture in the prolonged economic crisis beginning in 1982, they did so on new terms, bringing new capitalist relations into the organization of their production. Although older generations, including that of 1918, have experienced this change, the generation of 1942 is the first to come of age on these new terms.

The semiproletarianization of Zinacanteco labor was one important result of development trends in the 1970s. In 1967, the overwhelming majority of Zinacantecos had farmed milpa (Figure 2), even though important disparities in property holdings for agriculture had reappeared by 1967 (Figure 1). Wagework, with which many Zinacantecos had made a living before the advent of the *ejido* in 1940, was confined to men of the poorest households, who worked primarily for other Zinacantecos. It was ideally and statistically normative for adult Zinacantecos to farm milpa. But by 1981, a dramatic shift had taken place (Figure 3), with nearly three quarters of Apas's 189 married heads of households engaging partially or exclusively in wagework, many as unskilled workers in construction stimulated by the oil boom—of dams throughout the region and of

116

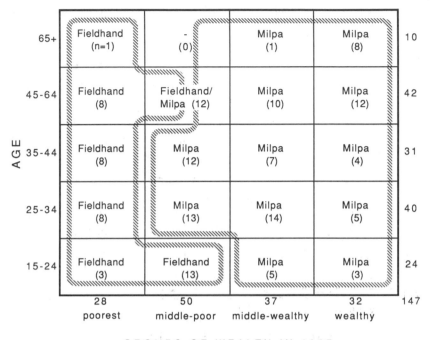

GROUPS OF WEALTH IN 1967

Figure 2. Productive activities of Apas men, 1967. The predominant occupation is shown for each group of married men of a given age and wealth. Most men farmed milpa, but a small underclass of poor Zinacantecos made their living as field hands for other Zinacantecos.

housing in Villahermosa and other cities. Although older household heads clung to agriculture during this period, most also took up wagework themselves. Younger Zinacantecos, including almost all of those born after 1950, deployed themselves extensively in wagework. Even today, six years into the post-1982 economic slump, wagework constitutes a major part of the productive repertory of all but the wealthiest or oldest household heads (Figure 4).

Important changes in agriculture also accompanied the oil boom and its subsequent bust. In 1967, the households of Apas had engaged almost universally in farming milpa on rented lands in the Grijalva Valley. By 1981 agriculture had declined to the extent that only 45 percent of married men made milpa as a primary or sole livelihood, while the acreage farmed dropped from an average 2.5 hectares per household in 1967 to only 1.2 hectares in 1981, barely enough for subsistence. Had it continued unabated, the oil boom seemingly would have eclipsed milpa farming from the repertory of principal Zinacanteco livelihoods. As it was, the 1982 economic crisis returned Zinacantecos to agriculture, but in milpa cultivation that has been irreversibly transformed. Although farming in

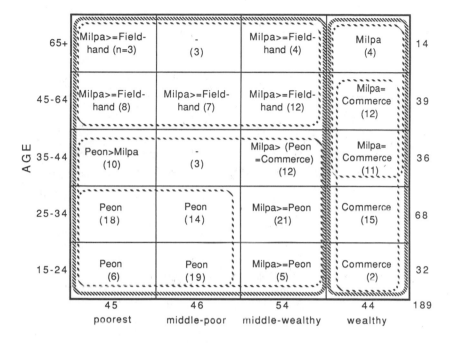

	45 poorest	46 middle-poor	54 middle-wealthy	44 wealthy	189
65+	Milpa>=Field-hand (n=3)	. (3)	Milpa>=Field-hand (4)	Milpa (4)	14
45-64	Milpa>=Field-hand (8)	Milpa>=Field-hand (7)	Milpa>=Field-hand (12)	Milpa= Commerce (12)	39
35-44	Peon>Milpa (10)	. (3)	Milpa> (Peon =Commerce) (12)	Milpa= Commerce (11)	36
25-34	Peon (18)	Peon (14)	Milpa>=Peon (21)	Commerce (15)	68
15-24	Peon (6)	Peon (19)	Milpa>=Peon (5)	Commerce (2)	32

GROUPS OF WEALTH IN 1981

Figure 3. Productive activities of Apas men, 1981. The oil-led boom semiproletarianized all but the wealthiest Zinacantecos. Most men in Apas reduced milpa farming to a minimum, shifting into wagework in the regional economy either as unskilled peons in construction, or as field hands for farmers outside their community. A minority of wealthier Zinacantecos went into regional commerce.

1986 once again involved the majority of Zinacantecos (79 percent of 226 married men), it was no longer predominantly of rented lands in the Grijalva Valley, but rather of communal and *ejidal* lands in the highlands. And while the average acreage farmed has increased slightly from 1981 to 1.4 hectares planted per household, farming has shifted from heavy reliance on manual labor to the use of chemical inputs—weedkillers and fertilizer—to intensify farming while minimizing labor inputs. For the brief periods during which Zinacantecos do need labor, they simply hire among the newly prevalent unskilled wageworkers of their community.

In the meantime, wealthy Zinacantecos, who devoted their energies primarily to large-scale rental farming of milpa in 1967, have taken to commerce (Figures 3 and 4), notably as truckers and vendors engaged in the long-distance transport and sale of agricultural crops throughout the state of Chiapas. Although primarily wealthy Zinacantecos entered into such commerce during the 1970s, even those of more modest means have taken it up, as is evident in the mix of commerce, wagework, and farming characteristic of most of my Zinacanteco age-mates of modest to moderate means in 1986.

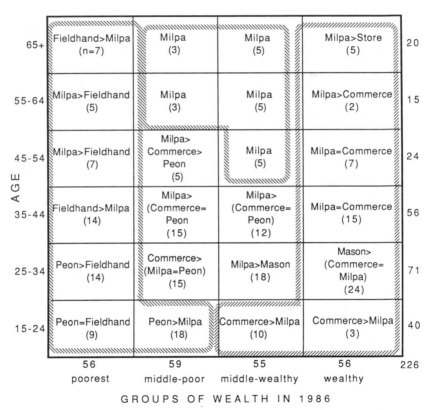

Figure 4. Productive activities of Apas men, 1986. The post-1982 economic crisis returned Zinacantecos to farming private or *ejidal* holdings in the highlands, although many younger men continued wagework in the regional economy as field hands, unskilled construction peons, or skilled masons. Wealthier Zinacantecos combined milpa farming with commerce.

Taken together, the semiproletarianization of Zinacanteco labor, the transformation of agriculture, and the move first of wealthy Zinacantecos and then others into commerce represent a major shift in relations of Zinacanteco production. In 1967 Apas was a community of milpa farmers employing labor-intensive methods of production, a community with a relatively small underclass of laborers working for other Zinacantecos. As long as Zinacantecos played the role of specialists in producing corn with intensive use of one another's labor, accumulating rights in the labor of youths through the marriage system and of the poor through big-man patterns of leadership, the community's internal stratification was largely self-reproducing. By 1981, however, Zinacantecos had pulled out of extensive agriculture and had begun to work for non-Zinacanteco task masters. The old relations of Zinacanteco class thus broke down, shifting to new productive relations between Zinacanteco peasant/proletarians and non-Indian employers, and between Zinacanteco middle men and producers/consumers of the broader marketplace of the region. Although Apas has returned to agriculture to some degree in the post-1982 economic crisis, the agriculture is much less labor intensive because of the utilization of chemical inputs. And the return has not brought a revival of the old productive relations emphasizing the accumulation of rights in others. The basic stratification in Zinacanteco society has come to be between those who do commerce and those who do proletarian wagework.

Changes in key Zinacanteco sociocultural practices, notably in marriage and in the system of ritual *cargo* participation, reflect these significant shifts in Zinacanteco stratification. The changes are particularly noticeable in the evolving lives of the generation of Zinacantecos born around 1942.

The bride-wealth-based marriage system of the 1950s and 1960s has receded markedly with the advent of new productive relations, beginning with the proletarianization of labor. Figure 5 shows that the once-normative unions after a house-entering ceremony or wedding have given way to elopements followed by the begging of pardon to the bride's family. Proletarianization of labor has freed Zinacanteco youths from the economic dependence on elders that the older bride-wealth system reproduced and reinforced.

Although the change has undermined the ability of all older Zinacantecos to subordinate offspring of marriageable age through bride wealth, it affects the generation of 1942 in a novel way. These individuals are among the last cohorts to marry in the "traditional" manner that flourished in the 1950s. At the same time they are the first, with offspring just now beginning to mature as young adults, to have raised families almost entirely in the era of new regional development and altered Zinacanteco stratification.

Xap Inas, for example, married at age twenty-one in 1963 after a costly courtship and was still working for his parents' household in lowland rental farming four years later, after the birth of children in 1965 and 1967. By 1973 Xap headed a household of his own, continuing to farm in the lowlands. During the oil-led boom Xap joined his contemporaries in taking up wagework. He continued to farm a minimum of milpa and began to trade in fruits and vegetables as his progeny grew to include seven offspring, four still living just before the economic crisis of 1982. Four years and two children later, Xap still undertakes a mix of wagework, commerce, and farming with fertilizer and chemical weed sprays. In 1986 his eldest son Antun eloped with a young woman after no formal courtship, settling accounts with his bride's family three months later with money earned in wagework. Elopements are now normative in Apas. Xap cannot expect any of his children to marry and to indebt themselves to him as he did through the extended courtship, which indebted him to his parents.

120

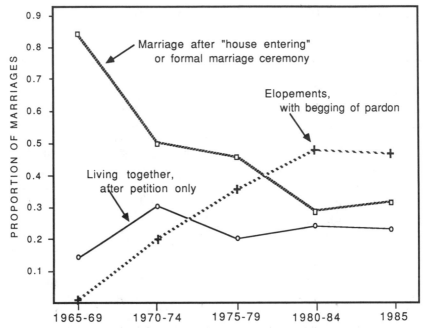

Figure 5. Marriage trends in Apas. Marriages after the "house entering" or more formal marriage have been in steady decline since 1965, whereas elopements have become the norm. The data concern first marriages only of people presently living in Apas.

There have also been changes in the Zinacanteco *cargo* system. Interpreting the *cargo* system in terms of its capacity to integrate the community by legitimating internal differentiation and other social relations, Cancian has repeatedly stressed participation as key to the *cargo* system's trajectory. Population growth in excess of that in *cargo* roles limits the possibility for the system to provide full participation, in Cancian's analysis. He notes that proliferation in hamlets of new civil posts connected with state modernization programs has deflected Zinacanteco participation in the ceremonial center's ritual system. Recent developments, Cancian points out on the basis of research in the hamlet of Nachij, have brought new economic roles and have heightened political factionalism in Zinacantán, eroding the *cargo* system's capacity to integrate the community as it "opens" to the world (Cancian 1983).

My research in Apas substantiates many of Cancian's findings for the Zinacanteco hamlet of Nachij (Cancian 1974, 1983, 1987) regarding new hamlet-based civil roles and the displacement of *cargos* as the dominant idiom of local stratification. By 1981 Apas *cargo* participation had shifted, with only older men still involved in ceremonial-center *cargos*. Younger men had opted almost exclusively for inexpensive entry-level *cargos* in the hamlet. More recent trends include withdrawal from the *cargo* system by Protestant converts who do not want to spend money on ritual and a proliferation of factional groups that mount private sponsorship of ritual.

The Apas data suggest that younger Zinacantecos differ from their elders in orienting their lives more to the hamlets than to *jteklum*, the ceremonial center. Whereas the advent of *ejido* linked elders to the ceremonial center, it gave youngsters a home and a locus for their early lives. As the *cargo* system proliferated in the 1960s, the establishment of chapels and entry-level *cargo*s in hamlets reinforced local, as opposed to municipal, allegiances, as did the proliferation of hamlet-level posts of civic responsibility. At the same time, growing factionalism in Zinacanteco politics sometimes pitted hamlet-based groups against those in power in *jteklum*, making hamlets more of an arena for public life.

In the case of Apas, the coming to middle age of my generation has centered around life in the hamlet, if the experience of the twenty-five living men born between 1942 and 1946 is indicative. Public roles, other than *cargo*s, held by these men in Apas include: service as shaman or sponsor for water-hole rites (eight men), fiesta musician (four men), chapel treasurer, chapel president (three men), sacristan, education committee member (sixteen men), fiesta tax collector (three men), committee member for communal land (two men), hamlet *principal* (nine men), and hamlet *agente* for one of the minority political factions. Yet only two of these men have done civic service in *jteklum*.

Virtually every member of this age group who has taken an entry-level *cargo* (twenty men out of twenty-five) did so in the late 1970s in Apas (eighteen men), where *cargo*s were established in 1960 and a chapel built in 1963, rather than in *jteklum* (two men)—in sharp contrast to the ceremonial center entry-level *cargo*s characteristic of elder Apas generations. It should be noted that *cargo* service has always been much less costly in Apas than in *jteklum*. Apas *cargo*s are thus possible to take at a younger age without resorting to borrowing. Although entry-level service was indeed at a younger age (thirty-three years for the 1942-1946 cohort as compared to forty-three and one-half years for the 1918-1923 cohort), a shift that would seemingly allow for fuller participation, in fact participation has become factional, reflecting political divisions that have become prevalent in Zinacanteco local-level politics over the past two decades. PRI and PAN factions nominally linked to national parties have contended for shifting followings in Apas since the 1970s, and a third group has recently formed. The majority PAN grouping has controlled Apas *cargo*s in every recent year except 1982. As a result, those born since 1940 who are not affiliated with PAN have been excluded from entry-level *cargo*s in Apas. Many have joined in the private, factional sponsorship of ritual and entertainment that now characterizes Apas fiestas.

These empirical findings augment Cancian's, but they lead me to a different interpretation rooted in my conceptualization of the "traditional" *cargo* system as having been an integral part of the stratification of rank that matured in the 1950s and 1960s. At that time, graded *cargo* service enabled would-be leaders of older Zinacanteco generations to substantiate their right to speak for others in the community. This helped them accumulate rights over others in the domains of hamlet affairs and kinship. In the 1980s, however, stratification has changed. With the emergence of new relations of class, younger Zinacantecos no longer depend on the old meaning of *cargo* service for advancement. Instead of taking *cargo*s in *jteklum,* they do so in their hamlet. Because entry-level hamlet *cargo*s are inexpensive, youths no longer accumulate debt, and elders do not accumulate followings. Nor do they need to, for in a class system, one's economic power speaks for itself, enabling one to hire others' labor outright. *Cargo* service ceases to confer the right to speak for others and becomes little more than a rite of passage to mark adulthood. Private sponsorship of rival ritual activities also has grown as an expression of new class relations. Private ritual allows men to display their economic power without having to speak for others. When the wealthy sponsor private ritual, they display their lack of interest in accumulating followings.

CONTINUITY AND CHANGE

As Vogt foresaw in his design of the Harvard Chiapas Project, longitudinal study of Zinacantán afforded the best possibility for understanding fundamental processes of cultural continuity and change. I have contrasted the life experiences of two generations of Zinacantecos to emphasize how historically specific Mexican national developments have affected Zinacanteco stratification and have brought about sociocultural change.

In emphasizing change, I do not wish to deny important continuities in Zinacanteco life. Continuities of place, of adherence to Tzotzil, of cosmology, of clothing, of ethnic stratification and difference all continue to play an important part in Zinacanteco life. The fact that Zinacanteco semiproletarian workers return to families they have left behind in the *municipio* is an important force for continuity.

Indeed, the overlapping of lives is an important source of continuity. The generation of 1918 was very much in evidence in Zinacantán during and after the López Portillo years, and it would be fallacious to interpret Zinacanteco life since the 1970s exclusively with reference to younger generations. Every generation stands, Janus-faced, between the future and the past. The two generations highlighted in my analysis are in dialogue with one another—often times as parents and offspring—to forge meanings for new stratification and to rework understandings of older relations of production. Together, these two generations thread continuity through the fabric of Zinacanteco life, much of which would be recognizable to their forefathers.

And yet, much would not. For Zinacantán has gone through two profound alterations since the Mexican Revolution. The state system that has held power since the time of Lázaro Cárdenas established Zinacantecos as peasants. As such, Zinacantecos forged an internally generated stratification of rank in the

1950s and 1960s, embodied in distinctly new marriage and *cargo* practices. The oil-boom 1970s undercut peasant agriculture, however. It thrust Zinacantecos into the regional class system, semiproletarianizing them and transforming their distinct sociocultural practices. It is true that Mexico's economic crisis of the 1980s has returned Zinacantecos to agriculture—but without reversing the significant changes in Zinacanteco lifeways that took shape in the late 1970s. Relations of class have now come to the fore within Zinacantán, eroding the rank stratification that once gave meaning to and borrowed strength from mid-century bride wealth and *cargo* service and to much of the distinctive life experience of elder Zinacanteco generations.

ACKNOWLEDGMENTS. This analysis has benefited from reflection on comments and suggestions from Frank Cancian, Jane F. Collier, Daniel Mountjoy, and Evon Vogt. It is based in part on field research undertaken with and funded by Frank Cancian in 1981. Fieldwork during 1987 was supported by the Andrew W. Mellon Foundation through Stanford's Center for Latin American Studies and was assisted by Daniel Mountjoy. The analysis draws on support from National Science Foundation Research Grant BNS-8804607.

INDIAN SUMMERS

Niko Price
Harvard University

with Richard Price and Sally Price
Anses d'Arlet, Martinique

The twenty-three summers since Sally Price and Richard Price became "Pashku" and "Telesh" (Price 1966) have witnessed significant changes both in the highland Maya community of Muk'tajhok' and in the field of anthropology. Muk'tajhok', then a relatively isolated community of Zinacantecos just south of the border of the *municipio* of Zinacantán, now boasts a road and a truck; three water tanks relieve the two-hour treks to the valley water hole for at least some of the community's women; there is electricity for all and television for some; and its thirty-nine households and 200 people have grown to eighty and 350, respectively. During these two decades, anthropology too has grown. The scientific paradigms that dominated the early years of the Chiapas Project have been joined by a more interpretative mode; reflexive and critical stances have come increasingly to supplement the search for ethnographic "objectivity."

In the eyes of its practitioners, the Muk'tajhok' fieldwork of 1965 (Price and Price 1970) now seems strongly dated. Centered firmly within prevailing anthropological canons, this predoctoral research drew explicitly on "network analysis" and "activity analysis" (see also Nash 1964) in an attempt to elucidate the "social organization" of the community. By investigating such questions as who drank (fought, carried water, farmed, attended weddings, or curing ceremonies, etc.) with whom, a "mapping" of people and activities was produced, and "principles" of social organization inferred. Unsurprisingly, given methodologies and expectations, coparticipation in such activities was found to be highly patterned, relatively invariant from one person to the next, and structured mainly by kinship ties, residential proximity, and the developmental cycle of the domestic group. The main portion of that study was followed by a briefer analysis of stratification in the community, revealing greater differentiation among men than one might have predicted in such an apparently homogeneous hamlet. Characteristic of Harvard "Social Relations" anthropology in the mid-1960s, the study even concluded with a passing reference to "*achievement*"! The following summer's research in Muk'tajhok' (Price 1968, 1974), devoted to land-use patterns and the methodological potential of aerial photos, continued these "scientific" concerns, but—perhaps because it dealt less with lived experience and more with directly measurable variables—strikes us as somewhat less dated than the first summer's research (though, in retrospect, hardly more interesting intellectually).

Over two decades later, when Niko Price, a Harvard undergraduate and veteran of E. Z. Vogt, Jr.'s Mesoamerica course, set out for Chiapas for his first summer of fieldwork, he neither expected nor particularly desired to renew the Price family link with Muk'tajhok'. But one rainy afternoon, after he had spent several days of orientation in Apas and San Cristóbal, George and Jane Collier (who were serving as his field advisors) dropped him off at the Muk'tajhok' school, suggesting that he contact the head of the household in which his parents had lived a generation before. The small children who had lived in that house now had homes and families of their own, and they soon became his friends. And so the circle was closed. What follows here is his analysis of an incident of factionalism in Muk'tajhok', revealing not only something of the changes that marked the community over the twenty-two years since it was last studied, but also some changes in the conventions of writing anthropology. For here is a case in which very similar experiences "in the field" have led, in their respective times, to very different written products, sharing nonetheless—we hope—an ongoing concern for the sensitivity of the ethnographic eye.

Late one night, about two weeks after arriving in Muk'tajhok', I (Niko Price) was at the end of a long evening of helping my friend Chep Ernantis Peres deal with drunk people in his bar, and we were both exhausted. The record player was emitting a few final *rancheros* for the several remaining men who were sitting at tables, contemplating their bottles of *pox* and smoking cigarettes. Chep picked up one of the record jackets, which featured a photo of the singer wearing a gaudy black and gold hat, and told me an interesting story about the man.

During the early 1980s, he had been *presidente* of Ixtapa, the *municipio* to which Muk'tajhok' belongs, and he had been a good one. People liked him because he had given many presents (hoes, cloth, fertilizer, etc.) to the people of Muk'tajhok'; no other *presidente* had ever done this. When I asked whether everyone had shared in this largesse, Chep replied that all members of PRI had.[1] This struck me as strange, since I had been told that everyone in Muk'tajhok' was a member of PRI. Chep explained that, until about ten years before, there had been two political parties, but that the town had then united because the *presidente* had distributed presents so generously; PAN members felt that they could no longer afford to be affiliated with PAN.

During the period of the two parties' coexistence, PRI members had met in Chep's bar and the one next door, which was owned by his brother, and PAN was centered in a bar across town, owned by Chep Ximenes. I had already noticed the concentration of wealth in the households of the three bar owners; not only did they own the only bars in town, but they had the only water storage tanks as well, which meant that the women in their households did not have to hike for two hours every day to get water in the dry season. Chep Ximenez also owned the only vehicle in Muk'tajhok'.

Later that week I asked Chep Ernantis Peres to tell me who had been in which party, and this led us into a general discussion about the parties. Until about 1981, he said, everyone had belonged to PRI, but then Xuntum Ximenez Peres, a relative of Chep Ximenez was appointed *comisariado,* a rotating administrative post relating to *ejido* affairs. He and Chep Ximenes joined forces in a political move designed to mobilize support from the community, and they convinced some other administrative officers to become PAN with them. Many people in Muk'tajhok' switched parties, and a rift in the village developed. Finally, an all-out fistfight one night prompted a vote, and a new *comisariado* was chosen; he was a member of PRI. Muk'tajhok' then made the change official; it bought a community rubber stamp that read "PRI," and the party war was over. In 1987 remnants of the party-based factions still existed in the form of "groups of friends," but the two sides were no longer openly hostile. Chep would not, however, rule out the possibility that the other group would make a second move for political power.

A few days after this discussion, I interviewed a man named Markux Ernantis Peres, who had been a member of PRI, about the party conflict. His version of the story dealt almost entirely with politics external to Muk'tajhok'. To summarize: in 1981, Manuel Salasar Oranta—*presidente* in Ixtapa, a member of PRI, and the singer in the black-and-gold hat—was caught embezzling money. The man who discovered this, Veto Cruz Paz, was a member of PAN and came to Muk'tajhok' to convince people to join him in ousting Salasar from the presidency in favor of a PAN candidate. About forty percent of the men in Muk'tajhok' went along with him; the others remained loyal to PRI. Each party brought lawyers in from Tuxtla, the state capital, in an attempt to persuade members of the other party to switch over, but with little success. The PRI government of Salasar distributed presents to PRI members in Muk'tajhok'.

During this time, members of opposing parties did not talk to each other, and it was not rare for a few men from one party to get drunk and come to the bar of the opposing party to pick a fight. Two autonomous political organizations were formed in Muk'tajhok', one for each party. The *comisariado* and the *secretario* both joined PAN at the beginning of the conflict, and PRI members immediately appointed two new, "legitimate," office holders of their own. PAN then responded by appointing their own treasurer and vice-president, since these posts had been filled by men from PRI.

After almost a year of conflict, a new *presidente* was appointed in Ixtapa (by PRI), and lawyers came to Muk'tajhok' to urge support from the entire community. People were getting tired of the friction that had been caused by the party split. One night there was a major showdown in the schoolyard when drunk men from each party met, but after a lot of pushing and shouting, a vote was called. A majority voted PRI, and the members of PAN agreed to switch over to support the new *presidente.* All this was according to Markux.

Three days after my talk with Markux, I arranged another interview, this time with Chep Peres Peres, since I had been told that he had been one of the first to switch over to PAN. But when I brought the subject up, he asserted that he had always been "pure PRI." I thought at first I might be talking to the wrong person (as there are three men named Chep Peres Peres in Muk'tajhok'), but further discussion confirmed that he was indeed the right one. I then went over the list of people in the village with him, asking who had been with which party, and the division that he described was identical to that given by my other informants. But there was one important difference in his version: those who the others had called PRI, he called PAN, and vice versa—for every single man in town. *His* party had not made any trouble; it was the *other* one.

At this, I speculated that no one was willing to admit having been a member of PAN, but after talking to Chep Ernantis Peres again, and then coming back to Chep Peres Peres, I discovered a more interesting truth: no one had *ever* become PAN. During the conflict, each side claimed to be PRI, and each one claimed that the other was PAN. "PRI" and "PAN" had little more meaning than "us" and "them."

Indeed, the conflict hardly reflected national party politics at all. In a discussion of party conflicts in Zinacantán in general, Stephen Roof has noted that "the important factor [for PAN] was the negative affinity for PRI, not the positive affinity for PAN. The PAN-istas of Zinacantán know little about PAN's platform, ideology, or national leadership; they only know that it is PRI's biggest opponent" (1980:62). Political parties in Zinacantán have often been used for the sake of local disputes; in the *paraje* of Nabenchauk, fierce disputes have led to frequent fights and even some deaths. Such disputes always center on local issues, yet they are invariably fought out between the members of PRI and the members of PAN.

The factionalism in Muk'tajhok', however, had even less to do with party politics than with other Zinacanteco *parajes*. The ousting of Salasar in Ixtapa actually would not have affected anyone from Muk'tajhok'. Both Chep Ernantis Peres and Markux Ernantis Peres described PAN's rise in terms of local bids for power, and the conflict in Ixtapa seems to have presented little more than the idiom for this community-centered issue. But most importantly, there were no differences, either real or perceived, between the goals of the different factions. Each claimed to be PRI, and both had the same basic political ideology.

The split that occurred is perhaps best explained in terms of the history of the regional economy, that of Muk'tajhok', during the preceding half century. Indeed, I would suggest that the waning of political factionalism in the mid-1980s can best be understood as part of these same economic developments, viewed within the context of community ideology.

The men of Muk'tajhok' have been, for the last half century at least, primarily corn farmers. Beginning around 1935, the Mexican *ejido* land reform program distributed land grants to Zinacantecos, including those of Muk'tajhok' (Price 1965), when the boundaries of the community's *ejido* were essentially frozen. Lowland (or hot country) field rental, however, lessened the land shortage problem. Men from Muk'tajhok' got together in groups (most often kin-based) and rented land from ranches in hot country. They took buses and slept by their fields during certain times of the year, farming the highland tracts the rest of the time.

Heads of household could usually count on year-round labor from those sons who were still living with them and sometimes also from sons and brothers living separately. Also, despite the egalitarian ideology of the *ejido* system, some men by this time had succeeded in amassing considerably more *ejido* than others.[2] The larger landowners depended on the labor of men with smaller plots to farm their extensive fields. A governmental program run through the *ejidal* bank in the 1960s loaned money to farmers at eight percent a season (about nine months), asking for full payment only in years of good crop return. Such loans financed both the renting of land and the hiring of labor.

The discovery of oil in southern Mexico and soaring oil prices in the early 1970s contributed to general economic prosperity in the region. Jobs opened up, not only in oil, but in road building, house construction, and other related activities. A large-scale hydroelectric dam was constructed on the Grijalva River, near Tuxtla Gutiérrez, an hour's bus ride from Muk'tajhok'. In 1980 Roof wrote that "the entire state of Chiapas is now undergoing a tremendous economic boom, and there are high-paying jobs available building hydroelectric dams or housing in the state capital" (1980:95). Muk'tajhok' men (like other Indians in the area) were poorer than most people in the *ladino* towns and were therefore willing to work for comparatively low wages. These wages were particularly attractive to men with small *ejido* grants (who therefore earned less from farming) and to the young men who had access to no land except that of their fathers. Because an *ejido* grant can legally be passed on to only a single heir, many younger men had little occupational security in farming. The new opportunities that were opening up in the cities were therefore especially appealing to them.

Such employment opportunities in nearby cities caused an ever-increasing outflow of workers from Muk'tahjok' during the 1970s and placed strains on the internal dynamics of the *paraje*.[3] Men with more land found themselves competing for laborers to work for them, and each employer pressured his laborers to ally themselves with him. Hiring became based increasingly on personal relationships between laborer and individual employer or group of employers.

By 1981, as these pressures were straining the unity of Muk'tajhok', two events in national and *municipio*-wide politics transformed them into an all-out factionalist confrontation. In connection with the Mexican presidential election of July 1982, campaigning took place not only in major cities, but also in small villages throughout the country. PRI presidential hopeful Miguel de la Madrid, although virtually guaranteed victory, made 1800 campaign stops in the eight months before the elections (*New York Times,* July 6, 1982). Representatives of both PRI and PAN gave speeches in even the smallest communities of Mexico, including Muk'tajhok'. People in Muk'tajhok' became accustomed to thinking about politics in terms of warring parties.

Veto Cruz Paz's speech urging people from Muk'tajhok' to help oust the *presidente municipal* of Ixtapa provided an excellent opportunity to reproduce such electoral battles within the village and to bring into the open the developing alliances between particular laborers and their employers. I suspect that the specific issue of corruption in Ixtapa was unimportant to people from

Muk'tajhok', but that the quarrel fueled itself, becoming all the more fierce as it became organized along the lines of the hiring that was being done for *ejido* labor. As members of the two sides became increasingly hostile, eventually refusing to talk to each other and forming separate local governments, even those seemingly uninvolved, that is, those men who worked away from Muk'tajhok, were drawn into the dispute. Soon the *paraje* was divided in two. The system of accumulated individual ties had been drawn together in the factionalist scheme, each laborer owing allegiance not only to a particular employer, but to a town moiety as well.

The forces that acted to split the *paraje* were essentially economic, stemming from the competition for rapidly disappearing labor sources within it. I believe that the cessation of hostilities a year later was linked both to the changing economy and the existence in Muk'tajhok' of a long-standing communitarian ideology. The people of Muk'tajhok' pride themselves on the communal manner in which their village functioned traditionally, and most dealings with the outside world (insurance, electricity, etc.) have been handled on a communal level for at least the past quarter century. Many people spoke to me of the absurdity and of the impracticality of a *paraje* where half the population does not speak to the other half. At the same time, the partial reconciliation that occurred in 1982, and the gradual lessening of factionalist tensions since then, would not have been likely without certain economic conditions that eased some of the pressures.

Among the presents that the government in power in Ixtapa had given to its allies in Muk'tajhok' when the party split first occurred was a large quantity of fertilizer (ammonium sulfate in crystal form). The members of the faction that received the gifts benefited from this fertilizer in 1981, a year in which the harvest was unusually good. At the end of the year they negotiated a deal with the Banco Rural del Ixmo to give them a credit to buy fertilizer, and they began to farm exclusively in the highlands where less large-scale hiring of labor was needed. These same men also used their increasing profits toward the purchase of a herbicide (perroquat), which eliminates at least one of the labor-intensive weedings a cornfield requires. The growing use of both fertilizer and herbicide redirected large-scale farmers' expenditures from labor to chemicals. Finally, when the bottom dropped out of the oil market in 1982, the economic boom came to a standstill. This coincided also with the drying up of the oil wells in the area, and suddenly, outside employment opportunities became less attractive. Jobs were still available, mainly in construction, and in 1987 many Muk'tajhok' men were continuing to work in Tuxtla and other cities, but these jobs were usually less rewarding financially than even small-scale corn farming and were mainly used as a supplement to cultivation during the slow periods. At that time the men who worked in cities on a regular basis were for the most part without land and without hope of receiving any and were among the poorest people in Muk'tajhok'.[4]

I would argue that this combination of factors served to ease competition for the local labor force, and that without the fierce pressures of the late 1970s and early 1980s, factions simply became superfluous. Moreover, the existence of factions threatened the social harmony of Muk'tajhok'. Since the showdown at 2:00 in the morning in 1982, the two factions in Muk'tajhok' have been gradually disintegrating.

In 1987 the existence of the factions was still recognized, but they represented mainly residual social allegiances, left over disputes that had already ended. Members of one group still tended to hang out in Chep Ximenez's bar on one side of town, while the others gathered in front of the school and in Petul Ernantis Xantis's bar every night. While I was in Muk'tajhok', three of the four fistfights that sprang up among men who were drinking were between members of rival factions. This may be seen as especially significant because members of the same faction drink together more regularly and thus would have more opportunities to pick fights with each other.

Finally, although the correlation is not nearly as absolute as it was during the 1981-1982 conflict, in 1987 richer men still tended to hire laborers from their own faction, even though the competition for these workers no longer existed.[5] I was told that there were at least enough workers at that time for anyone who needed hired labor, but there was not really any competition for these jobs, since men could work in Tuxtla whenever they needed money. The residual preference of employers for laborers from their own faction was based mainly on social ties on an individual level, which were slowly beginning to change.

During my fieldwork, Muk'tajhok' was experiencing a gradual breakdown of the social divisions caused by the factionalist episode. Had I not paid attention to the several diverting little stories that people told me over a bottle of beer or passing time in front of the schoolhouse, I would never have imagined the existence of what is probably the most important political occurrence in Muk'tajhok' in the past quarter century.

ACKNOWLEDGMENTS. Niko Price is grateful to George Collier, who supervised his 1987 fieldwork, the drafting of this paper, and the presentation of some of these materials at the 1988 LASA meeting in New Orleans, as well as to Jane Collier and Robert Laughlin, both of whom offered comments and encouragements. All three authors would like to acknowledge the very special support, encouragement, and friendship offered over the years by Evon Z. Vogt, Jr. There must not be many anthropologists who have played the key role in stimulating two generations of a single household to undertake ethnographic careers. The three of us salute Vogtie upon his retirement.

END NOTES

[1] PRI, the Partido Revolucionario Institucional, is Mexico's dominant political party. PAN, the Partido de Acción Nacional, is the largest opposition party.

[2] Price and Price (1965:part VIII) describe the successful efforts of three Muk'tajhok' *cargo* holders to acquire additional *ejido* grants for themselves through political connections. In Muk'tajhok' in 1966, the four most landed men controlled nineteen percent of the *ejido* land, while the thirty-nine least landed controlled only ten percent (Price 1968). This is

true in other Zinacanteco *parajes* as well; Collier (n.d.:chap. 3, p. 3) comments that in Apas in the 1930s, poorer individuals received grants averaging about one-third less than those awarded to richer farmers.

[3] Although there are no specific data available on Muk'tajhok' for this period, information about the region in general makes possible this tentative reconstruction of events leading up to the factionalist confrontation of 1981-1982.

[4] Working separately with three men, I elicited a ranking of the eighty households in Muk'tajhok' in order of wealth, one being the richest and eighty the poorest. Men who worked as manual laborers outside of Muk'tajhok' averaged fifty, while those farming exclusively in Muk'tajhok' (regardless of how much land they controlled) averaged thirty-three.

[5] Although factional hiring preferences had become weak by 1987, they had not disappeared. PRI employers hired thirty workers from PRI and ten from PAN; PAN employers hired seven men from each of the two factions. This correlation (which includes all the hiring relationships for which I elicited party membership) is statistically significant at the 0.1 level using contingency tables.

FISCAL SYSTEMS OF HIGHLAND CHIAPAS

Thomas Crump
University of Amsterdam

The object of this essay is to look at the way in which different Indian *municipios* in Chiapas have developed fiscal systems in support of local political autonomy. At first sight, this is not a promising research theme, since these *municipios* have very little autonomy under Mexican law, and what little there is bestows no powers of taxation. On the other hand, as any anthropologist who has worked in this area knows, there is a wide difference between appearance and reality. According to their own cognition, the Indians in these *municipios* retain a considerable measure of autonomy, but since this relates mainly to the organization of religious ceremony whose impact does not cross the local boundaries,[1] it does not offend any provision of the Mexican law. Indeed, such autonomy is protected by the provisions of the national constitution relating to freedom of worship. So also, if, within these local communities, means can be devised for placing the burden of financing such ceremony upon the local economy, then, because of the *public* nature of this operation, it may rightly be labeled "fiscal." The starting point for this essay is, therefore, the recognition of the need for such finance, which then leads to a discussion of the different means adopted for providing it.

Before proceeding to any discussion specifically related to the situation in the highlands of Chiapas, it is useful to understand the purpose, as well as the possible methods, of the fiscal process. The purpose is essential to provide the necessary economic base for the operations of a political corporation; the latter being defined as any public, corporate body which, as such, has the power to carry out and, therefore by necessary implication, finance such operations as are recognized as being within its jurisdiction by those subject to it. These "subjects" define the public for whose benefit the corporation purports to act; their consent is not essential to the definition, and indeed it is useful to forget, in the present discussion, any sort of traditional American rhetoric relating to government being by consent of the governed. (Of course, the lesson from history may be that if there is too little consent, a revolutionary situation may arise. This is particularly true when it comes to taxation; witness the Boston Tea Party.) If, however, the principle of public finance, which lies behind any fiscal system, is clear enough, it does nothing to solve the practical problem of raising it in any local situation.

At this level the discussion tends to shift from the sphere of politics to that of economics. Granted that the public corporation requires certain funds to finance its activity, upon what basis can these funds be raised? Now, although there are any number of theories of public finance,[2] they all suffer from a want of any general underlying principle beyond the recognition of the need for the existence of wealth, in some form or another, available for expropriation (Crump 1981:138). Since this condition may be taken to be satisfied so long as the physical survival of the subject population is not jeopardized by the deprivations imposed upon it, the threshold for imposing taxation is seldom critical. Certainly in any case such as that of the Indian highlands of Chiapas with a long history of exploitation by peasant proprietors, the potential for appropriation by means of taxation (where necessary in kind) can hardly be gainsaid. This is particularly true of this part of Chiapas during the past forty-odd years, in which period a reduction in exploitation by peasant proprietors has combined with greatly increased economic opportunities.

Now if there is one lesson from history, in its relation to public expenditure and finance, it is that there is no essential relation between categories of expenditure, on one side of the ledger, and methods of taxation, on the other. The same is true when it comes to defining the classes of beneficiaries and contributors. There is, for instance, no reason in principle why public education should not be paid for by individuals with no children at school. Neither in principle, nor even in practice, does taxation recognize any essential overlap between the two classes. The most that can be said is that where the generality of the class of contributors has no common membership with that of the class of beneficiaries, the actual composition of the public corporation in which the whole operation takes place will be somewhat anomalous. This is important in relation to the Indian highlands of Chiapas, as regards their formal fiscal status under Mexican law, since although they are certainly beneficiaries, they are only in a very restricted sense, contributors.[3] For this reason, the Indian *municipios* are denied any powers of raising taxation on their own, unless the right to recruit *corvée* labor for public works can be counted as such.

Once one recognizes among the Indian *municipios* the possibility of operating an informal taxation system,[4] there is, scientifically, no objection to looking for one. The question is simply whether it is a reasonable hypothesis that such a system exists, given that certain conditions are satisfied. Indeed it does no harm to look in any case; the worst that can happen is that no such system will be discovered. From a scientific point of view, it is a more serious failing to discover such a system and then fail to recognize it for what it is. This indeed is precisely what happened with Cancian's (1965) research into the *cargo* system[5] in Zinacantán, which can be taken as the first case study in the present essay.

In Zinacantán, following the common practice throughout the Indian *municipios,* those who, as *cargo* holders, have assumed the obligation to provide for the ceremonies in the ritual calendar, are expected also to bear the financial costs: the two go together. At the same time, these expenses are not accepted as a charge on the individual *cargo* holder's working capital. This leaves the problem of finance unsolved, since such a man, in his own right, will not command any alternative resources. In practice, the system is kept running by means of mutual interest-free loans, made by prospective *cargo* holders to those actually in office. If the right balance is maintained, then ideally, a man who enters a cargo has already accumulated half the cash necessary for his year's expenditures. . . . In general . . . it is considered normal and proper to borrow about half the money needed for a cargo. These loans are made at the moment the money is needed, and so it is expected that a man will reach the middle of his term before seeking loans. . . . Prospective cargoholders do not hoard the money they expect to use for their cargos but rather lend it out to other cargoholders in anticipation of repayment at the time they will need it for their own cargos. . . . the cargoholder who is borrowing money will seek to borrow from several persons who will expect to be repaid at various times in the future (i.e., when their cargos come up), thus securing for himself the advantage of gradual repayment (Cancian 1965:100-101).

Now, it is to be noted that this system of finance is quite separate from that relating to any other economic operations in which the participants are involved. Taking a Weberian perspective on the *cargo* holders, seeing them, therefore, as performing a purely bureaucratic function, the finance which they command will then attach to the function and not to the individual who, for the time being, happens to perform it. The individuals involved in this way will then, in every year, be contributors to the expenses of a public office, which, functionally, is one way at least of defining the class of taxpayers. The financial commitment of these individuals would be no different if, every year, they were to receive a tax assessment for a ratable contribution to the expenses of maintaining the *cargo* system. The reason why the system cannot work this way is that it is not the charge of a corporate body with the power to raise taxation.[6]

The argument is that the system, in substance, is essentially fiscal. As such it is but one example of the "informal" expedients adopted by marginal communities in developing countries to carry out functions for which the state makes no provision, even if it does not actively frustrate their performance. As far as the "state" is concerned, all that is happening in Zinacantán is that money is borrowed, and later repaid, for carrying out religious activities that in principle are entirely legitimate.[7] The Zinacantán system does not involve the interests of anyone outside the *municipio,* so it is not surprising that no one has tried to define it according to the standards of a strictly legal system of public finance. In this context the existence of a "public" in Zinacantán is simply not recognized, whatever part it may play in the Zinacantecos' own cognition.[8] This means that one is constrained to accept, in a case such as the present one, an "etic" definition of the fiscal system—which of course is unacceptable according to the canons of cognitive anthropology. In any case, the point will become clearer when other parallel systems in the Chiapas highlands are considered.

The obvious case to contrast with that of Zinacantán is provided by Chamula, where, "on the occasion of the major festivals, provision has to be made for the entertainment of the largest Indian population in the highlands" (Crump

1987:242). In this case, the year 1937 marks a turning point, for it was then that the state government granted the highest ranking officials the monopoly of the sale of alcohol at the time of the festivals for which they were responsible (Rus and Wasserstrom 1980:474). At the same time, a handful of young Chamulas who were literate in Spanish were appointed as municipal scribes, whose job it would be to supervise the supply of migrant labor to the coffee plantations, at the same time defending the local population "against the depredations of unscrupulous planters and enganchadores."[9] In practice, the scribes also kept the records relating to the appointment and commercial activities of the officials who relied upon the alcohol monopoly to finance their term of office. The scribes in Zinacantán had a similar function (Cancian 1965:45), even though the system there was quite different.[10] The point is interesting, for as Goody (1986:58) has pointed out, the use of writing for keeping records of income and outgoings in relation to religious activities occurs at a very early stage in the development of a literate culture.

The fiscal systems of Zinacantán and Chamula are without any doubt the most advanced, in terms of range and complexity, of those operating in the Chiapas highlands. This does not mean that the need does not exist elsewhere; it is only that the means adopted to satisfy it are more elementary. It is still useful to look at four other cases, those of Amatenango, Chenalhó, Larráinzar, and Pantelhó, simply to illustrate the point that different local circumstances lead to quite different solutions to the problem. As in the case of Zinacantán and Chamula, the systems described are contingent on different periods of time; this, indeed, is characteristic of fiscal systems, which must continually adjust to meet changes in the economies upon which they are based.[11] The present essay, therefore, consists of an incomplete mosaic, composed of separate instances, which hardly combine to give any synoptic view of the whole; indeed, it is only at the very deepest structural level that such a "whole" can be found.

Amatenango appears to have solved the fiscal problem simply by means of a drastic reduction in its scale. The historical background is given by Nash (1970:195):

> The hierarchy fails to provide sufficient prestige or power to motivate people voluntarily to undertake some posts. The most vulnerable post was that of alférez. In fulfilling obligations to the saints, alféreces used to spend over 3,000 pesos, twice the normal income of a man in one year. They were assisted by members of their immediate households either in land or in the sale of pottery to help pay for the house fiestas. The show of wealth at these fiestas, when up to one hundred guests were fed, excited the envy of neighbors, often among the invited guests. It was felt that this provoked witchcraft, and every former alférez I knew maintained that he suffered some catastrophe following his year in office. In its last few years before its demise in 1966 the post was accepted only under duress, and all those who had been nominated at first chose

to go to jail. The reason that it survived as long as it did was the insistence of those officials who served in this post that it was essential to maintaining good fiestas. The resolution of the contradictions by abolishing the post contrast with that of Zinacantán.

This last point is significant. In both cases, envy clearly plays a part, but in Zinacantán a term in office was seen, quite specifically, as a means of effectively equalizing wealth and reducing envy (Cancian 1965:98), so that the maintenance of the system was seen as being in the general interest of the whole *municipio*. This moral basis appears to have been wanting in Amatenango, where past *alféreces* were mainly concerned to maintain good fiestas. The historical differences here, although in part attributable to differences in the local economies, are probably better explained by the differential structures of the two systems of office. In contrast to Amatenango, where too much of the general burden was concentrated in a single office, the Zinacantán system was diffuse, which made much easier the development of a system allowing the burden to be spread over the whole class of successful corn farmers.

Chenalhó provides for the finance of religious offices by a system similar to that of Zinacantán, with the important distinction that advance loans and repayments are made in kind (Guiteras Holmes 1974:58). A relatively unimportant office, such as that of an *alférez* for a minor saint, will involve the provision of maize at a level equivalent to some two or three years' consumption by a normal family, or three or four years' production by one man; a major office may require four to five times as much. The obligation to lend and repay seems to be much the same as in Zinacantán, but there is an interesting distinction to be found in the obligation to open any negotiations with a *bocado* of a gift of hard liquor.[12] At the same time, no formal records are kept, presumably because these are only seen as being required by a money-based system, although it is clear from Goody's analysis that written temple accounts, at least in the earliest periods, dealt as much with produce as with money, although "money in the plate is a more flexible gift than goods in kind" (Goody 1986:59). The point about *flexibility* is important in relation to a fiscal system, since it is a characteristic of any such system that contributions need not be related to appropriations. The very liquidity of money makes it, par excellence, the means best suited to achieving this end.[13]

The Indian community of Pantelhó provides yet another example of financing religious office, which depends upon the marketing of coffee produced by the officials during their term of office. This case is somewhat exceptional, since responsibility for the religious festivals is shared with the *ladino* community, which occupies two out of the three barrios of the center of the *municipio*. The contribution made by the Indians is kept quite distinct and has its own method of finance. Coffee, which is the basis of the exchange economy of the whole *municipio,* is grown as much by Indians as by *ladinos,* but there is an important difference in marketing. The *ladino* growers sell direct to one or the other of the wholesalers operating in the area, at a price directly related to that of the world market. This requires sales to be made in bulk, measured in *quintal* sacks. This is beyond the means of the average independent Indian grower, who is forced to sell his comparatively meager harvest in small quantities and at a much lower price to local *ladino* shopkeepers. (The shopkeepers recognize this as making an important contribution to the local *ladino* economy.) The Indian officials, however, pool their production of coffee, so that they are able to sell in bulk, directly to the wholesalers, at the same price as is paid to *ladino* growers. This provides them with a considerable margin over the independent Indian growers; this margin then provides the means for financing the Indian officials' contribution to the periodic religious festivals. In this case, the officials can be seen as serving a corporation that preserves its identity over the years, even as that of its constituent members constantly changes. This, on a very small scale, is on the same model as the government agencies to be found in any number of developing countries, whose responsibility it is to sell primary commodities, produced locally, on the world market. If, in the present case of Pantelhó, this means that the financial institution is not fiscal in character, the point is still that it is fiscal in function, just as it is in the other cases already examined.

The last case to look at is that of Larráinzar, where the finance of religious office is largely provided by the rent yielded by land rented to Chamula corn farmers. The Chamulas, who are chronically short of land, are somewhat notorious for encroaching on land in other *municipios*. In the present case, the *municipio* of Larráinzar has turned this practice to its own advantage by effectively creating an endowment for the expenses of religious office out of land cultivated by Chamulas. In the history of the Catholic church this may be regarded as the normal means for financing its activities,[14] but in Mexico, the Lerdo Law of 1856—which expropriated church-owned land in favor of existing tenants—had made it next to impossible (Bazant 1971:53).[15]

This essay looks at six fiscal systems maintained by the Indian communities in the Chiapas highlands—those of Zinacantán, Chamula, Amatenango, Chenalhó, Pantelhó, and Larráinzar. It is not suggested that any of these systems are at all stable over the long term; indeed, all the evidence is to the contrary. The most that can be said is that these systems are expedient during their period of operation, being highly susceptible to revision as economic circumstances change—and of course economic change is the most pronounced characteristic of the history of this area in the last fifty-odd years.[16] The interesting point is that the pattern revealed by the microcosm of Chiapas is a sort of refraction of the world fiscal scene, in which different jurisdictions, both national and local, maintain a wide variety of systems for raising revenue for public expenditure, all equally unstable over the long term. It does not matter, then, that this essay hardly presents a synoptic view of the whole fiscal scene in the Chiapas highlands at a given moment in history. It is the diversity of the systems described, together with their susceptibility to change in the face of economic and political pressure, that is significant. The question that interests the economic anthropologist is why this should be so.

The answer is twofold. The first point has already been made: no fiscal system has any essential link between appropriation and expenditure. The absence of such a link then means that temporary expediency is the immediate answer to any demand for new expenditure. It is, of course, necessary to recognize the contours of the tax base, for no purely fiscal system can actually create wealth where none exists.[17] This process of recognition is, for the cultural anthropologist, also a process of cognition within the local culture. From this perspective, however, the local vision is somewhat blurred, which leads to the second point, which is that the moral basis of any fiscal system is extremely elusive[18]—except perhaps for Marxist theorists, whose views on this matter are hardly current among Indians of the Chiapas highlands.[19] As the young Queen Victoria only too clearly recognized, more than a hundred years ago, expediency is the worm in the apple in any strongly moral system.[20] On other hand, expediency is the hallmark of all political activity,[21] and the anthropologist does not have to go as far afield as Chiapas to discover that the spending of public money is the hard core of politics. The cases discussed in this essay are significant for showing that, in this respect at least, the main difference between Washington and, say, Zinacantán, is one of scale.

END NOTES

[1] The illegal manufacture of hard liquor in Chamula, for sale outside the *municipios,* must be seen as a special case of autonomy in the economic sphere, which had no claim to legitimacy according to the national law. The implications of this operation are discussed in much greater detail in Crump (1976, 1987) and Wasserstrom (1983).

[2] A number of these are discussed, somewhat briefly, in Crump (1981:chap. 9 and 13).

[3] The reverse case is not only possible, but has a number of important historical precedents. The Boston Tea Party, already cited, is not a particularly good example, since the main complaint by the taxpayers was that they had no political representation. A better example is that of the taxation of the Spanish Netherlands in the sixteenth century, whereby the richest part of the whole Spanish empire was forced to bear the lion's share in the public finance of military and naval operations relating to the Spanish colonies in America, which, if anything, were completely contrary to its own interests. This also led to revolution, so that in the seventeenth century the newly independent Dutch republic, freed from the financial burdens imposed by the Hapsburg emperors, was able to become the world's most prosperous trading nation (Schama 1988:40-42).

[4] This is, in principle, no more objectionable than an informal economy; indeed the two, as the case of Chamula illustrates, may well combine in one system.

[5] Cancian follows the custom established among anthropologists working in the highlands of Chiapas of using the Spanish word *cargo* to refer to the religious and political offices recognized within any *municipio*. Readers of the present essay are assumed to be familiar with this use, and to realize, also, that the number, types, and duties of *cargos* can both change over time and vary greatly from one *municipio* to another.

[6] Collier (1973:236) notes two kinds of taxes in Zinacantán, of which the second "used for religious fiestas, is legally a voluntary contribution because Mexican law recognizes the separation of Church and State. Zinacantecos, however, consider both taxes obligatory." No mention at all is made of Cancian's (1965) study, nor of the form that these "religious taxes" take.

[7] The fact that these activities involve the large-scale consumption of locally manufactured bootleg liquor (Crump 1987:243 f.) is not essential in the present context.

FISCAL SYSTEMS OF HIGHLAND CHIAPAS

[8] The notion of a "public" must, at the very least, be conceived of by any Indian population in the area in a quite different way to that of the outside world. In the Indian highlands, it is participation in the *public* religious activities of a *municipio* which, if anything, defines the public according to local cognition. This definition supports the present analysis.

[9] The term *enganchador,* if familiar to any anthropologist who has worked in Chiapas, may still require some explanation for those specialized in other areas. The *enganchador* was a labor contractor to the coffee plantations, which, for climatic reasons, were located outside the highest areas (which included Chamula); his operations depended upon the chronic indebtedness of the Indian population, which provided the *enganche* or "hook" by which the individual Indian was enticed to work for a season on the plantations and so discharge his own indebtedness (Crump 1987:241). Since this was largely created by excess consumption of alcohol, the reform was calculated to reduce the economic dependency of Chamula by establishing local autonomy in the supply of the most important consumer good.

[10] A photograph of part of a page from the waiting lists kept by the Zinacantán scribes in 1961 is to be found in Cancian (1965:110-111); so far as I know, no anthropologist has been allowed to publish any similar record from Chamula.

[11] The modern industrial state is almost obsessively concerned with fiscal reform, relying upon the advice of endless commissions of inquiry, investigating both the demands of different departments and the shifting configurations of the tax base available to satisfy them. The process, however, is an ancient one, for the essential problem of getting a quart out of a pint pot dates back to the beginnings of fiscal history.

[12] The *bocado* required by other transactions can take other forms and be on a quite different scale; as an institution it fits in well with Mauss's (1954:28) well-known analysis of the exchange of gifts.

[13] Douglas (1967:119 f.) notes a number of cases in which this property of money is counter-productive in relation to the needs of the individual user. One of the functions of accounting is to give different sums of money "labels" that are designed to inhibit conversion from one category to another. This practice is indispensable for all budgetary control, and indeed the process of "laundering" money, made familiar by Watergate, is no more than a means of removing the labels, generally to allow money to be used for illegitimate purposes. In relation to specie, that is cash in the form of coin or notes, *laundering* is in any case otiose, for no unit of specie carries any record of its own history, nor of its present ownership. In circulating it provides a quite adventitious link between a succession of holders, linked to each other by a succession of transient, unrelated, and largely untraceable transactions. This fact provides the only link between successive incidents in Yourcenor's (1971) novel, *Denier du Reve.* It also explains why revenue agents pay so much attention to large scale transactions paid for in specie.

[14] Bunzel (1952:164) suggests that in Chichicastenango (Guatemala), the *cofradías* responsible for religious festivals each had their own corporate endowment in land. This may be taken to be the basic model, although Mexico was certainly not the only "Catholic" country to expropriate church property.

[15] It is true that in 1858 the military government of Mexico, under Zuloaga, declared the Lerdo law null, but this was of little help to the church in regaining its expropriated property (Bazant 1971:136 f.).

[16] The major factor in economic development was the opening of the Pan-American highway in the late 1940s and the later development of the ancillary road network. Here it is significant that Cancian's (1972) study of the economic consequences for Zinacantán hardly mentions his earlier (1965) study of the finance of religious office.

[17] So-called tax incentives are almost invariably negative in the sense that they relieve certain sectors of the economy, which are to be encouraged for reasons of (government) policy, of fiscal burdens that would otherwise be imposed. In the economic climate

prevailing in an era of generally high taxation, the incentive effect of such relief may well lead to an increase in wealth, but this is the result of the *response* to the tax laws, which may still fail to materialize in the form envisaged by the legislators.

[18] In English tax law this principle is stated in the form, "There is no equity in taxation." These words have a specific legal referent, in the sense that such equitable principles as estoppel and rectification do not apply in the operation of tax law. The tax law operates, therefore, in a sort of moral wilderness, in which both sides may go back on their word with perfect impunity.

[19] Simply stated, this theory is summed up in the words "soak the rich." Allowing a somewhat flexible definition of "the rich" according to local Indian criteria, this is more or less the principle upon which the fiscal systems described in this essay operate.

[20] The Queen said to Lord Melbourn, her first prime minister, "expediency: I never want to hear that word again" (cited in Lord David Cecil's *Lord M.* [1954]).

[21] Who was it who first said, "Politics is the art of the possible"?

WHODUNITS AND WHYDUNITS: CONTRASTS BETWEEN AMERICAN AND ZINACANTECO STORIES OF CONFLICT

Jane F. Collier
Stanford University

The stories of conflict I collected from American students in my classes at Stanford University in the late 1970s are strikingly different from the stories of conflict I collected from Maya informants in Zinacantán, Chiapas, Mexico, in the 1960s. American stories resemble "whodunits." The students who were asked to keep diaries recording the conflicts they encountered in daily life produced accounts describing their feelings and actions as victims of perceived wrongful acts. Like writers of classic detective stories, they did not focus on the person "who done it," but on the person who found out who done it. They described the *victim*'s efforts to assess the extent of an injury and to allocate blame. Zinacanteco informants, in contrast, told "whydunits." Like good Zinacanteco gossips, they focused on a *wrongdoer*'s acts and motives and paid little attention to victims who reacted reasonably, and therefore uninterestingly. Even informants who told stories of wrongs they themselves had suffered did not dwell on their roles as victims, but instead concentrated on the acts and motives of those who harmed them.

Although anthropologists interested in law and conflict management have long collected stories of past or ongoing "trouble cases," none to my knowledge has analyzed these accounts as stories. Since 1941, when Llewellyn and Hoebel introduced the "case method" (1941), legal anthropologists have commonly supplemented their observations of cases with oral accounts of remembered conflicts in order to increase the data base they use for finding out which norms prevail when contested and/or for analyzing the alternatives open to people who feel aggrieved. Anthropologists have also focused on key words in remembered cases in order to analyze "folk models of social structure," the shared, public concepts people use for defining and handling conflicts (Barkun 1968). But while legal anthropologists have mined remembered cases for information on outcomes, procedures, available forums, and key concepts, they have been less interested in analyzing remembered cases as texts. I, for example, did not think of cases as stories until I discovered that American college students told very different stories from the case accounts I had collected in Zinacantán.

My first impression on reading the American students' conflict diaries was that they were about emotions. Students described how they felt (angry, upset, frustrated, mad, hurt, confused, bothered, disappointed, depressed, etc.) at what they perceived as others' wrongdoing. Even students who admitted having done wrong did not write about their actions but about their feelings at others' reactions (for example, "I was really mad at having to sit there while the policeman lectured me on speeding. After all, everybody speeds on Bayshore Freeway."). This focus on emotions contrasted with the apparently matter-of-fact accounts of actions and counteractions I remembered collecting from Zinacanteco informants. The only emotions Zinacantecos mentioned were anger and fright. In this essay, I analyze these differences between American and Zinacanteco conflict narratives.

Before discussing the narratives, however, I will briefly describe how they were collected. In the spring of 1963, and over the winter of 1966-1967, I interviewed eight Zinacanteco men, most of whom were past *presidentes* and hamlet leaders, about trouble cases they had settled or participated in. Most of the interviews were conducted in Spanish, although I interviewed one hamlet elder in Tzotzil with the help of an interpreter. I began collecting cases with the intention of discovering the "laws" of Zinacantán, defined as rules made obligatory by sanctions imposed and enforced by publicly recognized authorities. By 1966, however, I was more interested in discovering how Zinacantecos managed conflict. I mined the cases I collected to analyze the alternatives available to people involved in conflicts and to understand the key concepts that organized their understanding of wrongdoing and its consequences (see Collier 1973).

The American conflict diaries were written in the late 1970s by approximately forty-five Stanford University undergraduates who enrolled in the three classes I taught on "Law and Conflict Management." At the beginning of each course, I asked students to keep diaries recording the conflicts they encountered in their daily lives. At the end, I asked them to analyze their diaries using the concepts we had discussed. I told them to focus on the alternatives open to them for handling conflict and to analyze the key concepts they used to understand wrongdoing. Most of the students allowed me to read their diaries, but I did not keep copies of them. The analysis in this essay is therefore based on the notes I took at the time and on the joint analysis we produced in class. The students were as impressed as I by their stress on emotions and by their lack of interest in offenders' motives.

As is obvious, the Zinacanteco and American conflict narratives are not directly comparable. They were collected from different types of people who were given different instructions. All the Zinacanteco informants were adult men, and most were important community leaders. I selected them from among the Zinacantecos willing to work for the Harvard Chiapas Project because of their past experience in mediating disputes or in working closely with elders who had done so. Almost all of the interviews were held in my office in San Cristóbal, where I asked each informant to tell me about the cases he remembered. As the informant spoke, I took notes in mixed English-Spanish that I later typed into the English case summaries used for the analysis in this essay. In contrast, the Stanford students who turned in their conflict diaries were young women and men who had not begun their careers. They had no special knowledge. They were simply students who had enrolled in the class. When I told them to keep diaries recording the conflicts they encountered in daily life, some protested the vagueness of my instructions. Unlike the Zinacanteco informants, who produced oral accounts of past conflicts, the American students produced written accounts of ongoing or barely settled conflicts.

Neither set of informants can be taken as representative of their entire groups. While the Zinacanteco leaders I interviewed were spokesmen for their community with outsiders, they were hardly representative of the women, youths, and lesser men who made up the majority of Zinacanteco adults. Similarly, the American students cannot be seen as representative of Americans as a whole. They were attending a private university whose student body is largely drawn from West Coast upper middle and upper class families. Few of the students were involved in permanent relationships at the time of writing. Almost all of them were in the process of separating from their parents, and few had begun the process of creating families of their own. As university students, they were also protected from serious harm. Bicycle theft was the only real crime they encountered. Zinacanteco leaders, in contrast, told of murders and severe beatings, although marital disputes were, in fact, the most common conflicts in Zinacantán.

ANALYSIS OF THE CONFLICT NARRATIVES

In comparing the Zinacanteco and American conflict narratives, I will begin each section with a discussion of the diaries written by American students. I do this because they were responsible for sparking my interest in the narrative structure of "cases." In the 1960s, when I collected conflict narratives from Zinacanteco informants, I noticed nothing remarkable about their stories. I found them plausible accounts of troubles people had encountered and how they handled them. It was not until I read the diaries written by Stanford students that I became aware of Zinacanteco narratives as cultural constructions. The American students' lack of interest in offenders and their motives highlighted the Zinacanteco concern with offenders. The students' focus on the victims' feelings and actions revealed the comparative lack of attention paid to victims by Zinacanteco informants. And students' unwillingness to involve third parties raised questions about the apparent willingness of Zinacantecos to invoke outside authority.

At first glance, each of these contrasts between American and Zinacanteco conflict narratives could be attributed to differences in narrators and their instructions. Perhaps the stories told by American students focus on victims rather than wrongdoers because students were asked to write about conflicts they experienced. Few people think of themselves as instigators of conflict; they are more likely to portray themselves as victims. And perhaps Zinacanteco stories focus on offenders because the informants were political leaders who were asked to talk about cases they had settled. Such men could be expected to tell stories focusing on what offenders did and their reasons for committing wrongful acts. And it seems reasonable to expect that mediators will talk about their own roles as third parties.

Because of these considerations, I decided to limit the Zinacanteco cases analyzed in this essay to those most comparable to the American students' conflict diaries. I focus only on those Zinacanteco cases in which the narrator was the victim of another's wrongdoing. As we shall see, these twelve cases, told by six informants, reveal the same focus on offenders characteristic of stories told by Zinacanteco mediators.

Contrasting Accounts of Why Wrongdoers Did Wrong

On reading the conflict diaries written by American students, I was immediately struck by the brevity of students' accounts of why wrongdoers did wrong. I remembered Zinacanteco informants telling long stories of past actions and counteractions to explain why a particular fight, murder, or beating occurred. But the American students devoted almost no diary space to explaining an offender's motives. After describing wrongful acts in short phrases such as "my roommate used my toothbrush again last night," "my boyfriend didn't shave before we went to an expensive restaurant," or "some guy cut ahead of me in line," they tended to dismiss the offender's motive in a single phrase. Students commonly described wrongdoers as either thoughtless or selfish—"he didn't think how I would feel," or "he was in a hurry."

Students' lack of interest in wrongdoers' motives might be explained by the fact that they lived among strangers. Unlike Zinacantecos, who live in small hamlets surrounded by kin and neighbors they have known all their lives, the American students lived among people they had recently met. Perhaps they had little to say about why wrongdoers did wrong because they knew little about the people who harmed them. But this explanation for the brevity of students' accounts is not convincing. Students' accounts were equally short regardless of how long the victims and wrongdoers had known one another. Explanations for why parents, siblings, or lovers committed harmful acts were as short and superficial as accounts of why total strangers did so.

More striking, however, was the content of students' explanations for wrongdoing. As noted above, students commonly described wrongdoers as either selfish or thoughtless. The phrases they actually used, however, reveal that selfishness and thoughtlessness are indistinguishable motives. To be selfish is to think only of oneself, and so, by definition, not to think about others. To be thoughtless of others is, again by definition, to think only of oneself.

Because the American students equated selfishness with thoughtlessness, they did not posit deliberate malice on the part of those who harmed them. Wrongdoers were merely thoughtless. They had not put themselves in others' shoes to think about how they would feel if they were the recipients of their own acts. The only student who described another person as intending deliberate harm described the wrongdoer as "sick"—in need of psychiatric help.

A few examples will illustrate the observation that American students' explanations for wrongdoing were equally short regardless of how long wrongdoers and victims had known each other. These examples also illustrate the equation of selfishness with thoughtlessness that implies a lack of intent to harm on the part of wrongdoers. One student whose mother embarrassed him in front of his roommates by asking him if he remembered to change his underwear daily explained her action with a brief phrase: "She still thinks of me as her little boy" (i.e., she does not think of me as I am now). A woman whose boyfriend did not shave before taking her to an expensive restaurant observed that "he was too lazy to shave" (i.e., he never thought how she would feel being seen in that restaurant with a bum). Many women students explained why a professor told sexist jokes in his class with such phrases as "he likes to get laughs from the guys." Even students who suggested that the professor "liked to watch the women squirm" implied that the professor put his own pleasure first; he was thinking of his enjoyment at watching women squirm, not what it felt like to be a squirming woman. No student, even the most feminist, suggested that the professor deliberately wanted to humiliate the women in his classes. Other students explained wrongful actions by strangers with equally short phrases. One student wrote of another who butted into a long waiting line, "he must have thought he was the only guy in a hurry." Although sarcastic, the writer clearly did not believe that the offender butted into line in order to deliberately offend those who had been waiting there. And a student explained a saleswoman's refusal to wait on her with the comment that "she couldn't be bothered."

The equation of selfishness with thoughtlessness that is implied in students' explanations for wrongdoing is confirmed by students' emphasis on their own reactions to being harmed. Because diary writers carefully described their feelings as victims, they suggested that victims experience deep emotions. If a wrongdoer had fully understood how the victim would feel, these diary writers implied, he or she would not have committed the wrong. A mother who understood how embarrassed her son would be by her questions would have kept her mouth shut. A boyfriend who understood how humiliated his girlfriend would be by his sloppy appearance would have shaved; knowing the depth of her feelings, he could not have treated them as irrelevant or as her problem. A professor who empathized with women would never tell sexist jokes. And a person who thought seriously about others' feelings would not butt into lines or keep a client needlessly waiting.

In contrast to the stories told by American students, which focus on the victim's efforts to assess blame, the stories told by Zinacanteco victims of wrongdoing are primarily accounts of "why the offender picked a fight with me." Unlike the American students who dismissed wrongdoers as merely thoughtless/selfish, the Zinacanteco informants posited deliberate malice on the part of their opponents. Even victims who said the offender was drunk at the time the wrongful act was committed provided reasons to explain why the offender might have wanted to harm the speaker. No informant failed to consider reasons for an offender's actions. At a minimum, the narrator supplied them in the offender's supposed voice. One informant, for example, reported that a drunken curer he met on the path accused him of witchcraft because he owned the land around a famous cave; the drunk called him the "owner" of the cave. A different informant told two separate stories about an old curer who, when drunk, came by his house to accuse him of acting more important than his elders. In one case, the informant described the curer as accusing him of trying to boss the hamlet curers around and of thinking that he was more important than others just because he could read and write.

Most of the stories told by Zinacanteco victim-narrators, however, provided fuller accounts of why the offender wanted to harm the victim. In seven of the twelve cases, the narrator told stories of past conflicts. One informant who claimed to have been witched told about his previous quarrels with the offender. Another, who had been *presidente* of Zinacantán, described sending soldiers to capture an accused thief as a prelude to his story of how the thief's mother had complained to the *ladino* authorities in San Cristóbal about his tactics. Another informant who had been the victim of an attempted stabbing described the hamlet political conflicts that preceded the event. Still another, who first described the man who tried to beat him only as a quarrelsome person, later reported the offender's alleged reasons for focusing his anger on the narrator; the fighter blamed the narrator for telling the school authorities about his truancy.

In the remaining two cases, the victim-narrators did not tell of past conflicts between offender and victim, but did tell stories to explain why the offender wanted to pick a fight with the narrator. One man whose brother started a quarrel over their inheritance said that his brother's in-laws had put him up to it. And another informant, faced with an angry neighbor who was accusing his son of flirting with a married woman, blamed a local gossip for having told the woman's parents-in-law about her supposed affair.

In summary, no Zinacanteco victim-narrator suggested that the wrongdoer had been merely thoughtless or selfish. Instead, each informant carefully provided reasons to explain why the offender wanted to harm him, in particular. And the concern for an offender's reasons was echoed later in each Zinacanteco account. Informants described settlement hearings as focused on the wrongdoer's motives.

Contrasting Accounts of Why Victims (i.e., Narrators) Acted as They Did

The conflict diaries written by American students were primarily stories of the victims' motives and actions, in contrast to the case histories I collected from Zinacanteco informants, which focused on the motives and actions of wrongdoers. The American students wrote at length about their reactions to being wronged, particularly their feelings. Their diaries were filled with words describing emotions.

On first reading the diaries, I wondered if students wrote about emotions because most of the wrongful acts they described were trivial. Perhaps they felt they had to describe their emotions in order to explain why such trivial acts were experienced as conflicts. After all, it is not a crime for a mother to ask her adult son, in front of his roommates, if he remembers to change his underwear every day. But this explanation is not convincing. Objectively, many of the wrongs described by Zinacanteco victim-narrators were equally trivial. Drunken neighbors who make insulting remarks are hardly dangerous criminals, yet Zinacanteco informants felt no need to dwell on their emotions. And Stanford students who were victims of real crimes wrote as much about their emotions as did victims of trivial acts. No victim of bicycle theft, for example, omitted an account of how she or he felt on discovering its loss.

The brevity of students' explanations of why a wrongdoer did wrong suggests a more convincing reason for their concern with emotions. Because students described almost all wrongdoers as thoughtless—or selfish which meant thoughtless—students' accounts suggest that intentions cannot be directly inferred from actions. If wrongdoers did not intend the consequences that resulted from their acts, then student writers of conflict diaries must have felt that they, as victims, could not simply describe the actions they took in response to being wronged. Rather, they had to describe their intentions in order for a reader to understand the consequences they intended to produce.

In addition, the students probably felt a need to account for why they acted at all. Because they portrayed wrongdoers as not intending to harm their victims, they did not cast wrongdoers as initiators of conflict. Rather, their accounts suggest that victims, by calling wrongdoers to account, either initiate conflict with strangers or introduce conflict into formerly conflict-free relationships with kin and friends. As a result, writers of conflict diaries were faced with the task of explaining why they decided to pick a fight.

Most student diary writers provided careful cost-benefit analyses to explain why they decided to take the actions they did (or chose to do nothing). They wrote about their feelings in the process of justifying why a decision had to be made and of calculating the costs and benefits involved in particular strategies. When diary writers described the unpleasant feelings they experienced as victims of other peoples' wrongful acts, they suggested a reason why they, as victims, should wish to act to alleviate those unpleasant feelings and provided a yardstick for assessing the costs and benefits of taking action. Students who described themselves as merely annoyed had as legitimate a reason for wanting to act as students who said they were deeply hurt, but students who were deeply hurt could justify pursuing more costly and risky strategies because the expected benefits were greater.

The cost-benefit analyses offered by students seemed to divide naturally into two parts: a description of the victim-narrator's feelings and an analysis of the risks and advantages involved in taking action. The considerations that commonly appeared in analyses of risks and advantages involved estimations of a wrongdoer's probable responses to being confronted, estimations of how likely a wrongdoer was to be more thoughtful in the future, and calculations of how much future interaction the victim expected to have with the wrongdoer. For example, the young man who described himself as upset over his mother's comments wrote that "although I was embarrassed by how she treated me, I didn't say anything because it would only hurt her feelings." The woman whose boyfriend had not shaved before going out to dinner wrote that "I knew he would think I was silly for getting so upset over nothing, but I still thought I should tell him how I feel." The students who complained about the professor who told sexist jokes in class described how angry they were, or how uncomfortable his jokes made them, but none took any action except to complain to me and to other female faculty members. They justified their inaction by observing that the professor was too old or too self-centered to change his ways, that initiating administrative procedures against him would take too much time and cause more trouble than the offense warranted, that the course was almost over anyway, and that a woman could always tell her friends not to enroll in the class. And in cases where students were wronged by strangers, the victims either justified their inaction by implying that they were unlikely to see the wrongdoer again ("there didn't seem any point in making a scene") or they justified taking action with such statements as "I was so mad I couldn't keep quiet" and "even though I knew it would start an argument, I couldn't let him get away with that."

By first describing their feelings, and then the action strategies they considered, the students suggested that thinking about the consequences of one's acts on others is apart from, and subsequent to, a basic desire to act that derives from feelings. Victim-narrators' accounts of the motives behind their own actions were thus consistent with the motives they attributed to wrongdoers. In students' accounts, wrongdoers were selfish and thoughtless. They acted on their emotions without stopping to think through the effects of their acts on others. Victim-narrators, in contrast, were neither selfish nor thoughtless. As demonstrated in their diaries, they carefully thought through the consequences of their acts, although they, like wrongdoers, were first moved to act by selfish impulses.

In summary, American victim-narrators told stories that portrayed themselves as concerned, thoughtful people who were not responsible for the conflicts that motivated their accounts. By carefully describing their actions and reasons for acting, the students simultaneously absolved themselves of responsibility and provided the information a reader/listener would need to assess the offender's fault.

In contrast to the American students, Zinacanteco victim-narrators said very little about what they felt or did when an offender tried to harm them. Only two informants mentioned their emotions. One reported that when a drunken curer accused him of witchcraft, he wanted to fight back but his wife stopped him and took him home. The next day, after learning about the fight from his wife, the informant said he was frightened because his opponent had already killed four people he accused of witchcraft. So the informant and his wife decided to talk with the *presidente*. Another informant reported that when his wife told him a drunken man had shouted abuses at her, he got very mad and went with his wife to confront the offender at his house.

The remaining Zinacanteco victim-narrators told matter-of-fact stories that focused on actions rather than emotions. One informant who was sitting in his courtyard when he was insulted by a drunken curer reported that he tried to calm the man because he was drunk. Finally, he got the drunken man to leave and go home. The next day, the informant left for hot country to work in his fields for eight days. When he returned, the hamlet elders were having a meeting. The informant reported walking up to the curer, who was now sober, to ask him if he remembered what he had said eight days before. Not once did this informant mention what he felt. Nor did he bother to explain why he took the actions he did. Another informant, who was almost stabbed by an angry drunk when he was sitting in a hamlet cantina, simply reported that his drinking companion grabbed the offender and took the knife away. Then a group of men came up and carried the offender off to jail. In some cases, the informant did not even mention trying to calm a drunken assaulter. The informant whose drunken brother tried to pick a fight over inheritance reported only that he left the house and went to work on the highway for a few days. And the man who reported that a quarrelsome person tried to hit him did not mention any feelings of fright or anger. He simply reported that the assaulter failed in his attack, and that the informant later went alone to the cabildo to complain.

Informants who were not in direct contact with their opponents were equally silent about their emotions. One man who reported being told by others that his soul had been sold to the Earth Lord said he never did anything about it because he had too much work to do. And another who was told by a friend that a woman had cried out to the gods to make him ill reported that he did not get sick and so did nothing about it. Similarly, the *presidente* who said a woman accused him of abusing his office before the San Cristóbal authorities did not describe his feelings on being summoned to appear before them. He reported only that when the San Cristóbal authorities telephoned him, he told them he could not come into town that day because he was busy, but he would be there at nine the next morning.

The matter-of-fact way in which Zinacanteco victim-narrators discussed their reactions to being wronged conveys the impression that victims acted as any reasonable person would have done. Having established that the offender wanted to harm this victim, in particular, Zinacanteco informants suggested an obvious reason why a victim might want to take action. In Zinacanteco stories, the wrongdoer initiates the conflict. The victim is already involved, willingly or unwillingly. A victim may have to decide what to do, but he or she does not have to decide whether or not to interpret a wrongful act as initiating a relationship of conflict between the offender and victim.

Contrasts in the Use of Third Parties

When analyzing the conflict diaries written by American students, both the students and I were surprised by their reluctance to invoke third parties. In contrast to Zinacanteco informants, who routinely reported invoking third parties, no American student wrote of asking an outside person to hear both sides and propose a solution to the conflict. Students did report asking third parties for advice, or for help in answering a factual question, but students appeared to resent advisors and experts who tried to act like mediators. Instead of invoking third parties, the students who felt wronged reported doing nothing at all or they reported confronting the wrongdoer directly.

Although students wrote about their attempts to settle conflicts, such accounts were clearly not intended as conclusions to their stories. Instead, the accounts served the purpose of providing more information about what the narrators/victims did. Accounts of the victim's actions and the offender's reactions were offered as further evidence for assessing the extent of the victim's injury and the offender's blame.

Many students reported doing nothing at all about a perceived wrong. They described opting for avoidance either to preserve an air of harmony in a valued relationship or because they cared so little about the relationship that they were willing to break it. Students seemed to be particularly reluctant to do anything about wrongs committed by powerful people or impersonal institutions. When they did report complaining to another person about such a wrong, they did not expect that person to take action. Students who complained to me about the professor who told sexist jokes, for example, did not want me to confront the professor or alert the university authorities. At most, they wanted me to help them warn other women not to take the class. And the few students who reported taking direct action against a more powerful wrongdoer described subsequent events as confrontations rather than as hearings in which both sides told their stories before someone with authority to propose a settlement. The student who complained to a store manager about a salesclerk's behavior did not portray herself as appealing to a third party. And students who objected to grades they received in courses reported confronting their professors directly. Stanford University has an ombudsperson, but no diary writer reported having consulted him.

When students reported taking action against equals, they usually described confrontations. Some confrontations were indirect. A student who complained of a messy roommate reported picking up the roommate's belongings. The student who resented having his toothbrush used attached a "do not use" sign to it. Students who objected to housemates leaving dirty dishes in the sink complained at dorm meetings that "some people" were not cleaning up after themselves. Other confrontations were direct. Some victim-narrators reported voicing their complaints as jokes. Others reported speaking directly with an offender, explaining how his or her act had made the victim feel.

Students reported three common outcomes to confrontations. Some degenerated into yelling matches in which the opponents talked past each other. Some, particularly those between people involved in intimate relationships, led to "talking things out"; long conversations that explored many aspects of a relationship. Most frequently, students described confrontations as leading to understandings about goals for the future. Roommates agreed to respect each other's possessions, the dorm meeting produced a set of new kitchen rules, the store manager refunded the money, and the professor who graded badly either agreed to change the grade or told the student how to do better. No student reported a confrontation that focused on establishing past facts and allocating blame.

In summary, the students' descriptions of avoidance and confrontations were further installments in their accounts of what they, as victims, had done. By describing their attempts at settlement, they portrayed themselves as people who had actively sought to end the conflict. If it was still going on, their stories implied, their opponent was to blame. The victim had acted like a reasonable person. If reason had not prevailed, it was not the victim's fault.

Similarly, the "settlements" described by Zinacanteco victim-narrators were further installments in their stories of why the wrongdoer did wrong. Their lengthy descriptions of an offender's words as actions during settlement procedures provided further evidence for assessing an offender's motives.

Unlike the American students, who frequently reported doing nothing when wronged, only two Zinacanteco informants reported opting for avoidance. Both reported being told by others that someone was trying to witch them. Neither got sick.

The most frequent action reported by Zinacanteco narrator-victims was to invoke a third party to act as mediator. In nine of the twelve cases, the victim appealed directly to a third party, confronted the offender in front of people who could serve as mediators, or turned to a mediator who was already on hand. When describing settlement hearings, the narrators barely mentioned their own conversations with mediators. Instead, they focused on offenders. They told how the mediator (or the victim speaking in front of hamlet or municipal authorities) asked the offender to explain his/her actions. The offender either failed to answer or, after answering, had his/her reasons exposed as false or inadequate. The offender was then scolded by the authorities and told to refrain from further action. In only one case did a Zinacanteco victim-narrator report going to confront the offender directly without first enlisting the help of someone in authority to act as a mediator. In this case, the narrator reported that the offender admitted doing wrong and begged the victim's pardon.

In summary, Zinacanteco victim-narrators' descriptions of how conflicts were settled, like their descriptions of how conflicts began, focused on the offender and his or her motives. Zinacantecos began their stories with accounts of why the offender did it. And they ended their stories with accounts of how the offender's publicly stated motives were inadequate or inappropriate.

CONFLICT NARRATIVES AS STORIES

The striking differences between American students' conflict diaries and the case accounts I collected from Zinacanteco informants suggest that while conflict may be universal, cultures provide people with different scripts for narrating their troubles. The American students produced "whodunits." Student narrators assumed the role of detective. They gave careful accounts of the clues they uncovered, providing a reader/listener with the evidence he/she would need to assess responsibility and allocate blame. The Zinacanteco informants produced "whydunits." Narrators carefully described the actions and relationships of the wrongdoer, thus allowing a listener to infer the offender's motives.

The American students produced whodunits even though my instructions to them were vague and my use of the word "diary" encouraged them to adopt a semiconfessional stance emphasizing their inner feelings. Their conflict diaries were filled with words referring to emotions, but students were not confessing their feelings. Instead, they referred to emotions in the process of explaining why they, as victims of another's wrongdoing, took the actions they did. Like writers of detective fiction, the students carefully recounted their actions and their reasons for acting. They did not focus on wrongdoers. Given the pervasiveness of popular psychology in American culture and the students' evident concern with emotions, I expected them to attribute complex inner motives to wrongdoers, but they did not. Students had no difficulty producing psychological explanations when I pushed them to account for someone's actions, but they did not produce such explanations spontaneously.

In an article analyzing narratives told by American litigants in small claims courts, O'Barr and Conley observed that "most litigants come to court with a narrative that they want to tell and usually find a way to present it" (1985:665). The five uninterrupted narratives they transcribed are very similar in story line to the accounts produced by the American students in my classes. Although narrators in small claims court did not talk about their emotions, their stories were primarily accounts of what they themselves had done. People who were accusing others of having harmed them said very little about the offender's actions and nothing about motives. For example, a man suing a cleaning company over a spot in his suit told about his efforts to have his suit fixed or replaced (O'Barr and Conley 1985:678). Another man involved in a boundary dispute with neighbors told of repeated efforts to dig up the sumac trees that had invaded his property (O'Barr and Conley 1985:682). And a woman suing the man who had sold her a defective car engine told about her many visits to the mechanic (O'Barr and Conley 1985:687).

Like the American students, the litigants whose narratives O'Barr and Conley (1985) transcribed seemed to assume that wrongdoers had not deliberately intended to harm the victim-narrator. The cleaning company, bad neighbors, and engine salesman were selfishly trying to avoid responsibility, but they were not out to deliberately put spots in suits, plant invasive shrubbery, or sell defective engines. The litigants in small claims court thus put themselves in the same position as the students who wrote conflict diaries. They had to explain why a conflict existed. So, when the litigants were asked to tell the court "the reason you're bringing this action" (O'Barr and Conley 1985:678, 687), they produced narratives recounting the history of their reasonable attempts to obtain compensation or relief.

O'Barr and Conley (1985) concluded that American litigants who are allowed to tell their own stories, uninterrupted by questions from judges and lawyers, seldom deal explicitly with issues of blame, responsibility, and agency. Instead of beginning with a statement that posits a hypothesis about who is responsible for the harm and then marshalling evidence to support it, as a lawyer would do, the litigants appear to rely on the listener to come to an inductive conclusion. O'Barr and Conley compared their findings with those of Pomerantz (1978) who, in a study of everyday conversations, found that Americans are reluctant to attribute blame. She wrote that "initial work suggests that [conversational] sequences may be organized to permit and prefer attributing blame to self (e.g., apologies, admissions, confessions) over attributing blame to co-participant (e.g., blamings, complaints, accusations)" (Pomerantz 1978:120).

The findings of O'Barr and Conley (1985) and Pomerantz (1978) suggest that Americans tell whodunits because they want their interlocutors to assess blame. Narrators recount in vivid detail the actions a victim (or detective) took to decide if a wrong was committed and, if so, who did it, but they stop short of attributing actual blame. That is the interlocutor's job. Ideally, as in a detective novel, the offender will admit blame directly, either by tearfully confessing or by bolting for the door into the arms of the waiting policeman.

Americans appear to tell whodunits even in situations where they are not appropriate and may be harmful to the narrator's interests. O'Barr and Conley, for example, suggested that litigants in small claims court prejudice their cases by telling stories that "differ substantially in form and content from the accounts that judges are accustomed to dealing with by training and experience" (1985:685). By expecting the judge to infer fault from the facts recounted, rather than laying out a theory of the case for testing, the litigant risks having the judge rule in favor of the other party.

Just as the American students in my classes wrote conflict diaries with the same story line as the narratives produced by litigants in small claims court, so the Zinacanteco informants I interviewed in my office in San Cristóbal produced stories with the same structure as the gossip narratives John Haviland recorded in natural conversations in Zinacanteco houses (1977). Zinacanteco stories are basically whydunits. Gossips tell what an offender did and said, paying particular attention to the circumstances in which the offender acted and to the reasons the offender (supposedly) gave for doing what he/she did. Unlike American story tellers who try to provide the reader/listener with the facts needed to discover "who done it," the Zinacanteco gossip begins by identifying the wrongdoer and then providing the information a listener needs to assess the adequacy of an offender's motives. A good American listener is supposed to respond at the end of a story by confessing or blaming another person. A good Zinacanteco listener is supposed to supply the reasons for a wrongdoer's behavior. John Haviland recorded a gossip session that ended with a listener exclaiming, "Damn! So that's why his brothers-in-law jailed him" (1977:2).

The Zinacanteco informants I interviewed appeared just as determined to follow their cultural script as the American students were to follow theirs.

Despite John Haviland's observation that "the man who has to face a dumb audience is thrown into confusion and finds it hard to speak at all" (1977:51), the Zinacanteco men I interviewed managed to produce whydunits without help from me. My ineptitude as an interlocutor undoubtedly cramped their style, but did not deflect the course of their narratives. In looking back at the cases I collected, I can see that informants tried to identify the people in their stories so that I, as interlocutor, could understand who they were from some personal vantage (Haviland 1977:51). And even though I expected informants to tell me about particular wrongful acts and their consequences, they responded to my questions about *delitos* (crimes) with rambling stories about the backgrounds of quarrels. In the end, the Zinacanteco informants converted me into a semiskilled interlocutor. I can remember exclaiming, "so that's why he did it," and "that person is really crazy."

CONCLUSION

Although I do not have the space to develop my ideas about why American and Zinacanteco conflict narratives take the shape they do, I want to end by briefly suggesting that narrative styles are related to deeper, usually unstated, assumptions about the causes and consequences of conflict (see Collier 1988).

Because the Stanford students portrayed those who hurt them as acting without a deliberate intent to harm, they assumed a social world in which people unintentionally trespass on one another's rights. At worst, offenders selfishly thought only of themselves. And because students portrayed victims as choosing whether or not to respond, they assumed a social world in which individuals initiate the relationships they have with others, or at least determine the content of the kinship and contiguity-based relationships they cannot choose. Students thus assumed a society made up of separate, autonomous, equal individuals whose relations with one another are the product of individual free choice. In their assumed world, everyone has the right to life, liberty, and happiness—that is, the right to have others not infringe on personal space, property, or feelings. And everyone has the obligation to obey the golden rule. In order to live in such an atomistic society, people must do unto others as they would have others do unto them. Individuals have the obligation to think about the consequences of their acts on others.

In a social world where conflict results primarily from the selfish/thoughtless behavior of individuals, conflicts can be settled by having offenders "pay" for the harm they caused. Americans tend to think of the legal system as having the job of distributing punishments, or compensatory payments, in accord with assessed blame or responsibility. Given this assumption, the most important determinants of outcomes appear to be what happened and who did it. Once these facts are established, the outcome should follow automatically—if justice prevails.

It thus makes sense for American tellers of conflict narratives to structure their stories so as to provide interlocutors with the information they need to determine what happened and who did it. Whodunits understandably end when the wrongdoer confesses or bolts. And narrators appropriately stop talking when they have led their interlocutors through the inductive reasoning process they used to assess blame. Unfortunately for American narrators, however, the courts do not work the way lay Americans seem to think they should. Court officials probably imagine themselves making decisions based on assessments of blame and responsibility, but, unfortunately for lay narrators, judges expect litigants to prove the facts through deductive rather than inductive reasoning.

Zinacanteco conflict narratives also assume a particular, if unstated, understanding of the causes and consequences of conflict. Because Zinacanteco informants portrayed those who hurt them as intending to harm them, they suggested a social world in which people are involved in complex, ongoing relationships. Unlike the American students who pictured conflict as resulting from one person's failure to respect another's *rights*, the Zinacanteco informants tended to portray conflicts as resulting from one person's failure to fulfill his or her *obligations* toward a specific other. Zinacanteco informants told stories in which conflicts occurred because someone had not fulfilled the obligations implied in an ongoing relationship. An old curer has the obligation not to shout insults at a literate young man who uses his skills to help hamlet elders manage local affairs. A younger brother has the obligation not to ask his older brother to move out of the house. People have an obligation to refrain from spreading harmful gossip about their neighbors.

In a social world where conflicts result primarily from a person's failure to fulfill his or her obligations, conflicts can be settled by having offenders recognize and assume their appropriate responsibilities toward others. Zinacantecos tend to think of their legal system as having the job of working out solutions acceptable to both sides. They do not expect mediators to establish blame or responsibility. Rather litigants want mediators to work out solutions that will enable both sides to accept their obligations toward each other (Collier 1973).

Given Zinacantecos' assumptions about the causes and consequences of conflict, they have little reason to feel they must establish the truth of past events. Instead, they need to know whether an offender will comply with his or her obligations in the future. An offender's motives for wrongdoing are more important in determining the outcome of a dispute than what he or she actually did. It thus makes sense for Zinacanteco tellers of conflict narratives to provide their interlocutors with the information required to develop a theory of why a person acted in a noteworthy way. Narrators understandably hope to elicit a response of "so that's why he/she did it!"

ACKNOWLEDGMENTS. I owe special thanks to Professor Evon Z. Vogt, who introduced me to Zinacantán, urged me to study conflict management procedures, and constructively criticized my conclusions. I also owe thanks to the Zinacanteco informants who graciously told their stories of conflict to an inept interlocutor.

Professor Laura Nader deserves my gratitude for suggesting the idea of asking the American students in my classes to keep conflict diaries. She also shaped my understanding of American conflict management procedures by sharing her ideas with me. I am particularly grateful to the students who allowed me to read their conflict diaries. In this essay, I have not quoted directly from the diaries; rather, I have invented statements that hopefully preserve the flavor of their words.

Many people offered helpful comments on my original analysis of the American students' conflict diaries (Collier 1980). I would like to acknowledge the suggestions of Richard Abel, Rosemary Coombe, Robert Levy, William L.F. Felstiner, Michelle Rosaldo, and Renato Rosaldo. George Collier offered many suggestions for improving the present essay.

HOPEFUL MASTERS:
CULTURAL AND LEGAL PLURALISM
IN THE UNITED STATES

Carol J. Greenhouse
Cornell University

INTRODUCTION: PLURALISM AS A
CULTURAL CATEGORY

Recent developments in the anthropology of law have included a new attentiveness to the simultaneity of different normative orders in society. Legal pluralism interests anthropologists not only because it focuses questions on the relationship of legality (in the narrow, institutional sense of the term) to culture, but also because that relationship must be an articulate one. National legal systems everywhere must deliberate the relationship of official law to local governments, myriad administrative orders of both governmental and non-governmental agencies, local ideology and practice, and what used to be conventionally called "custom." When the national experience involves the active definition and negotiation of cultural sovereignties, the urgencies of descriptive, interpretive, and comparative problems in the understanding and maintenance of sociolegal orders become even more pronounced.

Such problems are by no means confined to postcolonial nations, although the postcolonial experience has occasioned a large and, increasingly, self-critical literature (e.g., Comaroff and Roberts 1981; Moore 1986). Jane Collier's research on law and normative ordering in Zinacantán has contributed an important and extended ethnographic chapter to this literature, as well as a comparative approach (1973, 1974, 1975). Specifically, Collier emphasizes the centrality of contradiction in culture and the engagement of legal actors with the always-shifting consequences of contradiction. Cultural contradiction necessitates legal improvisation (among other things), and so the question arises as how to "read" law and legal pluralism to find the multiple voices that invent and reinvent legal orders with words. Cultural pluralism and legal pluralism would seem to be connected, even obviously so, but how? This essay sketches a "reading" of the relationship between these forms of pluralism in the United States.

One of the more striking paradoxes of American life—especially visible in a presidential election year (this is written in 1988)—involves the central notions of pluralism, equality, and law. On the one hand, Americans refer to their society as an inclusive "melting pot," in which diversity is assimilated into a single nation that celebrates the law's appropriateness as a forum for resolving competing social visions and individual claims. From this perspective, legal pluralism perfects cultural pluralism as the basis for democratic capitalism. On the other hand, Americans also make manifest a view of equality that makes inequality the companion of difference. From this perspective, law use is problematic and carries with it the stigma of abuse and excess, because difference itself is believed to be intrinsically disruptive and disturbing.

These two views are emblematized in the dual fact that Americans believe their society to be an excessively litigious one, even though most people never litigate at all; indeed, the remedy of choice among Americans in conflict situations is avoidance. If people—including many lawyers and social scientists—persist in believing in "American litigiousness" in the face of ample evidence to the contrary, their persuasions are not just a commentary on the selective impact of the law and society field, but also a commentary on the ways in which Americans address the pervasive cultural paradox of believing simultaneously in inclusive equality and exclusive hierarchy. In this essay, I want to offer an analysis of the signs with which Americans sustain and claim to resolve this paradox, by drawing on ethnographic studies of American life.

The starting point of this essay is in the observation that Americans cannot escape taking a position on the meaning of pluralism, that it is—quite literally—a crucial cultural category. The very origins of the modern nation in European occupation of lands owned by indigenous nations, and the fact of successive waves of European, African, Asian, and Latin American immigration, involves most Americans in very personal ways in the negotiations of pluralism. Ethnicity might be carefully celebrated in public rituals of various kinds (see discussion below), but (I will argue) those very rituals preclude the translation of cultural pluralism into legal pluralism. While individualism might provide immigrants and their descendants with an idiom with which to organize and evaluate their personal successes and celebrate their cultural origins, public life subverts that idiom.

The title of this essay comes from a monograph by Evon Z. Vogt. In *Modern Homesteaders: The Life of a Twentieth Century Frontier Community,* Vogt (1955a) presents an analysis of the value system of the village he calls "Homestead." Located near the western border of New Mexico, Homestead was about thirty years old at the time of his research there, with a population of 200. The original Homesteaders were part of the wave of "new migrants" (Vogt 1955a:16) driven west from the southern Plains states by drought, wind, and a collapsing market in the late 1920s and early 1930s. Vogt's monograph forms part of a series of works on the region around Homestead, called "Rimrock" (see Vogt and Albert 1966 for a synoptic discussion of the Values Study and its findings, as well as Vogt 1951 for a study of Navajo veterans).

The Values Study investigators chose Rimrock for its diversity. In a relatively small region, five "cultures" (as they were identified by the project) shared the landscape: Texas homesteaders, Mormons, Spanish-Americans, Navajo, and Zuni. Each group was studied separately, as were the interactions among the groups over time.[1] The five chapters that comprise the heart of the book treat the central themes of Homesteaders' implicit and explicit value statements. The titles are "Hopeful Mastery Over Nature," "Living in the Future," "Working and Loafing," "Group Superiority and Inferiority," and "The Atomistic Social Order."

Read separately, each chapter can stand alone as an essay on the practical and spiritual preoccupations of modern pioneers struggling with difficulties of virtually every sort.[2] The account is fascinating, particularly because Homestead is a new settlement, still largely inhabited by its founders. Nevertheless, Homesteaders express their carefully worked out values, which situate individuals in Homestead as equals and Homestead at the top of a hierarchy in the local social and natural world. Within the limited scope of this essay, my aim is to sketch connections among American ethnographies to outline ways in which Americans conceptualize pluralism and its implications. Vogt (1955a:1) himself speculates that Homesteaders express "core American values," and it is in that spirit that I turn now to the general ethnographic problem of the cultural meanings of pluralism in the United States.

THE CULTURAL LIMITS OF EQUALITY

The idea that Americans situate their visions of equality within carefully circumscribed social boundaries provides a long-standing theme in the analysis of American life. Tocqueville's (1945) *Democracy in America* contains vivid descriptions and analysis of the exclusion of the indigenous nations and the slaves not only from participation in the new nation's social, economic, and political institutions, but also from the emergent culture's self-representation.

Early ethnographic accounts of American life emphasizes social stratification (e.g., Gorer 1964; Lynd and Lynd 1929; Mead 1943; Warner 1949) and focus on Americans' claims to resolve the paradox of believing in equality while aspiring to superiority with a temporal framework, that is, upward mobility over time. This temporal dimension pushes the concept of equality into motion, into a dynamic relationship between personal achievement and social progress. An important requirement of this model is the idea of nationhood; it is the invocation of the nation that separates the "American dream" from mere fantasies of personal success. The American dream not only tacitly and symbolically invokes a genealogy of dreams and dreamers—the European settlers, the founding fathers, the great presidents (notably Lincoln; Warner 1962)—but also establishes personal success as both the criterion and the standard of participation in the national life. Society and nation become one.

The cultural meaning of equality as first and foremost the apparatus of the convergence of personal, social, and national interests is presented and represented both in everyday life and in public ritual. Annual public commemorations—Memorial Day (Warner 1962), centennial celebrations (Warner 1959; Singer 1984), or multiethnic festivals (Errington 1987)—present themselves as suspensions of ordinary boundaries of status and identity for celebrants. The family reunions and summer camp meetings that are so important to American Protestants in the south offer "a root metaphor for the life of free enterprise and personal gain" (Neville 1987:143). The pilgrimages that these gatherings represent symbolically connect the individual to God and, simultaneously, asserts the individual's kinship with "the elect," past and present (Neville 1987:143). Such celebrations offer an individual multiple vocabularies with which to connect his experience to those of his kin, his town, his co-religionists, and fellow citizens.

In the United States, people are also adept at renegotiating such connections in their everyday lives, asserting instead their own individuality or some other preferred principal of exclusion. Chock (1986) analyzes family narratives by Greek Americans as deft deflections of ethnic invocations in favor of more individualistic themes. The college students whom Moffatt (1986) studied could resist the geography of their dormitory, which housed black and white students on the same floor, by developing an idiom of "friendliness" that allowed white students to define the black students as having chosen their relative distance. Varenne (1986), too, offers an analysis of the American rhetoric of hospitality ("drop in any time" is the eponymous example), in which social distance is carefully constructed, probed, and manipulated in tentative exchanges of hypothetical invitations.

The very landscape of the city reflects collective attempts to order a wide array of socially sanctioned personal and public meanings. Perin's (1977) cultural reading of American zoning categories and statements by developers, creditors, and others whose job it is to define the value of real estate shows in precise terms how it is that land use categories and social categories merge. Schools, neighborhood organizations, community health care delivering systems, and other institutions of urban life, can be read as reproducing not only the categorical terms in which hierarchy is expressed, but also the consequences of those classifications (in general, see Mullings 1987).

These examples converge in their cultural (and ethnographic) gestures toward the essential paradox of believing and disbelieving in pluralism as a basis for nationhood. Specifically, they suggest that while individualism may be appropriately inscribed with signs of difference (e.g., in autobiographical narrative), public narrative (e.g., in civic ritual) celebrates the transcendence—however ephemeral—of differences. Just as the American dream locates an individual's alienation in the past, so civic ritual places pluralism in the past. Here, the temporal symbols that claim to resolve the paradox of inequality emerge in stronger light. Warner's (1959:221-225) meticulous and trenchant analysis of Yankee City's tercentenary procession links these two movements in a discussion of public representations of time and its social meanings:[3]

> The importance of time in Yankee City is not in the here and now but as it once was, in an enduring yesterday that has remained while present time has gone elsewhere. . . . [From the perspective of the people in the reviewing stand,] time moved by them. The time-ordered events of the parade moved from the starting place in Yankee

> City through the streets of the city as *one* thing. The Procession
> itself, while trying to emphasize the rationality of time, played
> havoc with it [Warner 1959:221-223].

Warner's observation is literally essential, as it calls into question the temporality that Americans invoke in their ritualized representations of lineal time. The symbolic importance of time is clearly demonstrated in American ethnography as the cultural mechanism that allows people to reconcile their self-proclaimed egalitarianism and their experience of inequality (e.g., Warner 1962; Varenne 1977). From this cultural perspective, time seems to be about the very possibility of transformation. But on close examination, instead of mapping the channels of personal and collective transformation, public invocations of time (as Warner shows) *fix* time in decentered present, that is, a present *about to pass*. Thus, it is somewhat less surprising to find, as Singer (1984:140) does in his critical assessment and ethnographic follow-up of Warner's tercentenary project, that thirty years later, "one system of differences [in Yankee City], based on race, religion, ethnicity, and social class, is being transformed into another system of differences, based on local birth, duration of local residence, community acceptance, and lifestyle." History and genealogy are (in this context) alternate and reversible representations made possible by the symbolic fixing of time under the guise of passing time.[4]

Thus, while time is wildly invoked as the resolution to the paradox that this essay addresses, Warner's analysis (and Singer's reanalysis) allows us to see that it is a spurious attempt at resolution—spurious in that representations of time only call forth the same patterned juxtapositions of emblems of difference that beg reconciliation in the first place.[5] In symbolic terms, temporality yields to taxonomy; the culture of things yields to the nature of things. How is it that, in the United States, cultural pluralism—understood as conflicts of values and legal pluralism—understood as conflicts of interest, come to be assigned (respectively) to the cultural domains of nature and culture?

EQUALITY, HIERARCHY, NATURE, AND CULTURE

Herzfeld's (1986) exploration of cultural definitions of nationhood suggests that in western political thought, the elision, or blurring, of the distinction between nature and culture (both culturally conceived) constitutes a potent invocation of the nation. The nation structures personal meanings by fixing complex, shifting terms of "personal, moral evaluation" (such as terms of ethnicity and identity) into a "technical vocabulary of a . . . political order" (Herzfeld 1986:81). Specifically, he proposes that fixing the vocabulary of identity into a taxonomy of the nation *naturalizes* the categories of the taxonomy:

> Nationhood, especially as conceived by the Romantic nationalists
> of the early nineteenth century in Europe, was explicitly *cultural*;

yet it claims to eternal validity rested on the authority of a cultural-
ized *nature*. Thus, the concept of nation encapsulated a
paradox. . . . Nationhood represents both a naturalization of political centralization (in the sense of representing it as a form of logical
entity) and a "culturalization" of nature (in the sense that political
centralization is regarded as the finest achievement of reason)
[Herzfeld 1986:75-79].

Clearly, when Herzfeld uses the term "nature" here, he means it in a particular
sense, that is, a sense in which nature itself is conceived to compromise a
taxonomy and order.[6] The idea of an ordered nature also played a fundamental
role in the development of Western ideas of individuality (Dumont 1986:chap.
2). The idea of order connects these spheres to the extent that order is conceived
as having being authored by God and to the extent that "order" is *therefore*
inevitably singular.

European settlement in the United States imported a conception of nature
developed during the early modern period. The early modern view stipulated
not only an author of the natural order (God), but also a proprietor and
beneficiary: humankind (Thomas 1983). The very concept of nature, then,
carried within it specific ideas of dominion by men over things deemed natural.
Further, nature long symbolized a "moral vacuum" in Western thought: "[F]ron-
tiersmen acutely sensed that they battled wild country not only for personal
survival but in the name of nation, race, and God. Civilizing the new world
meant enlightening darkness, ordering chaos, and changing evil into good"
(Nash 1973:24). Nash compares the nineteenth-century pioneers' sense of their
own project as a "morality play," in which nature was the villain and the settler
the hero.

Indeed, in the mid-twentieth century, "[the] settlers of Homestead were the
type of frontiersmen who defined nature as something to be mastered, controlled, and exploited by man for his own ends and material comfort" (Vogt
1955a:63). While the chapter on Homesteaders' "hopeful mastery" of nature
focuses attention on the prospect of technological and rational achievements,
the monograph also hints at the extent to which local ideas of nature include the
other cultural groups with whom Homesteaders share the landscape.

Homesteaders invoke a caste distinction in expressing their superior status
vis-à-vis Spanish-Americans and lump Navajos and Zunis together. Vogt
(1955a:123) states unequivocally that although "Homesteaders believe in the
cherished American value of 'equality,' they apply it strictly to relationships
among 'white folks.'" Spanish-Americans and Indians are locally described in
somewhat different terms, whose ranges overlap in their shared stigmatizing as
"uncivilized." In particular, the Indians are "destined to disappear" in the local
view (1955a:130).

Like Homesteaders, other Americans, too, draw on a complex cultural
vocabulary to define the relationships to groups they define as "other." Warner's
informants, for example, employed stereotypes of class that ranged from repre-

sentations of the elite in terms of pedigree and social institutions to representations of the lowest class as "lulus" and "river rats" (Warner 1962:82-83). Contemporary ethnography suggests the enduring power of these sorts of images, which situate social conflict at the bottom of the hierarchy and restraint at the top (Greenhouse 1988; Yngvesson 1988).

Like the other American anthropologists of law have described, Homesteaders manage to sustain an effective double standard in the expression and evaluation of conflict in their everyday lives. On the other hand, they normalize conflict among those they deem equal by dismissing it as "fussin' and feodin'" that does not disrupt the perception of equilibrium which local people value highly. On the other hand, they point to differences in life style, as well as episodes of violent conflict, as ongoing sources of validation for their overall sense of hierarchy in the region. Parallels abound in more recent studies from widely separated regions (e.g., Engel [1984] in the Midwest, Greenhouse [1986] in the South, and Yngvesson [1988] in the Northeast).

CONCLUSION

The implication of this discussion is that cultural diversity and legal pluralism belong to two different realms in Americans' cultural thought. Cultural diversity belongs to the domain of nature. American interpretations of conflict seem to center on the untrammeled expression of personal desire, requiring some moral dominion from the mainstream. From this perspective, to the extent that society succeeds, cultural pluralism will disappear. From the same perspective, social failure will be measured (or guaranteed) in the persistence of cultural pluralism, since with diversity comes not only conflict but subversion of civilization itself.

Legal pluralism, on the other hand, is about other things. The cultural view at issue here portrays legal pluralism as the interplay of legitimate interests in socially sanctioned arenas. American ethnography is full of examples of the image of equilibrium Americans bring to discussions of democracy and their public institutions. Legal pluralism—again, in this worldview—is not an extension of cultural diversity into the public arena, but rather its restriction.

If it is valid, this distinction is relevant not only in understanding the shape of Americans' improvisations toward social justice, but also in questioning how and where American experience might serve as a point of reflection of international and cross-cultural questions of pluralism, difference, and order. My general point is that cultural pluralism provides points of refraction and dispersal through which the meanings of law are multiplied and negotiated. Legal pluralism is not just a rubric of difference, but also the name of ongoing processes of permutation that perpetually redefine and rearrange principles of inclusion, exclusion, order, disorder, winning, and losing.

END NOTES

[1] While this is not the place to assess the overall contributions of the Values Study to an understanding of American life, it is worth noting that both the conceptualization of the

project and its presentation represented innovations in social science and ethnographic writing. As Vogt (1955a:1) explains at the beginning of his book, the impact of culture on social life in Homestead demanded something new:

> [The] organization of this book represents a marked departure from the traditional organization of an anthropological study with the familiar categories of "economics," "social structure," "religion," etc. Because I am convinced that the course of events in Homestead can best be understood in terms of values, I am presenting the description of this particular community within the framework of value-orientations. As such, the book will constitute an experiment in method of presentation and in theoretical treatment.

[2] Vogt (1955a:4-5) is careful to discourage readers from concluding that their values are in any sense *caused* by these struggles:

> The phenomenon which the anthropologist calls "culture" has been conceptualized in various ways, but whatever view one holds, an important and distinctive aspect of culture is its *selectivity,* which often seems arbitrary. Certain "choices" that are not completely reducible to biological or social imperatives or to the physical environment seem to be made by human groups which "set off" the cultural process in one direction rather than another. . . . [V]alue-orientations . . . function as selectors in cultural processes. . . .

[3] See Neville (1987:142) for a discussion of American civic processions as secular ritual.

[4] Engel's study (1987) of the relationship between local conceptions of time and concerns with change in "Sander County" suggests that these representations of time might also be simultaneous. In "Hopewell," too, past and present are locally presented as frames around "insiders" and "newcomers" (Greenhouse 1988). Hobsbawm (1983:292), writing of nineteenth-century Europe and the United States, charts the process in the other direction: with the breakdown of institutions that had once marked the aristocracy, the elite "adapted" the "criterion of descent . . . to establish an exclusive upper stratum among the white middle class." Hobsbawm suggests that the context for such strategies was in the economic and social expansion of the period; Warner's analysis (which culminates in the quoted observation of Singer's) argues a period of contraction for Yankee City and its immediate region.

In part because of the pivotal importance Warner gives to his cultural analysis of representations of time in Yankee City, I cannot agree with Marcus and Fischer's (1986:127) assessment that "documentation or the description of reality was technically unproblematic" in Warner's work, or their view that the Yankee City series can be faulted for failing to offer an unambiguous prognosis of the future of American society. The work itself is conceived as an experiment of anthropological method (Warner 1959:4, 1962:chap. 2; see also Singer 1984:chap. 5) and calls into question the very possibility of securing a vantage point on social change outside of cultural representations of change. If the work involves improvisational attempts to do just that, it is no less a tentative and self-critical effort.

[5] I borrow the term "emblems" from Singer's (1984:125) discussion of emblems of identity in the work of Durkheim and Warner.

[6] Strathern (1980:177) argues convincingly against the "solipsism" of defining cultural conceptions of nature in terms of underlying concerns with order, that is, of making taxonomy the sign of nature (and vice versa). Herzfeld's usage is devised to present configurations of political thought in Greece and the West, more generally, that give rise to the solipsism as a solution to fundamental cultural problems.

THE TRANSITION FROM INFANCY
TO EARLY CHILDHOOD:
A DIFFICULT TRANSITION AND
A DIFFICULT THEORY

Carolyn Pope Edwards
University of Massachusetts, Amherst

INTRODUCTION

One of the most important uses of fieldwork in anthropology is to raise new questions and generate hypotheses about human behavior and culture. I am sure that Vogtie considered these to be important purposes in his vision of the long-term field project and a secret educational payoff in introducing undergraduate students to fieldwork.

As an undergraduate in Chiapas in 1968-1969, I studied Zinacanteco funeral and burial customs. Now, reflecting on the experience, I realize that the questions that were aroused in my mind to linger on after I left focused not on the life crisis ritual, but rather on topics closer to what I have gone on to study, child development and socialization in comparative cultural perspective. However, at the time I did fieldwork, I had not yet studied developmental psychology, and so my eye was still naive and untrained in observing child and parent behavior. When Vogtie placed me in several Zinacanteco households and instructed me to take field notes, I was not at all sure what I was seeking or finding out, because nothing happened related to my topic of funeral customs.

The two households that I observed most intensively included children. In the first were at least six children, ranging in age from adolescence down to a girl of two and a small infant. In the second were four children: two boys aged about six and eight, a girl of three, and an infant boy. The first household also included a grandmother, while the second was nuclear in structure. In Zinacanteco style, the men and older adolescent boys engaged in farming and other activities that took them away from the compound all day, while the women and adolescent girls were busy in and nearer to home with food preparation, weaving, collecting firewood, and, in one household, carrying water and pasturing sheep. The school-age children played in the yard or accompanied adults on errands and were seldom seen inside the hut. The infants spent most of the day sleeping under cover on their mothers' backs while their mothers worked. During intervals of nursing they got their best opportunity to look around, smile at people, and receive friendly attention from whomever was nearby.

What disturbed me was the two- and three-year-olds, "toddlers" in common American parlance, "knee babies" in Margaret Mead's terminology. In contrast to the rest of the family, they seemed unoccupied and dispirited. Each orbited quietly around her mother, or leaned against her body when she sat down, but received few of the touches or absorbed looks that the mother directed at the "lap baby." The mothers did not scold or send the children away, but neither did they attempt to cheer them up or find something to occupy them.

In the first household, evening was the time that the two- year-old showed the most animation. I noted one incident in particular, when two adolescent boys, just back from the fields, sat relaxing next to each other on little chairs, with the child standing cradled between one boy's knees being "taught to talk." The boys stated words and short phrases to her in loud, clear tones, and she repeated them back. The boys were exuberant in their praise, and she beamed and laughed.

In the second household, the three-year-old spent some part of the day outside playing with her older brothers, but seemed especially withdrawn and uninvolved in the evenings, when the rest of the family sat around the cooking fire while the mother prepared tortillas, and all talked, ate, and rested. On one occasion, the little girl fell asleep on the family bed behind the circle of people, just before the others began to eat. When she awoke dinner was over, and she began to cry for food. Although she cried for at least an hour, she was not comforted or given anything to eat, and she eventually subsided and fell asleep with the other children.

I noted that, in both cases, the households were considered highly successful by Zinacanteco standards. The parents appeared to be warm, competent, and sensitive to the needs of others, and the older children in each family were affectively positive and energetic. The infants also were healthy and had well-organized behavior. They ate vigorously and were anything but listless in their responsive smiling, gazing, and cooing in social interaction. Only the toddlers appeared to be in difficulty.

ANTHROPOLOGICAL PERSPECTIVES

Of course, what I was observing was not idiosyncratic behavior but rather a cultural pattern. Vogt (1969b, 1970b) describes infancy in Zinacantán as a time of almost total nurturance. The child is nursed on demand and held most of the time, either in its mother's *rebozo* or lying next to her at night. Until walking competently, the child is subject to no expectations. As a young toddler, the child is expected to keep clear of fire and other hazards, to notify someone when needing to be helped to urinate or defecate, and to stand back from the mother when she is very busy. Still, the child receives little pressure to master the basic skills of walking, talking, and toileting and is offered much attention and affection. All of this changes at about age two or three, when the next baby is born. Then "life becomes rough" (Vogt 1970b:65). The toddler is completely weaned and becomes vulnerable to dysentery and other diseases. At first, adults cater to the jealous child's tantrums and help him to master his aggression, but by age three, the child receives little attention or affection, many commands, and a general attitude from adults of "don't bother me."

Indeed, the combination of high initial indulgence and relatively severe weaning and independence training to make way for the next baby is a common pattern worldwide (Whiting and Child 1953; Whiting and Edwards 1988). For instance, Romney and Romney (1966) studied a group culturally related to the Zinacantecos, the Mixtecans of Juxtlahuaca, in Oaxaca, Mexico. Based on systematic observations as part of the "Six Culture Study of Child Rearing," they present a very full description of the transition from infancy to early childhood that is generally consistent with the Zinacanteco pattern. Romney and Romney discuss a post-infancy transition that is marked by three important changes in the child's treatment. The first is weaning from the breast, which takes place when the child is one or two years old. Weaning is always abrupt, and mothers report that the period following weaning is a difficult one in terms of the child "crying for no reason" and being vulnerable to disease and death. The second change is in the child's sleeping arrangements. During the nursing period, the child sleeps in the parents' bed or, more rarely, in an adjacent cradle, but after weaning, the child sleeps with siblings. The third change is that the primary care of the child is transferred from the mother to older siblings or courtyard cousins. Though the mother retains ultimate responsibility for the child's care, nevertheless she cannot do her work with young children underfoot. Therefore, she ceases carrying the child in her *rebozo* and insists that older children, especially sisters, provide the nurturance, including comforting the child after a fall or hurt and helping meet other requests. This third transition is not an abrupt one like weaning, but takes place gradually over the course of a year or so.

In recent anthropological theorizing, the pattern of abrupt withdrawal of maternal nurturance after infancy has been described as common in nonindustrialized peoples and is exacerbated by ecological stress. The pattern sometimes potentiates malnutrition and associated secondary infections in toddlers (Cassidy 1980), but, some sociobiologists argue, may serve adaptive functions to promote reproductive success of parents (by allowing high rates of fertility under conditions of high child mortality; see Burgess et al. 1988). In another sociobiological interpretation, Draper and Harpending (1988) assert that cultures generally use one of two grand reproductive strategies, with associated patterns of child rearing. The first, "parent rearing" (where even after infancy, parents or a few consistent adults provide material and emotional resources), is described for most contemporary hunter-gatherer groups, some horticultural groups, and relatively affluent socioeconomic classes in modern societies. The second, "peer and surrogate rearing" (where, after infancy, the child is discouraged from putting too many demands on parents and is turned over to the multi-age peer group) is seen in most middle-level agricultural and pastoral groups and in the poorer socioeconomic classes in modern societies.

Thus, anthropologists have long been familiar with this account of the toddler period as a stressful transition involving "weaning from breast and back" and loss of close physical contact with mother. However, few have commented on how discrepant this picture is from the classical psychological accounts of the developmental crisis of early childhood. It is interesting that so little has been made of this discrepancy, because both psychologist and anthropologists have made a major point of how the Western description of adolescence as a stormy period of identity-questioning and conflict with the older generation does not typically fit non-Western cultures.

PSYCHOANALYTIC ACCOUNTS OF THE TODDLER PERIOD

The classic psychoanalytic account focuses on issues surrounding control of bodily function. The child is portrayed as an assertive, willful being whose strivings for independence bring him or her into inevitable conflict with socializing, restraining adults.

At first, Freud (1905; see Mueller and Cohen 1986) described only two surges of infantile sexuality: an oral stage in early infancy gratified by sucking and a phallic stage at the end of the preschool period. In his later writings, Freud (1949) inserted a third impulse-ridden stage between the original two, the anal-sadistic stage. During this time, the rectum and anus are the locus of sexual excitement, and children resist toilet training because they wish to control the timing of such a pleasurable function.

Erikson's (1963) revision of Freudian theory has more commandingly influenced current conceptions of the toddler period. Erikson tempered Freud's biological determinism and constructed eight "psychosocial" stages, each a particular kind of encounter between the individual and the social environment. Influenced by the anthropologists in the Harvard Department of Social Relations, he explicitly considered the cultural and historical contexts when analyzing an individual's experience. Erikson's second stage (age one to three) begins with the child's push for autonomy, including control of bodily function. Toddlers wish to be in charge of their own processes of elimination and to do other things for themselves, but they must begin to submit to parental pressure for clean and appropriate behavior. When toddlers' attempts at self-control do coincide with what is asked of them, they are boosted by an enduring strength of will. When, in contrast, parents are too rigid, demanding, or degrading, they may be weakened by lasting anxieties.

These descriptions seem off the mark for the Zinacanteco child, as well as the toddlers in many other societies. Of course, the ethnographic evidence is not of a clinical nature, yet it hardly suggests that the locus of conflict is the child's push for autonomy. Toilet training and other elements of self-reliance are acquired with a minimum of parent-child conflict in most communities where children's clothing is simple and floors can be easily swept up. Parents allow children to gradually learn to toilet, feed, and dress themselves at their own pace, through observation and imitation. Cross-cultural data suggest that, in many communities, the far more difficult tasks for the knee child are accepting the mother's insistence on physical separation and learning how to get one's needs met and find a place in the pecking order of the multi-age peer group (Whiting and Edwards 1988).

A recent theoretical contribution by Mueller and Cohen (1986) appears more promising in terms of the cross-cultural data. They propose that the toddler period, age one to three, is a "little latency," a period of relative emotional calm in which children's energies are directed outward toward mastery achievements in language and communication and establishing meaningful bonds with others, especially child peers. This theory rings true in its de-emphasis of bodily control issues, as well as its description of the child's orientation to the world of children. However, the parent-child relationship is said *not* to be an issue for the child in little latency. Indeed, attachment (and reattachment) issues are salient only during early infancy, the late preschool (Oedipal) period, and adolescence. It is not clear how this theory can cope with the case of the Zinacanteco child who enters the second year with a secure attachment to mother, but then must accept a redefinition of their relationship as imposed by her, much more severe than is expected of the typical American toddler, at the same time as he establishes initial peer bonds.

Another recent psychoanalytic interpretation seems to square with the anthropological data insofar as it focuses on separation from mother as the key issue for the older toddler. However, even this description seems different from the kind of upheaval experienced by Zinacanteco toddlers, because we still see an assertive child driving away from an encircling mother. Mahler, Pine, and Bergman (1975) theorize that the first three years of life are devoted to the gradual achievement of psychological separateness and individuation. At age one, they describe the newly mobile child as engaged in a burst of joyful exploration of the physical environment. Between age two and three, however, children's moods darken when they make the intellectual discovery that they are not, after all, omnipotent: their mothers operate under independent volition. The children are precipitated into a period of negativism, resistance to adult authority, ambivalence, and demandingness. Only by remaining available and accepting do the mothers help their children gradually to come to terms with their necessary separateness.

All of these theories are important and serious, but they are evidently limited in describing the special quality of what must be a physically and emotionally challenging transition for children in cultures such as Zinacantán.

STEPS TOWARD RECONCEPTUALIZING THE TODDLER PERIOD

In reconceptualizing this period, there are three main theoretical questions with which to deal. The first question is whether the toddler period represents a distinct developmental phase with its own issues or just a continuation of infancy. We (Whiting and Edwards 1988) have used Margaret Mead's terms (*lap, knee, yard,* and *community* ages of childhood) to mark the great, culturally universal changes seen not only in the physical and social settings that children frequent, but also in the social behavior that they demonstrate to and elicit from

172

TRANSITION FROM INFANCY TO EARLY CHILDHOOD

their social partners. In our view, infant and toddler periods are distinct in these dimensions. Lap babies live in a bounded space centered on the emotional and physical presence of the mother and other people who share intimate space with her or take over the care-giving role when she delegates it. These infants elicit high frequencies of nurturant behaviors (offering of food, comfort, warmth, objects, etc.) from all other age grades of people. In contrast, knee children (ambulatory toddlers) can now move out to explore a larger environment, though still one constantly monitored by caretakers. Because their memory, attention, and symbolic capacities are now qualitatively more mature, they can engage in much more complex communication. Mueller and Cohen (1986) are correct when they focus on the fact that toddlers have a surplus of intellectual energy suddenly free for making major strides in language, rule learning, object play, and sustained, reciprocal social interaction with child partners who are more like themselves.

As a result of these increased powers and new motivations, knee children receive less nurturance than before but more dominance. They elicit commands whose intent is to see that they do not harm themselves or others in their explorations. They receive commands and reprimands intended to instruct them in the rudiments of appropriate behavior. They become subject to restrictions from people who wish to curtail interaction or contact with them, or simply to control their movements.

Interestingly, we have identified societal differences in the proportion of different kinds of dominance that knee children receive. In societies such as Zinacantán, where parents expect older siblings to look after their younger brothers and sisters, the older children adopt a prosocial and training style of dominance; they monitor the younger children's play, participation in tasks, and social behavior with an eye to normative social rules or family objectives. In societies where older children are not given legitimate authority and responsibility for the younger children, their dominance is relatively more overtly egoistic in style, intended to meet their own needs rather than those of the toddler or family as a whole.

The second question is how to characterize the developmental issues of the toddler period. Is there one central, emotionally charged issue faced in all cultures—whether a psychosexual one (as Freud claimed) or a psychosocial conflict (such as Erikson's autonomy versus shame and doubt, or Mahler's separation and individuation)? Or is the toddler period normatively one of relative emotional calm, in which the child engages in a cluster of ego-building tasks related to communication, play, and social skills (as in Mueller's little latency)?

While this question is surely still open, I would argue that a describable set of developmental tasks is typical of the toddler years, but that children need not invariably confront all of them in every cultural group, and there is no invariant order in which these tasks must be surmounted. These tasks are best conceived of as psychosocial issues, in Erikson's sense of specific, historically and culturally constrained encounters between the maturing individual and the environment. They include the following: (1) learning to do without close physical contact and concentrated attention of care givers (including giving up the breast and sleeping position beside mother); (2) establishing bladder and bowel control; (3) beginning to control one's behavior in accordance with social standards; and (4) establishing bonds with people other than primary care givers. The evidence indicates that the timing of these tasks is set by the culture. Some, such as weaning and sleeping away from mother, can be moved backward into the infancy period, or pushed forward until after the toddler years. However, it is clearly true that *when* and *how* the child is asked to face each task strongly affects how stressful and challenging it is likely to be. For example, weaning and sleeping apart are much more difficult for the child when initiated in the toddler period than when done either earlier or later. Normative data have established that bladder and bowel control are much more difficult when expected of younger toddlers (especially males) than of three-year-olds. Moreover, when children are given more initiative in the timing and pace of mastering the task, the emotional difficulty is less, as, for example, when Zinacanteco toddlers gradually acquire sphincter control.

The third question is how to characterize the mother's role during the toddler period. This is perhaps the most difficult question of the three to answer. Does she (or should she) have one central goal, such as supporting the achievement of autonomy (in Erikson's terms) or remaining emotionally and physically available (in Mahler's)? Or are the meaning and impact of the mother's behavior primarily determined by cultural factors?

When the observed behavior of mothers to children aged two to ten in twelve societies was coded according to a transcultural system focusing on the overt intent of each act (Whiting and Edwards 1988), we found that four summary categories comprise almost all maternal acts: (1) *nurturance*—routine care giving and offering help, attention, and support; (2) *training*—teaching appropriate skills, social behavior, and hygiene and restraining dangerous and inappropriate behavior; (3) *control*—commanding, reprimanding, and dominating to meet the mother's own personal wishes; and (4) *sociability*—exchanging information, laughing, touching, and otherwise expressing positive feelings. Comparing mothers across the cultural communities, it is evident that their behavior shows a transcultural similarity to each age grade of children, especially the three youngest grades (lap, knee, and yard children). In general, mothers direct the largest proportions of nurturance to lap and knee children, control to yard children, and training to community (school-age) children.

However, cultural differences are also prominent, and they are related to ecological constraints set on mothers by their workloads. Their workloads are of course determined by subsistence level, household and settlement patterns, the help provided by husbands and adult female kin, the number of children the mother has, and opportunities for adult female sociability.

In essence, the surrounding complex of social supports and daily routines influences which of three general patterns, or profiles, characterizes maternal behavior to children of knee grade and above. The mothers of the sub-Saharan

African samples have *training* as their most frequent category, and they bear the heaviest workloads in the study. They begin recruiting their children as young as three years of age to serve as their main assistants in economic and household work, as well as child care. The mothers of Juxtlahuaca, Mexico, and the North Indian and Philippines samples have a profile with *controlling* as their most frequent category. They have relatively lighter workloads and more opportunity for adult female sociability. They use their children, especially daughters, in child care roles, but assign them fewer tasks of other kinds and/or wait until they are older. These mothers tend to use reprimanding and commanding after the fact to reduce their children's annoying behaviors or intrusions. The mothers of Orchard Town (United States) are the only group with *sociability* as their most frequent category. They have the lightest workloads but the least opportunity for adult social contact during the day. These mothers encourage types of play and social interaction with their young children that are most intense and time consuming for the mothers and most egalitarian. Certainly, they expect toddlers to demand a great deal of attention and care, even when there is another new baby.

These data do not answer directly the question of whether there is, at an abstract level, a universal theme in the mother's role with toddlers. Yet they do suggest to me that we should begin to think in terms of neither one nor a multitude, but rather a *few* psychological accounts of normal toddler development, each with its own scenario of central issue(s), normative signs of stress and conflict, and themes of adequate or supportive maternal behavior. These accounts would surely draw on classic psychoanalytic concepts of sexual interests and ego mastery, but would be specified using observational studies of cross- and intra-cultural variation in child and parent behavior during the toddler period. A good place to begin looking for divergent scenarios may be in terms of the three profiles of maternal behavior. The evidence reviewed in this essay suggests how the scenario in cultures with the "sociable mother" differs from the other two, but it does not suggest how the scenarios for "training" versus "controlling" maternal profiles differ.

CONCLUDING REMARKS

As we come to learn more about general patterns of human cultural adaptation, we can begin to ask increasingly sophisticated questions about the influence of culture on child development. No longer does there appear to be an infinite variety of scripts for normal development (as many anthropologists once thought), or just one optimal script (as many psychologists claimed), but rather a determinable set of distinct patterns. This is probably true not only of the toddler period, but also of the other developmental stages. Human cultural variability no longer seems as extreme as it once did (Draper and Harpending 1988), and human learning appears to be constrained by biasing mechanisms tied to physical and cognitive maturation. Thus, a fruitful opportunity for interdisciplinary research and theorizing lies ahead. We seem further along the road of constructing a comparative understanding of early child development than when I got my first glimpse in Zinacantán of how different growing up in another society can be.

FROM BIRTH TO MATURITY IN ZINACANTAN: ONTOGENESIS IN CULTURAL CONTEXT

Patricia M. Greenfield
University of California, Los Angeles

T. Berry Brazelton
Harvard Medical School

Carla Price Childs
Madison, Alabama

"For in the newborn baby is the future of our world."
Zinacanteco saying

Romin Teratol, of Zinacantán, described the birth of his son Antun as follows:

Well, after we ate, my wife's stomach was massaged, kneaded. But she hardly sat down at all. Standing there she did what had to be done. She got her children's meal for them. When her pain kept coming then she knelt and leaned on a chair. . . .

Well, the midwife was kneading her back, but [the midwife] wasn't strong.

So then I, myself, kneaded her back and then in a minute or two the baby came. And in a minute or two the afterbirth which remained appeared, too. . . .

When she finished washing it off, finished bathing the baby, she dressed it in its little clothes. She wrapped it carefully in blankets. And then it was given three chilies to hold so that it would . . . know to buy chili when it grew up. It was given a billhook, a digging stick, an axe, and a [strip of] palm so that it would learn to weave palm.

Then when the midwife finished giving them to it she censed [the baby]. She prayed to the tutelary gods so they would gather up its little soul at the meeting place.[1] That's what the midwife prayed. When she finished praying she gave [the baby] to its mother to cuddle. It slept with her [Laughlin 1980:157-158].

Ontogenesis, the biologically grounded maturation of an individual, provides an opportunity to analyze development in the context of two interrelated environmental adaptations: adaptation for physical survival and adaptation to cultural goals, values, and practices. Romin Teratol's description of the beginning of a new Zinacanteco life reveals each of these elements. In so doing, it anticipates themes that we shall use to integrate a series of developmental studies carried out in Zinacantán from 1966 to 1970 (Brazelton et al. 1969; Greenfield 1974; Greenfield and Childs 1977, 1978; Childs and Greenfield 1980; Appendix A).

In Romin Teratol's description, the maturation of the developing fetus culminates in the biological event of birth. The physical well-being of the mother is attended to in the kneading of her back, which relaxes her muscles, enhancing the safe voyage (and survival) of the baby. The mother is guided by Zinacanteco cultural practice to give birth in a vertical position (Anschuetz 1966), thus letting the force of gravity and the position of the pelvic bones facilitate the baby's passage and, therefore, his chances for survival (Caldeyro-Barcia 1979; Russell 1969). Without the availability of medical intervention, the Zinacanteco culture cannot afford the "luxury" of the much more dangerous supine position common in our own birthing practices (Caldeyro-Barcia 1979). The midwife's prayer for the soul of the baby reflects awareness of the very real precariousness of a new Zinacanteco life.

In ritually placing the work implements of a grown man in the newborn's hand, Zinacantecos look to the baby's future, valuing his sex and identity and evoking and reinforcing the cultural goal of the baby's adult role. The baby's value as a future member of society is recognized and enhanced.

OVERVIEW OF THE DEVELOPMENTAL STUDIES

Between the years 1966 and 1970, several detailed developmental studies were carried out with Zinacanteco children. Brazelton, Robey, and Collier (1969; Brazelton 1972) studied Zinacanteco newborns, in the process developing the Brazelton Neonatal Behavioral Assessment Scale (Brazelton 1973, 1984). They also studied infants from birth to nine months, using the Bailey and Knobloch-Passamanick tests (Brazelton et al. 1969; Brazelton 1972). Greenfield and Childs undertook several different studies. In one, young children were asked to manipulate a set of nesting cups (Greenfield 1972b; see Appendix A for procedural details). Another study dealt with the acquisition of sibling kinship concepts (Greenfield and Childs 1978; Greenfield 1983). In a third, children were asked to classify and reclassify objects by different attributes (Greenfield 1974). In a fourth, children used colored sticks to continue and represent patterns (Greenfield 1972b; Greenfield and Childs 1977; Childs and Greenfield 1980; Greenfield and Lave 1982; Greenfield 1983). The last, and most complex, study concerned the teaching of weaving, an important skill for Zinacanteco girls (Greenfield 1972b; Childs and Greenfield 1980; Greenfield 1984). In this essay, we seek to draw all these developmental studies together for the first time.

Our studies primarily reflect the perspectives of pediatrics and cross-cultural developmental psychology. In this essay, we draw upon the predominantly anthropological and sociological perspectives provided by other members of the Harvard Chiapas Project to interpret our results (Anschuetz 1966; Blanco and Chodorow 1964; Bricker 1973b; Cancian 1963, 1964, 1971a, 1971b; Collier 1969; Haviland 1978; Cancian 1985; Laughlin 1980; Miyamoto 1969; Trosper 1967; Turok 1972; Vogt 1969b). Leslie Haviland's work is particularly valuable, for it provides an insider's perspective on socialization and child rearing, thereby permitting the systematic observations of outsiders to be understood and interpreted from the Zinacanteco point of view. By integrating our observations with those of others who worked in Zinacantán, we are able to obtain a clear picture of how the innate qualities of Zinacanteco newborns and subsequent patterns of interaction between children and adults work together with Zinacanteco values to maintain adaptations for physical survival, as well as the cultural continuity so valued in Zinacantán.

DEVELOPMENT THROUGH INFANCY

Zinacanteco cultural practices involving infant and child care were remarkably uniform. As in other nontechnological cultures with extended families, knowledge was passed on by experienced older family members at the time of birth and thereafter. No special rites or practices were carried out while a woman was pregnant, and no pharmacologic agents were given before or during delivery. The midwife, always present during childbirth, did not employ any particular obstetrical techniques, but supported and encouraged the mother in labor (Anschuetz 1966). She led the assembled extended family in supportive groaning with each of the mother's labor pains. The mother knelt in front of her own mother, who caressed her. Her husband was at her back, pulling on the cinch at her waist with each labor pain. This effectively put pressure on the fundus of the uterus and helped to deliver the baby. The atmosphere in the house was one of support and celebration, with the entire extended family participating.

Immediately after birth, elaborate rituals were performed, with the newborn lying naked near the fire, a blanket at his or her back. Prayers and incantations by the midwife exhorted the gods to bestow on the child all the manly or womanly attributes necessary for success in the Zinacanteco world. It was at this point that various appropriate implements were placed in the baby's hand, representing his or her future role as an adult male or female. Romin Teratol's description has introduced the reader to the implements given to a newborn boy. For a girl, cooking and grinding utensils, weaving tools, and flowers were placed in her newborn grasp to reinforce her future feminine role.[2]

The infant was then clothed.[3] A long heavy skirt extending beyond the feet, which was worn throughout the first year by both sexes, was held in place by a wide belt wrapped firmly around the abdomen. Then the newborn was swaddled in additional layers of blankets to protect the baby from "losing parts of his soul." This swaddling acted as a constant suppressant to motor activity (Brazelton et al. 1966; Brazelton et al. 1969), as well as defending the baby from outside evil. In the presence of outsiders, infants' faces were covered except during feedings, especially during the first three months, to ward off illness and effects of "the evil eye." Strangers who came into a household with a baby in it were not supposed to look the baby in the eye until having protected the baby from the evil eye by kissing and blowing the baby on the wrist (Leslie Haviland, personal communication, September, 1988).

During the first month after delivery, the mother was confined, with the infant held wrapped in her arms or laid supine beside her as it rested. Thereafter, the child was carried in a sling on the mother's or another woman's back when not feeding. Leslie Haviland provides a detailed view of the sling and how it operates both in relation to the baby's needs and development and in relation to the mother's work life:

> Infants up to the age of about one year spend most of their time bound to their mothers by a woven carrying cloth. The cloth is a broad rectangle folded in half to form a triangle, one point going over the mothers shoulder, one under her opposite arm, and the third tucked tightly up under the infant. The two free points are tied in a knot in such a way that it supports the head of a young infant; it also more or less immobilizes its feet and at least one of its arms. The infant faces the mother's back, its head turned to one side. As children grow bigger and stronger they begin to assume a sitting position in the sling, with legs bent and tucked to one side. By the time a child is nearing one year of age, it can almost stand in the sling, raise its head to see over its mother's shoulder, and it can use both hands. This sling method allows the mother to swing the infant around to a position to which it can nurse comfortably from her breast without removing it from the sling, while maintaining most of the support it affords.
>
> This method of carrying leaves a mother's two hands free to cook, to wash clothing, to walk around and carry things quite freely. Women can be seen carrying loads of wood or a jug of water by a tumpline, a child slung in its cloth hanging forward from her shoulder [Haviland 1978:239-240].

Siblings often cared for infants, carrying them on their backs in imitation of the mother, though rarely playing with them (Blanco and Chodorow 1964). The mother played with the baby when she was in the company of other women and children or close male family members. When other male visitors arrived, the baby was immediately covered up and put on the mother's back.

Because of how the baby was carried in the sling and positioned for caregiving activities, eye-to-eye contact was much less frequent than in our culture (Brazelton et al. 1969; Leslie Haviland, personal communication, September,

1988). Similarly, giving a baby objects or toys was not valued by the Zinacantecos and occurred infrequently (Brazelton et al. 1969; Leslie Haviland, personal communication, September, 1988).

While most babies were given short opportunities to crawl on the ground (Haviland 1978), babies were not put on the floor to explore on their own. This was a protective adaptation against disease in an environment where the floor was simply dirt, and outdoors the ground often had "organic" garbage, such as peach pits, on it. Because an open fire was the center of every one-room house, babies were "usually held or carried, to keep them out of danger" (Haviland 1978:240).

Striking in this culture was the frequent nursing of the infant, facilitated by the dress of adult women—a cotton blouse, slit deeply under the arms to provide easy access to the breast (Brazelton et al. 1969). Breast-feeding provided abundant opportunities for mother-infant interaction. In Zinacantán, social interaction occurred in a variety of sensory modalities. Because babies were carried, wrapped up, on the back, kinesthetic and tactile forms of interaction predominated over visual stimulation. Covering the baby's head to avoid the evil eye reduced visual stimulation in the first year of life.

On the other hand, Zinacanteco mothers, unlike mothers in the United States, were in almost constant bodily contact with their babies and did not feel comfortable being physically separated from them during the day. Zinacanteco babies were felt to require body contact with care givers to feel happy and free of fear (Haviland 1978:240). Leslie Haviland raised her own baby, Sophie, in a Zinacanteco environment. Zinacanteco mothers were horrified when they saw Leslie put Sophie down; they would display their reaction through comments like, "How can you put her down?". Indeed, they blamed Sophie's frequent crying (in comparison with a Zinacanteco baby) on the physical separation created by what they considered to be a most inadequate practice.

This reaction makes an important point about the study of rearing practices in different cultures: it is not fair to assess different cultures by the same measure. It is not simply a question of intercultural variation in child-rearing practices. Often there are two very different philosophies, each of which generates a different pattern of care and development (Ochs and Schieffelin 1984); people subscribing to one or the other philosophy will each consider the ways of bringing up children in the other culture as not just different but worse (cf. Cole and Bruner 1971).

Description of Newborn and Infancy Study

Brazelton, Robey, and Collier carried out the major portion of this study during the summers of 1966 and 1967. In both summers, two pediatricians participated for one month each, while an anthropologist and a Zinacanteco assistant located subjects and interpreted language and cultural practices. The study consisted of three parts. The first focused on characteristics of the newborn at birth and in the first week of life.

Procedures for Observing Newborns. We observed two deliveries and were finally allowed to examine a total of five neonates several times in this first week of life. Until we were allowed to participate in deliveries, we were considered "dangerous" and were not allowed to handle their vulnerable newborns, for fear of the "evil eye" we might convey.

The observations of the newborns fell into three categories:

1. An unstructured observation period of thirty minutes, in which the infant was with his mother. At this time, we recorded spontaneous activity and the neonate's responses to stimuli that occurred naturally—environmental sounds, light changes, handling by the caretakers, and internal stimuli from within the baby. Of particular interest to us was the infant's use of motor activity and states of consciousness, that is, how the infant moved from one state to another, the buildup of tension before nursing, and the mode of falling asleep afterward.

2. A pediatric examination was made on each visit, with special attention given to the infant's maturity, state of nutrition, and hydration.

3. A neurological-behavioral evaluation was given to each infant at different points in the first week of life (Brazelton Neonatal Behavioral Assessment Scale).

The Brazelton Neonatal Behavioral Assessment Scale. The Brazelton scale (Brazelton 1973, 1984) was developed to assess the dynamic processes of behavioral organization and development in the neonate. It is a psychological scale for the neonate and, as described by Als, Tronick, Adamson, and Brazelton (1976), views the infant as part of a reciprocal, interactive feedback system between infant and care giver. While the exam includes the assessment of reflex responses, it focuses on the infant's capability to respond to the kind of stimuli that care givers present in an interactive situation and is designed to capture the baby's coping and adaptive strategies (for a detailed description of the scale, see Brazelton 1973, 1984).

Procedures for Studying the Infant's Social Environment and Development in the First Year. The second part of the study focused on mother-infant interaction. Four-hour observations of interaction were made using infants of different ages from birth through the first nine months of life. Coding was based on Rheingold's (1960) categories; we focused on whether mother or infant initiated the interplay, its purpose, and its outcome.

In the third part of the study, we focused on developmental milestones during the first year. However, testing after nine months of age became almost impossible because of intense stranger anxiety. We used the Knoblock-Pasamanick (Knobloch et al. 1966) adaptation of the Gesell scales the first summer and the Bayley (1961) scales the second summer. These scales yield a score of "motor age," based on gross and fine motor performance. They also yield a score of "mental age," based on social behavior, language development, and behavior in response to test objects.

Innate Differences

Zinacanteco babies were born with physical and behavioral qualities that set them apart from Euro-American infants in the United States (Brazelton et al. 1969; Brazelton 1972) or African neonates (Keefer et al. 1982). Physically, they were small, averaging five pounds in weight and eighteen inches in length at birth.

Assessed with the Brazelton Neonatal Behavioral Assessment Scale, Zinacanteco newborns were characterized by slow, liquid movements of arms and legs, low-keyed startles and reflex behavior interspersed with long periods of alertness. The delicate motor activity supported their sensory alertness. For long periods (six to eight minutes at a time) they watched, listened, and attended to auditory and visual stimuli without a break in attention. In Caucasian newborns in the United States, after three minutes of continuous attention, the state of attention is broken by excited motor activity or startles. Compared with Caucasian and African newborns, the Zinacanteco babies were significantly different in the quality of their motor behavior and the prolonged states of attention and of autonomic stability (Lester and Brazelton 1982).

In addition to maintaining quiet, alert states for long periods, with slow, smooth transitions from one state to another, they manifest none of the deep sleep, intense crying, or intense sucking states observed in the United States. The Zinacanteco babies were both less excitable (e.g., less irritable, with fewer spontaneous startles) and more consolable at birth. The apparent smooth control of state and motor behavior in Zinacanteco infants seemed to be of a higher order, facilitating the more developed sensory responses (visual and auditory). Their quiet motor behavior enhanced the prolonged period of attentiveness. The Zinacanteco babies habituated faster to a repeated stimulus from birth through the second day of life; habituation is considered a good measure of infant information processing/learning (Bornstein and Sigman 1984).

The Roles of Nature and Nurture

To what extent were the observed innate differences genetic; to what extent were they environmentally caused?

Nature. The argument for genetically caused behavioral differences in the newborn period is supported by empirical evidence concerning the behavior of newborns from other ethnic groups. Chinese-American, Navajo, and Japanese (Goto Island) babies differed from Euro-American babies in many of the same ways that Zinacanteco babies did—for example, in their controlled state behavior, their smooth motor movements, and their prolonged attention to sensory stimuli (Brazelton et al. 1969; Freedman and Freedman 1969; Freedman 1979). While the Chinese-American sample shared most environmental features with the Euro-American sample, the behavior of the newborns differed in the two groups. On the other hand, Zinacantecos, Navajos, Chinese-Americans, and Goto Islanders, sharing almost nothing in the physical and cultural environment, did share a common pattern of newborn behavior. Given the absence of environmental commonality, the common behavior must, logically, have a genetic basis. Indeed, these groups may have common genetic roots. It is now thought that

Navajos have been part of a migration from Asia (Freedman 1979); Maya Indians also have Asian roots.

Prenatal Environment. The beauty of studying babies at birth is that the extrauterine cultural environment has not yet had a chance to exert its influence. It is still possible, however, that prenatal environment has had its effects. There are three logical candidates for *prenatal* environmental factors: subclinical malnutrition, high altitude, and movement of the pregnant mother.

The first seems unlikely but cannot be entirely excluded. The general Zinacanteco diet is based on two complementary vegetable proteins, corn and beans (Lappe 1971), supplemented with small quantities of eggs, meat, greens, and fruit (Vogt 1969b). Emphasis is placed on the pregnant mother's diet to ensure that she have a good baby (Chávez et al. 1974). The Zinacanteco infant emerges from a mother who, during pregnancy, has been given a special high protein diet, consisting of what Zinacantecos consider "warm" foods, such as extra meat, eggs, and beans (Anschuetz 1966). This diet seems adequate to maintain caloric and iron requirements of the fetus. Their babies at birth do not appear stressed or IUGR (intrauterine growth retarded) (Als et al. 1976).

The Zinacantecos took a very practical approach to pregnancy and childbirth (Anschuetz 1966) and, over the years, have, without modern medicine, evolved practices that enhance the survival and fitness of their babies. Zinacanteco babies, in spite of their small size, showed none of the signs of being under-hydrated, undernourished, or behaviorally stressed, which we have noted in other groups of babies around the world (Brazelton et al. 1976).

The possibility remains that high rates of intestinal infection adversely affected Zinacanteco mothers' ability to absorb food and that their babies were, in turn, affected. However, this hypothesis is inconsistent with the fact that Zinacanteco newborns shared behavioral patterns with middle-class Chinese-American newborns born in Kaiser hospital (Freedman and Freedman 1969), a group whose mothers would be expected to have excellent nutritional status and extremely low rates of intestinal infection.

The second environmental factor, high altitude (approximately 5500 to 8000 ft), could account for a portion of one of the observed differences—the difference in movement patterns. Babies born at a high altitude (e.g., Denver at 5000 ft) can show slow liquid movements of the same type, but not as extreme as the Zinacanteco newborns. These babies have polycythemia, slower responses to autonomic demands because of relative hypoxia (Lubchenco 1970). Given, however, that the same basic motor movements are found in newborns born at a low altitude (e.g., the Goto Islands in Japan), an environmental factor (altitude) would not seem sufficient to account for the newborn behavior pattern. Nevertheless, the high altitude, with its attendant polycythemia, could serve to reinforce the behavior pattern.

The third prenatal environmental factor is the shaping of intrauterine behavior by the mother's movements and reactions to her own environment. The specific action of this factor is the most speculative, although current research indicates that prenatal behavior is responsive to environmental stimuli. One possibility is that intrauterine shaping enhanced genetically programmed behavioral patterns. For example, the controlled movement patterns of the Zinacanteco mother (Haviland 1978) and the quiet, rhythmic environment provided as she ground corn for tortillas or wove could have added to genetic influences in influencing the baby toward quiet, motor patterns.

Very likely, a number of factors worked together. The influence of relative hypoxia at this altitude, along with the nutritional effects of infection and the effects of constant, regular motor activity by the pregnant female, may have intensified the slow, liquid movements of neonates. This fluidity, lack of interfering motor activity, and well-regulated state and autonomic control, then, lent a potent background for what appeared to be auditory and visual competence in the immediate neonatal period.

Postnatal Environment. This apparent sensory competence may have depended on a lack of interference from the baby's own motor activity, coupled with a quiet environment immediately after delivery. The innate behavior of the neonate must be a powerful shaper of the nurturing environment provided by its parents.

The immediate perinatal experience—no drugs, no interference with the natural course of labor and delivery, emotional support for the mother, emphasis on subdued participation of the mother in the delivery—was then reflected in a similar experience for the newborn. The newborn was left undressed for a period. Even though he or she had a blanket at his or her back and was in front of an open fire, this would have been a highly stressful period, from an autonomic point of view, for a Euro-American baby. However, the Zinacanteco baby managed the necessary temperature control and was then placed in a swaddled, face-covered position beside the mother.

Breast-feeding occurred an average of sixty to eighty times a day over the first year, in several time samples, with up to ninety times a day in early infancy (Brazelton et al. 1969). These figures, obtained in the formal home observation situation, probably represent a maximum. Under the pressure of visitors, breast-feeding was performed in response to any activity on the part of the infant, rather than to any more direct expression of hunger. In more relaxed circumstances, an active baby on the back would first elicit patting from the mother, then rhythmic movement. If these procedures failed to quiet the baby, the mother would then nurse (Leslie Haviland, personal communication, September, 1988). A baby was never allowed to cry from hunger nor to become too active.

The mother's frequent nursing, sometimes in response to any movement, sets up a model of immediate, contingent responsiveness to the baby's needs, even before they were expressed. The baby, carried in a sling on the mother's back throughout the day, was cradled, rocked, and frequently breast-fed—rather than allowed to cry or to become frustrated.

Zinacantecos believe that an infant nurses for comfort as much as for nourishment, and that it should nurse when it wants to, whether out of hunger, or because it is frightened or disturbed in any way. It is essential, then, that its mother be readily available to it at all times, or its distress will make it ill

(Haviland 1978:241).

The tendency of these babies to remain quiet and slow in reactivity was reinforced by their subsequent handling in infancy, based on Zinacanteco child care philosophy. The infants' role in shaping the environment's response to them was visible in their neonatal behavior, which, in turn, provided the basis for appropriate reactions from the environment to reinforce their characteristics.

The force of the extrauterine cultural and physical environment began to be felt as early as the second half of the first week of life. Zinacanteco babies enjoyed a relatively quiet and inactive start in life, when compared with babies born in the United States. This difference in level of physical activity increased in the first week. Different care practices appeared to be responsible for this increase. Zinacanteco babies, in addition to starting life relatively quiet and inactive, were further constrained by being swaddled and carried horizontally on their mother's backs. In contrast, the typically more active Euro-American newborn, physically unrestricted in a crib, is left free to flail about. Patterns of nurture amplify those of nature.

Adaptation for Survival: Distinctive Newborn Behavior in its Cultural and Developmental Context

Clearly the example of motor movement in Zinacanteco newborns illustrates how the innate nature of the baby can be adapted to infant care in a particular culture. Even more important, it reveals how a fit between the nature of the baby and a cultural infant care practice functions to enhance survival in a particular niche of the physical environment. Note that swaddling is a successful adaptation to the cold. What if the Zinacanteco baby were very active and resisted swaddling? A newborn who kept kicking off its covers, as babies in the United States often do, would have small chance of survival in the cold climate of highland Chiapas, living in a house that was totally unheated during the night.

Anschuetz, in her field report, "To be Born in Zinacantán," speculated that "restrictive swaddling inhibits the child's motor development" (1966:20). This hypothesis was borne out by developmental testing (using the Bayley and the Knobloch-Pasamanick tests) (Brazelton et al. 1969; Brazelton 1972). While overall scores in Zinacantán generally lagged about one month behind norms established in the United States, the lag was consistently greater for motor skills than for mental skills.

Motor development was, nevertheless, normal. The close tactile and kinesthetic stimulation from being carried all day on the mother's back may have served as the necessary sensory input or fuel for the developmental program to proceed. Although not obvious to the casual observer, babies did a lot of leg stretching in the sling (Leslie Haviland, personal communication, September, 1988). Most important, the inborn program for motor development must have driven the baby on, given much less practice and what we think of as direct reinforcement from the environment. Although mothers did not encourage motor activity, they responded positively to the baby's need for it when his or her motor program reached a certain stage of development. For example, at four or five months, Zinacanteco babies would no longer tolerate being carried in a horizontal position and covered on their mothers' backs; mothers responded to the older babies' frustration by letting them sit up with their heads uncovered in the sling carrier.

More important than the slight advance of infants in the United States in the area of motor development is the adaptive significance of the developmental difference. LeVine (1977) has noted that the survival of the infant is an overriding cultural value in societies in which there is a high infant mortality rate. In such societies (of which Zinacantán is one), survival overrides the goal of optimizing development. Surviving the cold is more important than speeding up motor development. Hence, what we might consider a deficit from our point of view becomes a necessity in the ecological niche of another society (Harkness and Super 1982).

Indeed, Zinacantecos did not seem interested in "optimizing" motor development. Based on an intensive study of ten Zinacanteco families, Francesca Cancian reported that, "For babies, as for older children, there was little pressure from adults to master basic skills, and little pride on the part of parents over the speed with which their children learn to walk or talk" (1963:60).

Going one step further, Leslie Haviland's observations indicate that, far from being neutral, Zinacantecos were actually negative about early walking and that this attitude was based on very real risks in early walking. Sophie Haviland walked at nine months of age; in Zinacanteco eyes her precocious walking made her a "monster" because, in their particular environment, it was dangerous for a child to walk before understanding language. For example, Zinacanteco houses always have an open fire in the center. Because Sophie could propel herself motorically, yet lacked the understanding to stay away from the fire, there was a constant danger that she would fall in.

Walking before the development of rational sense and understanding was also considered disruptive to others—as when Sophie would stagger into somebody's weaving. Zinacantecos were horrified at the problems that Sophie caused by her too-early development of walking and were amused that her parents, unlike the typical Zinacanteco family, had to be on guard all the time to keep her from hurting herself or inadvertently creating some kind of damage (Leslie Haviland, personal communication, September, 1988).

Breaking cultural norms often reveals most dramatically what the norms are. In the case of motor development, reactions to Sophie's deviation from the normal walking age made it clear that Zinacantecos do not merely tolerate but actually value late walking. Even more important from a theoretical perspective is the fact that this norm is much more adaptive for survival in the Zinacanteco environment than our norm of maximizing motor development would be.

Developmental Similarities

Given Zinacanteco attitudes and the fact that the tests were extremely foreign to them (e.g., Zinacanteco infants were never placed in the prone position required for certain motor items on the tests nor generally given objects to play with), it is interesting that Zinacanteco babies lagged *only* one month behind American norms in developmental testing. Even more important, they passed developmental milestones in the same sequence as do babies in the United States. This common sequence is theoretically important: most likely it reflects the human genetic program for infant development.

Adaptation to Cultural Continuity versus Innovation and Individual Initiative

For Zinacantecos at the period of study, a key concept was *batz'i*, the true way, synonymous with the Zinacanteco way. In order to maintain the "true way" in the face of influences from modernization and the surrounding *ladino* community, it had to be transmitted to the next generation in every area of life—work roles, familial roles, and religious roles. We came to realize as a result of our developmental research that the culture not only transmitted the *content* of socialization, it also transmitted *processes* of learning and teaching by which cultural continuity was maximized and cultural innovation was minimized. The first such process to appear in infancy was imitation of a model for learning.

All babies imitate. However, the innate foundation of *special* skill in imitating a model lies in the Zinacanteco newborn's unusual attentiveness and sensitivity to visual and auditory stimuli: the first step in imitating a model is to observe and comprehend it. Indeed, an excellent ability to imitate surfaced in the developmental testing in the first year of life (Brazelton et al. 1969). Repeatedly, infants watched us carefully as we demonstrated the use of test objects, then imitated each movement we had made to score a success on the test, subsequently dropping the object without any of the exploration or experimental play we would have seen in babies from the United States. In addition, novel objects met with impassive faces in tested children and parents alike.

While exploration, experimentation, and novelty are highly valued in our culture, they may constitute a danger to a culture that wants to transmit a replication of itself to the next generation. Possible outcomes of exploration, experimentation, and attraction to novelty are innovation and cultural change. In similar fashion, individual initiative, a highly valued quality to us, also brings the danger that the individual will use this initiative to inaugurate new ways that deviate from the traditions of the group. More valued should be the ability to respond to the initiative of others, especially those older than oneself. The initial encouragement of this quality could be seen in the Zinacanteco infant's first interaction, breast-feeding.

Breast-feeding was an immediate response to any activity on the part of the infant, not just hunger. It therefore served a general quieting function, perhaps dampening self-initiated behavior. In addition, the infant's need to suck or feed was satisfied instantly—before he or she could build up to feel the importance of a need, make a demand, and then find it gratified. We speculate that feeding therefore did not contribute to the framework for self-motivated demand, frustration, and then gratification—a cycle which must be important in fueling a model for self-initiated independence (Brazelton 1972).

To continue our speculative interpretation of nursing, we may here have the ontogenetic roots of what, from the point of view of our own culture, is a discouragement of the child's individual initiative. From the Zinacanteco point of view, however, frequent nursing may in fact lay the groundwork for a view that the individual receives what he or she needs from *responding to others* rather than from *taking the initiative* to make others respond. This way of thinking is consonant with the ideal of fitting into a communal society.

Perhaps even more important from the Zinacanteco point of view is the fact that, in the nursing situation, the *younger* person is responding to the initiative of the *older*. An all pervasive concept in Zinacanteco culture is the contrast between *bankilal* and *itz'inal,* older and younger brother.[4] This senior/junior principle serves as a model for relative age or time as the basis for rank (Vogt 1969b). Applied to social relations and interaction in the family, the basic rule is that older people have authority over and command respect from younger people (Cancian 1963).

Under this analysis, Zinacanteco practices organized around nursing could form the roots of socialization into a society that values intact transmission of culture from the older generation to the younger. As we shall see, emphasizing the *responsiveness* rather than the *initiative* of the younger member of a dyad in social interactions in early infancy continued into childhood, when "good" children were assessed by their obedience to their parents (Blanco and Chodorow 1964), and commands were a dominant strategy for teaching new skills (Childs and Greenfield 1980; Greenfield 1984).

COGNITIVE DEVELOPMENT AND INFORMAL INSTRUCTION FROM ONE TO FIVE

Strategies for Nesting Cups

One aspect of the lack of experimentation with objects noted in the developmental testing was lack of investment in objects.This quality continued to be observed in Zinacanteco children carrying out a manipulative task (nesting cups inside each other) at one year of age (see procedural details in Appendix A). A one-year-old Zinacanteco child was able to let go of a nesting cup after placing it inside a second cup. An American child of the same age could not; the cup became part of his or her hand in a seemly egocentric fashion. The Zinacanteco behavior was more advanced in the sense of being less egocentric, less centered on the self as reference point; perhaps this is related to the greater other-centeredness of early interactions. At the same time, the dropping response cut off manipulation of the objects at an early stage of task development. These behaviors seen in testing and experimentation were also noted in home observation of babies in the first year of life (Brazelton et al. 1969; Brazelton 1972). In four hours, the modal number of times an infant played with a toy was zero; the maximum was seven.

The nesting cup study indicates that lack of object investment rather than early movement away from egocentrism explains the results. In this study, the older the Zinacanteco child, the more likely was he or she to utilize rather than let go of the first cup (see Table 1, Appendix A, for quantitative details). Our kinship concept results (to be described later) make it unlikely that egocentrism would increase with age. Therefore, increasing object investment remains as the only plausible factor. It seems that object investment developed later in a culture in which interaction with objects was deemphasized in the play of infants and children. A large (and therefore early) investment in objects and their manipulation is a functional necessity for socialization into a technological society such as ours. It is much less relevant, however, for a technologically simpler society such as Zinacantán.

Given the seeming lack of investment in the experimental materials, it is interesting that the basic developmental sequence of strategies used by Zinacanteco toddlers and children for combining the cups was identical to that found in the United States. We had identified three combinatorial rules that constituted a developmental sequence of grammarlike rules. The three rule-bound strategies—the grammar of action—are depicted in Figure 1. In the first phase (pretest) of the experiment, children played with the cups on their own during two trials, after seeing a demonstration of Strategy 3, the subassembly method, at the beginning of each trial. With Zinacanteco children of nine to fifteen months of age, we found that Strategy 1 was predominant, with a minority of children favoring Strategy 2. From twenty-one to thirty months, Strategy 2 was predominant, with a minority using Strategy 3. So far, both sequence and age norms are similar to those found in the United States. However, Zinacanteco children from thirty-five to seventy months of age, unlike their United States counterparts, did not progress to Strategy 3 on the pretest (see Table 2, Appendix A, for a quantitative analysis).

In the second phase of the experiment, we asked the mothers to teach their children how to nest the cups, using Strategy 3. In the third phase, an independent posttest following the teaching session, nine out of fourteen children in the oldest group (thirty-five to seventy months of age), who earlier had predominantly used Strategy 2, progressed to dominant use of Strategy 3. In four of the nine cases, practice alone (as assessed by performance in a third pretest trial) produced Strategy 3, the subassembly.

Though it is hard to compare age norms in the two cultures for Strategy 3, since some of the Zinacanteco children were older than the United States sample, the addition of practice and instruction actualized the latent third stage. The appearance of this sequence, in spite of the fact that the materials and task were totally foreign to Zinacanteco infants and their mothers, provides evidence for a transcultural and possibly universal development of grammars of manual action.

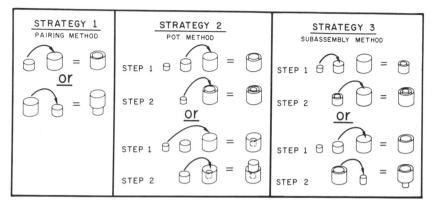

Figure 1. Strategies for combining seriated cups. In Strategies 1 and 2, a cup has a single role: it is either a stationary cup or a moving cup. In the most advanced strategy, Strategy 3, a cup or set of cups has a double role: it is first stationary and acted upon and then becomes a moving or acting cup. This dual role of a single element parallels the dual role of a grammatical element as both object and subject in an embedded sentence (e.g., "man" in "The man I love has a dog" or "I saw the man who lives there").

Maternal Teaching Strategies

The mothers' verbal and nonverbal teaching styles were also coded and characterized in the following ways.

Verbal comments were categorized as commands, statements, questions, or explanations, generally following the system used to characterize the verbal aspects of weaving instruction (Childs and Greenfield 1980). In line with the cultural importance of obedience from younger to older in Zinacanteco culture (see later section, "Commands in an Age-Ranked Society"), the overwhelming majority of maternal verbalizations were commands (see Table 3, Appendix A, for percentages).

The nonverbal styles were divided into three types originally identified by Kaye (1977) in a study of six-month-old babies being taught a sensorimotor problem-solving task by their mothers. *Shape* was an instructional style in which task simplification predominated. *Show* was an instructional style in which demonstration and pointing were dominant. *Shove* was a style in which the mother moved the child's hand for him or her.

Like the teaching style of the mothers studied by Kaye in the United States, the Zinacanteco mothers' teaching style was sensitive to the developmental level of the child being taught. (Because task performance was so related to age, it was hard to tell from these results alone if the mother's sensitivity was to the child's *age* or *stage* of task performance; the results of our study of weaving instruction make stage the likely factor.) Shaping, or task simplification, predominated for the mothers of children using Strategy 1; it declined for each successive developmental level. Showing was most predominant for the mothers of children using Strategy 2; it declined somewhat for mothers of children initially using the most advanced strategy. Shoving did not predominate at any stage, but reached its height for children using Strategy 3 (see Table 4, Appendix A, for a quantitative analysis). Kaye (1977) had also found that shaping was used more by mothers in the United States whose babies had the poorest pretest performance. Having only two levels of task performance in his study, however, he did not find a differentiation of showing and shoving according to the child's developmental level.

Like Kaye (1977), we found that mothers often combined strategies and that the developmentally correlated strategy was not necessarily more successful. Nor did active teachers achieve more success than did passive ones. Success seemed more related to the child's age than to the mother's teaching. The role of maturationally based readiness is demonstrated by the fact that almost half of the oldest children who progressed from the pot to the subassembly strategy did so on the basis of a few practice trials, even before the mother began her instruction.

The fact that the Zinacanteco mothers showed the same type of developmental sensitivity as Euro-American mothers is striking, considering that this type of task and materials were so very foreign to the Zinacantecos and that a correspondence between mother's teaching style and child's developmental level was not reinforced in either country by more successful learning on the part of the child. These results suggest the hypothesis that the mother/teacher's sensitivity has some sort of built-in biological basis. In addition, there may be an innate foundation for the one difference that emerged between mothers in the United States and Zinacantán: Zinacanteco mothers were less often "shovers." This style difference seemed to reflect the innate Zinacanteco quality of low motoric assertiveness first displayed by newborns.

LATER COGNITIVE DEVELOPMENT AND LEARNING

Mirroring our findings with infant and toddler development, the striking result of our studies of later cognitive development was the appearance of the same sequences of development from age four to adolescence as one would expect in the United States or Europe. Whether the task was conceptual understanding or visual pattern representation, this finding was the same. In the area of conceptual understanding, we explored culturally central kinship concepts (Greenfield and Childs 1978) and the classification of culturally relevant flowers and culturally irrelevant rods (Greenfield 1974).

A Study of Kinship Concepts: Transcultural Patterns of Cognitive Development in Childhood and Adolescence

Our study was a developmental one, involving children and adolescents at three age levels: four and five, eight to ten, and thirteen to eighteen years old.

The procedure we used is presented in Appendix B.

We tested the effect of the structure of Zinacanteco kinship terminology as worked out in two componential analyses by Jane Collier (1969), as well as applying a system developed by Haviland and Clark (1974). None predicted our results. We also considered the impact of the Zinacanteco emphasis on age ranking, including the *bankilal/itz'inal* distinction. This factor also failed to predict the order of acquisition or the errors of our three age groups of subjects. In sum, the developmental pattern could not be attributed to any factor specific to the Zinacanteco culture.

We found that the youngest children were able to list their sibling group as young as we tested them. Because Zinacanteco households do not normally have cousins or unrelated children living in them, we do not know if, at this point, the child has the relational concept of common parentage or the more absolute concept of members of an age group living in the same household. Common parentage seems more likely, as siblings in Zinacanteco households can sometimes be old enough to be members of the next generation.

The next stage was the acquisition of the ability to discriminate sibling terms that differentiate males from females. One possible reason for the early acquisition of these conceptual dimensions, siblingship, and sex, suggested by the theoretical analysis of Hirschfeld (n.d.), is that they could have an innate basis in the child's conceptual apparatus. Our ability to rule out culture-specific factors affecting the pattern of development provides evidence in favor of this speculation.

At the same time, terminological differentiation of the sibling group involved the developmental process of decentration (movement away from egocentrism), a key element in Piagetian theory. This development is shown in Figure 2, where it can be seen that the children are able to answer ego-centered questions (e.g., "What is the name of your older sister?") before other-centered questions (e.g., asking the child to name his older brother's older sister), and that the ability to answer other-centered questions involving a reversal of perspective ("As for your younger brother Petul, what is the name of his older brother?" Answer: "Me.") develops last of all.

This developmental sequence is exactly that predicted by Piagetian theory. Having ruled out culture-specific factors as a causal influence, we may conclude that a genetically based program for human development, operating across a wide range of genetic and cultural variability, is responsible for this common pattern of cognitive development.

Although our questions were adapted to Zinacantán and differed in form from those of Piaget (1928), the ages for the final decentered stage agree with Piaget's age norms in Switzerland. A common rate, as well as a common sequence of development, indicates equivalent stimulation for this domain of knowledge in the two cultures. Given that Zinacanteco children seemed to master a more complex system of sibling terms at the same age as children in the United States, it is even possible that Zinacanteco culture was providing *greater* stimulation for the comprehension of kinship terms. This speculation fits with the greater importance of sibling relations in Zinacantán as compared with the United States.

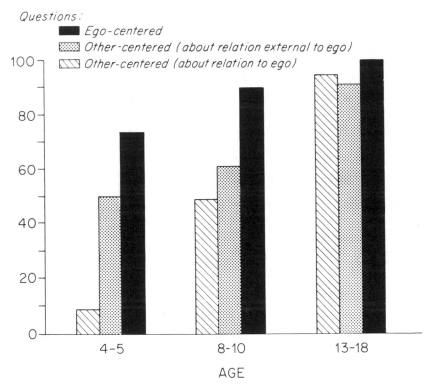

Figure 2. Percentage of different types of question answered correctly at different ages.

A Study of Object Classification:
Transcultural Patterns and Cultural Constraints

The same general agreement with stages and ages in the United States and Europe appeared in the second study of conceptual understanding, the object classification study. The stimuli are shown in Figure 3. A child might first be asked to tie the flowers into a red bouquet and a white bouquet. Then the bouquets were untied, and he or she had to sort by species. The last step was to make bouquets by length. In the second stage of the experiment, the child had to sort and re-sort the rods by color, circumference, and length. Different attribute orders were used for different children. Our subjects fell into the same three age groups as in the kinship study.

According to a Piagetian analysis, one would expect the ability to re-sort, an instance of two-way classification, to become fully developed in the second age group, eight-to-ten-year-olds; this age group did, in fact, show this ability, thus conforming to a Piagetian description of concrete operational thought.

FLOWERS

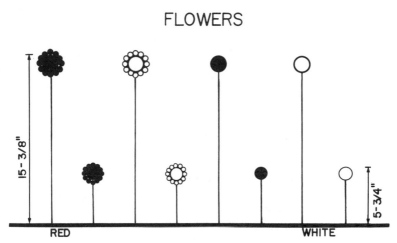

Flower length varied somewhat from day to day.
Lengths shown are illustrative.

RODS

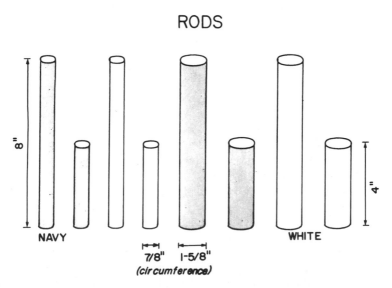

Figure 3. Flower and rod stimuli for object classification study.

From Piaget's scheme of ages and stages, one would have also predicted that the youngest group, age four and five, would be able to sort but not re-sort. With the rods, this prediction was confirmed: a majority of the four- and five-year-olds were able to sort, while only a third of the group could re-sort the rods. Sorting performance was not as good with the culturally more familiar flowers: less than half the youngest children could do the first sort, although, again, a third could also re-sort.

Neither the familiarity of bouquets of flowers nor experience as a flower seller helped performance. In fact, for the youngest children, performance was best with the unfamiliar, but perceptually simpler rods. Over the sample as a whole, re-sorting of the flowers seemed further hindered by the fact that it made no cultural sense to take apart perfectly "good" bouquets (sorted by species or length) to make "inferior" ones (sorted by color). Logical manipulation by the experimenters led Zinacanteco subjects far away indeed from the *batz'i* way. Miyamoto (1969) had found a parallel cultural constraint in his developmental study of concept development.

Once again, the general sequence of development was predicted by a universalistic theory, that of Piaget. Similarly, the rate in which this sequence progressed indicated fairly equivalent environmental stimulation in general, with one exception: Zinacanteco emphasis on the *batz'i* way was in conflict with and therefore hindered unlimited reclassification of the familiar flower stimuli.

Pattern Representation: Effects of Weaving Experience and Cognitive Development

In a visual pattern continuation task, we asked schooled and unschooled Zinacanteco children from four to eighteen years of age to use sticks in a frame to represent striped patterns. We found that pattern representation passed through stages of increasing differentiation and hierarchical integration, as posited by Werner's (1948) universalistic theory of development (Greenfield and Childs 1977).

Against this background of similarity, there again appeared a specific cultural effect related to our observations of Zinacanteco infants. One of our pattern continuation tasks could be treated by going beyond the given information. In this pattern, the child was shown a series of red and white stripes in the following configuration: 1 red, 1 white; 2 reds, 2 whites; 3 reds, 3 whites; 4 reds, 4 whites —a so-called growing pattern (Figure 4). Of the Zinacanteco children who did not go to school, no child at any age could complete this pattern by making it grow (Progression strategy, Figure 4)—the oldest unschooled children succeeded only in repeating it directly or in mirror image; these are valid, but more imitative, representations. In the Zinacanteco culture there was but one clearly prescribed way to do every task. Our task was most often treated the Zinacanteco way: the growing pattern was copied stick-by-stick. We see this behavior as fitting with the observations of Zinacanteco infants. They showed good imitative ability, but lack of motivation to go beyond the model and experiment with objects.

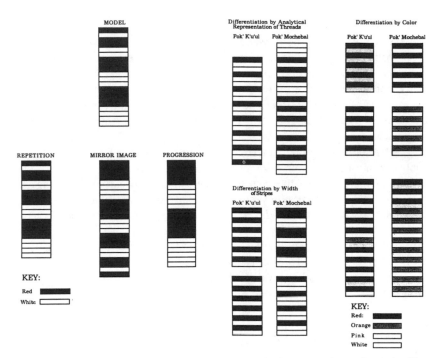

Figure 4. Model for growing pattern and three possible continuations.

Figure 5. Representations of two familiar woven patterns: *pok' k'u'ul* and *pok' mochebal*. *Upper left*: differentiation by analytical representation of threads, maintaining pattern configuration. *Lower left*: differentiation by width of stripes. *Right*: differentiation by color. (In each pair, the *pok' k'u'ul* representation appears on the left, the pok' mochebal representation on the right.)

We also used the pattern representation task to look for effects of an out-of-school learning experience—learning to weave—on cognitive processes. Among the older groups of subjects, some knew how to weave; others, being male, did not. Some of the males had, however, been to school. First the subjects were asked to represent the red-and-white striped patterns of two familiar woven garments—the *pok' mochebal,* worn by all females, and the *pok' k'u'ul,* worn by all males—by using wooden sticks in a frame to construct the designs.

There were interesting differences between the female weavers and the male nonweavers. A substantial proportion of the girls used the sticks accurately to represent the colors and configurations of the two patterns as they are actually constructed with threads (see Figure 5, upper left). In contrast, the boys generally differentiated the two patterns by using the sticks to convey the visual impression created by the garments at a distance, violating thread configurations and even colors in the process (see Figure 5, left lower and right). In the case of each group, the representation was closely related to the function the patterns served in the real world. Girls who are responsible for weaving the patterns must analyze their construction. Boys, who merely wear and observe the patterns in the clothing of others, are more concerned with a general overall impression. Cultural functions, differentiated by sex, influenced representation of familiar woven patterns.

The question of whether pattern skills would transfer from weaving to a new context was raised in our research. Subjects were asked to continue novel patterns, culminating in the growing pattern described earlier. Weaving experience was a detriment: nonweaving boys performed significantly better. For the girls, who were directly involved in the weaving patterns and had less contact with the outside, modern world, perhaps deviation from the "true way" was simply out of bounds. In our culture, we put a very positive value on transfer of skills to new situations. Transfer is a learning process that involves novelty and can lead to innovation. From the Zinacanteco point of view, therefore, transfer must have had a negative value.

The Teaching and Learning of Weaving:
An Example of Informal Education

In 1970 we made a video study of Zinacanteco girls learning to weave on back-strap looms (Childs and Greenfield 1980; Greenfield 1984).

Observation and Modeling. Learning by observation continued to be extremely important long after infancy in learning adult skills central to the culture. One obvious fact was that girls of eight to ten years of age, sitting down at a back-strap loom to weave their first piece of cloth, already knew a tremendous amount about weaving, although they had not yet taken part in the process. Leslie Haviland notes that, "The girl's mother or an older sister will have been watched carefully for some months by the young girl" (1978:215).

While the novice was weaving, an adult (most frequently the mother) intervened at difficult parts, often taking over from the beginning learner. In so doing, the adult simultaneously provided a model and got the job done with maximum efficiency. Thus, observation of another person continued to be critical, even at an older age. Like Zinacanteco newborns, the weaving learners are extremely attentive: first-time weavers watched more than they wove, and they attended to the model eighty-four percent of the time. Observation rather than experimentation constituted the crucial learning technique.

The learners also listened more than they spoke. With the exception of the one schooled girl in the sample, the rate of verbalization was very low. Once again, initiation of an interaction by a younger person was not part of Zinacanteco culture; as in nursing, the younger person's role was to respond.

As the weaver became more experienced, the role of modeling and imitation decreased. The teacher gradually withdrew from the active task role, and the learner increasingly participated, rather than merely watching the teacher. At the next stage there was an increase in cooperative activity with the teacher, as well as in independent weaving. Finally, somewhere around age thirteen to fifteen, and after many completed pieces of cloth, the teacher withdrew completely, and the experienced weaver was on her own. At this point, the Zinacanteco female had "graduated" from her informal education. As an experienced weaver, she now possessed a skill that was said to contribute to her marriageability (Trosper 1967).

Shaping. In harmony with the strategy used with children six or seven years younger in the nesting cup experiment, "shaping," or task simplification, was used with the most novice weavers: they were first given small items requiring less strength to weave. This conclusion is supported by Leslie Haviland's (1978) observation in the same hamlet of Nabenchauk that girls generally started by weaving small bags.

Scaffolding: The Match Between Teacher Techniques and Learner Needs. The teacher's sensitive adjustment of teaching techniques to skill level and task difficulty was evident in other responses as well. In general outline and even in some specific features, it is reminiscent of Zinacanteco mothers' adjustment of teaching techniques to their children's skill level in the nesting cups task. Because girls start to weave at a variety of ages, our results made it clear that the adjustment was based on learner skill level, not chronological age.

Commands in an Age-Ranked Society. Commands played an important role in the informal education of Zinacanteco children. "A Zinacanteco parent's highest praise of his child is 'He obeys well, he works well'" (Blanco and Chodorow 1964). A younger person is obliged to carry out the commands of an older one (Cancian 1963). Cancian's comparative study in Zinacantán and Cambridge showed that, in Zinacantán, mothers commanded children more frequently than in the United States, while Zinacanteco children gave direction to mothers less often than children in the United States (Cancian 1971a). This comparative finding shows how the hierarchical structure of Zinacanteco society, with its emphasis on the senior/junior principle, was reflected in the very nature of parent-child interaction.

Normally commands are considered in terms of their power connotations; in Zinacantán their role in informal instruction was also important. As we saw in the nesting cup situation, commands dominated mothers' verbal strategies for teaching very young children how to nest cups. Similarly, commands dominated the verbalization from teacher to first-time novice weaver, constituting ninety-one percent of the teacher's verbal output.

Commands, however, declined dramatically in proportion to the learner's experience. By the time a learner had already woven two to four pieces of cloth, commands constituted only about half of the teacher's output. Statements had become quite important, though explanations continued to be virtually nonexistent. Indeed, it was the paucity of explanations that led Leslie Haviland to conclude that "rarely does anyone verbalize the method" (Haviland 1978:215, personal communication, October, 1988).

FROM BIRTH TO MATURITY IN ZINACANTAN

Because a major implication of the junior-senior principle in the Zinacanteco family is the obligation of the younger person to obey the older, the weaving "teacher" had the weight of the culture behind her commands. The specialized use of commands as a teaching technique for novices comes out when we compare our data with that of Francesca Cancian (1963), who studied family interaction in Zinacantán across a wide range of household situations. In her data the proportion of commands uttered from mother to child was much lower than for our weavers of comparable age, indicating the specialized function of commands in helping novices to accomplish a new task.

Obeyed commands not only teach, they also get the task done. As Greenfield and Lave (1982) and Wertsch, Minick, and Arns (1984) have pointed out, informal education often occurs as a byproduct of task accomplishment. This is very much the case for Zinacanteco weaving education (Haviland 1978, personal communication, October, 1988).

If the *bankilal- itz' inal* or senior/junior principle operates as precisely as Vogt (1969b) claims, then we could predict that the tendency to carry out commands would be a function of *how* junior the "commandee" was to the "commander." We reanalyzed some of Francesca Cancian's (1963) thesis data to test out this hypothesis, looking at the ratio of obedience to disobedience. As predicted, children were most obedient to their grandmother, next most obedient to their mother, and least obedient to their older sister: as age span between junior and senior increased, so did obedience. However, at worst, in the case of the older sister, children still obeyed almost twice as often as they disobeyed.

Development intervened to modify this relationship between obedience and junior-senior distance, however. Although the distance is less for an older girl than for a younger girl vis-à-vis her mother, obedience was more, not less, frequent. With development, a more collaborative and responsible relationship seemed to develop. The number of commands went down in this relationship (Cancian 1963); at the same time, the older daughter did more self-initiated chores (Blanco and Chodorow 1964). Our weaving study also showed an increase in initiation as the learner became older and more experienced. Completing this picture of a relation that becomes increasingly collaborative with age, we found *no* instance in Francesca Cancian's (1963) data in which the mother failed to obey directions from the grandmother, her own mother.

Reinforcement. We explored the use of verbal reinforcement in the teaching of weaving. Blanco and Chodorow (1964) had reported very little verbal reinforcement for household chores, with very occasional rewards. In our weaving data, there was also very occasional verbal reinforcement; almost all of it was negative (e.g., "You don't know how."). More frequently, reinforcement took the form of saying something to another person within earshot of the learner. Again, this was almost always negative. Despite the disagreement with Blanco and Chodorow's findings in this respect, the dominance of negative rather than positive reinforcement, which we found in weaving instruction, accorded well with the broader cultural pattern of genres of ritualized insults identified by Bricker (1973b).

We also wonder if there might not be a connection between this negative evaluative approach to teaching and the self-disparagement that occurs in Zinacanteco ritual prayers, for example:

Grant pardon to my lowly back,
Grant pardon to my humble side,
To me, who am Thy lowly dog,
To me, who am Thy humble pig,
To me, Thy dunce,
To me, Thy fool,
[Dedication of a new house; Laughlin 1980:226].

Perhaps the negative evaluation from others during childhood becomes incorporated into a negative self-image in adulthood. In the absence of psychology, religion may then provide a ritualized way of dealing with a culturally induced psychological problem.

Failure-Free Learning, Observation/Imitation, and the Maintenance of Tradition. Perhaps the most striking feature of the ensemble of weaving instruction was that it constituted failure-free and relatively errorless learning. Most likely because of observing models of weaving expertise at earlier points in time, the novice weaver already looked very proficient when she sat down to weave for the very first time, and the teacher always intervened when the going got tough, thus preventing errors. This method contrasted with the trial-and-error methods of learning weaving observed in Cambridge, Massachusetts (by Greenfield), Akwete, Nigeria (by Lisa Aronson), and in highland Guatemala (by Maria and James Loucky).

In seeming contrast with our formal study, Leslie Haviland describes the role of the instructor as being "to correct mistakes and to untangle problems as they occur" (1978:215). During our formal observations, potential mistakes were most often prevented before they became problems. Therefore, we saw error prevention on the part of the weaving "teachers," rather than the error correction mentioned by Haviland (1978). However, the difference may be more apparent than real. Haviland (personal communication, October, 1988) noted that, unlike our more formal videotaped observations, a weaving learner did not always have her mother or other "teacher" available to watch her. Hence, the presence of our camera probably elicited more intense watchfulness and more successful error prevention by the "teachers" than would take place in everyday life. Nonetheless, the process of error prevention through "teacher" intervention was also observed by Haviland and should, at the very least, represent a cultural ideal.

Haviland (1978) also noted that the small items woven by beginners were full of mistakes. Weaving "teachers," under the constraints of other household work in everyday life, prevented failure but allowed small errors that affected the looks but not the function of the woven items. Still, these small mistakes were a far cry from the full-scale trial-and-error experimentation observed in the Cambridge back-strap loom weaving class.

In a trial-and-error approach, it is always possible that the learner will discover new patterns or methods. For the Zinacantecos, however, there was but one correct method, the *batz' i* or true one, and there were only three patterns woven for clothing, one worn by all men and the other two worn by all women. (The top left of Figure 5 gives a good sense of the two major patterns, the *pok' k'u'ul,* for men, and the *pok' mochebal,* for women.) Learning by observing and imitating a model was a method for exact transmission of these culturally defined patterns. These patterns then constituted the foundation of the culturally defined or *batz' i* manner of dressing. The power of this norm is revealed in the following anecdote: Once we asked a Zinacanteco girl why some Zinacanteco people who passed by were dressed in different clothing. The reply was, "they don't know how to dress."

Conformity and Individuality. Despite the Zinacanteco emphasis on conformity to tradition, there was still room for individuality. As in our culture, individual personality was expressed within culturally defined limits; the limits were simply narrower in Zinacantán. In the arena of weaving and textiles, for example, each of the standard woven patterns had variants within its general configuration, and woven clothing was trimmed with embroidery defined as to location but freely variable as to pattern. Leslie Haviland writes: "Far more than any other activity weaving gives expression to a Zinacanteco woman's personality. Even if, to the untutored eye, the degree of variation in Zinacanteco textiles is so minute as to speak more loudly of the narrow conventions of style within which it is contained than of the individuality of which it is the manifestation, it remains a clear signal of personality to the Zinacanteco beholder" (1978:207).

Contrast with "the American Way." Our analysis of the implicit differences between instruction and learning in Zinacantán and the United States was dramatically validated by Marta Turok's (1972) description of the conflicting cultural assumptions that were revealed when she, a Harvard student, began learning how to weave from a Zinacanteco teacher:

> When I began taking back-strap loom weaving from Tonik, an older Zinacanteco woman, I became increasingly restless, when after two months of what I termed observation and what she termed learning, I had not touched the loom. Many times she would verbally call my attention to an obscure technical point, or when she would finish a certain step she would say, "You have seen me do it. Now you have learned." I wanted to shout back, "No, I haven't! Because I have not tried it myself." However, it was she who decided when I was ready to touch the loom, and my initial clumsiness brought about comments such as, "Cabeza de pollo! (chicken head) You have not watched me! You have not learned!" [Turok 1972:1-2].

This description affirms the contrasting role of observation and active experimentation in the two cultures. It also reveals that relatively errorless learning did not merely "happen"; it was expected. Finally, Turok's description confirms the tendency toward negative rather than positive reinforcement in informal instruction.

THE INFLUENCE OF SCHOOLING AND GENDER

In all of the studies of cognitive development in middle childhood and adolescence, there were samples of schooled as well as unschooled subjects. In the study of learning to weave, there was one schoolgirl in the sample. What difference, if any, did schooling make? First, it is necessary to state that all schooling occurs in Spanish, a language that is not spoken at home by the children. Second, Spanish introduces reading and writing into an otherwise oral culture.

On the basis of Greenfield's (1966, 1972a; Greenfield and Bruner 1969; Greenfield et al. 1966) previous research in Senegal , it was expected that schooling would have a large and positive impact on cognitive development as measured in an experimental situation. However, this was not the case. For example, there were no differences between schooled and unschooled adolescents in the development of skills in classifying familiar and unfamiliar objects. In the development of kinship concepts, the only difference favored unschooled children: unschooled eight-to-ten-year-olds were, more often than schooled, able to answer kinship questions in which the subject had to view a kin relation to self from the perspective of another person. As in object classification, schooling made no difference at all in the development of pattern representation.

Why should schooling not have been an advantage to overall cognitive development, as measured by our tasks? There are a number of possibilities, some lying in the tasks, some in the nature of schooling, others in the Zinacanteco concept of intelligence, and still others in the Zinacanteco nature itself.

As for the tasks, all the major cognitive tasks given to school-age subjects were highly structured, unambiguous, and left little room for alternative cultural interpretations. In addition, a number of the major tasks—kinship, flower sorting, representations of woven patterns—were based on Zinacanteco culture. Indeed, traditional Zinacanteco education was *more* effective than school-based education in developing decentered comprehension of sibling relations, a culturally central domain for Zinacantecos.

Only one task—classifying rods—was culturally irrelevant. Yet among the Baole of the Ivory Coast, Dasen (1984) found that the logical ability involved in such tasks is correlated with parental judgments of a child's respect and obedience at home, qualities also highly valued by the Zinacantecos. Therefore, even this seemingly irrelevant task may somehow have tapped traits considered culturally desirable for Zinacanteco children.

As for the nature of schooling, the local schools went through third grade only and were staffed by non-Tzotzil speakers, many of whom had not even completed high-school level teacher training (Trosper 1967). While differences in

Senegal between school and unschooled children appeared as early as the first grade, the predominantly Wolof children (also from an oral culture) were taught primarily by African teachers, bilingual in Wolof and French. Finally, among the Zinacanteco adolescent subjects, many were undoubtedly no longer in school and making little use of their school learning (Trosper 1967).

As for definitions of intelligence, all Zinacantecos agreed that school makes a child intelligent (Trosper 1967). Although far from definitive, this agreement could mean that the indigenous definition of intelligence was in harmony with what was taught in school: this is not the case in many African cultures (e.g., Wober 1974; Dasen 1984). For example, among the Baole, some people saw school intelligence as distinct or in conflict with the indigenous concept of intelligence (Dasen 1984; Dasen et al. 1985). Therefore, it could be that, unlike several African societies, schools in Zinacantán were developing qualities of mind that were already valued and encouraged in the Zinacantecos' informal education. This point must, however, remain speculative until such time as someone investigates the Zinacanteco, as well as the Wolof, concept of intelligence.

The final factor, Zinacanteco nature itself, relates to the excellent attentional qualities shown by Zinacanteco newborns. Insofar as infant visual attention (especially habituation) predicts later cognitive development (Bornstein and Sigman 1984), perhaps the "head start" provided by the Zinacantecos' innate attentional skills, in combination with their traditional informal education, suffices to bring children to the level of cognitive development expected in our culture, overshadowing any possible effects of relatively poor quality formal education.

Despite the similarities in the major patterns and rates of cognitive development between schooled and unschooled children in Zinacantán, schooling did, nevertheless, produce some differences. The differences were particularly interesting because they seemed to fit in with Zinacanteco adults' fears about the effects of schooling on their young people and, most important, potentially interfered with the maintenance of cultural continuity.

One very common Zinacanteco fear was that children, especially girls, would stop obeying their parents (Trosper 1967). While we do not have direct evidence on this point, there was an interesting piece of indirect evidence. If we consider obedience to be a particular manifestation of taking a passive role in relation to an authority figure, then another manifestation of this role was the general conversational dominance of teacher over learner during weaving instruction. The one girl in our weaving sample who had been to school was an exception in this regard: she was almost *four* times as active verbally in relation to the teacher as an unschooled girl with equivalent weaving experience. Schooling may make the *itz' inal* (junior) member of a pair more dominant, in this way weakening cultural norms.

Anxiety about cultural continuity was expressed in the universal Zinacanteco fear that a child who had been to school might decide to leave Zinacantán (Trosper 1967), thus breaking his or her ties to the culture. Indeed, literate, schooled Zinacantecos participating in a study of cultural norms considered "wants to be a non-Indian" to be an attribute of good behavior (Cancian 1971b).

One important threat to cultural continuity is to go beyond the model provided by an authority figure to produce a novel result. Among our experiments, there was one task, continuation of the "growing pattern" in the pattern-representation study, in which this was possible. In the "progression" strategy, the subject transcends the model to produce novel elements. It seems significant that the only Zinacanteco subjects who used this strategy were boys who had attended school. Here is an indication that schooling posed a threat to cultural continuity by influencing students to go beyond the models presented by authority figures.

Another important aspect of cultural continuity was the distinctive education of girls and boys, foretold in the birth ritual described at the beginning of this essay. But a key characteristic of school, one which we generally take for granted, is that, in school, boys and girls are generally (in principle if not always in practice) taught the *same* rather than *different* things. Indeed, we did find evidence that boys, as a result of going to school, acquired some cultural knowledge (analytic representation of Zinacanteco woven patterns) that, without school, was reserved for females. Thus when it came to representing woven patterns, using sticks in a frame, the oldest schoolboys resembled the female weavers, rather than the unschooled boys of similar age, in taking the analytic approach to the task described earlier (and shown at the top, left of Figure 5).

Given the Zinacantecos' concern with differentiating the education of boys and girls, it is noteworthy that, where differences in rate of cognitive development were found in our studies, it was gender rather than schooling that made the difference. In both cases where a gender difference was found, the tasks were culturally irrelevant ones—(1) sorting rods and (2) representing culturally novel patterns. In each case, boys developed more rapidly or farther than girls, while the performance of schooled boys did not differ from that of their unschooled male peers. These results probably reflect the fact that, in traditional Zinacanteco informal education, Zinacanteco males were given broader experience in the world outside Zinacantán and were expected to develop the more general problem-solving skills useful in economic transactions with the *ladino* world.

THEMES FROM BIRTH TO MATURITY IN ZINACANTAN

Several themes anticipated at birth appeared repeatedly in these developmental studies.

Transcultural Nature of Developmental Stages and Adult Behaviors

The sequence of behavioral milestones exhibited by Zinacanteco babies are indicative of a universal, maturationally based plan of infant development. In the nesting cup task, Zinacanteco children showed the same developmental sequence of strategies as United States children. Given their lack of familiarity with toys, this sequence must also have had a maturational foundation. In teaching their children how to nest the cups, Zinacanteco mothers, like United States mothers, adapted their teaching strategies in relation to the skill level of their children, not to the success of one strategy over another.

Comprehension of kinship terms showed the same developmental process of decentration posited by Piagetian theory, despite our different predictions based on the complexity and cultural importance of the Zinacanteco sibling system. Given that factors in the cultural environment cannot be responsible for the sequence, a maturationally guided plan of development must once again be the key. Similarly, the children in the classification study were in the same stages at the same ages as United States and European children. In the pattern representation tasks, stages of development followed the sequence of increasing differentiation and hierarchical integration predicted by Werner's (1948) universalistic theory. In the weaving study, teachers showed the same sensitivity to the skill level of the learners that appeared in the nesting cup study, adjusting both the difficulty of the task and their teaching techniques. This pattern of results has also been found in the United States (e.g., Kaye 1977; Greenfield 1984).

Physical Activity Level

The low level of physical activity apparent in Zinacanteco infants at birth was further reinforced by the practice of swaddling. Nursing at the slightest sign of movement further reduced motor activity. Children tested in the first year of life, when compared to United States norms, showed a delay in the development of motor skills that was greater than their slight delay in mental skill development. A low level of motor response at birth was consonant with a small amount of fine motor (eye-hand) experimentation during the first year of life. There was additional evidence of low motoric activity in older children who sat observing for long periods when learning to weave and in adults in the nesting cup task, where mothers infrequently used the more physically aggressive teaching strategy of "shoving" the baby's hand.

A low level of physical activity was the norm in Zinacanteco adulthood. Restricted motion was adaptive for the Zinacanteco mother who nearly always had a baby on her back and, during her childbearing years, must perform work under this condition (Haviland 1978). "Never a people given to wild gesticulation even at their most excited, Zinacanteco physical restraint is most marked in the behavior of women" (Haviland 1978:243). Quite astonishingly, Leslie Haviland's description of female body movement is remarkably reminiscent of Brazelton, Robey, and Collier's (1969) observations of Zinacanteco newborns: "Feminine body movement is highly controlled and carried out in a narrow circumference. Women keep their upper arms tight to their bodies and rarely raise their hands or arms over their heads. . . . In short, Zinacanteco women never engage in sweeping, expansive gestures, nor do they allow their limbs to stray outward from their bodies, whether in work or in fun" (Haviland 1978:243). This is not merely the way Zinacanteco women *actually* move, this is also the way they are *supposed* to move. Creating striking ontogenetic continuity, an innate newborn behavior ultimately becomes a culturally valued adult behavior.

Response versus Individual Initiative

Zinacanteco newborns, quiet and alert, attentively observed their surroundings, laying the foundation for later observational learning. They did not cry intensely or flail about, demanding that someone react to them. The pattern of response versus initiation that first appeared when the newborn received the tools that symbolized its predetermined role in Zinacanteco society was reflected again and again in the Zinacanteco child's later development.

Infants showed little interest in playing with an object beyond imitation. In frequent nursing, infants found their needs satisfied probably before they were aware of them and could take the initiative to express them. Children playing with nesting cups did not hang on to them in an egocentric fashion as year-old American children did. They developed investment in objects later and seemed to have less interest in manipulating them on their own.

We had expected children who were asked to classify and reclassify flowers and rods to find the culturally familiar flowers easier to work with. This was not the case. We asked them to sort flowers in ways that flowers were not ordinarily sorted, and they, influenced by the Zinacanteco concept of there being only one true, or *batz' i,* way to do things, found the familiar flowers harder to sort than the unfamiliar rods.

This lack of ability to innovate also appeared in the pattern representation study. The "growing" pattern was treated imitatively by all the unschooled children, and the weaving girls had less success than nonweaving boys in continuing all the unusual (i.e., not Zinacanteco) patterns. Boys, and schooled boys in particular, showed the influence of the outside world in their superior ability to transfer skills and to treat the tasks analytically. That schooling could promote individual innovation was indicated most dramatically by the fact that, in representing culturally novel patterns, the only subjects to transcend the model and take a "progressive" approach to the "growing pattern" had been to school.

Like Zinacanteco newborns, the girls in the weaving study showed a remarkable ability to observe an adult attentively for long periods of time. They did not often initiate conversation. Commands from teacher to learner were of primary importance as a teaching technique, illustrating the Zinacanteco principle of senior/junior, or *bankilal/itz' inal.* There was no encouragement of individual initiative through trial-and-error learning.

Behind this predominance of response over initiative on the part of Zinacanteco children lies the traditional culture of Zinacantán with its *batz' i* way of doing things and its emphasis on the *bankilal/itz' inal* relationship. Cultures can change, however.

Actual and Potential Effects of Culture Change. Now, in the 1980s, fifteen to twenty years after the developmental studies were done, Zinacantecos own and operate many of the trucks used for commerce and transportation in the highlands around San Cristóbal de las Casas (Cancian 1985). Zinacanteco culture is currently becoming more entrepreneurial and technological.

Although child-rearing practices are very resistant to change, we would predict that methods of early socialization would very gradually come to place relatively greater emphasis on innovation, individual initiative, and manipulation of objects, and relatively less on maintenance of tradition. Going one step further, we predicted that new methods of weaving instruction would follow and would lead, in turn, to new woven patterns and constant pattern innovation. The prediction about novel patterns has been borne out; new woven patterns are now rife in Zinacantán (Frank Cancian, personal communication 1987). It only remains to return to study the instructional process and patterns of senior-junior interaction to see if there has been further disruption in the beautiful continuity of the traditional way.

CONCLUSIONS

Our set of studies may offer what is to date the most comprehensive view of cognitive development, learning, and cultural values in a nontechnological culture. Such a variety of experimental and observational methods across such a broad age range is, to our knowledge, unique in the literature.

From a theoretical point of view, these themes show, on the one hand, that it is possible to find continuity in developmental style from birth to maturity and that the source of this style continuity lies in a specific cultural context—in this case, the culture of Zinacantán. On the other hand, we see that culturally defined style occurs within the framework of transcultural patterns of child development and maternal behavior. The force behind these transcultural patterns of *child* development would seem to be genetically guided patterns of maturation. At the very least, the transcultural similarities in *maternal* behavior must reflect the capacity of our species to adapt to the functional requirements of an instructional situation.

We seem to have found a new answer to the old question concerning the relationship between culture-specific and universal forces in development. Universal forces—a maturational genetic program supported by cultural universals of basic care and socialization—fuel the *basic patterns of qualitative developmental change*. Culture-specific forces, in contrast, shape the *stylistic* aspects of these patterns, providing continuity in behavioral style across diverse developmental stages.

Our themes of cultural continuity could become visible only through a close analysis of the cultural context from the perspective of its members. Here we were uniquely fortunate: first, in being able to plan our studies on the foundation of ten previous years of ethnographic fieldwork; second, to have been given cultural training and colleagueship by Zinacanteco associates and American researchers experienced in Zinacantán (including members of our own team); and, now, to have twenty-five years of multidisciplinary study of Zinacantán upon which to base our cultural analysis and interpretations. All of this was made possible by the Harvard Chiapas Project, founded and continuously directed by Professor Evon Z. Vogt, to whom this volume is dedicated.

ACKNOWLEDGMENTS. As a pediatrician, Vogtie opened my eyes to how deep cultural differences can be and to the variability in human behavior. He had the vision to encourage interdisciplinary collaboration and provided a unique opportunity to develop the Brazelton Neonatal Assessment Scale. He has been a dear friend ever since.

T.B. Brazelton

At a time when my cross-cultural research had been cut off by family responsibilities (a baby, a three-year-old, and a husband still in medical training), the context provided by Vogtie and the Harvard Chiapas Project made meaningful short-term cross-cultural research possible, allowing me to continue in the field of cross-cultural developmental psychology.

I am particularly grateful that Vogtie gave me Carla Childs, then a junior at Radcliffe, as an assistant. She was an experienced fieldworker in Zinacantán with excellent Tzotzil skills and a strong interest in child development and education. The research could not have been done without her, and our friendship made the fieldwork a great pleasure.

Now, more than ever, I appreciate Berry Brazelton's invitation to go to Chiapas to follow up his exciting and challenging research with Zinacanteco babies. The task he set—to place Zinacanteco infancy in a broader developmental and cultural framework—has finally been achieved in the present essay.

But Berry's contribution was far more than a scientific one. If I had not had my pediatricians with me in Chiapas (Berry one month, J. Robey the other), I would never have dared to go into the field with a baby who had been seriously ill most of his short life.

I am most appreciative to Victoria Bricker and Gary Gossen, whose (heroic) efforts as editors stimulated this essay and enabled me to work once again with Carla Childs and Berry Brazelton.

I am grateful for the careful tending that Nan and Vogtie gave to the Chiapas Project archives over the years and for Vogtie's generosity in making the archives—a unique and precious resource—available to me for this paper.

My special thanks to Leslie Haviland for sharing her thesis and, especially, her incisive unpublished observations. Thanks also to Francesca Cancian for help in tracking down a paper missing from the Chiapas Project archives, to Laura Weiss for graphic illustrations and help with manuscript preparation, and to Pierre Dasen for comments on an earlier version of the paper.

Manuscript preparation was carried out with the aid of the UCLA Gold Shield Faculty Prize.

P.M. Greenfield

Most of the important learning in my undergraduate experience took place as a result of my association with the Harvard Chiapas Project. As a sophomore, I felt lucky to be chosen, but I really had no idea where that first forty-eight hour bus ride would lead. I found myself not only in the world of Zinacantán, but also in the equally fascinating world of the ideas and personalities of my Harvard associates. Vogtie and Nan made me feel as welcome as if I had always been there. My interest in other cultures was deepened and made more specific. I was thrilled to be able to take on the challenge of learning to use a new and strange language. The other researchers taught me the value of examining an idea from different viewpoints. My enjoyable and enduring partnership with Patricia Greenfield introduced me to the field of developmental psychology and forced me to think more rigorously.

I am thankful to Vogtie for giving me the opportunity to participate in the Harvard Chiapas Project, and to both Vogtie and Nan for making my years with the project such a warm and rewarding experience.

C.P. Childs

We would also like to express our collective thanks to George Collier and John Robey, who worked with Brazelton, to Xun Pavlu, who served as the assistant to Greenfield and Childs, and to Xunka Pavlu for her unfailing hospitality and kindness during Greenfield and Childs' work in Nabenchauk. We are especially grateful to all of the Zinacanteco families who participated in our studies.

Finally, we want to acknowledge Nan Vogt's important contribution. Her warmth and generous hospitality—combined with extraordinary skills in creating festive occasions for people to come together—provided the chemistry that made the Harvard Chiapas Project work.

END NOTES

[1] "The tutelary gods are ancestral gods who watch over the town. The 'meeting place' is Calary, the principal shrine overlooking Zinacantán Center" (Laughlin 1980:161).

[2] This role was further reinforced in early childhood when "girls have toy looms for make-believe weaving, and little grinding stones and pots for making tortillas and carrying water" (Cancian 1963:63-64).

[3] Differing slightly from this observation, note that Anton Teratol had been clothed *before* the ritual proceedings, according to his father's description.

[4] Actually, male's older brother versus male's younger brother.

APPENDIX A
ZINACANTECO NESTING CUP STUDY

Because this study has not previously been published, details of method and results are presented in this appendix.

METHOD

Subjects

The participants in our study were thirty Zinacanteco mother/child pairs from the hamlet of Nabenchauk. The age of the children ranged from nine to seventy months. Age was assessed by asking for age in years and finding out the month of birth. There were sixteen girls and fourteen boys in the sample. Analyses of the manipulative behavior of the babies and the nonverbal teaching strategies of the mothers were based on the full sample. Analyses of the verbal teaching strategies of the mothers were based on a subsample of eighteen mothers for whom complete Tzotzil transcripts were available.

Procedure

Testing took place in an empty Zinacanteco house. The baby or child was seated with the mother on the floor of the house. (This is the normal position for Zinacanteco women.) The experimenter (Childs) was seated on the floor facing mother and child. A recorder (Greenfield) coded nonverbal responses and audio recorded verbal dialogue.

First phase (pretest). In the familiarization portion of the procedure, the experimenter laid out five blue plastic nesting cups of different sizes ranging from 1 7/16 inches in diameter to 2 5/8 inches in two rows in a nonseriated order. She then said to the mother: *Ak' o takinuk schi' uk ixtolal, schiuk basoetik, lavole,* "Let your child play with the toy, with the cups." For the first trial in the pretest, the experimenter then said to the mother: *Ta ora ak' o spas stuk. Mu xachanubtas. Mu xavak' be yil,* "Now let him/her do it alone. Don't teach. Don't show him/her." The experimenter then demonstrated the subassembly method of nesting the cups (see Figure 1) and said to the child: *Tahinan schi' uk ixtolal, schi' uk basoetik,* "Play with the toy, with the cups."

The concept was that the nature and extent of the child's imitation would reveal his or her stage of cognitive processing or comprehension of the demonstration.

The second trial of the pretest was the same as the first, except that the experimenter gave the child the largest cup to start with. The point here was to see whether the child was able to put down the cup and start with a smaller acting cup required to seriate the cups or whether the child would make an egocentric identification of cup and hand.

Trial 3 consisted of a repetion of Trial 1. Trial 3 was the baseline from which the impact of maternal teaching was assessed. Trial 3 was also compared with performance on Trials 1 and 2 to assess the impace of practice without teaching.

If in any part of the pretest or posttest, the child succeeded in seriating all five cups, the experimenter gave him/her a sixth blue cup, intermediate in size between the third and the fourth cup, saying: *Tik' o li hun basoe. K' elo mi x' och,* "Stick in this one cup. See if it goes in."

Second phase (teaching). The experimenter then introduced the teaching phase of the experiment as follows to the mother: *Chakak' be avil. Chahchanubtas. Paso yech,* "I'll show you, I'll teach you. Do it this way."

The experimenter then demonstrated the subassembly method, handed the mother the smallest cup, and let her do it. The experimenter corrected any errors. After the mother got the cups together in the demonstrated manner one time, with or without help, her practice was stopped. The experimenter then said: *Chanubtaso lavole,* "Teach your child." The experimenter took her cue from the mother as to when to end the teaching.

Third phase (posttest). For Trial 1 of the posttest, the cups were put back on the floor and the experimenter said: *Ak' o spas stuk. Mu xavalbe,* "Let him/her do it alone, don't speak to him/her."

In Trial 2 of the posttest, the experimenter demonstrated the subassembly method and laid out the cups, as in the first part of the pretest, instructing the mother as follows: *Mu xachanubtas. Mu xavalbe,* "Don't teach. Don't speak to him/her." Then the experimenter said to the child: *Tahinan schi' uk ixtolal schi' uk basoetik,* "Play with the toy, with the cups."

Table 1

Percentage of Children at Different Ages Showing Investment in First Cup[1]

	Months	
9-15	21-30	35-70
(N=5)	(N=8)	(N=15)
20%	62.5%	87%

---

[1] This measure is based on Trials 1 and 2 of the pretest. If on either trial, the first cup touched became the moving or "acting cup," this was counted as egocentric identification or investment. On Trial 1, the child chose the first cup; on Trial 2 , the experimenter handed the child the biggest cup to start with. If the child tried to use this cup as the moving or "acting" cup, such a move would be incompatible with seriation. It was planned to use only this trial as a measure of egocentrism, but very few of the youngest children responded at all to this situation.

Table 2

Percentage of Children at Different Ages Utilizing Different Dominant Strategies in Trials 1 and 2 of the Pretest

TYPES OF STRATEGIES

MONTHS	Strategy 1 (Pairing Method)	Strategy 2 (Pot Method)	Strategy 3 (Subassembly Method)
9 - 1 5 (N=5)	80%	20%	0%
2 1 - 3 0 (N=8)	0%	87.5%	12.5%
3 5 - 7 0 (N=15)	0%	93%	7%

Table 3

Mothers' Verbal Instructions
Average Percentages of Different Types of Verbalization[1]

MOTHERS' VERBALIZATIONS

AGE OF CHILDREN IN MONTHS	Commands	Other Types of Verbalization (Statements, Questions, Explanations)
9 - 1 5	90%	10%
2 1 - 3 0	89%	11%
3 5 - 7 0	87%	13%

[1] The percentages in the table are based on the verbalizations of 18 mothers: four mothers of 9-15 month olds, five mothers of 21-30 month olds, and nine mothers of 35-70 months olds. Due to equipment problems, we lacked auditory records for the other mothers who participated.

Table 4

Percentage of Mothers Using Different Dominant Teaching Strategies with Children Utilizing Different Dominant Manipulative Strategies

	MOTHER STRATEGY		
CHILD STRATEGY	**Shape**	**Show**	**Shove**
Strategy 1 (Pairing) (N= 4)	75%	25%	0%
Strategy 2 (Pot) (N=18)	41.7%[1]	52.8%[1]	5.5%
Strategy 3[2] (Subassembly) (N=3)	11%[3]	44.3%[3]	44.3%[3]

[1] One mother used "shape" and "show" equally; she contributed one-half to the raw score for each category.

[2] Includes children producing equal mixtures of Strategies 2 and 3.

[3] One mother used "shape", "show", and "shove" equally; she contributed one-third to the raw score for each category.

APPENDIX B

Before asking our subjects any question, we elicited family trees from their mothers which gave the names of all the household members and showed the kinship relationships between them. Here is the sibling portion of a sample family tree.

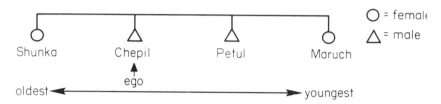

Figure 6. Sibling portion of a sample family tree.

We used these family trees to compose a personal set of questions for each subject. Because we wanted to test comprehension rather than production of kinship terms, we phrased our questions so that they included the kinship terms and required one or more proper names for an answer. Zinacantecos use six sibling terms: older brother of a boy, younger brother of a boy, older brother of a girl, younger sister of a boy, older sister of a girl or boy, and younger sibling of a girl.

Our questions using Zinacanteco sibling terms were of two types: "ego-centered" and "other-centered." Ego-centered questions concerned the relationship of an individual subject to his siblings. For the sample family tree above we would compose three such "ego-centered" questions for the boy Chepil, for example:

Tzotzil:	K'usi	sbi	lavixe?
English (literal):	What	his-name	the-your-older sister?
English (free):	What is the name of your older sister?		
Answer:	Xunka		

For the same sample family tree we would address seven such "other-centered" questions to Chepil, using each of his three siblings in turn as the reference point, for example:

Tzotzil:	A	laviz'in	Petul
English (literal):	As for	the-your-younger brother	Petul
	k'usi	sbi	lisvixe?
	what	his-name	the-his-older sister?

English (free):   As for your younger brother Petul, what is the name of his older sister?

Answer: Xunka

For the sample tree, three of the "other-centered" questions would involve a reversal of perspective. The answer would contain the name of the subject himself, for example:

Q: As for your younger brother Petul, what is the name of his older brother?
A: Chepil (or me)

We asked all of the questions in the singular form, even when a complete correct answer included more than one person. After each response, we asked subjects a follow-up question like the following:

Tzotzil: Mi   oy   to   svix?
English (literal): ?   there is   still   his-older sister?
English (free):   Does he have another older sister?

We repeated this question until the subject had told us that there were no more.

LIFE, DEATH, AND APOTHEOSIS OF A CHAMULA PROTESTANT LEADER: BIOGRAPHY AS SOCIAL HISTORY

Gary H. Gossen
University at Albany, SUNY

FORETHOUGHTS

Miguel Kaxlan, a Chamula Tzotzil, was born in 1912, on the eve of the Mexican Revolution, and died in 1982, at the age of seventy. His life and role as founder and leader of the post-1965 Protestant movement of San Juan Chamula, surely do not count as great historical documents, perhaps not even in the context of highland Chiapas. However, his life provides a glimpse, from a very local perspective, of the incredible transformation and abundant contradictions of Mexico in the twentieth century.

This essay charts new territory for me. It is an effort to place the biography of a remarkable person in a matrix of embedded contexts, from highly local cultural drama to Mexican national life. This biography developed over the twenty years of my association with the Harvard Chiapas Project as an almost clandestine undertaking, for any public association with Tzotzil Protestants would not have been politically appropriate for me in my dealings with the Chamula traditionalists with whom I had friendships and good working relationships. In fact, I have never heard anyone—Tzotzil Protestants, Chamula traditionalists, local *ladinos,* INI (Instituto Nacional Indigenista) officials, or Protestant missionaries themselves—talk openly or eagerly about the subject of this essay to any but established or potential allies. When they do address the subject, the rhetoric is accusatory or defensive; it is not a subject for casual conversation. My association with the Chamula Protestant Movement has never been open or close, yet my interest has been nothing short of intense, for it was hard to hear hymns that I had known as a child in Kansas translated to Tzotzil and sung with the abandon of a full-blown revival, without feeling some deep sense of *déjà vu.* How could this be happening in Chiapas?

While "objective" information on the subject of Protestant evangelical activity is hard to come by, there can be little doubt that this work of religious conversion has been one of the major agents of social change in the Chiapas highlands in the last few decades. One has only to observe, in the middle of the 1980s, the Indian Protestant entrepreneurs in the San Cristóbal market or the dozens of new Indian Protestant squatter settlements and refugee camps around the San Cristóbal Valley, or the relatively prosperous farming settlement of Betania on the Pan-American highway south of San Cristóbal, to realize that Protestant converts are major players in the modernization process and contemporary demographic picture of the region.

Data for this essay come from hearsay, opinion, oral history, and everyday conversation; that is, conventional fieldwork. They also come from Protestant publications (notably Steven 1976), as well as from an extensive biography of the protagonist of this essay that was commissioned by me and written in Tzotzil by his son Manuel Gómez Hernández. I first sought Manuel's help with his father's biography in 1977, after he sought work with me as a translator. One of the fruits of his association with the United States Presbyterian missionaries of San Cristóbal was a remarkable facility in written Tzotzil and with Spanish translation. He had in fact been employed by the mission for many years as a New Testament translator. I was less interested in his translation services than in what he could tell me about his remarkable and notorious father who, in 1977, was in the midst of a major political drama that I hardly understood. I was eager to find out more, for I was at the time engaged in a project on Chamula out-migration, and I found that Miguel Kaxlan was the topic of choice in many conversations with Chamula traditionalists. They regarded him as a harbinger of evil, being a bearer of the "new and dangerous words" that could easily, in their view, destroy the community of San Juan Chamula. How could one resist the desire to get to know him, or at least, about him?

DEATH OF MIGUEL KAXLAN

In the autumn of 1982, several weeks before the festivals of All Saints and All Souls (November 1 and 2), a group of Chamula men kidnapped their compatriot, Miguel Kaxlan, in broad daylight from the marketplace in San Cristóbal de las Casas, the old colonial town that today, as in the past, serves as the major trade center of the central Chiapas highlands. After capturing him, they bound his legs and arms and blindfolded him, telling him simply that they planned to take him to the town center of San Juan Chamula, his home *municipio,* in order to discuss with him the status of land and personal property that had recently been expropriated from his band of Protestant convert followers. On the surface the subject matter and purpose of the "trip" made sense. He was both the founder and leader of this movement, dating from 1964. His followers, indeed, had serious property claims against the public officials of Chamula who had, since 1965, systematically harassed the converts. At the time of the kidnapping in 1982, these officials and their predecessors had stripped the converts of their right to live in the community, thus effectively expropriating their land and property.

Once the kidnappers were well within Chamula, on a relatively isolated and very steep truck road that leads from the San Cristóbal Valley into the Chamula hamlet of Milpoleta, they murdered their victim and hacked him to pieces with their machetes. The dismembered corpse was found and taken for burial in San Cristóbal de las Casas. At the present time, some six years later, no suspects have been arrested, nor even identified. The case is as though it never happened, as though it were a dream. Even if Miguel Kaxlan simply "disappeared," a view that is commonly held by all interested parties—Tzotzil Protestants and traditionalists and *ladinos*—it is nevertheless the case that he lives as a symbol of the life and times of contemporary Mexico.

With Miguel Kaxlan's death, apparently carried out with knowledge of, if not at the behest of then-ruling municipal authorities, a bitter chapter in the recent social history of the Tzotzil area of Chiapas has come to a close. Although the initial charismatic moment has passed, the victory clearly belongs to Miguel Kaxlan and others like him. Protestantism is now a full contender for the hearts and minds of the Tzotzil and Tzeltal peoples of highland Chiapas. There is now, more than ever before, a broad range of choices for Indians who live under the political sovereignty of Mexico. Will they retain Indian identity in custom and language? Will they become mestizo laborers, farmers, merchants, and traders? Will they become Protestant Mexicans? Will they become radicalized advocates of pan-national guerrilla movements? Will they become Vatican II modern Catholics? Will they continue, as many have been, into the late twentieth century, as Indians who coexist with the Mexican State? Or will they become Christians or socialists for whom nationality is not the most important question?

In San Juan Chamula, as in other thousands of small communities in Latin America, the quest for modernity moves forward inexorably. Miguel Kaxlan, the Chamula, is not a great historical figure, even regionally; his murder was not even reported in the press of the state capital of Tuxtla Gutiérrez. Yet, even as "Mr. Nobody," his life and times are worth exploring, for his religious and political career allow one to glimpse possible answers to an important question: to what extent is a historical movement toward modernization and social change (e.g., Protestantism) to be understood as local, national, or global? Is Protestantism any of these? Or is it all of them? Or is it simply a convenient vehicle for the political and economic ambitions of individuals who can no longer live in their traditional communities? Or, is Protestantism but one more overlay in the complex mosaic of alien cultural forms that have been, over the centuries, "encapsulated" by the Indian communities of Chiapas to make these alien forms their own (see Vogt 1965a)?

LIFE OF MIGUEL KAXLAN

Miguel Kaxlan was born in 1912 in the small hamlet of Ya'al Vakax in the *municipio* of San Juan Chamula. Then, as now, Chamula was a circumscribed, conservative, monolingual Tzotzil Indian community. Although the community's public life was radically transformed by colonial and Mexican national institutions, its domestic and economic life at the hamlet level was Maya in content and style, with most people making a living as subsistence farmers and artisans. Many Chamula men, then as now, also went as seasonal laborers to work on the distant coffee plantations and cattle ranches of the Pacific coastal lowlands. Chamula of that time was part of the great ethnic mosaic of Chiapas that continues into our time, a complex picture of hundreds of local Indian communities that live in strained coexistence with the dominant Mexican mestizo culture of the region.

Miguel Kaxlan was born in one of the poorest hamlets of a land-poor, densely settled community, made even more miserable by mestizo land encroachments that occurred in the nineteenth century. Eight days after Miguel Gómez Chakoj-chu was born, his mother died from complications of childbirth and influenza. Seven days after his mother's death, his father also died of influenza. Miguel, now an orphan, was grudgingly taken in by his paternal uncle. In this household he spent his early childhood. At the age of eight, hunger and domestic strife over his unwelcome presence drove him to seek a place as an intern in the community's first and, at that time, only school. This was located in the ceremonial and civic center of San Juan Chamula, at some half-a-day's walk from his uncle's home. At this school he studied Spanish and standard beginning primary subjects. He turned out to be an excellent student. In 1922, in recognition of his good performance, he was given the honor of raising the flag over the school on the occasion of the visit of a distinguished Federal Education Ministry visitor to the school This visitor was so taken by the child's promise and so moved by the orphan's tattered, torn Indian clothing that he gave him a set of new clothes from his own valise. These included a shirt, pants, and shoes and socks, all European style. Since the clothes were the only ones he had, he wore them all the time, and he was apparently the first Chamula ever to wear European clothing in the community. Hence, he was nicknamed Miguel Kaxlan (Kaxlan is Tzotzil for Castellano, referring to being of Hispanic or *ladino* origin). This nickname stuck and he was known from the age of ten by this name, which roughly translates as "Miguel the *ladino*." The name would prove to be both a curse and a self-fulfilling prophecy. He would never really go home again.

In 1925 he went off to another government school called Cerro Hueco, which was located in the lowland area of the state of Chiapas, near Tuxtla Gutiérrez, the capital. This school brought together students from dozens of Indian communities of the state, thus obliging all of them to seek fluent Spanish as a lingua franca. In this multiethnic context he met and apparently had a fast love affair with a girl whose community of origin was ironic and prophetic. Her home was Rincón Chamula. This community is of historical interest in that it was settled in large part by political exiles from Chamula, who fled there following their defeat in a political and religious movement known as the "Pajarito Rebellion," that took place in San Juan Chamula in 1910-1911. Rincón Chamula was thus ethnically Chamula, but physically and socially removed by relatively great distance from San Juan.

Miguel, at the age of fifteen, married the girl from Rincón and moved there to join the community of his own exiled countrymen. In these surroundings, Miguel, an orphan among exiles, became aware of the political circumstances in San Juan that had produced the Pajarito Rebellion and defeated the leaders of the movement. He became increasingly bitter when he realized that some of the forces—notably poverty and marginality—that had driven him to leave San Juan and to move toward the *ladino* world had also driven out his wife's family as political and social exiles.

Miguel Kaxlan abandoned his first wife in 1929, at the age of seventeen, in order to continue his studies. He went to the state capital of Tuxtla Gutiérrez, specifically to the office of Public Education, in an effort to find a way to go to Mexico City to seek further education. Arrangements were made and he departed for Mexico. He went by train from the Pacific lowland town to Arriaga. This was his first experience on a train and it caused an extraordinary impression of fear and amazement. Upon arriving in Mexico City, he was astonished to find that there were more Spanish speakers than English speakers, for he understood, from his own teaching and background, that Mexico City was so strange as to be labeled the "Land of the English" (*slumal inklex*). While he was studying in Mexico City he had various amorous adventures. But, most significant to him was his study of the Mexican Revolutionary Constitution of 1917, a subject that captured his young imagination, for there was, stated there, the promise of social justice for all Mexicans, particularly the poor, the marginal, and the oppressed. At the same time that he learned these things, he was keenly aware that his being Indian in Mexico City, a fact that was apparent from his still-imperfect Spanish, led to ill treatment and rudeness from native Spanish speakers.

The *coup-de-grâce* came in the form of modern medicine. He became very ill and willingly submitted to receiving some injections as a cure, even though this mode of medical treatment was totally strange to him. By chance, the shots were not administered correctly and he suffered a temporary paralysis in his arm. This was enough. In 1931 he left Mexico City and returned to San Juan Chamula where his uncle felt obliged to take him in, although grudgingly. They allowed him to farm the land that had been his parents', but which had been passed, by custom, to his guardians upon his parents' death, as a way of compensating them for the burden of rearing their orphaned children.

Miguel married again, the wife in Rincón Chamula apparently forgotten. As a poor couple with no land for maize production, they became potters, an economic pursuit that required little more than house and patio and access to communal forest land as a source for charcoal. Between 1931 and 1940 they had six children, but things did not go well for them. Miguel apparently drank a great deal and frequently beat his wife. Furthermore, their children did not have adequate food or clothing. The younger ones apparently had no clothing at all. Miguel's disastrous domestic circumstances ruined his reputation and blocked his aspirations to become a political or religious official in the town center.

In 1940 he abandoned his second household and went to work on the coffee plantations of the Pacific lowlands. Here he spent seven years, never returning to San Juan during this period. The support of his family fell to his uncle's household. Between 1947 and 1950 he worked as a day laborer on the construction of a section of the Pan-American highway that was being constructed between Tuxtla Gutiérrez and the Guatemalan border. During this period Miguel embarked on a third long-term relationship with a Tzotzil woman, this time with a Zinacanteco. In 1951, with the Pan-American highway construction project completed and this source of income gone, his third living arrangement broke apart due to some of the same problems that had caused his other domestic misfortunes. These were poverty and alcohol.

Ruin was complete. He returned to San Juan broke, alcoholic, and totally disillusioned, for he had not, by any reckoning, achieved economic or social mobility, or even material goods, from his lifelong effort to master Spanish and the life style of the Mexican mestizo world. Not only had he not prospered in the *ladino* world, but he had nowhere to go but back home to Ya'al Vakax where, remarkably, his second wife and her family took him in. He had little choice but to revert, however grudgingly, to the traditional life style. A few days after his uncelebrated homecoming he took a sweat bath in the household *temascal* and had an unexpected revelation. A vision came to him. He was sucked up into the vortex of a whirlwind and was bodily lifted out of the sweat bath and carried 10 m through the air and dropped on the ground. After this extraordinary event, he became desperately ill and dreamed continuously. During this period, an unspecified sacred being appeared to him and "called" him to a new career as a shaman. The vision was complex, but basically carried a single message: he was to return to the traditional life in Chamula and was commanded to become a shaman. The "man" in the vision spoke to him, using these words:

> All that I have given to you,
>   All that you have received,
>
> It is yours,
>   I wish to leave it to you.
>
> From this moment you will serve me,
>   You will help me to care,
>
> For my children,
>   For my offspring.
>
> Receive my gift.
>   Do not fail me.
>   Take good care of it.
>
> For it will serve you in caring
>   For my children,
>   For my offspring.

From 1951 to 1958 Miguel Kaxlan lived in San Juan, earning a very modest living as a curer. Once again, however, his old problems returned. He began again to drink heavily and to fight with his wife and in-laws. He lost most of his curing clients and his source of income. His life was again where it had been so often in the past, in complete ruin. The last blow in the destruction of Miguel's attempted life as a traditional Chamula came from an act that may or may not have happened as reported. Whatever really occurred, he was publicly accused in 1958 of stealing the clothing from a mother and a daughter when they were washing their hair at a water hole. The accusation said that he stole the clothing so as to disorient them so that he could rape the daughter. Then he was said to have left both mother and daughter naked in order to go off and sell their clothing. These events reached the village elders, and policemen were sent to arrest him. Public shame was heaped on him during the hearings, and he was sentenced to several days in jail and had to pay a fine of 1500 pesos. This sentence and payment of damages were perceived by the community as too light a punishment for the crime. Most of them felt that the women's family ought to have killed him. That he got off so "easily" was attributed to the mediation efforts of Erasto Urbina, then mayor of San Cristóbal de las Casas. This intervention itself is noteworthy, for Urbina was (and is still) regarded as a great hero by the local Indian community, for he was bilingual in Tzotzil and Spanish, being of mixed Tzotzil and *ladino* heritage. Although he was a successful merchant and politician in the *ladino* world, he constantly worked to improve the economic and social circumstances of Indians by guaranteeing their equal status before municipal and state law. In the context of his hardware business, he always found ways to offer short-term credit to Indians without requiring collateral or charging interest.

Erasto Urbina's help with Miguel's legal problems after the rape and the scandal left Miguel with an indelible impression of gratitude and awe. Urbina was a compelling role model as a man of Tzotzil background who had "made it" in the *ladino* world. With his shamanistic career in ruins, and public shame that would not vanish, Miguel clearly had little alternative but to leave home once again. Perhaps he could follow the path of Erasto Urbina. From 1958 to 1965, Miguel literally lived at the edge of two worlds, Indian and *ladino,* a pattern of social marginality that had characterized much of his life.

However, by now his choices were dwindling. He could never really go home again to Chamula. His children would no longer speak to him. His wife abandoned him. His in-laws would not have anything to do with him. His only choice at this point in his life was to work as a day laborer in San Cristóbal and in the Pacific lowlands. His drinking problem grew worse. Fate had dragged him to a low ebb. Even his carefully cultivated Spanish language skills and willingness to "go *ladino*" in custom and dress would not deliver to him his lifelong aspiration of becoming someone of note.

In 1964 his brother Domingo got a job as a gardener at the San Cristóbal home of the North American Presbyterian missionaries Kenneth and Elaine Jacobs. They had already spent some ten years in the missionary effort in the Indian communities of the Chiapas highlands, though their work had not yet penetrated San Juan Chamula. Their presence in Chiapas was with the full blessing of Mexican government agencies. This support reflected the honest commitment of the secular government to the complete freedom of religious belief and practice. The Protestant evangelical agenda also meshed with government goals of supporting modernization, literacy, and Western health programs for Indian communities. The Protestants did these things as part of the missionary enterprise, so it did not "cost" the government anything.

Domingo, Miguel's brother, converted to the Presbyterian sect and he, in turn, converted his brother. Miguel felt he had little to lose. His conversion provided for him both a place to live (in the missionary compound) and, best of all, a job as a New Testament translation assistant to the missionaries. For the first time ever, his Tzotzil-Spanish skills were worth something. He set to work translating selected books of the New Testament to the Chamula dialect of Tzotzil.

In time, both Miguel and his brother joined the missionary cause itself and began proselytizing among friends and relatives in Chamula. By 1965 there were 35 converts, among them (a bizarre symbol of reconciliation) the family of Miguel's son, Manuel Gómez Hernández. Manuel was among those who had suffered hunger and hardships in childhood due to his father's neglect. Between 1965 and 1969 the number of Chamula converts reached 120, a relatively small number, but enough to send waves of anxiety across the red hills and oak and pine thickets of San Juan. A clear and present menace to Chamula's jealously guarded ethnic conservatism and central authority system was loose.

Among the cherished articles of faith and practice of the new Presbyterian sect were concepts that truly threatened the traditional order. Among the most unthinkable and intolerable were the following: (1) refusal to pay municipal taxes to support the fiesta cycle, which in their view was a cult of paganism; (2) refusal to participate in any way in the public religious life of the community; and (3) refusal to consume alcoholic beverages, a major source of revenue for the civil-religious hierarchy.

The traditional oligarchy was also worried because a system of fairly workable relations had evolved over the years between the small group of politically prominent Chamula families and Mexico's (then) one and only official political party, the PRI (Partido Revolucionario Institucional). The Chamula oligarchy felt threatened for obvious reasons. First, the precedent for a tax rebellion was in place, even though the present numbers were few. Second, the Protestants refused to recognize the moral authority of the central town government in their own lives. Finally, the Protestants in no way respected the finely tuned understandings that provided for Chamula cooperation with state and federal political authorities in exchange for a hands-off policy regarding Chamula autonomy in religious and judicial matters that were essential for the maintenance of a traditional Chamula community with no apparent Mexican federal presence.

By 1967 the threat was perceived to be intolerable and the converts' homes were burned to the ground, with no subsequent investigations or formal charges brought against anyone. The municipal authorities looked the other way and the state authorities were unable to respond. The burned-out Protestants found themselves obliged to flee to San Cristóbal, where they took refuge in the Presbyterian missionary compound.

It happened that the fires that destroyed the Protestants' homes in Chamula killed several members of one family, including three girls. Two other girls escaped the blaze with severe burns and fled heroically to San Cristóbal in the middle of the night. These girls survived and became quasi-martyrs for the Protestant cause. They became active missionaries themselves and traveled widely through the United States soliciting funds for the Chamula mission.

The confrontational episode that involved the burning of homes caused a great deal of negative publicity and the state government was forced to intervene on behalf of the Protestants, who did, after all, enjoy protection of land and property under Mexican law. There followed several years of peace and reconciliation, and the Protestants were allowed to return to cultivate their cornfields and pasture their sheep, although living permanently in the community was out of the question. In 1974 the peace collapsed. The Protestant numbers had increased significantly by that time and they were blamed for fomenting an embarrassing rebellion of several thousand people who sought to prevent the elected chief magistrate (*presidente municipal*) from taking office. Being a member of the oligarchy, he had been duly elected by the usual PRI-supported machinery. The rebels accused the oligarchy of financial and electoral fraud and sought, at gunpoint, to keep the elected official from taking office. The oligarchy responded to this challenge by jailing 200 Protestants, who were reputed to be the leaders of the electoral rebellion. They were subsequently taken to San Cristóbal and forbidden ever to return to Chamula. The state officials looked the other way. This episode of violence broke the strained coexistence of the Protestant Chamulas with the traditionalists. Most important for this narrative, the key players in the persecution of the Protestants were the very people who, almost twenty years before, had been the ones who had jailed Miguel Kaxlan on the occasion of the rape and theft trial. The ingredients of vengeance and honor were unquestionably present and Miguel Kaxlan sensed an opportunity to rectify past grievances.

After the events of 1974, Miguel Kaxlan moved quickly into the arena of religious politics, since Protestantism was proving to be a useful tool for vengeance against those who, for decades, had succeeded, in his view, in excluding him from participation in Chamula traditional religious and political life. He proceeded to ally himself with the PAN (Partido de Acción Nacional) which, nationally, was associated with the economic and religious right wing of Mexican politics. In reality, it was but a vehicle of protest against the PRI establishment, and it was, in its way, useful to Miguel. He was able to mobilize large numbers of his compatriots for the cause of antiestablishment political alignment with the PAN party, if only because it was against PRI, with which the Chamula oligarchy, his enemy, was associated. He was able to convert many people to Protestantism as an adjunct to their antiestablishment sentiments, for Miguel's antipathy for the ruling families was shared by many of his compatriots. With this political ploy, it was not difficult to turn religious conversion into a political statement. Indeed, many who could not have cared less about the tenets of the faith, became Protestants precisely because of its antiestablishment political posture.

The cynical alliance of Miguel Kaxlan with PAN and Protestantism enraged both the oligarchy and the PRI. The reasons were clear. PRI responded by allying itself with the traditional oligarchy against the Protestants. No action was taken against the land claims. Why? Because the Protestants and PAN could easily end, with lightning speed, the comfortable cooperation that the state and federal governments had enjoyed for several decades with the Chamula oligarchy. This mattered more than a little bit because Chamula was, and is today, the largest and most influential Indian community in the state. It also has a long history as an epicenter of rebellion and violence in recent Chiapas history. What had Miguel Kaxlan wrought?

Miguel spent the years from 1976 to his death in 1982 trying to convince the state and federal authorities that the oligarchy of San Juan Chamula had acted against federal law, which guarantees freedom of religion and benefit of the usufruct of property. Miguel Kaxlan took these issues to the highest levels of grievance that were available to him, even to Mexico City, claiming that the authorities in San Juan Chamula acted against federal law by depriving citizens of freedom of religion and use of their land and property. This was a compelling, if not convincing, allegation, since over 2000 Chamula Protestants lived as exiles in the San Cristóbal Valley in 1976, unable to return to their homes. Neither the state nor federal authorities chose to respond to their grievances about alienated or estranged property.

As a consequence of the imbroglio that followed Miguel's attempts to get higher authorities involved in the Protestant grievances, he became a despised enemy, not only of the Chamula traditionalists, but also of the local Mexican political officials and of the Presbyterian converts and missionaries themselves. The Chamula traditionalists became infuriated because he was attempting to destroy their authority in the community. The local and state PRI officials were stung by his public accusations that suggested that Mexican laws and constitutional guarantees were empty shells. The officials were also alarmed because Miguel Kaxlan had well over 2000 followers whom he might mobilize for a full-scale rebellion. This was to be avoided at all cost because Chamula had an impressive track record of trouble. In fact, the ringleaders of two violent Indian social movements, those of 1868-1869 and 1910-1911, were Chamulas. Both movements had been directed against the established *ladino* political and religious authorities. Finally, the missionaries and the new Chamula Protestant converts were upset and embarrassed by the turn of events, for Miguel Kaxlan caused a factional split in the fledgling Chamula Presbyterian sect. One group, led by Miguel's son Manuel, was convinced that pacifism, spiritual purity, and an entirely new life style were required for their survival. They should simply abandon their property claims in San Juan and build new lives elsewhere. The other faction, led by Miguel Kaxlan himself, consisted of converts who saw the Protestantism as a useful medium for political protest and economic improvement within their own community.

Such was the inflammatory stage on which Miguel Kaxlan moved in the last years of his life. Thanks to Miguel and his son working with the missionaries, the two wings of the Protestant movement had in 1982 more than 2000 adherents. At this time nearly all had been exiled from San Juan. Most lived in slumlike temporary settlements around the San Cristóbal Valley, earning a miserable living as menial laborers and domestic servants in their new town. Many received support from the church. Still others took advantage to buy private tracts of land with favorable payment plans guaranteed by funds from the mission. Yet others became prosperous middlemen in the San Cristóbal market. For every winner, however, there were many losers, and the climate was very tense. When at last in 1982, his own countrymen abducted and murdered Miguel Kaxlan, the whole community seemed to breathe a collective sigh of relief and joy. Indeed, to this day, the circumstances of the murder have not been investigated. No one has accused anyone. The Mexican politicians are silent, as are the Chamula traditionalists and the Protestants. It is as though all wish to forget him, as though he had never lived.

APOTHEOSIS OF MIGUEL KAXLAN

I believe that Miguel Kaxlan lives in both the conscious identity and unconscious psyche of modern Chiapas, perhaps also in the soul of Mexico itself. His words, deeds, and death are both a small footnote to and the table of contents of Mexican life in the twentieth century.

Miguel Kaxlan was born, like Mexico itself, with an Indian soul. This means, in its Tzotzil variant, that his life and body were collective social entities that were predestined to develop in a certain manner since the moment of his conception (see Gossen 1975). His Indian identity and soul were not of his making, nor were they subject to his control. All that he was to be, as a Tzotzil, was given, or so it seemed. In spite of his birthright, he was from birth systematically cast out of the Tzotzil world. Both parents died within two weeks of his birth. His aunt and uncle did not want him around, for they could barely feed him. His own community rejected him and, in effect, sent him away. His nickname tells the tale. "Miguel the *ladino*" was his identity from the age of ten, for the Mexican clothes that the government official gave him were his only clothes. Acculturation through changes in language and life style seemed to be his only alternative for survival.

In spite of his obligatory plunge into the *ladino* world, he tried to, in very traditional ways, go home again. Tzotzil women and Indian domestic life were the strategy of choice. He married or lived with at least three such women; indeed, they symbolized several variants of the Tzotzil world: an exile community, the home community, and a non-Chamula Tzotzil community, Zinacantán. He also tried to come home again through a career in traditional curing and through his abortive efforts to join the civil-religious hierarchy. He even tried in his last years to defend Indian rights generically; that is, to point out the contradictions between Mexican law and local practice when the matter of Indian property rights was at stake. In the last analysis, all efforts failed catastrophically. He was doomed to shed the Indian soul.

From birth, it would seem, the circumstances of the Western soul were imposed upon his Indian soul. He was compelled to become a pragmatist and opportunist, to exercise free will, albeit in a flawed and destructive manner. To become what he might through his own devices was thrust upon him. In his lifelong flight from the status of being a poor orphan, his newly discovered Western soul, identified with self determination, personal liberty, and free will, found expression through the only means that were available to him: education and acculturation.

In spite of his efforts to "re-dress" (in the sense of Spanish *revestir*) himself as a Westerner, his efforts to become modern, Mexican style, and to make his own destiny, did not work out. Indeed, these efforts utterly destroyed him. He could live neither with the contradictions of the Tzotzil world nor with those of modern Mexico.

Miguel Kaxlan tried all his life to be a member of the community into which he was born. This never worked out, nor did the alternative. With every turn, his every effort to move successfully in the *ladino* world turned sour. Each time he sought refuge in a Tzotzil household, and each time he abandoned it. In every case, it was wives, lovers, even burn-scarred little girls (the Protestant martyrs), who gave him his chance to become a credible Tzotzil male, to become someone in the native context. Each time he played this card, he failed, most catastrophically in the theft and rape case. The women outlasted him, in every case. They stayed; he went on to die.

Miguel Kaxlan's linguistic skill in Spanish and Tzotzil was noteworthy. He was in fact effectively bilingual from the age of twenty. He tried earnestly to use this skill to carve out a niche for himself in the Tzotzil world. He sought a job as a municipal scribe and later as a political official, yet he could not find a place in the Indian system, for the authorities did not believe that he was trustworthy, for he had spent so many years wandering through the *ladino* world. He even attempted to use his bilingualism and translation skills to create an Indian Protestant church, with its own Tzotzil texts, so that it would not become a de facto acculturation tool. This effort to act as an advocate for the Indian community failed as well, for he was swept away by his political agenda, also ironically, in defense of his people. He moved on to try to put his knowledge of Mexican law and of the 1917 constitution at the service of his people; all to no avail.

As he approached the end of his life, Miguel Kaxlan witnessed the chilling irony of the traditional Tzotzil community in open alliance with the federal and state political authorities in a concerted effort to circumvent constitutional guarantees having to do with freedom of religion and property rights. Miguel's own son abandoned him to found his own faction of their common adopted religion. In effect, his son seemed willing to write off the Protestant converts' legal rights to their land and property in order to get on with their lives, in spite of an overwhelming case for legal grievances under the Mexican Constitution of 1917, which Miguel knew well.

Toward the end, he came to believe that corruption, dishonesty, and compromise were failings not only of the traditional Tzotzil social order, but also of the Mexican government, the *ladino* social order, and of the Protestant movement itself. All the identities that he aspired to have—Indian, *ladino,* Protestant, even Miguel Kaxlan—turned out, for him, to be impossible, for none was, in the last analysis free of contradictions. In the end, I believe it is likely that he faced death with relief rather than with fear.

THE CALENDRICAL MEANING OF RITUAL AMONG THE MAYA[1]

Victoria R. Bricker
Tulane University

In the highlands of Chiapas, Mexico, the most elaborate dramas are performed during festivals associated with the Maya New Year. The traditional solar calendar (the *hab*) consisted of eighteen months of twenty days each, plus a short five-day intercalary "month," known as *uayeb* or *xma kaba kin,* "nameless days," in Yucatec Maya and as *ch'ay k'in,* "lost days," in Tzotzil and Tzeltal, the principal Indian languages of highland Chiapas. The New Year's dramas typically occur during the "lost days" that end the old year, rather than during the first days of the new year, and they coincide with the dates of the Catholic festival of Carnival in many modern Maya communities.

The township (*municipio*) of Chamula, in the Tzotzil sector of the Chiapas highlands, still uses the traditional solar calendar to schedule its festivals, and it has preserved some very ancient rites in its New Year's ceremonies. The meaning of those rites has not survived in the oral traditions of the community and therefore cannot be elicited in interviews with Chamula informants. It must be sought in the historical record, in sixteenth-century Spanish documents and Late Classic Maya hieroglyphic texts. The latter appear on stone monuments and in pre-Columbian books known as codices, where they are associated with artistic representations of calendrical rituals. The scenes on many of those monuments and on several pages of the *Dresden Codex* and the *Madrid Codex* highlight the very elements in the New Year's ceremonies of Chamula that the traditional ethnographic methods, participant observation and interviewing, have failed to explain. Their meaning lies in the accompanying hieroglyphic texts and in eyewitness descriptions of the same rites recorded by Spaniards in the sixteenth century.

Portions of three Chamula New Year's rituals resemble scenes carved on Classic Maya stelae and painted on several pages of the *Dresden Codex* and the *Madrid Codex.* One of the Chamula rituals, the Bull Sacrifice, occurs at the beginning of the festival of Carnival. Another ritual, in which all the leaders of the community run over a track of burning thatch, occurs at the end of the festival. The third ritual, a dance in which the leaders of the community take turns wearing a jaguar skin and carrying a spear that is also a banner, is repeated at various times throughout the five principal days of the festival. At present, these rituals have no obvious relationship to each other, nor with other rituals that take place over the same five-day period. In various parts of the Maya area during the pre-Columbian past, rituals like them were performed in different years of a four-year ceremonial cycle, where they had specialized and unrelated functions.

THE BULL SACRIFICE

The five "lost days" begin on the Saturday before Ash Wednesday in Chamula. However, preparations for the festival get under way several weeks earlier, and the Bull Sacrifice takes place on the Tuesday preceding the first "lost day." The festival is sponsored by six religious officials who are known as "Passions" (*paxyon*) in Chamula. The three senior Passions who are finishing their terms of office offer banquets of beef stew on Sunday and Tuesday during the festival. Each of these Passions purchases a bull in the lowlands and brings it into the highlands to be slaughtered in the open space in front of his house. The bull is thrown to the ground, its front and back legs are tied together, and its head is pulled back to expose the neck arteries, which the slaughterers use as a guide for finding the right place to insert their knives.

Before stabbing the bull in the neck, the butcher asks for mint leaves, which he places in both nostrils to flavor the meat, and for a bucket in which to collect the bull's blood. The blood is taken immediately to the cooking compound, a brush-enclosed area not far from the slaughtering post where all the cooking for the festival takes place, to be cooked with mint into a pudding that will be served at midday together with some of the bull's internal organs.

After bleeding to death, the bull is skinned, its internal organs are removed, and its penis is cut off. The bull's head and feet are removed with the skin intact. The skin and flesh are stripped away from the lower jaw, and the head and the feet are tied to the center post of the porch of the Passion's house, where they remain for the next ten days. The meat will be cut up into small pieces and served in soup during the Passion's banquets.

What makes this event a sacrificial ritual, rather than simply a butchering procedure, is the treatment of the bull's head, especially the defleshing of the lower jaw.[2] Some obvious parallels between this ritual and scenes on Classic Maya stelae and in the *Dresden Codex* are discussed in a later section of this paper.

THE JAGUAR SKIN DANCE

At various times during Carnival, the sponsors of the festival and the civil authorities of the community participate in the Jaguar Skin Dance. The Chamulas' name for the dance is *ak' ot chilon*. The word *ak' ot* means "dance," and *chilon* refers to the cow or sheep bells sewn to a leather band attached to the neck of a jaguar skin. Another leather strap fastened to the animal's head permits the pelt to be slipped over the head and worn during the dance.

The other prop for the dance combines the characteristics of a spear with those of a flag. A socketed metal spear point (Figure 1) is tied at the top of a long pole by red and green ribbons, the ends of which dangle over a flowered chintz banner (Figure 2).

Figure 1. Sketch of socketed spear point used on flags in Chamula.

Figure 2. Jaguar Skin Dance in Chamula. Drawing by Mariano López Calixto (Bricker 1973a:111).

The civil and religious officials line up in rank order and take turns holding a flag and dancing with the jaguar skin on their backs, while a "Bell Ringer" (*jtij chilon*) walking behind moves the pelt back and forth to make the bells on it jingle. Another man walks in front of the official, holding a wooden staff with ribbons attached by one end at the top. They circle two drummers seated on little chairs, who are tapping small clay kettledrums with their fingertips. After circling the drums three times, the official is lifted off his feet and carried for a few steps by an "Embracer" (*jpetvanej*). The Embracer walks him three steps into the center of the circle, then three steps away from the drums, while he waves his flag in the four cardinal directions, and finally carries him over to a nearby cross, where he sets him on his feet. The Bell Ringer immediately snatches the jaguar pelt from his head, the man with the ribboned staff seizes the flag, and both run off to recruit someone else, the next-highest-ranking male present, to take part in the dance. The lifting episode is described as being "raised beside the kettledrum" (*muyel ta bin*) (see Bricker 1973a:109-112 for a more detailed description of this dance and Figure 2 for a Chamula's sketch of it).

Chamulas interpret this dance in terms of the Passion of Christ. They say that the spear point symbolizes the head of God (*sjol jtotik*) and the jaguar skin represents God's jaguar, who defended him when the demons, or Jews, tried to kill him. Formerly, jaguars wore bells around their necks so that they could signal each other's presence in the forest. That is why bells are attached to the jaguar skin. Whenever a man puts on the jaguar skin, he is impersonating the jaguar who tried to defend Christ. The lifting sequence beside the kettledrums symbolizes the resurrection of Christ.

I believe that this ritual has a much older meaning that predates the introduction of Christianity in the Maya area by many centuries. The modern Chamula exegetical explanation does not account for the fact that the jaguar dance is performed during the "lost days" that end the traditional Maya solar year. And the lifting ceremony has a calendrical significance of which Chamulas are no longer aware.

THE FIRE-WALKING RITE

On the last day of the festival, a group of men and boys remove old thatch from the roof of an abandoned house and carry it to the plaza in front of the town hall. They carefully arrange the thatch in a 5-m-wide track running from the atrium of the churchyard to the opposite end of the plaza. The thatch is set afire at about 2:30 P.M.; it blazes up and then dies down, leaving a thin bed of glowing coals. At this point the Passions and all their assistants run back and forth across the coals.

Chamulas regard this activity as a rite of purification. Carnival is a period of license and evil when many men release their inhibitions by drinking, fighting, and impersonating monkeys. The monkey impersonators symbolize the Jews, or demons, who harassed Christ. They must run over the fire to rid themselves of evil. The Passions and the other civil and religious officials with whom they have associated have become tainted with their evil. If they do not also run through the fire at this time, their ghosts will go to hell after they die. But if they run through the fire while they are still alive, they will not receive further punishment after death.

Like the Jaguar Skin Dance, the calendrical implications of this rite have been obscured in an exegesis that relates it to the biblical Passion. Although the rite itself is demonstrably pre-Columbian in origin (see below), its present meaning is Christian, not Maya.

PRE-COLUMBIAN CALENDRICAL RITUALS

More than a century ago, Cyrus Thomas (1882) demonstrated that pages 25-28 of the *Dresden Codex* and pages 34-37 of the *Madrid Codex* are concerned with the New Year's ceremonies described by Diego de Landa in his *Relación de las cosas de Yucatán* (Tozzer 1941:136-149). Landa conducted his investigation of Yucatecan customs in the middle of the sixteenth century. At that time, the Maya were using the "Mayapan Calendar" (Edmonson 1976), and the yearbearer days were Kan, Ix, Muluc, and Cauac. The "yearbearers" were the days on which the Maya New Year could begin. Each day in the year was given one of twenty names (Imix, Ik, Akbal, Kan, Chicchan, Cimi, Manik, Lamat, Muluc, Oc, Chuen, Eb, Ben, Ix, Men, Cib, Caban, Edznab, Cauac, and Ahau), only four of which could fall on New Year's day in any one Maya calendar

(Edmonson 1976:713; Satterthwaite 1965:609). The Early Classic yearbearers, Ik, Manik, Eb, and Caban, were first used at Tikal and are therefore said to represent the "Tikal Calendar." A different set of yearbearers, Akbal, Lamat, Ben, and Edznab, were used in the vicinity of Campeche in Yucatán after 672 A.D. and constitute the "Campeche Calendar." Another shift in yearbearers in 1539, on the eve of the Spanish Conquest, initiated the system in use when Landa was recording the customs of Yucatán (Edmonson 1976:713).

The New Year's ceremonies of Yucatán were cyclical, with different rituals repeating every four years. In the days before a Kan year was to begin, a hollow image called Kan u Uayeyab was fashioned of clay and placed on one of two piles of stones at the southern entrance of a town. A statue was made of a god called Bolon Dzacab and placed in the house of the sponsor of the ceremonies for that year. After clearing and decorating the road to the southern entrance of the town, the lords, priest, and other men stood before the image on the pile of stones and censed it with forty-nine grains of maize ground up with incense and made it an offering of a headless hen. Then they placed the image on a standard called *kante* and carried it to the house in which the statue of Bolon Dzacab had been set up. The hollow clay image was placed opposite the statue of Bolon Dzacab and offered food and drink. Then these offerings were passed out to everyone present, with the priest receiving a leg of venison as a special portion. Some men drew blood from their ears with which they anointed a stone called *kanal acantun*. A heart-shaped piece of bread and another bread made of gourd seeds were offered to Kan u Uayeyab. At the end of the "nameless days," the statue of Bolon Dzacab was carried to the temple, and the image of Kan u Uayeyab was borne to the eastern entrance of the town, where it remained for a year (Tozzer 1941:139-143).

In the days preceding a Muluc year, the priests and nobles made an image of the god Chac u Uayeyab and placed it on a pile of stones at the eastern entrance to the town. They also made a statue of the god Kinich Ahau and placed it in the house of the man who sponsored the ceremonies for that year. After clearing and decorating the path to the eastern entrance of the town, they censed the image of Chac u Uayeyab with a mixture of fifty-three grains of ground maize and incense and cut off the head of a hen as an offering. Then they carried the image on a standard called *chacte* to the house where the statue of Kinich Ahau had been set up. On the way they performed some war dances, which they called *holcan okot* and *batel okot*. Once again, food was offered to the idols, and men and boys drew blood from their ears to smear on a stone called *chac acantun*. At the end of the five days of the festival, they took the statue of Kinich Ahau to the temple and carried the image of Chac u Uayeyab to the northern entrance of the town to be left on a pile of stones for a year (Tozzer 1941:144-145).

The ceremonies that ushered in an Ix year involved an image called Sac u Uayeyab and a statue of the god Itzamna. After being censed and offered a headless hen, the image was carried from the northern entrance of the town on a standard called *sachia* and was set up in front of the statue of Itzamna in the sponsor's house. As before, offerings were made to the idols, and men drew

CALENDRICAL MEANING OF RITUAL

blood from their bodies to smear on a stone called *sac acantun*. At the end of the festival, the statue of Itzamna was carried to the temple, and Sac u Uayeyab was placed on a pile of stones at the western entrance of the town (Tozzer 1941:145-147).

In the ceremonies that anticipated the beginning of a Cauac year, an image was made of a god called Ek u Uayeyab, and a statue was made of a god called Uac Mitun Ahau. After being censed and offered a headless hen, Ek u Uayeyab was placed on a standard called *yax ek*. A skull and a dead man were placed on the shoulders of the image, Ek u Uayeyab; " . . . and on top of all, a carnivorous bird, which they called *kuch* [a vulture]" (Tozzer 1941:147). The men who accompanied the image to the center of town performed several dances along the way, among them *xibalba okot,* "dance of the underworld." Offerings were made to both Ek u Uayeyab and Uac Mitun Ahau, and men drew blood from various parts of their bodies with which they anointed a stone called *ekel acantun*. When the ceremonies were over, the statue of Uac Mitun Ahau was carried to the temple, and the image of Ek u Uayeyab was transported to a pile of stones at the southern entrance of the town (Tozzer 1941:147-149).

Landa mentions that the years in which Cauac was the yearbearer were noted for droughts, and he describes a special ceremony for averting such calamities that was performed during the five-day festival that preceded those years:

> they made a great arch of wood in the court, filling it on the top and on the sides with firewood, leaving in it doors for going in and out. After this most of the men then each took bundles of sticks, long and very dry, tied together, and a singer, mounted on the top of the wood, sang and made a noise with one of their drums. All danced below him with great order and devotion, going in and out through the doors of that arch of wood and thus they continued to dance until evening, when each one leaving his bundle there, they went home to rest and eat. When the night fell, they returned and many people with them, for this ceremony was held in great esteem among them, and each man taking his torch they lighted it and each one for himself set fire with them to the wood, which at once blazed up and was quickly consumed. When there was no longer anything but coals, they levelled them and spread them out wide, and those who had danced having come together there were some who set about passing over those coals barefoot and naked, as they were, from one side to the other [Tozzer 1941:148-149].

A more detailed description of this ceremony appears in the *Relación de Valladolid*:

> And at the quarter (*cuarto*) of dawn the same procession came bringing the priest before it clad in their kind of alb with many small snail shells sewn on the lower part, and their kind of chasuble, a

miter on his head; there were depicted on it many faces of demons. With his acolyte he came to the place where the bed of hot wood was, which could not be approached nearer than a stone's throw, and when he arrived he carried a hyssop with many tails of vipers and poisonous snakes tied on it, and, the acolyte bringing to him a vessel of the kind of wine they used, he sprinkled with that hyssop and on all four sides of the fire he performed his ceremonies and sprinkled the coals with it. And then he ordered them to take off his sandals and he went on the bed of hot wood sprinkling, and behind him the whole procession of Indians [quoted in Tozzer 1941:148 n.733].

The references to sprinkling in the passage from the *Relación de Valladolid* imply that the priest was performing a rain-making ceremony to forestall a drought during the coming year. The Maya of Yucatán usually wait until the first heavy rains have fallen before planting their fields. In good years, the rains begin during the first week of May, not long after the men have finished burning the trees and bushes they have cut down and left to dry earlier in the year. In bad years, the rains may not come until June or July, and the crops suffer accordingly. I suspect that the fire symbolizes the yearly burning of fields in the spring, and the sprinkling is a kind of sympathetic magic to influence the rains to fall on the recently burned-over fields, so that the crops can be planted on time.

A number of ceremonies described by Landa are illustrated in pictures on the New Year's pages of the *Dresden Codex* and the *Madrid Codex* and on period-ending monuments of Late Classic date. The glyphs for two sets of yearbearers, representing both the Tikal and Campeche calendars, appear on the left side of pages 25-28 in the *Dresden Codex*. The glyphs along the left margin of pages 34-37 of the *Madrid Codex* refer only to the colonial yearbearers, the ones in use when Landa wrote his *Relación de las cosas de Yucatán*.

A different system of dating seems to be associated with scenes of New Year's rituals on carved stone monuments. The dates on these monuments are based on the 360-day *tun*, rather than the 365-day *hab*, and they were usually erected at 5-*tun* intervals, rather than at the end of every *hab* or *tun*. I call them "period-ending monuments" because they mark the endings of *hotuns*, or 5-*tun* periods.

The New Year's pages of the *Dresden Codex* are divided into three registers (Figure 3). According to Thompson (1972:90): "the top third of each page . . . illustrates the induction of the patron of the incoming year. He is perched rather precariously on the conventionalized representation of a carrier frame on the bearer's back, the tumpline passing across the bearer's chest, not across the forehead, the usual Maya method of supporting a pack." The four patrons depicted in the top third of these pages are Bolon Dzacab, a jaguar, the corn god, and the death god.

The figures on three period-ending monuments at Tikal, Stelae 19, 21, and 22, are shown in profile with packs on their backs. The "burden" in each case is a head

238

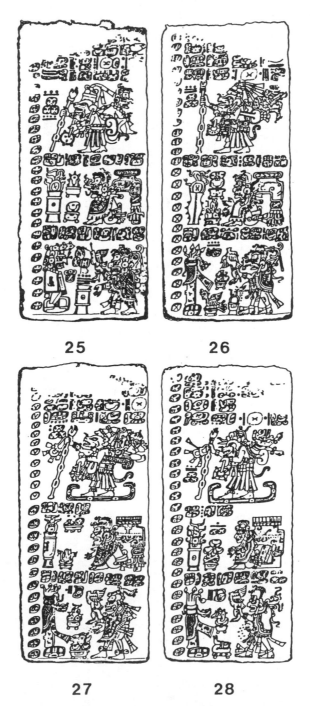

Figure 3. Pages 25-28 of the *Dresden Codex* (after Villacorta C. et al. 1976:60, 62, 64, 66).

with a fleshless jaw that resembles the death god on the back of the bearer on Dresden 28a (compare Figure 3 with Figure 4). Stela 30, which unfortunately cannot be dated, shows the head of the corn god in identical circumstances. The corn god appears in similar contexts on period-ending monuments at Piedras Negras, Yaxchilán (Figure 5), and La Pasadita (Figure 6).

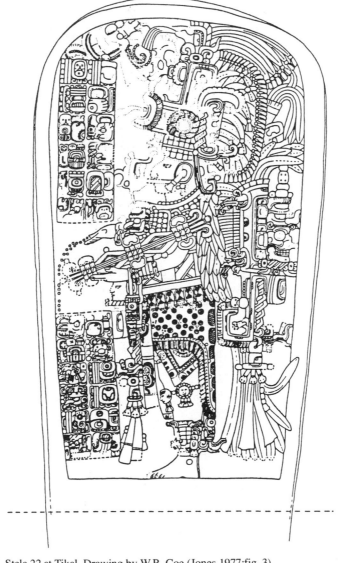

Figure 4. Stela 22 at Tikal. Drawing by W.R. Coe (Jones 1977:fig. 3).

CALENDRICAL MEANING OF RITUAL

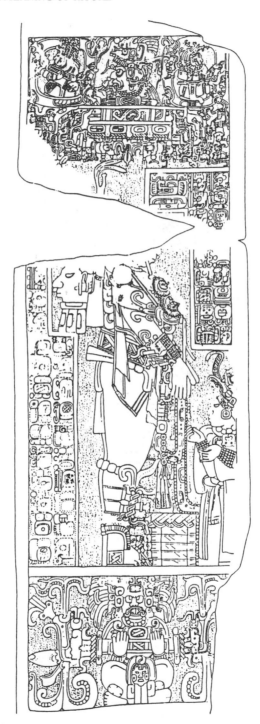

Figure 5. Stela 1 at Yaxchilán. Unpublished drawing by Ian Graham.

Figure 6. Lintel 2 at La Pasadita. Drawing by Ian Graham (Simpson 1976:fig. 4).

CALENDRICAL MEANING OF RITUAL

I have found no examples on period-ending monuments of the other two gods pictured as burdens on *Dresden* 25a-28a. It is possible that the jaguar on the north face of Stela A at Quirigua represents the burden of the figure on the south face of that monument (Figure 7). The complete head and pelt of a jaguar cover the back of the yearbearer on page 36a of the *Madrid Codex* (Figure 8), instead of being carried in a pack. And although Bolon Dzacab, the burden shown in the upper register of *Dresden* 25, frequently appears in the form of a manikin scepter on Classic period monuments (compare Figure 3 with Figure 9), such representations are not limited to period-ending contexts.

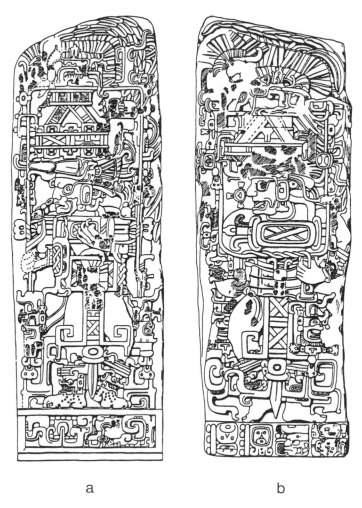

a   b

Figure 7. Stela A at Quirigua. *a*, north face; *b*, south face. Drawing by A.P. Maudslay (Marcus 1976:137).

36a   37a

Figure 8. Pages 36a-37a of the *Madrid Codex* (after Villacorta C. et al. 1976:296, 298).

Thompson (1972:90) notes that the bearer of the patron of the incoming year on the top third of *Dresden* 25-28 "holds a peculiar staff which terminates in a human hand. . . . This staff terminating in a hand has a sporadic distribution in the art of Middle America, but its significance is unknown." Another distinctive characteristic of this staff not mentioned by Thompson is the series of three oval expanded elements spaced at regular intervals along its length (Figure 3). The figures on Stelae 19, 21, and 22 at Tikal also carry staves, but the expanded elements on them are diamond-shaped instead of oval, and they do not end in human hands (Figure 4). Nevertheless, it is possible that they represent stylistically different examples of a similar object with a similar function.

The figure on Stela 3 at Bonampak holds a staff that confirms this interpretation. Only one expanded element is visible on this stela, but it has the same rounded shape as the expanded elements on the staves of the *Dresden* pages, and it terminates in an open-mouthed serpent's head (Figure 10). I suspect that the "human hand" at the top of the staves on *Dresden* 25a-28a was not intended to represent a hand, but is actually the glyph that provides the *chi* reading in the collocation for *chikin,* "west." The word *chi* means "mouth" in the Yucatecan languages, and I believe that the glyph substitutes for the serpent's mouth in this context. I submit that the staves that appear on *Dresden* 25a-28a are the codical equivalents of the "ceremonial bars" and "serpent bars" that appear on period-ending monuments (see Proskouriakoff 1950:201, 204 for definitions of these terms). The ceremonial bars lack the serpent heads found at both ends of the serpent bars, but the intertwined bodies of the two serpents are represented in the diamond-shaped expanded elements on them.

Rulers are usually depicted wearing elaborate sandals on Classic Maya monuments, but the figures on Stelae 19, 21, and 22 at Tikal are barefooted (Figure 4), as are the figures at the bottom of pages 25 and 27 of the *Dresden*

CALENDRICAL MEANING OF RITUAL

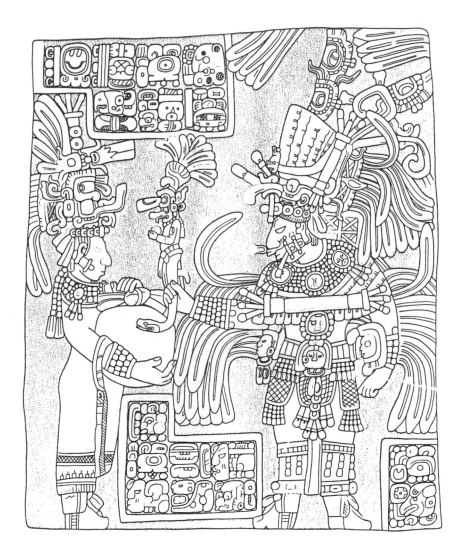

Figure 9. Lintel 53 at Yaxchilán. Drawing by Ian Graham (Graham 1979:115).

Figure 10. Stela 3 at Bonampak. Drawing by Peter Mathews (Mathews 1980:fig. 4).

CALENDRICAL MEANING OF RITUAL

Codex (Figure 3). According to the *Relación de Valladolid,* the New Year's ceremonies that were performed to usher in the years over which Cauac presided ended with a Fire-Walking Rite during which the officiating priest removed his sandals and ran over hot coals (see above). The right hand of the figure on Stela 22 at Tikal is slightly inverted, with circlets shown falling between the thumb and forefinger (Figure 4). The priest who ran over the hot coals in the Fire-Walking Rite sprinkled them with his hyssop of viper tails as he went.

The rite illustrated on Stela 22 at Tikal (Figure 4) conforms to the description of the Fire-Walking Rite in the *Relación de Valladolid* in several respects: (1) the figure is barefooted; (2) the figure is sprinkling or scattering something with his right hand; and (3) the figure is holding an object in his left hand that could represent a hyssop with the bodies of snakes intertwined (i.e., the "expanded elements" are the twisted bodies of snakes). Other parallels with the New Year's ceremonies described in ethnohistorical sources and depicted on the New Year's pages of the *Dresden Codex* and the *Madrid Codex* are: (4) the figure carries the death god on his back; and (5) the figure wears a garment with what could be shells sewn to its lower edge.

The middle section of each of the New Year's pages in the *Dresden Codex* depicts one of the gods mentioned by Landa seated in a building. The gods are (in order): Bolon Dzacab, Kinich Ahau, Itzamna, and Uac Mitun Ahau (Thompson 1972:90). According to Landa (Tozzer 1941:136-149), two gods were involved in each of the New Year's ceremonies. The image of one god was associated with a pile of stones at one of the entrances to the town; the statue of another god was first placed in the house of the sponsor of the ceremonies and later taken to a temple. Different gods are depicted in the top and middle portions of pages 26 and 27 of the *Dresden Codex* (Figure 3).

Only one monument in my sample, Stela 40 at Piedras Negras, depicts a god seated in a building. It is also the only relevant monument which is divided into two registers, with a top portion that corresponds to the top third of the *Dresden* pages and a bottom portion that corresponds to the middle section of the *Dresden* pages. The top register of Stela 40 shows the yearbearer with the head of the corn god as his burden. The bottom register shows a god, possibly Kinich Ahau, resting on a stool in a building that resembles the building shown on *Dresden* 25b-28b (Thompson 1970:pl. 12).

The bottom third of pages 25-28 of the *Dresden Codex* illustrates the rituals that take place at the four entrances to the town (Figure 3). The captions above the pictures contain the glyphs for the four directions where the entrances were located in Landa's time: east (D. 25c), south (D. 26c), west (D. 27c), and north (D. 28c). Each picture contains a figure holding a decapitated bird in its right hand, which must be the headless hen described by Landa. Censers are depicted on D. 25c and D. 26c, and the figures on D. 26c-28c are sprinkling grains of what I take to be the mixture of incense and maize in Landa's description of the ceremonies in honor of the Kan and Muluc years. The glyph for stone (*tun*) appears at the left-hand side of the pictures at the bottom of each page, and in three cases, the glyph for wood (*te*) appears directly above it. Together they must represent the wooden idols on piles of stones observed by Landa at the entrances to a typical sixteenth-century Yucatecan town.[3]

The left-most figure on Stela 1 at Yaxchilán is shown standing over a censer while grains of incense fall upon it from his open hands (Figure 5). The same is true of the left-most figure on Lintel 2 at La Pasadita (Figure 6). In both cases, the burden is the corn god shown strapped to their backs. The date on the first monument refers to the *hotun* ending on 9.16.10.0.0 1 Ahau 3 Zip (15 March A.D. 761). The date on the second monument, 9.16.15.0.0 7 Ahau 18 Pop (17 February A.D. 766), also falls at the end of a *hotun*. I assume that the scenes on these monuments are related to the New Year's rituals described by Landa. They may refer to the burning of incense at one of the four entrances of a town.

Thus each of the three registers of the *Dresden Codex see*ms to have counterparts on stone monuments, as well as in the New Year's rituals described by Landa. The hieroglyphic texts on those monuments specify that the men who carry the patron of the incoming year or *hotun* on their backs are the rulers of the sites at which they are found. The yearbearers were human beings (perhaps personifying gods, perhaps not), and the responsibility for conducting the rituals in honor of the New Year quite literally rested on the shoulders of the political head of the community.

CHAMULA PARALLELS

Two of the four gods that are shown as burdens in the top register of *Dresden* 25-28 can also be found in the New Year's rituals of Chamula. The bull with the defleshed jaw must correspond to the god that presided over the Cauac years, who is represented as a skull on D. 28a and on Stelae 19, 21, and 22 at Tikal (Figures 3 and 4). Evidently, human beings were still being sacrificed for this purpose in Landa's time (Tozzer 1941:147). The Spaniards eventually succeeded in their efforts to abolish human sacrifice, and Chamulas now use bulls as sacrificial victims. The special treatment of the bull's head—displaying it prominently on the central post of the porch and exposing the lower jawbone—link the modern ceremony to Landa's description of the Cauac rites and to the skull burdens on the three stelae from Tikal.

A jaguar is the yearbearer's burden on *Dresden* 26a (Figure 3). A complete jaguar skin, including the animal's head, is draped over the head and back of the figure on the corresponding page of the *Madrid Codex* (Figure 8). That page, M. 36a, has a column of Muluc glyphs at the left of the hieroglyphic text. A jaguar pelt is worn in exactly the same manner when the political and religious officials take part in the Jaguar Skin Dance of Chamula (compare Figures 2 and 8). The significance of this dance is now clear. It represents the yearbearer ceremony of the Muluc years. Like the ruler on Stela A at Quirigua (Figure 7), the political and religious officials are serving as yearbearers when they don the jaguar skin and dance. The bells on the jaguar pelt were probably originally shells, and the entire garment may represent the "alb with many small snail shells sewn on the lower part" referred to in the quote from the *Relación de Valladolid* above. Landa says that war dances were performed during the "nameless days" preceding Muluc years (Tozzer 1941:144), and the so-called flag (*vantera* Sp. *bandera,* "flag") carried by the dancer wearing the jaguar skin syncretizes two military symbols, the pre-Columbian spear and the colonial Spanish flag. Lintel 8 at Yaxchilán depicts a strikingly similar spear, in which feathers, perhaps from the green quetzal and the red macaw, substitute for the ribbons that now festoon the pole between the metal point and the cloth banner (compare Figure 11 with Figures 1 and 2). The ribboned staff of the man who walks in front of the person wearing the jaguar skin may be the modern counterpart of the serpent staff described as a "hyssop" of viper tails in the *Relación de Valladolid.* And the clay kettledrums that are played during the dance are depicted on page 37a of the *Madrid Codex* (compare Figures 2 and 8). Finally, the lifting of the official with the jaguar skin on his back may symbolize the carrying or "bearing" of the New Year.

Figure 11. Lintel 8 at Yaxchilán. Drawing by Ian Graham (Graham and von Euw 1977:27).

The parallels between the Fire-Walking Rite of Chamula and descriptions of a similar rite by Landa and in the *Relación de Valladolid* have been commented on before (e.g., Blom 1956:282). What has not been recognized until now is that it is not an isolated survival, but is part of a trait complex that includes the Bull Sacrifice and the Jaguar Skin Dance. The Fire-Walking Rite and the Bull Sacrifice are derived from the New Year's ceremonies in honor of Cauac. The Jaguar Skin Dance is a Muluc ceremony and should not be performed in the same year as the other two rituals.

Thus the meaning of these rituals is ultimately calendrical and Maya, not biblical and Spanish. The epigraphic and ethnohistorical data suggest that the were once performed over a vast geographical area that encompassed the Yucatán peninsula, including the Peten, the eastern highlands of Guatemala, and the highlands of Chiapas. We see in Chamula the most recent expression of an ancient religious tradition whose formal characteristics have been preserved on stone monuments, in hieroglyphic books, and in ritual drama for at least fifteen hundred years.

END NOTES

[1] The ethnographic data which are the subject of this paper are drawn from Chapter 5 of my book, *Ritual Humor in Highland Chiapas* (Bricker 1973a). Since that book was published, I have turned to ethnohistory and epigraphy for information on the meaning of Maya ritual and drama. The utility of analyzing ethnographic data from a historical perspective is exemplified in my recent book, *The Indian Christ, the Indian King: The Historical Substrate of Maya Myth and Ritual* (Bricker 1981), as well as in this essay.

[2] I am grateful to Thor Anderson for pointing this out to me.

[3] Two piles of stones can still be seen on either side of the entrances to the modern Yucatecan town of Ebtun. Although wooden crosses have replaced the pre-Columbian idols, they continue to echo the "wood-on-stone" motif shown hieroglyphically in the pictures at the bottom of the New Year's pages of the *Dresden Codex*.

SOULS AND SELVES IN CHAMULA:
A THOUGHT ON INDIVIDUALS, FATALISM,
AND DENIAL

Priscilla Rachun Linn
Arlington, Virginia

Fatalism is a concept at once terrifying and fascinating to post-modern Western anthropologists, often caught in a struggle for independence from the tentacles of a seemingly preordained universe. We may recognize the presence of fate, but we would almost surely deny fatalism as a prevailing philosophy of life. This leads to a question: has the denial of fate ever been explored systematically in the contexts of the Maya?

Creeping ethnocentrism and an adherence to one's own values may no doubt be attributed to asking this question, but again creeping ethnocentrism also may be attributed to not asking it. It is curious that we readily accept the denial of fate and full or partial rejection of fatalism for ourselves, but not for individuals in a culture with a belief system that endorses fatalism. Surely the bottom line among any people who value life must be survival. And at times, in order to survive, people must renegotiate and therefore deny what seem to be events or circumstances prescribed by fate.

Where, then, can contemporary evidence be found about individual response to fatalism among Maya people? Dreams are one index, for certainly among the Tzotzil-speaking Zinacantecos and Chamulas of highland Chiapas deep prophetic significance of a person's fate appears attached to dreams. *Cargo* holders, curers, and midwives are called to their duties by dreams, and many tales of fortune and misfortune, including murder and fatal illness, have been foretold in dreams. Indeed there is often a negative cast to the prophecy. For example, only 30 of 132 motifs Laughlin (1976) tabulates in his extensive book on Zinacanteco dreams have favorable import.

Laughlin is careful to state, however, that the Zinacantecos would agree with Jung, whom he quotes, that "the interpretation of dreams and symbols largely depends on the individual circumstances of the dreamer and upon the condition of his mind. . . . [there are] private motifs that do not seem to be shared with other dreamers. . . . [other dreams can] constitute a powerful ego-building force, reinforcing a man's or woman's relationship with the gods and with self." (Laughlin 1976:10). The above statement holds true for Chamula.

Laughlin's observations lead to another question: if, indeed, fatalism is a primary influence on Maya life, then must the fate prescribed always be negative, and must it lead more often than not to passivity in the face of destiny? One Chamula elder told me how in his youth he avoided the fate of death presaged by an owl's night hooting by throwing incense on the hearth fire and praying. He changed his negative fate for a positive one.

In Chamula, the community of approximately 60,000 where my fieldwork took place in 1970-1972 and 1975, relatively few channels of expression for optimistic statements about fate exist, though there are people for whom positive statements might be true. I never heard anyone say, for example, "I am enjoying good health, Thank God," or, "I am taking advantage of life's opportunities and seeking out everything favorable offered in my environment." Even in the United States, where people are openly oriented to self-assertion and success, tongues might cluck at such hubris. For here, as in Chamula, it is more acceptable to appear to be done unto than to do unto. This observation was first made to me by a wise psychiatric social worker in her expert search for hidden anger, but I believe it can also be applied to the highland *municipios* of the Chiapas Maya (Marlene Halperin, personal communication 1978).

For some Chamulas a quasi-despairing but socially acceptable exterior regarding the proscriptions of fate leads Gossen to state that "what Westerners might call 'spiritual peace' or 'general happiness' . . . does not occur in the Chamula repertory of emotion" (1975:459). While fully acknowledging the aptness of Gossen's statement for some Chamulas, I cannot help but wonder if what they say ever differs from what they do when confronting fate.

I found that for some a set of personal rules for operating came into play when a serious problem arose, such as an illness, accident, or financial difficulty. These rules do not appear to indicate a "fatalism and apparent passivity before the inevitable" (Gossen 1975:459). Such rules involve manipulating spiritual resources and powers, using as many channels of communication with the deities as available to them, including curers from many Indian communities, *ladino* spiritual healers, and if necessary witches; interpreting ambiguous dreams favorably and transforming souls into a set of personal symbols whose actions and escapes from peril reflect a sense of personal power in achieving gain or triumphing over evil.

It is hard to tell how much these operational rules are influenced by emotional states such as despair and depression, anger and elation, and how much they are influenced by cultural parameters. Thus a passive fatalism may indeed be the choice for some according to the interpretation, manipulation, and operation of spiritual resources, but not necessarily the choice for everyone. One choice might be to reject fatalism, hence possibly also to reject certain Maya values, while another choice might be, as stated above, to choose to appear to accept fatalism while indeed acting in a manner that challenges the seeming inevitability of fate.

My field observations reveal, for example, that Chamula behavior towards illness can range from resigned fatalism to active intervention in finding a cure. Family members of the Chamula gardener who worked for the Harvard Chiapas Project showed marked individual variation to illness. Two of the sons in the gardener's family met very different ends when they both contracted tuberculosis. Twice the father forbade them antibiotics. The younger son, first diagnosed, rebelled, accepted medical treatment from an American anthropologist, and lived. He ultimately severed his ties in Chamula and became more citified in his ways. Several years later, the more traditional older brother obeyed his father's orders and died.

In contrast, other field assistants from different families willingly accepted Western medicine as well as pursuing native cures. One sought relief for his wife's mysterious and incapacitating neurological ailment from a doctor who is *ladino* (the term for Mexicans following a Hispanicized, rather than Indian, way of life), as well as from numerous curers in Indian and *ladino* communities within a 250 km radius of Chamula. The gardener accepted his perceived fate without seeking outside intervention, whereas other Chamulas appear to have intervened in their fate by using expanded sources of traditional and nontraditional healing.

INDIVIDUAL EXPRESSION AND SOUL BELIEFS

We may never know why some people are more inclined towards a negative fatalism than others in any of the highland Indian communities, but we may have a clue about people's perception of the impact of fate on them. Each person's soul is intimately linked to his or her destiny—especially that part of the soul known as a *chanul* or an animal spirit companion. The *chanul* appears in dreams, which have already been mentioned as prognosticators of an individual's fate. The animal soul's well-being (which intimately affects the well-being of its human counterpart) can be foretold by interpreting the events in a dream.

Vogt (1965b, 1969b, 1970a, 1976) has written definitively about animal souls in Zinacantán, and Gossen (1975) has discussed animal souls and human destiny in Chamula. Indeed, it is from Gossen's seminal paper that the thoughts for this essay evolved. Childs (1968), Foster (1944), Guiteras Holmes (1961), Holland (1961), Linn (1982), Pitt-Rivers (1970), Pozas A. (1959:200-204), Saler (1967), and Silver (1966) have all contributed to the exploration of Maya soul beliefs. Due to the constraints of space, however, some of the more detailed information on soul beliefs, not included here, can be found in the above works.

In looking at the connections between perceptions of fate and souls, this essay departs from the quest for an "essential notion" to render soul beliefs intelligible and reduce confusion (Pitt-Rivers 1970:186). I find that in the very inconsistencies and vagaries of soul belief we receive some of the most valuable information about people's personal symbolic systems, their perception of personal power, and their belief in their ability to manipulate—or even reject—destiny.

Individuals and Soul Research in Chamula

Unfortunately, while I was actually in the field, I was stymied by the inconsistent information about animal souls I now find so revealing, and so I turned my attention to the more concrete matters of the yearly festival cycle. Since direct correlations between personalities and interpretations of the soul were not made in the field, doing so here would be quite speculative. Where possible, I make some general observations about personalities and souls, offering this information as an explorative theory in the spirit of inquiry Professor Vogt ever fostered. Perhaps some future anthropologist may find merit in examining the personal symbolic expression of animal soul beliefs suggested in the remainder of this essay.

Perhaps, too, future anthropologists will be able to continue this examination within any of the highland Maya communities. Indeed, comparing the responses of individuals from Maya communities may contribute towards understanding the unique differences between the cultural personalities of the many communities with their diverse histories and contours of their social and political organizations.

Personalities of Field Assistants. A word about the diversity of the nineteen field assistants I contacted indicates how I came to the variations I found so frustrating in 1970. Each brought an outlook on life as varied as his or her soul beliefs. Some were assertive, others more passive; some were confident, some more diffident; some were insecure, some deferent, and some cocky.

The boy, between nine and twelve years of age, reflected hesitantly and sketchily on matters reserved more properly for adults. Two were curers: an unmarried woman in her late twenties and a respected elder, renowned in the community hierarchy of civil and religious office holders. Others included four young men in their late teens (two pairs of brothers from different families) who had not yet achieved stature in the community; a literate woman in her twenties who was quite poor and affected by the scandal of her illegitimate child; an elderly woman, the wife of a former religious office holder; and other adult males, including three elders who had served prestigious religious offices and sponsored major festivals.

In dealing with individual variation, there is always the possibility that information is invented to mislead the anthropologist probing sensitive matters. In the interpretation I put forth, the inventions are a part of the personal symbolic system and can be interpreted as such.

ESSENTIAL SOUL DATA: GENERALIZATIONS AND VARIATIONS

To underscore the range of information collected about souls, and to show how this information varies among field assistants and according to fieldworkers, I use the research of several anthropologists. In setting out the information below, I first present general information that appears in every source. This includes Pozas's short account, which reveals no apparent idiosyncrasies (1959:201-204). This is followed by Gossen's (1975), Linn's (1970-1972, 1975), and Childs's (1968) reports. Gossen's data on souls is clearly the result of meticulous interviews, but he does not state how many were interviewed. Childs interviewed some twelve Chamulas, mostly adult men.

Ownership and Types of Souls

General: A benevolent deity, either St. Jerome or Our Father in the Sky (also called the Sun/Christ by Gossen), assigns every ordinary person, Indian and non-Indian, a *chanul* that exists outside the body as a living wild animal. There is no mention of who assigns witch souls. Children do not necessarily inherit the soul animal of their parents. Ever since the humans of today have existed, a baby *chanul* is born at the same time and is the same sex as its human counterpart. Humans and animals mature at the same rate. *Chanuletik* (plural of *chanul*) have five toes on each paw. Other wild animals have four toes.

All souls have a junior and senior aspect which will be discussed below. Witches may have domestic animals as souls, which no doubt reflects a strong influence of seventeenth-century European witchcraft beliefs on native soul concepts.

A core list of *chanuletik* includes: large jaguars, smaller felines (pumas, ocelots, tigrillos, margays), coyotes, grey foxes, weasels, opossums, and raccoons. A core list of witch familiars includes: goats, sheep, horses, cattle, dogs, cats, chickens, turkeys, and pigs. Domestic black animals are particularly suspect.

Gossen: Rabbits, skunks, and squirrels are added for ordinary people; wild birds and insects may be witches' souls. St. Jerome and the Sun/Christ assign the *chanul.*

Linn: Hawks and buzzards can be souls for ordinary people. Some Chamulas state that rabbits cannot be souls. Men, women, and children can possess three souls, or men possess three and women only two or even one soul. Only Our Father in the Sky is mentioned as assigning souls.

Childs: Hummingbirds, owls, whippoorwills, and kinkajous can be souls for ordinary people; monkeys, deer, and snakes can be souls for witches. Again, some state rabbits cannot be souls. Only Our Father in the Sky assigns souls.

Dwellings and Junior/Senior Aspect of Souls

General: All wild animal souls live away from human habitation in caves and woods. As stated above, all manifest a junior and senior aspect. The jaguar, strongest and largest of soul animals, dwells far from the highlands in hot low country. Witch souls can be devious domestic animals living in human compounds.

Gossen: Both the junior and senior aspect have thirteen parts. "The junior aspect of the *chanul* lives in the sacred mountain named *Tzontevitz* located in Chamula municipal territory. . . . The senior aspect of the soul animal lives on the third level of the sky. . . . During the day, these associated animals roam the woods and fields of their territories much as an ordinary animal would. However, at night, St. Jerome, in both his junior and senior aspects, herds them into corrals—the junior one on the sacred mountain, the senior in the third level of the sky" (Gossen 1975:451).

Linn: Souls have both a physical and spiritual presence. Senior animals can live both on earth and in heaven, or it is only junior animals who live on earth. Variations include the ideas that senior animals never contact junior animals or, quite the opposite, that senior animals care for the juniors. Animals may sleep during the day and hunt at night, or vice versa. Junior animals roam about freely or remain in caves, too delicate to fend for themselves. Souls (both junior and senior aspects) may live in a variety of places, including *tzontevitz, muktavitz* (the traditional home of Zinacanteco souls [Vogt 1969b:371]), *mispia* (a sacred mountain for rain-making ritual), or in unnamed woods, caves, and mountains all over Chamula and in low country. Some state that felines sleep in caves while coyotes and weasels repose in grassy caves.

Childs: Curers can have two junior animals and two senior. Junior animals can leave the cave, seniors might not. Seniors and juniors might live apart, seniors in *tzontevitz,* juniors in *ojovitz*—another sacred mountain in Chamula and home of the earth gods. Soul animals can also live in *muktavitz* and in the caves around each barrio cross in Chamula. (These three barrios form the geo-socio-political divisions of the municipality.) Jaguars might live in deep forest, and jaguars and hummingbirds might live apart from other souls. *Ladino* souls live very far away from human habitation, for *ladinos* do not get as sick as Indians.

Caretakers of Souls

General: The carved figure of St. Jerome (*htotik hermin*) poses with a lion in the Chamula church, hence it is called the patron saint of souls by most Chamulas, but not all believe that he feeds or herds souls in a heavenly realm. Curers often pay special attention to St. Jerome if the animal soul is possibly sick, wounded, or neglected, but animal souls are not the cause of every illness.

Gossen: St. Jerome cares for animals on earth and in heaven, protecting them at night in corrals.

Linn: Our Father in the Sky and St. Jerome can supervise food distribution and rescue animals in distress, as well as the capricious and at times cantankerous earth gods (see Gossen 1974 and Linn 1976 for more information on these earth and rain deities). A combination of Our Father, St. Jerome, and the earth gods can also care for souls. In the sky, Our Father and St. Jerome feed stationary senior animals the essence of meat. Animals can sit in a cave on chairs around a large table with bowls of food, dining every day in the same manner as religious and civil officials during festivals. Adult souls can feed child souls, while senior souls can supernaturally hunt birds, chickens, and rabbits for junior animals. Alternatively, junior animals can hunt for themselves, while senior animals, too important to be endangered, remain behind in enclosures such as corrals or caves.

Childs: The saints, St. Jerome, ancestral spirits, earth spirits (or a combination of these beings), and the barrio saints —John, Peter, and Sebastian—can all be seen to exit from the barrio cave shelters at night to feed souls. Or senior animals can feed junior animals.

Soul Endangerment

General: Souls remain most secure if they stay put inside a wilderness enclosure protected by their guardians. Outside their enclosure they may be hurt by the vicious hooves, claws, and teeth of witch souls, or they may be hurt by guns and traps of humans angered by marauding animals they do not recognize as souls. When the animal suffers and dies, three days later, so also does the human, and vice versa.

Gossen: Souls may also loose one of their parts due to human activity such as "sexual intercourse, fright, excitement, pleasure, anger, or accident" (Gossen 1975:451).

Linn: Animals may fight about sharing food inside the corral and may be shoved from the feeding table. If not rescued, they starve and die. Junior animals may be unable to get food, and some ornery animals may just cause brawls.

Childs: Soul animals may steal food from earth gods. Angrily they expel the animal, and a hunter shoots it. Supernatural guardians can also withdraw protection from souls, if humans refuse to offer the guardians candles. Souls can also then be shot and killed.

Traits and Social Ranking of Souls

General: Each individual interprets how soul animals symbolize the power, energy, intelligence, health, appearance, and ability to cure illness of their human owners. Animal souls exist not only as a physical presence in themselves, but also as metaphors of their human counterparts. A powerful curer or witch may have a large jaguar for a soul, while a weak, scrawny, sickly person might have a raccoon, opossum, skunk, or lesser animal. Witches—who can be either poor or rich—usually are linked with domestic animals.

Gossen: Souls come in three rankings: rich and powerful, who are mostly shamans and political leaders, usually associated with a jaguar; moderately successful, linked with coyote, weasel, and ocelot; and humble and poor, linked with rabbit, opossum, and skunk. The powerful and poor ends are consistent, but the moderately successful level "is not consistently reported from individual to individual" (Gossen 1975:452).

Linn: Characteristics of animals and their owners vary with individual interpretation. Some see a strong curer having three separate souls, for example, a jaguar and two coyotes, while a lesser person has two weasels and a coyote. The character of the coyote and weasel seem to vary the most. All speakers attribute strong spiritual qualities or leadership to the jaguar. Aside from jaguars, powerful curers can also have smaller felines, coyotes, gray foxes, and weasels for souls.

Wealthy people might have traditionally lucky blue green colored souls, while poor people have traditionally unlucky red colored souls. Drunkards might have jaguar souls; wife beaters might have coyote souls. For some, strong people can have opossums, for this animal does not die easily. For others, noncurers or only very minor curers, hence not strong people, will have possums, skunks, or raccoons for souls. Some Chamulas state that coyotes and weasels may belong to smart people, some to stupid people, or some say only to neighboring Tzotzil-speaking Huisteco Indians, or only to *ladinos,* or not to *ladinos* at all. *Ladinos* from Chiapa de Corzo are said to have vultures for souls.

Childs: Rich people own nice big jaguar souls, while poorer folk have ocelots, pumas, possums, weasels, skunks, and kinkajous. Big jaguars accompany strong curers, but ocelots, weasels, and coyotes accompany noncurers only. Weasels, especially, might belong to poorer people, for they eat chickens and get shot. *Ladinos* and Indians from the municipalities of San Andres, Tenejapa, San Miguel, San Pedro, and Zinacantán have strong animal souls due to the many good curers living there. Indians from Huistán have coyotes. Indians from Tenejapa might have jaguars and supernatural fireballs called *poslom* for souls, but Indians from Oxchuc and Cancuc, feared as witches, possess screech owls, horned owls, and whippoorwills, while some say *ladinos* have jaguars, coyotes, and hawks.

Humans Perception and Divination for Souls

General: Souls are the figures perceived in dreams, whether they have human or animal form, but only a shaman can determine the kind of soul a person has from a dream. If Chamulas know their souls, most do not readily discuss this intimate matter with anthropologists, although they discuss general soul matters quite openly. Stories abound of people shooting souls mistaken for profane wildlife, especially coyotes, weasels, and raccoons, but jaguars may also be targets (Gossen 1974:256, 284). Extremely unfortunate people may even kill their own souls, which is not taken as suicide. Usually the soul has committed some misdeed, like stealing corn from the fields.

SOULS, CONFORMITY, AND DESTINY

A strong message of conformity, humility, and acceptance of destiny may be read in the beliefs outlined above. To remain safe, animal souls should stay confined in a cave or corral rather than roam freely like wild animals. This implies that human survival is based on staying within the bounds of social decorum. Soul animals are often described as marauders and predators potentially damaging human settlements or each other, implying that Chamulas are also easily capable of social destruction through fights, envy, suspicion, and anger, which lead to lethal witchcraft. Animals should keep a set distance from humans, so in Chamula should social distance be observed in acknowledging principles of seniority, male superiority, social and economic rank, property rights, and so forth (see Gossen 1974). The jaguar, most dangerous of all, emphasizes overt fear in Chamula of extreme power, for they relegate such an animal to a safe distance from humans in the lowlands. Curers with jaguar souls are set apart from ordinary Chamulas by their great spiritual power, which can be perverted into witchcraft. When this power is controlled, however, the jaguar guides, leads, and protects ordinary souls.

Feeding pattern also expresses caution and conformity. Souls and humans must eat correct foods in the correct manner. In Chamula, peacefully eaten meals are a paradigm of social order, especially those consumed during festivals given by *cargo* officials or at curing ceremonies. Just as stronger religious officials support the weaker festival onlookers, or the host of the curing ceremony provides a meal to the assembled participants, so animal souls should eat communally and willingly share food, with the stronger caring for the weaker. Antisocial eating habits, such as cannibalism of the soul, hoarding, gluttony, or wastefulness, lead to accusations of witchcraft, much as soul animals face death from hunters if they steal food.

People often mention the dangers surrounding eating, which is the essence of survival for soul animals. Rationality may not always prevail when souls eat. An animal may escape its approved confines to eat forbidden food, thus endangering its own life. Furthermore, animals may be neglected to starve. There is no telling when emotionally uncontrolled witch souls jeopardize survival by stealing food or fighting, clawing, or stealing food from feeding animals.

The above statements underscore the boundaries of approved behavior and the lack of overt room for strong, direct speech, reflecting a lusty quest for personal power, fortune, or success. Such talk clearly invites witchcraft or accusations of being a witch. The ambitious, vengeful, or strident individual must therefore seek other modes of individual self expression.

INDIVIDUAL METAPHORS FOR FATE AND AUTONOMY IN SOUL BELIEFS

It is perhaps in the very way people express the numerous variations in soul beliefs that they are able to put forth symbolic expressions of individual power, self-determination, and denial of fate. Ten obvious variations will be highlighted here, but numerous others, subtle and detailed, must await further discussion.

1. Each person creates his or her own list of animals and assigns his or her own relative powers, dangers, and characteristics to them. Animals can be as strong, brutal, weak, cunning, caring, treacherous, stupid, lazy, beautiful, or ugly as the person interprets them to be. Several of the elder men, powerful in their community, only mentioned the weaker soul animals when I asked if they existed, indicating that perhaps some speakers hardly identify with lesser souls and their inferiority. Excluding a rabbit shows a sense of personal survival, since rabbits are probably the easiest highland game to capture.

2. None of my field assistants thought that soul animals were hereditary. A child born of jaguar soul parents is not necessarily a jaguar. Parental souls therefore do not appear to create or influence a sense of family destiny or inherited fate. It would be extremely interesting to know how Chamulas explain differences in the outcome of siblings judged to have the same soul animal and how children as they grow up come to differ in soul beliefs from the influential adults in their lives. People who believe that soul animals are destined to be

inherited may have a stronger sense of fate's influence than those who do not and may hold more strongly to traditional beliefs and the word of their parents than those who see the soul animal unrelated to the elders.

3. The interaction between soul and human makes it hard to tell how much the soul influences human behavior, and vice versa. Gossen (1975:453) relates a story about a woman killing her own soul and dying three days later, but Childs (1968) collected a story about an astute person who saved his soul. One night he recognized that a small wild feline was his soul. Instead of shooting it, he rescued the cat and placed it in a cave, demonstrating an active metaphor of self-preservation and survival.

4. Numbers of souls and their complexity reveal a metaphoric sense of social flexibility, ingenuity, adaptability, and opportunity. It is my hunch that the more complex the soul beliefs, the more complex the world of the speaker, with the more diverse choices and positive attitudes towards influencing life. Ordering souls in definite hierarchies, both social and sexual, provides a metaphor for the speaker's perception and evaluation of social and sexual hierarchies. The child I interviewed provided a very limited list of souls with very sketchy beliefs about their organization, reflecting the limited perception of the world around him that a child might have. Conversely, the village elder who was also a curer described an intricate set of beliefs about souls being arranged in hierarchies matching his experience with social hierarchies.

Equally important is how quickly people assign souls to *ladinos*. Some people considered *ladino* souls immediately without probing questions, indicating an awareness of the *ladino* world and perhaps the options that world offers, despite Indians' basic dislike and distrust of it as seen by the often disparaging comments about *ladino* souls.

5. Residence of souls also indicates metaphoric vulnerability to danger, for animals thought to come in easy contact with humans are far more likely to encounter harm than those safely ensconced in a sacred mountain under protective custody of the saints or spirits. Anthropologists need to explore what kind of life experiences put forth a view that souls lead a precarious wandering existence and what experiences lead to the concept of relative security.

6. Another marked variation occurred in the degrees of dependency required for survival by the animals. Some see animals quite happily foraging for themselves, fairly removed from divine intervention, while others perceive close divine supervision, with souls sitting at tables like humans. Perhaps dependency on spiritual care ties in with a metaphoric sense of individual self-determination—strong dependency revealing a need for divine custody to survive and a weak dependency on individual autonomy and self-will. If the autonomy is viewed as dangerous, however, the attitude might be easy abandonment by the divine caretaker, hence an individual prone to insecurities and perhaps despairing fatalism.

7. Concomitant to expressions of general soul autonomy are ideas about soul feeding patterns. The image of souls eating independently differs from penned-up creatures waiting for food to be doled out. In the latter case, the guardian

directly supervises and punishes nonconforming vicious souls that flaunt social control by instigating fights over food. Independent eating suggests a metaphor of relative safety from witches and a free choice tolerable for human survival, without constant spiritual supervision. Those who discuss eating independently, such as the young men, may indicate a distance from the supernatural world, perhaps indicating a sense of autonomy rather than fatalism.

8. The kinds of caretakers for souls may also reflect relative self-security and self-determination. People who see senior souls caring for juniors may expect real people to rely more on one another than the gods when help is needed. If the earth gods are envisioned as caretakers, people may feel more unsettled and subject to unpredictable fate than those who turn to the more trustworthy, kindhearted, and steadfast St. Jerome. Indeed, often when the gods such as St. Jerome of Our Father in the Sky allow illness to occur, the sick person has brought on trouble through some sin, such as failure to make offerings to the gods, greed, or irascibility without cause.

9. Some speakers readily emphasize that souls may be easily and suddenly harmed (such as by sudden fright, sexual excitement, and so forth), while others may talk about soul activities before they discuss how souls are harmed. Speakers preoccupied with harm tend also to emphasize that witches abound, and the gods readily abandon imperfect humans to witches. Some speakers do not mention witch familiars until well into an interview, while others mention them right away and focus much of the discussion on them. Reasons for preoccupation with witches may have to do with sickness in the family or a recent run of bad luck. How the speaker responds to misfortune is some indication of fatalism. The degree to which gods are hard and intolerant or more patient and forgiving also indicates how speakers perceive the harshness of fate. The way the soul reacts to spiritual abandonment and the means to rectify the abandonment through help from the gods shows different perceptions of spiritual power, limits of personal control, and the inevitability of fate.

10. Chamulas may undergo marked personal and psychological change. Chronically sick people may become well, poorer people may become better off (though not often), alcoholics may become teetotalers, lay people may become curers. It is said that people may change animal souls or have a curer reinterpret the kind of soul they have. Few data have been collected on the phenomenon of soul change to see, for example, if reinterpretation correlates with change in state of life. It is my hunch that better understanding of these changes would further reveal important insights into the use of animal souls as personal symbols of self-destiny.

I am the first to admit that the ideas above are quite speculative and most certainly subjective, based on my perceptions as much as on any cultural reality. However, it is not just Chamulas who manipulate personal symbols, but all people. The differences in the way Gossen and I perceive the effect of fate on Chamula may reflect differences in our own perceptions of life, as much as any differences in the Chamulas we interviewed. We anthropologists all bring our own personal symbols into any project we undertake, hence our struggle with

262

objectivity, but that is yet another weighty matter.

WHOLE COMMUNITIES AND PARTIAL BELIEFS: A PARTING COMMENT

The question of fate leads to a concluding, more general thought about the role of the personal in anthropology. The intricate interplay between the individual and his or her culture remains one of the great mysteries of anthropology. At the cultural level, everyone in Chamula has a *chanul*; heretics are absent, for no one denies, or even questions, the existence of this animal spirit companion. Soul beliefs are much like the traditional clothing of Chiapanec Indians. At first the distinctive style of each community seems almost uniform, yet upon closer inspection each garment reveals a personal style. The variety of clothes is as much a statement about one's place in the community as is the variety of soul beliefs.

In the Harvard Chiapas Project, Professor Vogt has achieved one of the great contributions to anthropology. Enough research has been culled on a level of cultural abstraction by a widely diverse group of anthropologists to begin to explore some of the most subtle and complex questions of an individual's perception of self in his or her culture.

The personal response to fate as an expression of self in Chamula culture impacts not only on issues of individual psychology, but also, as Gossen (1975:460) suggests, on Chamula response to such crucial matters as development projects and community improvements that affect the well-being of the entire municipality.

ACKNOWLEDGMENTS. I would like to thank the Doherty Foundation for Latin American Studies for a grant awarded in 1970-1971 and the Harvard Chiapas Project for a grant in 1972, which made my fieldwork possible. I would also like to thank Professor Evon Z. Vogt, leader of the Harvard Chiapas Project, and his wife, Catherine C. Vogt, for all their gracious and generous assistance throughout the course of my graduate research, both at Harvard and in the field.

ELUSIVE ESSENCES:
SOULS AND SOCIAL IDENTITY
IN TWO HIGHLAND MAYA COMMUNITIES

John M. Watanabe
University of Michigan

INTRODUCTION

Evon Z. Vogt's pioneering research on the Tzotzil Maya of the Chiapas highlands in southeastern Mexico exemplifies both close-grained ethnographic analysis of the community of Zinacantán (Vogt 1969b, 1976) and an abiding concern for controlled comparison within the Maya culture area as a whole (Vogt 1964d, n.d.). As a scholar, he first impressed me with the importance of understanding ethnographic particulars in their own terms before waxing too theoretical about them; as a teacher, he challenged and inspired me to plumb the "native's" point of view as deeply as possible, while keeping in mind wider comparative issues and implications. In this essay, I hope to demonstrate lessons well-learned through an analysis of Maya concepts of "soul" in the Mam *municipio* of Santiago Chimaltenango in the Cuchumatán highlands of western Guatemala. I begin with a brief discussion of Zinacanteco "souls," then examine the analogous Chimalteco concepts, in the process evaluating the relevance of each case for understanding the other. I will argue that in addition to issues of mortality, morality, and social control, Maya "souls" figure importantly in questions of local ethnic identity, in this sense perhaps resembling American black notions of "soul" more closely than metaphysical essences. I conclude with the implications of this comparison for including soul concepts in the "systemic patterns" of Vogt's phylogenetic model of Maya culture.

"SOULS" IN ZINACANTAN

The Tzotzil Maya of Zinacantán recognize two types of "souls" (Vogt 1969b:369-374). First, the *ch'ulel* constitutes an "inner soul" located in the blood and heart. The ancestral gods place this soul in each embryo at birth. Most Zinacantecos say that these souls pass down the patriline, drawn from a "pool" of souls previously held by members of the same descent group. In this sense, children represent the literal as well as figurative *k'exoliletik,* "replacements, substitutes," for deceased relatives. Although apparently eternal and indestructible, the *ch'ulel* consists of thirteen parts, one or more of which can leave the body during sleep when dreaming or "drop out" when the person experiences strong emotions, especially fright. If not remedied by the proper curing ritual, such "soul loss" leads to illness and eventual death.

The second type of soul is the *chanul* or "animal spirit companion." This soul takes the form of a wild animal, such as a jaguar, coyote, ocelot, or smaller animal, cared for by the ancestral gods where they live inside a large mountain near the town center of Zinacantán. The different species of animal souls in part account for personal differences between individuals: successful Zinacantecos have strong animal souls like jaguars, less notable townspeople more humble opossum or rabbit souls. Each day, the ancestors release these animal souls to graze on surrounding mountainsides disguised as sheep or cows, but at night they gather them into corrals inside their sacred mountain to protect them from witches and other dangers of the dark. Such protection proves indispensable since every Zinacanteco shares his or her *ch'ulel,* "inner soul," with one of these animal souls and so shares the same life fate with it; what happens to one must happen to the other. As with the inner soul, the animal soul can be "lost" in the sense that, for any number of reasons, the ancestral gods may choose to abandon an animal soul to roam untended in the woods, leaving its human self to suffer whatever misfortune befalls the forsaken animal.

Vogt interprets Zinacanteco soul concepts in two ways. Socially, they function as a ready mechanism of social control, since having a soul relates directly to behaving in appropriate Zinacanteco ways. The corralled animal soul dramatizes ancestral—that is, community—mastery over unruly individual behavior or tendencies. If a Zinacanteco fails to conform to accepted standards of work, speech, social conduct, community service, or dress and cleanliness, the ancestral gods can either knock out all or part of the offender's inner soul, or release his or her animal soul from their protective custody. In both cases, the mortal jeopardy of such punishment compels miscreants to seek a ritual cure that at once reintegrates them into Zinacanteco society while reaffirming the moral sovereignty of Zinacanteco custom (Vogt 1976:86-89). On a more abstract level, Vogt also suggests that Zinacanteco souls conceptually balance the categories of "culture" and "nature" in Zinacanteco thought (1970a:1158-1160). In particular, animal souls represent both a "culturalization of nature" and a "naturalization of culture." Zinacantecos become "naturalized" by sharing their souls with animals, yet at the same time these "wild" animals remain corralled, controlled by the ancestral gods as quintessential arbiters of culture. Consonant with Lévi-Strauss's theory of totemism, Vogt argues that this double transposition serves to explain organizational principles and structural relations of Zinacanteco society by grounding them in the "natural" distinctions of animal species.

Several elements stand out in Vogt's description and analysis of Zinacanteco souls: the unequivocal association of souls with ancestors, linked metonymically by blood and descent; the deep attachment of both the inner soul and the animal soul to local community places, epitomized by the mountain abode of the ancestors; and the intimate connection between having a soul and behaving properly. I now turn to the Mam concepts of soul in the Guatemalan town of Santiago Chimaltenango to see to what extent these characteristics of continuity, commitment, and comportment pertain to what at first appears to be a contrasting set of conceptualizations.

"SOULS" IN SANTIAGO CHIMALTENANGO

The *municipio* of Santiago Chimaltenango lies on the southern slopes of the Cuchumatán highlands in the department of Huehuetenango, Guatemala. Charles Wagley (1941, 1949) first carried out research there in 1937, and I did so in 1978-1980, with brief return visits in 1981 and 1988 (Watanabe 1984, 1988). The people here speak Mam, the most widespread language of the Mamean branch of Eastern Mayan languages, and appear to have occupied the area since at least A.D. 500 (England 1983:6). The town center of Santiago Chimaltenango, or "Chimbal" as Mam speakers call the town, stands at nearly 7400 ft (2242 m), with township lands falling to below 6000 ft in the lower valleys and rising to well over 9000 ft on the highest peaks. Unlike other Maya towns, over two-thirds of Chimbal's 3500 inhabitants live in the town center rather than scattered in outlying hamlets. Rapid population growth in recent years has undermined local subsistence corn farming, leading to greater dependency on migratory wage labor outside the community, as well as diversification into cash cropping in coffee, petty trading, and transport (Watanabe 1981). The advent of electoral party politics after 1944, along with Catholic and evangelical missionization since the 1950s, have vitiated the former ritual obligations of the town's civil-religious hierarchy and discredited much of the old "folk" Catholic religion. Despite this apparent assimilation to *ladino* ways, Chimaltecos have retained their language, their land, and a resolute self-identity that continues to distinguish them from both their *ladino* and Maya neighbors alike (Watanabe 1988). Chimalteco notions of "soul" play an essential part in fostering this local distinctiveness.

Like Zinacantecos, Chimaltecos recognize an "inner soul" called *aanma*. The concept of *aanma*, however, lacks explicit reference to local ancestors and adheres more closely to Christian notions of an immaterial personal essence. Derived from the Spanish *ánima*, "soul" (cf. Maldonado et al. 1986:16), *aanma* means both "heart" and "soul" in Mam. Chimaltecos say that the spiritual aspect of *aanma* resides in the breath, *xeewbaj*, and survives death to become *taanma kyimni*, "soul of the dead." Although Chimaltecos formerly said that after death souls abided inside nearby peaks or volcanos with the *taajwa witz*, "owners or masters of the mountains," these *witz*, or "mountains" as they were often simply called, figured not as ancestral gods but as capricious *ladino* supernaturals rich in money, clothes, plantations, and livestock, for whom the dead toiled. In fact, Chimalteco *witz* bear striking resemblance to *yahval balamil*, the greedy *ladino* Earth Lord in Zinacantán (cf. Wagley 1949:60, 67-68; Vogt 1969b:302-303). Today, Chimaltecos generally associate souls with a distant but all-powerful, largely Christian God, whereas *witz* evoke images of the Devil. Similarly, the Chimalteco term *-kleel*, which once referred to guardian spirit animals akin to Zinacanteco animal souls (cf. Wagley 1949:65-66), now denotes a protective angel or saint who watches over a person (Watanabe 1984:95-96).

Despite such obvious Christianization, the Chimalteco concept of *aanma* represents more than an artless reflection of Christian metaphysics. It retains strong reference to the physical body, especially the heart and even one's "sense of touch" (cf. Maldonado et al. 1986:16). Also, like the Zinacanteco *ch'ulel, aanma* can be "lost": it leaves the body during sleep when Chimaltecos dream; it "goes out" if the person suffers *seky'pajleenin*, "fright." One Chimalteco reasoned that fright "makes the soul think that the body is already dead," and so it leaves. Mothers will sweep the ground with a sprig of brush or a broom where a child has gotten hurt, repeating several times in a low voice, *we7ketza! we7ketza!*, "Get up, get up," to the child's *aanma*. Even a grown man who slips on a muddy path will sometimes strike the spot with his machete so that his startled "soul" will not remain behind.

As in Zinacantán, soul loss corresponds to illness—for Chimaltecos, a loss of appetite, listlessness, insomnia, headaches, "sadness." The cure here, however, entails not a ritual "soul calling" (cf. Vogt 1969b:442-444), but spraying the patient's face and chest with a potion made mostly of *aguardiente,* raw bootleg sugar cane rum, mixed with black pepper, rue (*Ruta graveolens*), and a patent medicine sold in local pharmacies (cf. Gillin 1948; Rubel et al. 1984:33). This dousing, plus drafts of the tonic over several days, "heats" the patient's blood and so induces the soul to return, literally putting the person "back in touch" with normal activities. That *aanma* refers to one's immaterial "soul" as well as corporeal "heart" more than coincidentally links spiritual and physical well-being in Chimbal. Christian overtones aside, *aanma* still inheres in the condition of one's blood and in how one behaves, much like the Zinacanteco *ch'ulel.* This "social" as opposed to metaphysical quality of Chimalteco souls relates directly to another kind of "cognitive essence" that Mam speakers call *naabl*—what might be termed a person's "social soul," or more positivistically, a people's particular "way of being."

"Souls" and Social Life in Chimbal

Even to native Mam speakers, the concept of *naabl* remains somewhat elusive. Various dictionary translations include "thought, idea, feeling" and "mentality, attitude" (Maldonado et al. 1986:206); or more obtusely, a person's "normality" or "beginning of conscious life" (Robertson et al. n.d.:801). Although these definitions testify to the intriguing scope of the concept, none adequately captures its full import. Linguistically, the word derives from the transitive verb root *naa-*, "feel or perceive," and the instrumental suffix *-bil* (England 1983:118); taken literally, *naabl* means "that used to feel or perceive." Syntactically, *naabl* always occurs in possessed form, but unlike other similar Mam nouns belonging to human beings, such as body parts, food, clothing, and kin terms, *naabl* lacks an absolute form independent of possessive markers, perhaps suggesting that it remains semantically more integral to its possessors than these other things (cf. England 1983:68-70). Notably, only human beings and words possess *naabl, tnaabl yool* being "the meaning of a word." More than simply thoughts, ideas, or feelings, *naabl* refers to the "normal"—yet distinctly—human capacity to do things like think, imagine, and feel, or perhaps like words, to be meaningful.

In trying to define this term, one Chimalteco observed, *ok nuul itz'j juun xhku7l, minti7 txiimbitz peero at tnaabl,* "When a baby is born, it does not have thoughts but it has *naabl.*" He went on to explain that a mother must be careful getting out of bed because her sleeping baby will sense what is happening and wake up crying. Such awareness, however, remains particularly human, since animals obviously have such perspicacity but lack *naabl* in Chimalteco eyes. Closer scrutiny of the verb root *naa-* reinforces this supposition: in addition to "feel or perceive," *naa-* in its various forms can also mean "remember," "guess," "behave (properly)," and even "pray," implying that *naabl* serves to do these things as well. The word also occurs in idiomatic expressions meaning "be careful" and "assume or suppose," further reinforcing notions of purposive judgment and reasoning. In other words, if *naabl* means "sense" as in general sense perception or consciousness, it also means "having sense" as in being humanly sensible both to oneself and to others—including those to whom one prays.

Elaborating on this point, the Mam phrase *te tuul tnaabl xjaal,* literally "when the person's *naabl* arrived here," has three possible meanings. Depending on the context, it translates variously as "when the person woke up," "at the time of the person's earliest childhood memories," and "when the person recovered from an illness." In each case the "arrival" of *naabl* relates to emergence from an anomalous social state: sleep, infancy, and sickness. During sleep, a person is alive but unaware and unresponsive. In infancy, a baby is aware but neither fully capable nor responsible. When sick, the invalid is socially "invalid"—absent from the normal activities that sustain, structure, and so give meaning to Chimalteco life. Thus, having *naabl* not only implies a personal "sense and sensibility" private to individuals, but it also involves unequivocal and continual public demonstrations of such understanding that others can recognize and respond to socially. Without such mutual recognition, there can be no *naabl,* regardless of one's own conscious state.

In keeping with this conjunction of personal sense and public sensibility, *naabl* holds two principal referents for Chimaltecos, one physical, the other social. Physically, *naabl,* like *aanma,* relates directly to the condition of the blood, *chiky',* because it is the "heat" in the blood that allows for sense perceptions. Normally, the blood is "hot," evidenced by a ruddy, healthy complexion; notably, the Mam word *kyaq* means both "red" and "hot." When heated through physical exertion, experiencing strong emotions, or ingesting "hot" substances like alcohol, the blood becomes increasingly sensitive until it "overheats," and the person passes out—most typically when someone gets drunk. Conversely, sickness, *yaabil,* robs the blood of its heat, immediately obvious in the invalid's pale, wan complexion. During serious illness, the blood is said to "go down" or "go back," leaving the victim cold, weak, and insensate. Cures attempt to restore the blood to its typical hot state by warming the patient with alcoholic potions and sweat baths. As with *aanma,* physical well-being conventionalized by "normal" sensitivity of the blood constitutes one self-evident measure of *naabl.*

Equally self-evident, however, is the social nature of this individual well-being. If in one sense *naabl* refers to a general human perspicacity rooted in the blood, Chimaltecos also fully appreciate that human beings do not exist independently of particular times and places and that people from different places possess different social "sensibilities." Consequently, *naabl* refers not only to individual existence but also to the particular "way of being" of the community to which an individual belongs. Chimaltecos continually comment on the behavior of their *ladino* as well as Maya neighbors, implying both a distinctive and superior Chimalteco *naabl*—more composed, more well-spoken, more enterprising. What differentiates Chimaltecos from others, however, lies less in the uniqueness of what they do or how they do it than in where, and with whom, they do whatever they do. In this regard, *naabl* remains highly personalized, grounded in the trust and familiarity of ongoing, lifelong associations between known individuals rather than in mutual but individual conformity to some immutable, impersonal, Chimalteco ideal. By making a sincere effort to live in Chimbal with Chimaltecos, one eventually comes to demonstrate—as well as validate—a local *naabl* born of shared experiences, common expectations, enduring—if at times conflicting—commitments, and the inescapable intimacy of personal reputation. These associations also extend back in time through one's parents, from whom one learned to be Chimalteco, back to those ancestors who first united people to place by building the church where it now stands at the center of town. Although not quite racial in essence, the particular genius of Chimalteco *naabl* inheres in the personal interactions and shared understandings of a local people rooted collectively in the enduring place that is Chimbal.

The reality of physical well-being within a familiar here and now makes *naabl* conventionally self-evident to Chimaltecos. This "humanly innate" yet "socially emergent" quality of *naabl* also qualifies it as a kind of "social soul." As Roy Wagner (1981:94) has said of souls in general, *naabl* represents that personal "spark of conventional discernment, of moral 'rightness' or humanity" that recognizes and responds to itself in others; "it sums up the ways in which its possessor is similar to others, over and above the ways in which he [or she] differs from them." For Chimaltecos, this similarity refers most immediately to a social as opposed to metaphysical identity. Quite simply, *naabl* is that "something" that makes Chimaltecos socially transparent—and thus intelligible—to one another. While some Chimaltecos obviously make "better" sense to, and of, other Chimaltecos, these differences remain one of degree, not kind. When a person's *naabl* is "complete," *tz'aql tnaabl xjaal,* he or she is resourceful, intelligent, purposive, and self-controlled. Those who speak nonsense, who cannot control their emotions, who do not pay attention—who literally do not "make sense" or are "out of touch"—have "incomplete" *naabl.* A common *naabl,* however singularly shared, nonetheless enables Chimaltecos to relate meaningfully to one another.

Ultimately, such shared sensibilities also validate the "metaphysical" soul *aanma*. As one Chimalteco observed, *qa kyuw tnaabl, jaka tz'aajtz ti taamna tu7n xnaq'tzbil,* "If [someone's] *naabl* is 'hard' [i.e., a short-tempered, stubborn, impatient person], [the person's] *aanma* can come back through instruction"— implying that "incomplete" *naabl* indicates a deficient *aanma* as well. Without the equanimity, sensibility—even sensitivity—of *naabl,* one hardly has much of a soul either. Interestingly enough, Tzotzil speakers in Zinacantán recognize a similar correspondence between sociality and soul, but with no lexical distinction between the soul's metaphysical and social aspects. In Tzotzil, the same word *ch'ulel* that refers to the "inner soul" can also mean "dreams," "ritual speech," and "sense," as in "Don't you have any sense?" (Laughlin 1975:139). Like Mam, Tzotzil appears to cluster ideas of individual consciousness, proper form, and social sensibility around a notion of "immaterial essence," but here this same essence also carries metaphysical as well as pragmatic import.

Despite its "soul-like" aspects, Chimaltecos clearly distinguish the "social soul" of *naabl* from the "metaphysical" *aanma.* Although the two concepts overlap semantically in reference to individual existence, *naabl* refers more to the cognitive and behavioral understandings that hold between individuals, whereas *aanma* primarily concerns an inner animating "life principle" held by individuals singly. Where common understandings or expectations fail, Chimaltecos allude to an absence of *naabl.* While this often coincides with soul loss as privation of a personal essence, it is not soul loss per se. The presence or absence of *naabl* remains existential rather than essential; individuals either exhibit *naabl* to others or they do not. Nonetheless, Chimaltecos presume a direct relation between *aanma* and *naabl,* "essence" and "existence," since proof of one's soul lies in outward social behavior and sense perceptions, as much as a lack of normal sensibilities indicates "soul trouble." The dialectical rather than causal nature of this juxtaposition suggests that soul concepts in Chimbal serve more than simply to mystify animate existence. Instead, they objectify a particularly Chimalteco "way of life," then internalize this essence in individuals as long as they continue to affirm this life's dictates. Rather than meditations on existential truth or human destiny, both *naabl* and *aanma* pertain to the "rightness" of feeling, of thinking, of reasoning, of acting, of praying—in short, of living—in Chimalteco ways, whatever these might be, given time and circumstance. While Chimaltecos neither ignore nor prove incapable of abstract or ultimate concerns, their concepts of soul have yet to divorce the "mystery of life" from the concrete immediacies of their own—and others'—lives.

"SOULS" AND SOCIAL IDENTITY

In their outward expression, Chimalteco concepts of soul contrast noticeably with Zinacanteco souls. Where Tzotzil *ch'ulel* and *chanul* evoke images of parental authority and pastoral husbandry, Mam *aanma* and *naabl* allude to errant shades and elusive sensibilities. The Maya in both communities, however, consistently relate ideas of personal "immaterial essences" to blood and ancestry, to ancestral places, and to proper behavior. In fact, the contrasts in their respective cultural notations serve largely to reinforce the common significance of "soul" in the two communities. Regarding blood and ancestry, Zinacantecos speak explicitly of ancestral gods who both pass on the souls of former Zinacantecos to their patrilineal descendants and watch over the doings of their townspeople. Chimalteco conventions remain more circuitous but nonetheless culturally self-evident. Souls, in both their metaphysical and social aspects, inhere in the blood, which in turn implies physiological as well as cultural parentage extending back to the first Chimaltecos who founded the town. Socially, Chimaltecos do not speak of their ancestors as watching over them, but having a soul does imply demonstrating proper Chimalteco sensibilities that ultimately derive from ancestral precedents. Although Chimalteco souls may at first glance appear more "pragmatic" and Zinacanteco conceptions more "mystical," to most Zinacantecos the worldly presence of ancestral gods remains as patent as the mountains in which they reside. In both towns, souls precipitate in individuals abiding yet immediate affinities to the ongoing present as well as to the collective past. They remain essentially "this-worldly" rather than "other-worldly" (cf. Vogt 1969b:371).

Similarly, ancestors bind the living souls of Zinacantán and Chimbal to the particular places where they reside, but they do so in inverse fashion. Chimaltecos identify ancestors with the local church at the center of town, instead of with nearby mountain peaks as Zinacantecos do. For whatever reasons, Chimaltecos long ago claimed the church in Chimbal for their own, not necessarily out of greater Catholic piety but because their ancestors originally built it. Older than living Chimalteco memory, the church testifies unequivocally to ancestral existence and accomplishments. Conversely, Zinacantecos still choose to "encapsulate" Catholic church and chapel within the embrace of their ancestor-mountains (cf. Vogt 1969b:586), looking to the immutable landscape to embody the ongoing presence of their forebears. Despite this centripetal versus centrifugal transposition of ancestral metonyms, both ageless church in Chimbal and eternal mountains in Zinacantán actualize the past in the present, joining living souls to their ancestors through the physical continuity of known ancestral places. In this regard, I would agree wholeheartedly with Vogt that concepts of souls and ancestors do indeed "naturalize" culture and "culturalize" nature, but perhaps more in the sense of reifying culturally constituted claims about local sovereignty, that is, making communities real by "literally" embedding their origins in—and thus also giving meaning to—the legitimate, "natural" order of things.

This mutual identity of people and place, however, turns not simply on ascription of the appropriate kind of soul, but more precisely on mastery of the social propriety that having such a soul presupposes. Souls articulate an identity inclusively defined by ongoing behavior, rather than exclusively determined by such things as birth or physiognomy. Indeed, inadequate or improper behavior often corresponds to the actual loss of one's "innate" soul, proof enough of the locus of mutual identity in these communities. As before, this conjunction of souls and social propriety finds contrasting yet congruent expression in Zinacantán and Chimbal. Zinacantecos say that ancestors embody cultural ideals, and excessive or persistent deviation from these ideals prompts the ancestors to punish offenders by knocking out their "inner souls" or by forsaking their animal soul companions. In contrast, Chimaltecos acknowledge no explicit ancestral exemplars and instead refer to irregular behavior as lacking the common—that is, the shared as well as normal—"sense and sensibility" of human souls. Rather than provoking soul loss as in Zinacantán, misbehavior in Chimbal itself intrinsically evidences soul loss. Paradoxically, despite the obvious correspondence between souls and propriety, in neither community does having a soul ever guarantee proper behavior, because souls get lost precisely when someone with a soul behaves improperly. In other words, having a soul need not signify strict conformity to some preemptory cultural standard, but missing souls always denote a conspicuous departure from the ordinary. Souls appear more to validate a diffuse sense of what is right and appropriate rather than stipulate explicit behavioral norms. Like the cultural "rules" that John Haviland (1977:chap. 8) discusses in relation to Zinacanteco gossip, souls become most apparent by their absence; that is, when the "normal" social state of affairs that they imply is violated in some obvious way.

Ironically, then, soul concepts in both communities regulate social behavior without actually dictating rules of social conduct. Even in Zinacantán, ancestral ideals remain largely putative rather than precise because only shamans can "see" inside the ancestors' sacred mountains, but even they still evidently differ on what exactly they remember seeing there (cf. Vogt 1969b:384, 416). Rather than sanction specific social behavior, souls sanctify—that is, assert the motivated rather than arbitrary nature of—"acceptable" conduct by grounding the vagaries of individual behavior in the presumed constancy of cultural propositions about individual and social existence. As long as soul concepts remain culturally self-evident, that is, accepted by the community at large, their pure conventionality leaves them unfalsifiable—no one can prove that souls do not exist—and their resulting sanctity thus makes them personally compelling and socially powerful (cf. Rappaport 1979). Such self-evidence also makes having a soul largely self-referential: soul must be what souls actually do because every normal person supposedly has one. Nonetheless, keeping one's soul rests on mutual acknowledgement rather than on mere self-assertion, so no one is free simply to do as they please and call it "soulful." What souls actually mean depends on agreed upon—that is, morally constituted—canons of behavior that oblige individuals to recognize an authority beyond their own personal volition. That such social control remains "emergent" rather than "dictated" makes it no less real or potent. After all, soul loss not only denies to nonconformists moral legitimacy but robs them of their existential validity as well. The pure conventionality of soul concepts leaves their precise dictates ineffable, yet for all that, the more inescapable as long as one wishes to remain part of the community that acknowledges them.

Thus, through images of shared continuity, enduring propinquity, and self-evident "common sense," Maya souls foster an identity between members of the same community that remains at once internalized in each individual yet potentially errant depending on their actions. This tacit, behaviorally immanent, yet clearly canonical quality to having a soul can perhaps be likened to having "soul" in North American black culture. In his book, *Urban Blues,* Charles Keil observes that "soul" engenders black identity as well as black solidarity by articulating a "common experience, [and the] shared modes of thinking about and expressing that common experience" (1966:180). On one hand, soul alludes to an "unspeakable essence," "a mixture of ethnic essence, purity, sincerity, conviction, credibility, and just plain effort" (Keil 1966:160, 164); it arises from having faced the same adversities of life, from "knowing what that slavery shit is all about," but persevering nonetheless (Keil 1966:169-170). On the other hand, soul comprises more than knowing or being; it demands the commitment of deeds as well, of engaging in the soul brother's and sister's improvisational style of speech, dress, walk, and repartee, but doing so as an expression of mutual understanding and recognition, as a kind of communion, rather than simply to demonstrate personal accomplishment (Keil 1966:160-162, 180-181). For all its apparent worldliness, black soul also retains a sacred quality (Keil 1966:176-177), a transcendent purity impossible to describe, but instantly recognizable; whatever "it" is, those in the know perceive immediately those who have soul from those who do not. Consequently, soul's all-pervasiveness makes almost any social interaction a potential ritual of self-affirmation and collective affinity.

Like black soul, Maya souls precipitate social identity out of a people's common history, shared experiences, and knowing familiarity; they then conventionalize individual behavior less as approximations of some stated ideal and more in terms of how one's actions express commitment to the spirit of that history, experience, and knowledge. Soul remains behaviorally immanent yet culturally transcendent, definitive of social boundaries yet ultimately undefinable in its own terms. Both usages of soul ultimately sanctify each people's ethnic identity. This by no means implies that Maya concepts of soul perfectly replicate black soul. The communities that Maya souls precipitate remain much more localized and circumscribed than the ethnic identity articulated by American black soul. The Maya also speak of souls in a plural rather than singular sense, relating the common understandings and actions that substantiate their souls to definite notions of shared substance. As a result, Maya souls adhere even more closely to the ritual of identity that everyday life becomes, because to disregard that life, whether willfully or inadvertently, demonstrates more than a lack of soul, it provokes the loss of one's own personal soul. Although far from exact, the analogy serves at least as a reminder that souls need not always be mystical or mystifying but also pertain to the immediate, palpable, and pervasive concerns of social being.

CONCLUSION

Through a comparison of two Maya communities, I have argued that Maya concepts of soul, particularly the "inner" soul associated with the blood, inextricably link individual mortality and social morality to particular local, ultimately ethnic, places. Maya souls fuse this personal and community identity through images of continuity with local ancestors, commitment to ancestral locales, and comportment literally, given the conjunction between souls and behavior, "in the spirit of" the ancestors. I conclude with a brief discussion of some theoretical, ethnographic, and comparative issues entailed in this argument.

Theoretically, I have attended closely to Maya words and their meanings, but not because I take them to be the essence, or perhaps I should say "soul," of Maya culture. Far from a meaningful totality in themselves, these words constitute the largely tacit framework of cultural propositions and conventional associations that these people acknowledge in communicating with one another and thus making sense out of their lives. The self-evident, and thus self-referential, nature of Maya souls would suggest that, in fact, much of this "sense" actually lies outside culture proper in the emergent contingencies of personal encounters and particular situations. Conventions of soul, however, do culturally impute an intrinsic meaningfulness to individual behavior that becomes problematic only when individuals wax odd, or eccentric, or offensive enough to attract notice. Precisely when or what is "enough" to prompt the social estrangement of actual soul loss remains culturally unspecified, but nonetheless apparent to those involved. In this sense, Maya souls clearly exemplify how cultural "symbols and meanings" remain not extrinsically authoritative in regard to behavior, but intrinsically informative of it. Close attention to words reveals the cultural logic, but not the experiential substance, of Maya souls. In this essay, I have dealt only with the first, knowing full well that without the second, the meaning of Maya souls remains at best incompletely appreciated.

Ethnographically, the self-referential quality of Maya souls—that soul is what souls do—constitutes an important counterpoint to their equally real but tacit canonical sense. The myriad, often unspecifiable, transgressions that provoke soul loss lead some anthropologists to see in Maya souls the fatalism of a world beyond human control (cf. Gossen 1975:459; Foster 1944:98), or conversely, the Maya's quest for security through "compulsive" conformity (cf. Gillin 1951:123-124). Such negatively rather than positively defined cultural precepts regarding souls, however, also lend souls the potential flexibility to sanctify a wide range of social behavior. As I have tried to demonstrate in this essay, having a soul means behaving in sensible ways, not just mechanically cleaving to established ways. Soul indeed demands a mastery of cultural convention, but this need precludes neither personal opportunism nor cultural innovation as long as one has the eloquence to persuade others of one's propriety. Although souls unequivocally situate individuals within a community, they constitute that community more as an inclusive, continually negotiated ground of social interaction rather than as an exclusive nexus of essential traits or institutions. I would suggest that greater appreciation of these "emergent" qualities of Maya souls might well clarify the tenacity of Maya ethnic identity in the face of rapid, and in Guatemala, increasingly violent, social change (cf. Watanabe 1988).

Finally, regarding cross-cultural comparison within the Maya area, Vogt (1964d:32-35), in his initial discussion of the "phylogenetic" model of Maya cultural development, argued that ancestors and soul concepts comprise "systemic patterns" in Maya culture. He drew particular attention to the ancestral care of animal souls as a distinctive Maya configuration. Given the variation in Maya concepts of animal souls (cf. Saler 1964; Gossen 1975), I would simply reiterate Vogt's briefer mention of "inner" souls associated with the blood and behavior as an equally important, if perhaps less diagnostic, Maya pattern. I remain uncertain, however, to what extent the specific argument about Maya souls presented in this essay can be projected back in time, especially to before the Spanish Conquest. Post-Conquest realities of resettlement and Catholic missionization would make it surprising if contemporary Maya souls had simply endured unchanged. Also, comparison of soul concepts in Zinacantán and Santiago Chimaltenango clearly reveals rather different cultural notations, making any substantive reconstruction of ancient Maya concepts even more problematic. Nonetheless, the underlying logic of elusive Maya essences does suggest a common pattern here, a pattern that may also reveal something of what ancient Maya souls were once about.

It is this beguilement with the Maya, both past and present, and the wisdom of "soul" rather than ego, that as teacher and exemplar, Evon Z. Vogt has shared so generously. I only hope that this offering has proven worthy of its inspiration.

ACKNOWLEDGMENTS. I gratefully acknowledge the Frederick Sheldon Fund of Harvard University and the Michigan Society of Fellows, University of Michigan, Ann Arbor, for support during the various phases of research, reflection, and writing that led to this essay.

COGNITIVE ECONOMY, COHERENCE, AND DIVINATION IN THREE CIVILIZATIONS

Benjamin N. Colby
University of California, Irvine

Culture is continually in change as individuals drawing from cultural patterns in their world are confronted by different types of problem situations and have to make adaptations. Since people are uniquely situated in history, and since culture is continually in process, cultural phenomena are rarely seamless. Lowie (1920) once referred to culture as a thing of "shreds and patches"; Vogt's description of cosmology in Zinacantán begins with the caveat that the concepts he reports "are not entirely uniform and consistent" (1969b:297). Though ethnographers in the field are continually aware of those shared aspects of culture that contribute to a general sense of configuration, the imperfections in Ruth Benedict's configurational ethnography have deterred investigations of any native sense of coherence that might exist. Critical attention has been focused on contradictions between ethnographers, rather than on mechanisms of cultural coherence. But it is precisely those cultural phenomena which provide a sense of coherence to the people of a social group that are the most significant for understanding cultural dynamics. These phenomena are varied, but religion is a primary area in which they operate. As the work of Vogt and others has shown, religious data gathered in Mexico and Guatemala are indeed varied from one informant to the next, and even in the information provided by a single informant. Given this variation, then, we might ask what keeps it in check? What keeps cultural systems from flying apart in different directions? What is the "glue" that holds cultural systems together?

Among the integrative mechanisms in religion, divination can be especially powerful. As a pattern system it organizes much that is of concern to individuals facing an uncertain world, and it covers a broad range of human topics. Most of the ancient civilizations have used divinatory systems over extended time periods. Among these, in addition to Maya divination, are the Greek oracles and the Chinese I Ching. The oracles were the foci for a large complex of knowledge processing and political structures that lasted, at least at Delphi, for a thousand years. The perpetuation of patterns requires a natural/material and social environment that makes these patterns useful. When individuals choose to use a particular pattern, they do so on the basis of having interpreted the cultural ecology in which they live and having determined the optimal goals for well-being in that ecology. When the ecology is changing rapidly, we would expect greater selective pressure to bear on any pattern, because it may not always produce the same results, or because a changing ecology can lead to a

COGNITIVE ECONOMY, COHERENCE, AND DIVINATION

change in goals or goal priorities involving that pattern. The oracles at Delphi, and elsewhere in the classical world, disappeared within a narrow band of time compared to their prior long survival. The Chinese I Ching is widespread to this day.

Among the Maya, the integrative force provided by calendar tie-ins with divination provide a doubly strong source of cultural coherence. As represented in the codices, the system goes back to the earliest times. Among the Maya groups that still practice this ancient art, the Ixil are especially interesting because their system links to ancestor worship, a characteristic of the Classic period, but which has been greatly attenuated if not extinguished in most , Postclassic Maya (Colby 1976). Usually reference to ancestral deities among the modern Maya is made to mythical deities (as is true in most mythologies), rather than to the recently departed souls of people who were known when alive by their progeny, relatives, and others.

There is currently a tremendous change, indeed, a revolutionary upheaval, in Ixil life, which surely will affect the future of divination among those people. The description that follows is based on data collected prior to the current revolutionary resistance.

In Ixil divination, people who were sick or down in their luck would come to a native priest or day keeper for a divination. By laying out special seeds and using the pre-Columbian calendar to count them, the day keeper would determine the cause of his client's problem. The system includes codings and metaphoric linkages that apply to other expressions of Ixil culture as well, particularly myths and dreams. Such linkages across different genres and domains have a dual function. First is that of cognitive economy, where individuals can utilize the same components of cognitive organization in more than a single domain of perception and behavior. The second is the sense of coherence provided, which in itself has been shown to relate to physical health (Antonovsky 1987). A primary means by which these functions are accomplished is through metaphor.

In his extensive survey of the anthropology of metaphor, Fernández (1974) outlines a theory that involves quality spaces, transformations, latent themes, plans, and a process of pronominalization in which the self (and one's views of others in the world) takes on meaning and makes cognitive "conversions" that facilitate the living process. Culturally given or ready-made metaphoric linkages exist in systems of symbolic usage to assist in this pronominalization process. Some of these metaphors are used heavily because they have a guiding function for systems of symbolic usage that are important, especially in religion. Fernández (1972) speaks of such metaphors as "organizing" human endeavor.

Such organizing metaphors, one would expect, will effect some degree of cognitive economy. Among the more traditional Ixil there is one particular metaphor that organizes key religious ideas and permits cognitive economy in a variety of domains. It is familiar to Maya specialists, for it exists in Zinacantán and many other groups (Vogt 1969b). This is a metaphor that links sickness with captivity. For the Ixil, sickness is an indication that one's soul is being held in captivity by one of the supernatural beings populating the Ixil supernatural world. There are Ixil folk tales in which the protagonist is transported either to the underworld (under the aegis of the earth god) or to the sky world (under control by a syncretic Christian-sun god) and released in connection with ritual of a curative nature. The diviner, Shas Ko'w, has described a dream in which he was given the keys to a supernatural jail (Colby and Colby 1981). This symbolized the conferring by the gods of the ability to release people from sickness.

The equating of captivity with sickness is an organizing or structuring process that has important entailments among the Ixil. The reason for the captivity is always some supernatural displeasure with the individual. Often this can be ancestral displeasure. In either case, the reason is due to the individual's wrongdoing. Sometimes there is a delay in a god's notice of wrongdoing until another mortal, perhaps the wronged person, notifies the gods via a ritual for redress. The usual therapy is to discover the sin or wrongdoing, perform rituals of atonement, and lead a better life.

A complete divinatory system can be seen as having a system for providing a reading stimulus, a set of interpretive rules for obtaining a reading from the stimulus, and a knowledge and procedure structure of at least three components: an ethical system, a worldview, and a series of linking procedures interfacing people, situations, and problems.

In the analysis of this divinatory process, one can go beyond a merely interpretive study to a goal-guided one. In a goal-guided mode, models or analytical explanations are developed which duplicate or predict some known or future outcome, an attempt to mechanically arrive at the same reading a day keeper has produced. This involves a constant testing process, which requires sufficient data and many cases of actual divinations. Such a built-in validity check presupposes a working system at a fairly rational level. It ought to work for a system like the Chinese I Ching, but one would not expect it to work for anything as subjective as crystal gazing (another technique used among the Ixil), nor, perhaps, for the Greek oracles, though here we lack information. There is much room for ambiguity and idiosyncrasy in between this range from internal subjectivity to externalized rational systems. But if the system is closer to the externalized rational end, and if the analysis is restricted to a single individual and involves a long and extensive examination of that individual's divinatory decisions, it may be possible to arrive at a reasonably stable set of predictive mechanisms. The ultimate goal is not so much the successful prediction as the validation of the theory and native or possibly "emic" categories which the prediction confirms.

Prior to the theoretical model described here for Ixil divination, two other models have been developed. The first was an application of artificial intelligence (AI) to a cognitive anthropological approach. This was a working computer model, a LISP-based system (Colby and Knaus 1974) that produced readings. The procedures and data structures commonly used for sentence comprehension in AI are helpful for such models. Their chief advantage is that

COGNITIVE ECONOMY, COHERENCE, AND DIVINATION

they require complete specification, thus forcing the analyst to recognize and make explicit the full extent to which underlying presuppositions are utilized in such a process. AI is still not widespread in cognitive anthropology. Scarcely a handful of researchers might be mentioned. Hinz, (1979), Kokot (1982), and Werner (1978) have made contributions in the study of belief systems, and a programming system has been developed to facilitate anthropological applications (Colby 1985; James and Colby 1979). But other researchers can be included if we go beyond specific modeling attempts to more discursive writings that are informed by AI or cognitive science, for example, the writings by Agar and Hobbs (1985), Beaugrande (1980), and Hutchins (1980). The forerunner for much of this, though rarely recognized as such, was the early work by Metzger and Williams (1963a, 1963b).

The second divinatory model (Colby and Colby 1981) was a more differentiated set of procedures for reading and transforming material presented in a series of charts, some of which were a direct mapping of data elicited from the day keeper in explicit recited form.

The current approach is a systemic pattern-matching in which a divinatory layout is interpreted, weighted, and then used in a pattern search of a "cognitive text" involving prototypical sequences. These sequence prototypes are used as part of a general behavioral logic used in interpreting processes of types other than divination (for example, sickness episodes, court disputes, and other case histories, but these are beyond the scope of the current task).

In the layout, each seed stimulus on the table is linked with one of twenty day-god names and one of thirteen numbers. The seeds are placed in columns and rows, and those in the far right-hand column are chosen as the days that speak.

Each day-god name is an entry mnemonic for a domain network that links day-god domains and types with a causal condition for the sickness and with salient participants in that condition. This first system will be called the layout system. Thus for example, if the day god, 'Imush, should appear in one of the talking positions after the seeds have been laid out, the diviner has to construct a story that contains at least one of the features from the layout system for this day in the story line itself. Therefore, he must somehow use the following characteristics: day-god domain—house; causal condition—(insufficient) penance; participants—female, clothes. The decision of which of these features to use for the pattern-matching search depends first on salience weightings. The procedure for determining the salience of speaking days are first to assign all talking positions an initial salience value of 1. To this is added any additional amounts that accrue from the following number prefixes of the talking day: for the numbers 6, 8, 9, or 13, add 2; for 4, 12, 5, or 11, add 1. Then for 'Alkaalte days add 2, and for the following "attributes" add 1: Earth Lord, Tiix, Soul, Death, Anger, Transgression, Fine, Wealth, or Money. The resulting pattern is actually a set of patterns ordered by salience weightings. These are matched with the view of alter system.

Given the age and sex of one of his clients, there are certain general assumptions that are made about the client unless the diviner has information to the contrary. Some of these are "default" assumptions about client attributes, others come from a knowledge about the client gained before or during the consultation. This information, both default and verified, comprises the view of alter system that, during a consultation, is presumed to be held in "short-term memory."

This system has the following components:

1. Ascriptive attributes
   age of generation
   gender
   physical attributes
2. Events or occasions
   failed courtships
   marriages
   divorces
   bought or sold property
3. Acquired attributes
   wealth—ownership
   prestige—religious positions, etc.
   alcoholic
   quarrelsome
   care of shrine and surroundings

In the behavioral logic of the diviner, there are particular problems that often are associated with these attributes of the client. The diviner can thus select several likely problems that link to the client's attributes in the view of alter system. That is, each particular attribute of the alter can be associated with particular problem prototypes that are enabled through that attribute. For example, one can not have a dispute with one's wife if one does not have a wife as an attribute in the system.

The task then becomes one of choosing from among these. This is done through a likelihood or probability weighting (a neglected aspect of cognition in anthropology). Probability weighting works through a set of salience rules that produce an ordered list (rank-ordered in terms of likelihood) of likely problem or sickness causes. This list is given salience weightings according to the type of descriptive attributes of the alter that link to it (in the view of alter system).

Since the three categories of the view of alter system are increasingly salient in the readings, with the first category having the lowest salience and the third the highest, a salience value reflecting this gradient can be assigned to each of the three categories, with a 1 for the lowest and a 3 for the highest. Since attributes point to more than a single problem, and problems have multiple attribute inputs, there may be repeats of problems in the resultant weighted list, so these problems have to be aggregated along with their weights. The numerical

COGNITIVE ECONOMY, COHERENCE, AND DIVINATION

values used in this process represent a marking system or a hypothesized neural excitation level and are arbitrarily given magnitudes of 1, 2, and 3. Through trial and error they have worked reasonably well so far. These weights are the same that were used in the second model of divination, which was created before an extensive body of literature on life events, stress, and coping (Lazarus and Folkman 1984; Thoits 1983) had built up. The life events literature suggests indirectly that in terms of stress effect the weighting order for the three categories, ascriptive, events, and acquired, is not only valid for the Ixil but universal.

Thus the day keeper builds this list of likely problems into his view of alter system. This list of likely problems is then matched with salience values derived from the reading.

In constructing a model that can produce readings I have attempted to match actual readings produced by Shas Ko'w, either in a real divination situation or during interviews when Shas Ko'w was on the University of California, Irvine, campus and worked with me to produce hypothetical readings. Since the model is not a test of correlation between a small number of variables, but rather a test of something much more specific—the actual content and syntax of a reading— a successful matching involves a judgment of whether the predicted reading is a reasonable paraphrase of the actual reading. The decision of whether a prediction is an acceptable paraphrase of the actual reading would ideally be made by an Ixil day keeper, or at least an Ixil informant. In this new model of the process, that test was not possible, and a judgment has to be made by the analyst. Another caveat is that many of the cases used in deriving this model were hypothetical ones suggested by the diviner, Shas. Attending a real divination among the Ixil is akin to accompanying someone at a psychotherapy session in our own society; comparatively few real cases were collected, including an unusual one that was filmed. In addition to the cases I recorded in the field and at the University of California, Irvine, were those recorded in the field by John Clement.

One of Shas's hypothetical examples can be used to further explain the process. There are three talking days: 9 Kaoo, 2 Kan, and 9 'Ee. The client is an unmarried woman. We first choose a predicate from the talking positions. For Kaoo we have two predicates in the system, a general "transgression" and a more specific "envy." But because Kaoo is associated with the earth god, we also can get the predicates associated with that god generally (i.e., rather than Kaoo specifically). These are: sex with another, cutting wood without license, and gathering relics without license. Applying the salience rules to the number 9, which precedes Kaoo, we get a value of 4.

From 9 'Ee there is no specific event or associated state, but since this is one of the four 'Alkaalte days (on which the new year can begin), we get the more general list of transgression predicates: any transgression, and two very specific ones: resisting the call to be day keeper and performing ritual when not qualified. These all have a salience value of 5 because of the number 9 preceding 'Ee.

To determine the client attribute problem salience in the view of alter system, we apply the rules previously given. The ascriptive attributes that filter through, neglect of household duties or the spurning of a suitor, are each given a value of 1. There are no circumstantial attributes and the last type gives angry suitor a value of 3 + 1.

Matching up the possible predicates with the possible problems yields a single solution: sex with another. From the reading template (the same as in model 2; Colby and Colby 1981) we look at the communication module. We come up with the participant, a male, who complains to the punishing being. Drawing on general knowledge, in the behavioral logic system we take this to be the former suitor who is angry that the client is seeing another man. Finally the punishing being module produces the 'Alkaalte as the one who causes the client to be sick. The reading thus has the following substance: The woman client has been seeing a man, causing a rejected suitor to notify the gods of this wrongdoing. God 'Ee caused her to be sick as a result. Shas's actual reading was: There is a transgression against the earth god with a man. There is an enemy (who complains to the gods). When she was younger many men wanted her, were jealous.

In this more direct and simplified model of divination there are four components: (a) the layout system, a system for providing a reading stimulus; (b) the view of alter system, the view that the diviner holds of his client; (c) an attribute-problem system, which derives from (d) a behavioral logic, which includes problem sequence prototypes. These last two, (c) and (d), are not confined to divination alone, but form part of an individual's general knowledge, a store of interlinked schemas about beliefs, goals, plans, and other procedures. These are called upon in other domains, which for the Ixil can be tapped as myths, life histories, texts of folk philosophy, and ritual texts, as well as more mundane matters like court cases, village happenings, and neighborhood problems.

For a comparative perspective in the matter of cognitive economy, I shall review the two other divinatory systems that are prominent in history, Chinese and Greek, to consider how cognitive economy might be seen to influence the rate of social change and the development of scientific thinking.

The great Chinese divination system is the I Ching or Book of Changes (Wilhelm 1967). The traditional stimulus material was a set of yarrow stalks cast in a way that could be represented by six lines, either solid or broken. There are sixty-four possible combinations or "hexagrams" of solid or broken lines in groups of six. Anyone who can read the Book of Changes can follow directions and arrive at a reading. There are various ways of organizing readings according to how the elements in a casting are grouped. In one grouping each hexagram is composed of two trigrams. The lower trigram usually refers to internal life and to what is coming in the future or what is being created, while the upper trigram concerns the external world and what is receding or dissolving. Each trigram has a particular name and set of attributes.

Another way of grouping the six lines is by pairs. According to the I Ching, there are three cosmic potentials for explaining action in the world: heaven, man, and earth. These sometimes are correlated to three pairs of lines: top, middle, and bottom.

Still another grouping is by even and odd positions. The first, third, and fifth are positions of light or *yang*, while the second, fourth, and sixth are *yin* or darkness.

Finally, there is a set of attributes that are associated with each of the six positions alone. Thus, with these groupings and their associated attributes, there is latitude for a great number of interpretive combinations.

There are thousands of writings on I Ching interpretations. The Book of Changes contains the most important ones historically. These interpret the hexagram generally, their component trigrams and individual lines. There are several different authors, and the commentary has been written at various periods.

The I Ching is noteworthy because it has lasted so long and continues to be taken seriously by millions of people. It is also one of the chief causes offered in commentaries by writers on China who speculate about why science never developed in that country to the extent that it did in the West. Joseph Needham (1956:335-344), the great historian of Chinese science, technology, and folk theories, sees the impeding of Chinese science as due to a "cognitive formalism," which goes back at least to the sixth century B.C., back to the early use of the I Ching. The Chinese had in the I Ching a powerful means of pigeonholing the universe and an associative or categorical rather than a causal mode of thinking. It is this mode of thinking, Needham speculated, that held back the development of modern science in China. Richard Baum (1983) agrees with Needham's assessment about categorical thinking, and he sees it continuing to characterize Chinese thought even in its modern Marxist manifestation.

An efficient system for categorizing the universe is strong, indeed, for here cognitive economy can touch a broad range of phenomena at a high level of organization. When we reason, converse, tell stories, or do other things, we draw upon understandings and knowledge structures that exist as systems of varying size, conviction, and affect. If these cognitive phenomena can be generalized across a wider series of domains and genres, we are likely to be dealing with fairly coherent systems that are resistant to change. We have an innate need for such coherence. We like to use mental packages that allow a variety of "takes" on a situation, but which require a minimum of cognitive effort. Divination provides just such a system.

Divination had a powerful influence among the Greeks as well as the Chinese and Mayas, particularly through the oracular complexes at Delphi, Delos, and other centers. But unlike the I Ching and Ixil divination, much less is known about the mechanism for deriving a reading in ancient Greece.

The consultation process for an oracle in those times has been reconstructed by Flaceliere (1965:30). The clients go to an office to arrange an appointment. At the proper time, they go to the temple and walk through a vaulted passage to a special room. There they remain while the seer and attendants proceed by another passage to a lower underground room containing a sacred spring. In this room is a prophetess who has been underground and isolated. The seer delivers the question to her. She then pronounces the message she receives from the god. The message is taken back and given to the client. In a careful study, Fontenrose (1978) concludes that the oracular message is not first expressed by the Pythia (priestess) in a strange idiom that has to be translated (as many had previously thought), nor were all the messages put into verse and committed to writing.

What actually happens to produce a reading is not known. Sometimes lots were drawn, and many think that a trance state was required (Littleton 1986). But we know much more about actual readings and the history of the oracles, particularly through Plutarch, who was a priest at Delphi.

If historians are correct in attributing the impeding of science in China to the I Ching divination, why is it that divination in Greece failed to impede science in that country? Greek scientific thought is the chief source of modern science. Writings on mathematics and empirical verification stretch over a thousand years of ancient Greek history. Why was there such a difference between China and Greece in the growth of science?

And why did science do so poorly among the Mayas? Except for an amazingly precise astronomy and mathematics associated with it, the Mayas were still further behind than the Chinese. Even if extensive written historical records were available for the Maya area, it is doubtful that a case could be made for a more developed body of scientific thought than the Mayas are now thought to have had in pre-Columbian times.

One possible answer is that in Greece the system was less mechanical, more inspirational, and it was concentrated in a few famous places, not spread throughout the population among a large number of curers or among the laity. Thus it did not freeze up categories of thought as it did in China and among the Maya. Another possible answer closely related to this might be that there was less pressure for maintaining cognitive economy at a higher level of cognitive organization. The principle of cognitive economy seems to have operated much more extensively among the Mayas than either the Chinese or Greeks, and more among the Chinese than the Greeks.

Cognitive economy makes for low diversity of cultural patterns. The benefits of cognitive economy and those of cognitive diversity involve trade offs. There seems to be a certain balance between the known and unknown, the familiar and the strange, the old and the new that people need to have in all societies. A kind of cultural redundancy seems necessary. But where this balance point, or feeling of comfort, exists along the continuum from old to new seems to vary across societies and from one domain to the next. The whole question of rate of change has still not been adequately addressed in anthropology, though the differential rate of development for different spheres of culture have been shown by Carneiro (1973).

Cognitive economy among the Mayas surely must have been especially strong through divination, which was integrated with two calendars and the deification of time. These, in turn, integrated all high cultural activities. The three surviving codices of Maya hieroglyphics treat ceremonies and divinations organized by this structure of time, gods, and attributes associated with them.

COGNITIVE ECONOMY, COHERENCE, AND DIVINATION

Everything in life was, in one way or another, brought under the purview of the religious system. This must have been an extensive form of cognitive economy and cultural coherence.

That the Mayas never surpassed the splendor of their Classic period and that successor states, for example, the Aztecs at the time of Conquest, never reached the level of the Maya Classic period suggests that, in Mesoamerica, diversity of cultural patterns and the creation of new cultural patterns were not as high as in China and certainly not as high as in ancient Greece.

Turning once more to the modern-day Ixil, a syncretic culture of ancient Maya and seventeenth-century Spanish culture, what can be said about the evolution of variant culture forms and meta-level political thinking among that group today?

In Ixil country, there are some important changes that have been taking place over the last few decades. The first significant change was introduced by the Catholic missionary priests seeking to bring modern Catholicism to the Ixil. They organized many Ixil, particularly young literate ones, into Catholic Action groups to study the catechism and modern church ideas. Over time, these groups became progressively more aware politically and active in a process of consciousness raising, where priests and others engaged Ixil members of Catholic Action in dialogues that involved meta-level thinking.

The next, and by far the most important, turn of events is that the Ixil area became the epicenter of the revolution in Guatemala. In reaction to this, the main towns have been converted by the government to military strongholds, where Ixil peasants from outlying areas have been brought into the town, and the inhabitants are unable to leave without passes. With the revolution has come a sharp break which creates great cultural stress.

Protestants have gained the most from this in the short run. Before the war, missionaries found little success in gaining converts, except through the provision of medical consultation and treatment. Now they have the added advantage of military backing. The Protestant notion of personal sin certainly has its similarities to the Ixil notion of sickness as a state of disfavor. In this state of disfavor, responsibility is placed on the individual, though instead of multiple punishing gods and spirits there is a single punishing deity. Thus a move toward Protestant fundamentalist religion is a move away from the organizing metaphor for Ixil divination.

In further contrast to both traditional Ixil religion and fundamentalist beliefs, some members of the Catholic Action groups came to another notion of sin, yet further removed from the Ixil sickness metaphor: a notion of collective sin externalized to oppressor elements of the larger society. It is sinful for children to die of malnutrition and curable diseases. It is sinful to be denied access to land when there is so much available. It is sinful not to be able to read or write.

In both Protestant and Catholic groups, and for different reasons, then, the old idea of personal sin as the cause of sickness has changed radically. Whether a collective notion of sin among revolutionaries or a fundamentalist notion, both strike at the very core of Ixil divinatory practices. In addition, day keepers are forbidden to practice their rituals in the mountains, and some who did so were killed by the army. Whether the divinatory system and everything associated with it can survive remains to be seen. This prediction is made on the basis of reports from many sources, including Ixil friends, as well as reporters and other anthropologists who have been in the Ixil area. The sweeps through Ixil and other Maya towns have been of holocaustal proportions. But in one highland area, the Ixcoy, where there has been significant combat, Eike Hinz (known for his work on Aztec belief systems; 1979) was able to collect cases of Maya divination in 1983 and in 1987. So the system may be more resilient than one might expect.

The detailed description of how divination works is necessary if we are to go beyond a study of the system itself to wider questions of cultural ecology. The internal workings of the system can lead to an understanding of its coherence and persistence in an unchanging world. But these internal workings also provide a clue to how the system may be changed in an unstable world. Any cultural pattern, systemic or not, is subject to a process of cultural selection. A pattern is used by people. The concerns and goals of people thus become a necessary part of the picture.

A society has competing systems for dealing with problems in the world. The I Ching and Greek oracles had rivals in the matter of interpreting the world, dispensing wisdom, and suggesting courses of action. In Greece the development of a scientific approach was one such rival. In China, however, the scientific approach never gained strength, and this has been one of the great puzzles of historical analysis.

The internal mechanisms of a system such as were postulated in the decision model given for the Ixil explain, in part, the persistence of such a system. But external forces must be considered for an understanding of how systems change or die out. This requires consideration of a different order of sociocultural data. As cognitive anthropology develops and broadens its scope, some of the most anthropologically interesting results are likely to emerge from analyses that span both internal and external forces.

COMPOSITION AND CONTENT
IN MAYA SCULPTURE:
A STUDY OF BALLGAME SCENES
AT CHICHEN ITZA, YUCATAN, MEXICO

Linnéa H. Wren
Gustavus Adolphus College

Through over twenty seasons of fieldwork in Zinacantán, Chiapas, Mexico, Evon Z. Vogt became an acute observer of organizational principles in Maya culture. He recognized that the contemporary Maya have systematically patterned their lives in such a way that "certain ritual behaviors are replicated at various structural levels in society, and certain concepts . . . are replicated in various domains of the culture" (Vogt 1961:342; 1969b:571). It is the purpose of this essay to argue that conceptual patterns shaped the beliefs and directed the actions of the ancient Maya of the northern lowlands, just as they presently do those of the modern Maya of the highlands of Chiapas, and, further, to propose that these conceptual patterns imbued pre-Columbian Maya art not only by means of specific symbols and motifs, but also by means of general characteristics of style.

Twentieth-century critics have interpreted the development of artistic styles as differing responses to an aesthetic emotion that is paradoxically both universal and particular. It is universal in that it is shared by every culture at every period, but it is particular in that it is experienced within any culture by only a few individuals, that is, those who evidence the ability to respond to artworks in purely aesthetic terms. These terms dictate that both the creation and appreciation of art be dependent solely upon formally significant compositional arrangements of visual elements, such as line, color, light, and texture, and be divorced from cultural issues, such as context, content, function, and meaning. According to this viewpoint, the appreciation of art in terms of stylistic qualities and the interpretation of art in terms of its illustrative purpose, its narrative content, or its religious meaning are, at best, distinct and, more often, disjunctive activities (Bell 1913; Fry 1920).

I would like to propose, however, that for the ancient Maya, composition and content, rather than being functionally independent of each other, were conceptually fused with each other. Through the analysis of two figural scenes depicting the Mesoamerican ballgame as it was played at Chichén Itzá, I will argue that the meaning of Maya sculpture rested upon the implicit cultural patterns that were conveyed by characteristics of style, particularly the treatment of time and space, as well as upon the explicit information that was communicated by an elaborate repetoire of symbols and motifs. I will seek to show that, for the Maya, compositional formats were not arbitrarily chosen in response to artists' aesthetic preferences. Instead, different compositional formats defined different types of involvement between the spectator and the artwork and revealed different patterns of relationship between the individual, society, and cosmos. In doing so, I will draw upon the studies of ancient Near Eastern art by Henrietta Groenewegen-Frankfort (1972) and Irene Winter (1985), of Netherlandish art by Svetlana Alpers (1983), and of Maya art by Flora Clancy (1980) and Marvin Cohodas (1978).

The Mesoamerican ballgame was a game of skill, daring, and danger. Evidence suggests that the game, in some form, dates to at least the second millennium B.C. In the Aztec version witnessed by Europeans in the sixteenth century, the game involved players competing, in pairs or in teams, on an I-shaped court to drive a rubber ball into the opposing end zone or through a ring mounted in mid-court. The players struck the ball with their arms, torso, or legs, but were prohibited from directing its course with their hands. Popular as a sport, the game was also used as a form of gambling, and stakes could be high, including not only private property such as precious jewelry and textiles, but also pledges of servitude from individuals and, in one case, the fate of a kingdom (Stern 1948; Schele and Miller 1986).

The ballgame was also important to the Maya. Masonry ball courts are found at almost all Maya sites of the southern lowlands and highlands. The courts generally consist of two parallel structures with sloping inner walls flanking a paved, open-ended playing alley, and they are frequently located near the palace and temple compounds associated with the elite. Representations of ballplayers are frequent in Maya relief sculpture and on Maya polychromed ceramic vessels (Schele and Miller 1986:pl. 95, 96, 96a, 98, 101-104). Players are shown with specialized equipment such as protective yokes and knee pads, as well as *hachas, palmas,* and handstones, and often with the elaborate headdresses, jewelry, and costume elements indicative of elite status. The depiction of Bird-Jaguar's victory over Jeweled Skull on the hieroglyphic stairs of Structure 33, Yaxchilán (Graham 1982), indicates that the ballgame and the accompanying human sacrifices may have served as a public celebration in which a ruler re-enacted his defeat of an important enemy. Similar events are recorded in inscriptions from Seibal and Naranjo (Schele and Miller 1986:249-250). The assumption of ballgame titles by Bird-Jaguar at Yaxchilán and Chan Bahlum at Palenque further indicates that the ballgame verified the ruler's right to office (Freidel and Schele 1985).

In addition to contests between human protagonists, ballgames between pairs of humans and divinities and between pairs of divinities were also represented by the Maya. The three carved ball court markers at Copán depict underworld deities as ballplayers. On the Center Marker a game takes place between a contestant who can be identified as the God of Zero and the death god of sacrifice and a contestant who is glyphically named as Hun-Ahau and who can be identified with Hunahpu, one of the Hero Twins of the *Popol Vuh* (Schele and Miller 1986:251, fig. VI.10 and VI.11, pl. 102). The *Popol Vuh* is an account of

Maya mythology transcribed into a Latin alphabetic adaptation of the Quiché language in the mid-sixteenth century by a young Maya nobleman in Guatemala. In this account the lords of Xibalbá, the Maya underworld, defeated two brothers, 1 Hunahpu and 7 Hunahpu, in a ballgame and sacrificed them. The victory of the lords of the underworld, however, was followed by defeat on the ball court at the hands of the Hero Twins. The twins were miraculously conceived when the spittle of the severed head of 1 Hunahpu fell on the hand of the daughter of an underworld deity. When they were invited to play on the ball court of the underworld lords, Hunahpu and Xbalanque outwitted their opponents, dismembered their bodies, and achieved immortality in the celestial sphere either as the sun and moon or as the sun and Venus (Tedlock 1985).

Ball courts are encountered far less frequently in the northern Maya lowlands than in the other regions occupied by the Maya. Only twenty-one ball courts have been found at nine archaeological sites situated in that part of the peninsula north of the road connecting Escárcega and Chetumal. Of these, thirteen are located at Chichén Itzá (Robertson et al. 1985). The importance of the ballgame to the inhabitants of Chichén Itzá is evident not only in the number of courts at the site, but is further underlined by the impressive size of the Great Ball Court, the largest ball court in Mesoamerica, by the prominent location of the Great Ball Court on the North Terrace, the most important ceremonial precinct in the site, and by the frequent depictions of ballplayers in the sculpture at the site.

The Great Ball Court measures approximately 167 m in length and 70 m in width at its greatest points. The I-shaped playing field is surrounded by vertical walls in which stone rings have been tenoned at the center. Four temples, the Lower Temple of the Jaguars, the Upper Temple of the Jaguars, the South Temple, and the North Temple, are associated with the Great Ball Court. The figure of a ballplayer costumed in a yoke, kneeling pad, and specialized foot gear and wearing circular eye rings and a mouth mask on his face is the focus of the reliefs covering the interior surfaces of the Lower Temple of the Jaguars (Maudslay 1889-1902:vol. 2, pl. 49). Six panels depicting the sacrifice of a defeated ballplayer are carved on the benches abutting the walls of the playing field. Each panel shows two teams of seven players facing each other. In the center is a large ball, possibly made by being molded around the skull that is inscribed on the ball's surface. On one side a kneeling decapitated player is shown with streams of blood stylized as six serpents and a flowering vine issuing from his neck. On the other side his victorious opponent is shown with a knife in one hand and a severed head in the other (Marquina 1951:266). Similar scenes are represented on the interior surfaces of the Monjas Ball Court (Bolles 1977:220-234) and the Casa Colorada Ball Court (Folan 1968:49-60).

More recently, several ballgame scenes have been identified in two new contexts at Chichén Itzá. A hemispherical stone combining figural relief with a hieroglyphic inscription has been located by Peter Schmidt, director of the Regional Museum in Merida, and myself (Figure 1). The stone, which we have termed the Great Ball Court Stone, was initially discovered during the 1923 restoration of the Great Ball Court conducted by the Instituto Nacional de

COMPOSITION AND CONTENT IN MAYA SCULPTURE

Antropología e Historia. It was reported only briefly in two erroneous reports by Cesar Lizardi Ramos (1936, 1937) and in a misleading discussion of a supposed Initial Series date by J. Eric S. Thompson (1937).

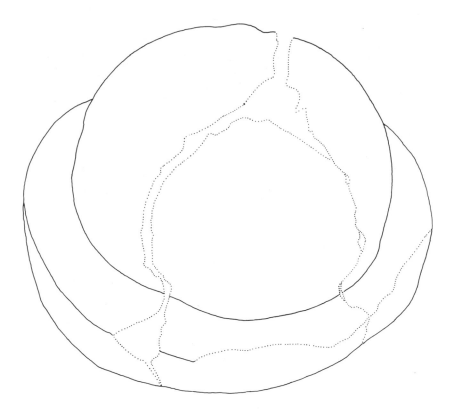

Figure 1. Great Ball Court Stone.

The Great Ball Court Stone measures 52 cm in height, 99 cm in diameter, and 311 cm at its outer circumference. It is similar in shape to altars used at Chichén Itzá for heart extraction sacrifices, such as those illustrated on Gold Disc H from the Sacred Cenote (Lothrop 1952:fig. 1) and on the west vault in the Upper Temple of the Jaguars (Coggins and Shane 1984:fig. 19). The purpose of the stone as an altar on which ritual sacrifice was practiced in the Great Ball Court seems clear.

Three figural panels are carved on the upper surfaces of the Great Ball Court Stone, and a band of twenty-four hieroglyphs is inscribed on the rim on its base (Figure 2). One figural panel, Area 3, depicts four serpent warriors and a reclining *bacab* figure (Figure 3); two panels, Areas 1 and 2, depict decapitation scenes of ballplayers similar to those represented on the ball court benches (Figures 4 and 5). The inscription (Figure 6) includes one glyph, Glyph 5, which clearly refers to the ballgame event (R. Krochock, personal communication 1985), and a phrase, Glyphs 21-24, that includes a name which may be identified as an ideographic variant of Kakupacal and the Chichén Itzá emblem glyph. Glyphs 6 and 7 record a Calendar Round date, 11 Cimi 14 Pax, that may refer to the Long Count date 10.1.15.3.6 or A.D. 864 GMT (Wren 1986). Thus, the construction of the Great Ball Court complex and the execution of its associated artworks appear to date to the Terminal Classic period.

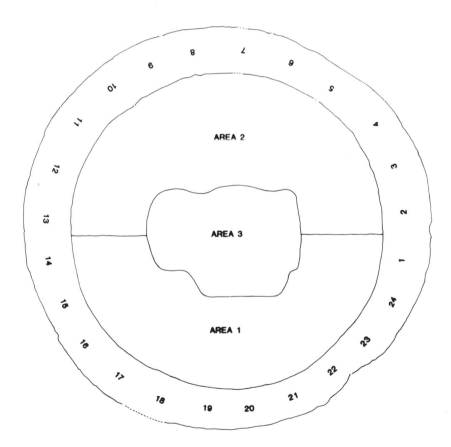

Figure 2. Great Ball Court Stone. Schematic drawing by Linnéa Wren.

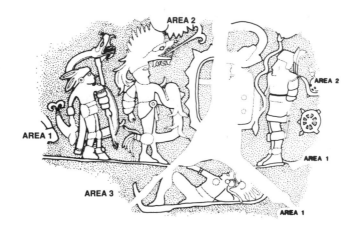

Figure 3. Great Ball Court Stone, Area 3. Drawing by Ruth Krochock after Peggy Diggs.

Figure 4. Great Ball Court Stone, Area 1. Drawing by Ruth Krochock after Peggy Diggs.

A second previously unrecognized context in which the ballgame is represented is in the North Temple on the east wall (Figure 7). The interior walls and vaults of the North Temple are decorated in low relief carving, which was originally covered with stucco and paint. Areas of the relief, including the east wall, were drawn by Adela Breton in 1907. As published by Breton (1917:187), the design in the center of the east wall is an indistinct shape. But a careful study of the carving reveals a decapitated ballplayer from whose neck pours blood in the shape of seven serpents. The player, who kneels by a large ball, is bound by a rope held by a standing figure wearing the jester god headdress, an indication of chiefly status. As in other sites in the Maya region, the ballgame at Chichén Itzá thus appears to be connected to the themes of conquest and kinship.

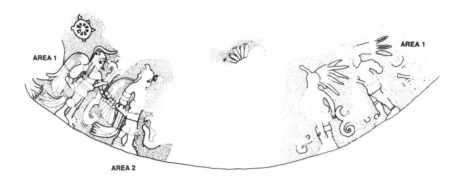

Figure 5. Great Ball Court Stone, Area 2. Drawing by Ruth Krochock after Peggy Diggs.

Large sections of relief have flaked off the surface of the north wall since the time of Breton's visit. However, additional scenes from the North Temple have been recovered by Schmidt, who has located approximately thirty percent of the stones from the collapsed south arch above the building's entrance (Figures 8a and 8b). Several skeletal figures suggest that this portion of the temple relief depicts an underworld scene. The complete cycle of reliefs in the North Temple, which includes scenes on the north wall (Figure 9), west wall (Figure 10), and north arch (Figure 11), appear to indicate an elaborate series of ritual activities that included the ballgame as an important component. Schmidt and I have argued elsewhere that these reliefs may represent the designation, accession, and death of a ruler (Wren and Schmidt 1986).

The depictions of ballgame scenes in Areas 1 and 2 of the Great Ball Court Stone and on the east wall of the North Temple raise the issue of the relationship between the formal principles of composition and the expressive purposes of imagery. Although the scenes are similar in their subjects, they are different in the compositional formats in which they are presented.

The ballgame scenes on the Great Ball Court Stone are presented in a static format. In this format, the space is flattened and time is stilled. The human figure is shown through a combination of frontal and profile views that renders the body as flat as possible. The background is emptied of landscape and architectural elements, and its depth is reduced to a two-dimensional plane filled, in places, by scroll designs. Movement is arrested by the use of horizontal and vertical axes.

The static format is the compositional arrangement most commonly used in

COMPOSITION AND CONTENT IN MAYA SCULPTURE

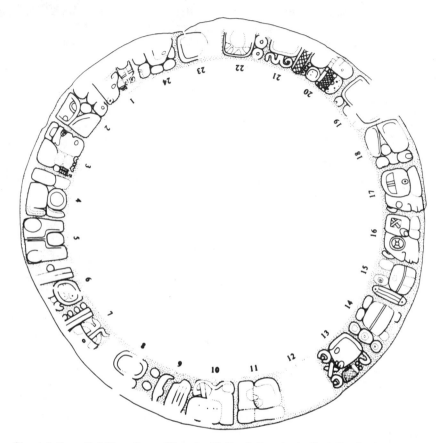

Figure 6. Great Ball Court Stone, Hieroglyphic Band. Drawing by Ruth Krochock.

Maya monumental sculpture and most often employed at Chichén Itzá. It is applied to the walls, piers, jambs, and benches of monumental structures such as the Lower Temple of the Jaguars (Maudslay 1889-1902:vol. 2, pl. 49), the Temple of the Warriors and the Northwest Colonnade (Morris et al. 1931), and the Mercado (Ruppert 1943), as well as to the bench reliefs of the Great Ball Court and other ball courts at the site. Its function as an important communicative device rather than merely as a conceptually neutral aesthetic framework for the subject is evidenced by the insistence with which it is adapted to the curvilinear surfaces of the Great Ball Court Stone. In each of the three areas of relief, the superimposition of figural compositions organized along horizontal and vertical axes upon the hemispherical shape of the stone results in distortions in the figures and in perceptual confusions for the viewer.

The static format creates a sense of permanence that transcends the temporal. The figures presented in this format appear to be neither active nor in repose.

Figure 7. North Temple, East Wall. Drawing by Linnéa Wren.

Their gestures are fixed, and their actions are stilled by the flat space that surrounds them. Balanced on ground lines but simultaneously situated in ambiguous and unspecified localities and suspended in a timeless moment, the figures are removed from the immediacy of actual events and historical time. The static format serves a means of translating the ephemeral nature of actual individuals and concrete occurrences into events of lasting significance and universal relevance.

The static format further serves as a means of distancing the actor in the artwork from the audience. It can be compared to a screen, which permits the viewer to see reflections of the natural world but prevents the viewer from entering into the illusory space or from sharing in the unfolding of the depicted event. Action and actors are remote. The meaning of the scene is imposed upon the viewer. Because he cannot experience the scene, the viewer can only accept rather than question, modify, or judge the interpretation and ideals presented in the artwork.

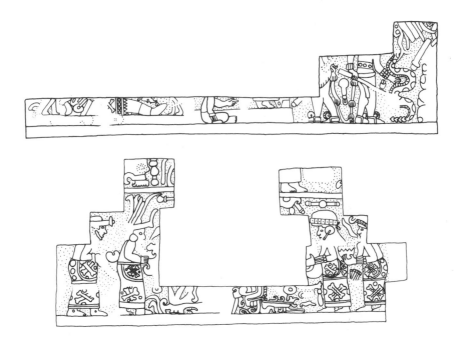

Figures 8a and 8b. North Temple, South Arch. Drawings by Peter Schmidt and Linnéa Wren.

In contrast to the Great Ball Court Stone, the ballgame scene in the North Temple reliefs is depicted in a different compositional arrangement that may be termed an active format. In the active format, space is deepened, and time is no longer static. Horizontal and vertical axes are relaxed, while diagonal axes are introduced. Physical settings are defined by the inclusion of natural and architectural elements. Movement in space and action through time are suggested by the wide variety of poses assumed by the human actors.

The active format is utilized by the sculptors of Chichén Itzá in the Temple of Xtoloc, the Temple of the Sculpted Wall Panels (Ruppert 1931:pl. 11), and, most impressively, in the North Temple. Unlike the static format, which is employed in sculpture throughout the Maya region, the use of the active format in monumental sculpture at Chichén Itzá represents an artistic innovation. Parallels may be found in non-Maya regions in the sculptured columns and

Figure 8b

panels at El Tajin (Kampen 1972) and the reliefs of the Pacific coast of
Guatemala (Miller 1984), and in Maya regions in the paneled stelae of northern
Yucatán (Proskouriakoff 1950) and the recently discovered sculpture from
X'Telhu (Robertson 1986). But nothing comparable to the North Temple in its
scale or complexity is known from the contemporary sculptural tradition of
Mesoamerica.

The active format may be compared to a window rather than a screen. Because
space is three-dimensional, rather than flat, the viewer can enter the space
created in the reliefs; because the settings are specific in landscape and architectural detail rather than anonymous, the viewer can identify locations; because
time is shown to unfold gradually in a series of events rather than being frozen
into a single moment, the viewer can re-enact the events and can participate in
the sacred and secular actions of the actors. As a result, the meaning of the

COMPOSITION AND CONTENT IN MAYA SCULPTURE

Figure 9. North Temple, North Wall. Drawing by Linnéa Wren (after Marquina 1951:photo 439; Breton 1917:pl. 3).

artwork is actively appropriated by the viewer.

As the treatment of space and time become more dynamic, the sense that the subject transcends the transitoriness of actual circumstances diminishes. At the same time, the immediacy of the scene increases. The active format, thus, enables the viewer to structure the collage of fragmentary and often incomprehensible experiences of daily life into concrete physical relationships with the supernatural forces believed to control the natural order.

The utility of the active format was not unrecognized by Maya artists during the Classic period. The active format was used in media such as ceramic vessels (Coe 1973, 1978) and mural painting (Barrera Rubio 1979) designed for visual contemplation by the elite class in personal settings. The innovation at Chichén Itzá was that artists began to use the active format in monumental reliefs designed for settings accessible to a much larger public, such as the Monjas complex, where the Temple of the Sculptured Wall Panels is located, and the Great Ball Court complex, where the North Temple is located. The reasons for this innovation can be found, I believe, in the changing nature of the Maya polity at Chichén Itzá.

During the Terminal Classic period, when the Great Ball Court was constructed, Chichén Itzá became one of the most important polities in the northern Maya lowlands. Traditional interpretations of the history of the site have divided its occupation into two distinct phases: a Late Classic phase, during which Maya occupants built Puuc-style buildings, and an Early Postclassic phase, during which Toltec bands of conquerors from the central Mexican site of Tula, Hidalgo, imposed foreign beliefs, practices, and architectural and sculptural styles upon the native population (Tozzer 1957).

Figure 10. North Temple, West Wall. Drawing by Linnéa Wren (after Breton 1917:pl. 4).

300

Figure 11. North Temple, North Arch. Drawing by Linnéa Wren (after Cohodas 1978:fig. 31).

This reconstruction of the history of Chichén Itzá has recently been challenged (Proskouriakoff 1970; Lincoln 1986). It now appears that the history of the site cannot be divided into two discrete periods, during the first of which the Maya social order was unchallenged by outside influences, and during the second of which Maya rulers were replaced by Toltec leaders, and Maya cultural patterns were subordinated to those of central Mexico. Instead, it appears that strong foreign influences were present in northern Yucatán throughout the Classic period (Miller 1985) and that Maya culture proved a resilient receptor. Instead of permitting their culture to be either subordinated to influences from without or stagnated by factors from within, the Maya responded by absorbing outside influences into native traditions (Freidel 1986).

At Chichén Itzá, this response resulted in a dynamic syncretism between contemporaneous Maya and non-Maya traditions of Mexico, Veracruz, and Oaxaca, and, possibly, other regions (Wren and Schmidt 1986). It also appears to have resulted in the inclusion of greater numbers of the populace into the elite class.

Evidence that a much larger percentage of the occupants of Chichén Itzá was permitted to share the power and prerogatives once restricted to a tiny elite can be seen in the architecture and sculpture of the site (Wren 1986). At Chichén Itzá, builders learned to combine the colonnades connected by wooden lintels found in central Mexico with the corbelled vaults employed in the Maya region. As a result, monumental architecture at Chichén Itzá dramatically exceeded the scale of masonry-roofed buildings built at any other Maya site. The massive enclosed spaces appear to have been constructed in order to give an increased number of people access to the rituals and events enacted in their interiors.

The expanded size of the elite is also reflected in the multiplication of figural images that decorate the architecture of Chichén Itzá. In contrast to the individuals' lives that are memorialized in the figural sculpture at other Maya sites, large numbers of important personages are celebrated at Chichén Itzá. Hundreds of warriors and priests appear singly and marching in files on the surfaces of structures such as the Temple of the Warriors, the Northwest

Colonnade, and the Lower Temple of the Jaguars.

The simultaneous use of two distinct compositional formats addressed the needs of the changing social order at Chichén Itzá in several ways. The static format continued to be used to maintain traditional Maya beliefs that the elite possessed an inherently and immutably different nature from the non-elite class and that this nature was based upon a special relationship with supernatural deities. At the same time, the active format was adapted for monumental relief sculpture in public settings to acknowledge that a growing portion of the populace was now allowed to participate in the sacred ritual behavior represented.

Thus, compositional formats as well as symbolic imagery conveyed conceptual formulations about the individual and his role in the social order and the cosmic realm. Visual form, that is, the treatment of space and time, was used as a means of communicating culturally significant messages concerning the cultural patterns by which an individual's life was structured on all levels of experience. More succinctly, the art of Chichén Itzá appears to demonstrate the axiom coined by Marshall McLuhan that, "The medium is the message" (1964:7).

THE SOCIAL ECOLOGY OF ETHNIC DIFFERENTIATION IN THE SIERRA TARAHUMARA AND CHIAPAS HIGHLANDS

Jerome M. Levi
Harvard University

A THEORETICAL FRAMEWORK: BEHAVIORAL ECOLOGY AND SOCIAL ANTHROPOLOGY

This brief study addresses the following question: What types of spacing behaviors, territorial signals, and displays of aggression, competition, or dominance are used to communicate the existence of ethnic boundaries, and under what circumstances will one repertoire of mutual avoidance be used rather than another? An attempt is made to answer this question by suggesting some reasons why the communication of ethnic boundaries differs between two indigenous zones in Mexico, namely among the Tarahumara of the Sierra Madre and the Tzotzil and Tzeltal of the Chiapas highlands.

Since many of the most important factors influencing these features appear to be ultimately correlated with a society's settlement pattern, subsistence strategy, and level of internal differentiation, an understanding of these issues requires one to undertake an investigation that is social and ecological, in both method and theory. Outlining a theoretical framework and an ecological model of ethnic differentiation, I then compare the Sierra Tarahumara and the Chiapas highlands in terms of how these two regions represent contrasting forms of ethnic differentiation regarding adaptive strategies, clothing styles, and modes of public ritual. Consequently, this essay does not pretend to offer an exhaustive discussion of ethnicity in these two regions. Rather, employing Tarahumara, Tzotzil, and Tzeltal ethnography, its goal is to test several hypotheses concerning the possible ecological determinants of the signals of ethnic differentiation. In the process, I hope to stimulate new ways of thinking about a familiar set of ethnological topics.

There are at least three ways in which social anthropologists have found the arguments first developed by ecologists for nonhuman species to be of value in the interpretation of sociological data. One method involves the use of ecological analogy, that is, the appropriation of biological models that are then applied to certain social anthropological settings. Vogt's discussion of Maya cultural development in terms of adaptive radiation, what he termed the "genetic model," is a particularly ingenious example of an argument based on ecological analogy:

> In brief, the genetic model assumes that genetically related tribes, as determined by related languages, physical types, and systemic patterns, are derived from a small proto-group with a proto-culture at some time in the past. The model resembles that of a zoologist who views a certain species of animal as evolving and making an adaptive adjustment to a given ecological niche and then radiating from this point as the population expands into neighboring ecological niches. As the population moves into different ecological settings, further adaptive radiations occur in the species. But these variations are traceable to the ancestral animal, or, in other words, back to the proto-type.
>
> In the genetic model, as applied to human populations, we assume that a small proto-group succeeds in adapting itself efficiently to a certain ecological niche and in developing certain basic systemic patterns which constitute the basic aspects of the proto-culture. If the adaptation proves to be efficient, the population expands, and the group begins to radiate from this point of dispersal. As members split off from the proto-group and move into neighboring ecological niches, they make appropriate adaptations to these new situations and begin to differentiate—that is, there are adaptive variations from the proto-type over time as the members of the genetic unit spread from the dispersal area [Vogt 1964d:11-12].

Another type of ecological argument used by social anthropologists explicitly examines the way that specific populations are locally adapted to given habitats (e.g., Goldschmidt 1959; Kennedy 1978; Leach 1961; Lee 1979; Rappaport 1968; Steward 1955). These studies have in common the view that there exist certain constraints—such as physical environment, subsistence, and technology—which, in the final analysis, condition social forms to the extent that they impose limitations on the range of possible adaptations.

A third type of ecological argument used by social anthropologists investigates man-land relationships, but does so by taking a broader view of the environment. The ecological system that these studies are concerned with is not a single society per se, but rather the connections between different societies (e.g., Barth 1956, 1969; Geertz 1963; Leach 1954). These studies examine intergroup dynamics in terms of how the utilization of different niches differentiates between populations. Though there are a number of fine studies of interethnic relations in Mesoamerica (e.g., Colby and van den Berghe 1961, 1969; De la Fuente 1967; Friedlander 1975; Gillin 1951; Hawkins 1984; Warren 1978), most have tended to employ other than ecological paradigms. Notable exceptions are George Collier's (1975) and Siverts's (1969) superb analyses of ethnicity and intergroup relations in the highlands of Chiapas, which focus on man-land ratios and the economic interaction spheres of different communities.

During the last decade there has also emerged a new body of research on human spatial organization (Abruzzi 1982; Durham 1981; Dyson-Hudson and

Smith 1978; Harpending and Davis 1977; Hayden 1981; Smith 1981), the results of which are more sophisticated than the earlier debate on whether human territoriality is innate (Ardrey 1966:1; Cohen 1976:55) or acquired (Reynolds 1966:449), and the biological underpinnings of which are more rigorous then the generalized ecological orientations of most previous studies of hunter-gatherer group dynamics. Utilizing recent developments in the study of animal territoriality and group size, and equipped with the theoretical armature of ethology, sociobiology, and evolutionary ecology, these investigations have begun to apply more formal biological models to human populations. The theoretical orientation of this essay is based upon this latter behavioral ecological framework—together with the previously discussed types of ecological arguments that employ the notions of ecological analogy, habitat adaptation, and intergroup processes.

A MODEL OF ETHNIC DIFFERENTIATION AND TERRITORIAL SIGNALING

I postulate that human populations respond to conditions of resource availability and resource competition in ways similar to the responses exhibited by nonhuman populations. Comparisons between different species are justified on the grounds that the relation of similarity is suggested to be one of analogy rather than homology. Because culture is the most important facet of human adaptation, it is predicted that there is an important fit between cultural practices and ecological variables.

Various devices, known as isolating mechanisms, maintain boundaries between contiguous populations by preventing random interbreeding. There exist both premating and postmating isolating mechanisms. The most numerous and significant class of isolating mechanisms are premating behavioral or ethological barriers. The importance of ethological isolating mechanisms in the process of species differentiation has been elaborated by Mayr (1963, 1970) and recently applied to the process of ethnic differentiation by Abruzzi (1982).

In animal species that are sympatric—that is, populations that are capable of occupying overlapping ranges without loss of identity due to interbreeding—premating isolating mechanisms foster this reproductive isolation by heightening recognition among members of a given population via specific behaviors and stimuli. These ethological barriers may be visual, such as the coloration and mating dances of birds, auditory, such as the calls of insects and frogs, or olfactory, as is widespread among mammals (Abruzzi 1982:18).

Following Abruzzi, I suggest that processes analogous to isolating mechanisms function in human populations to foster ethnic differentiation:

> Isolating mechanisms among human populations are just as varied as those that separate nonhuman populations, and premating mechanisms are likewise the most efficient and the most susceptible to selective improvement. Premating mechanisms that foster "eth-

> nic visibility" are quite common. Such mechanisms limit or stereotype the interactions of local populations and, by heightening the recognition of ethnic identity, reduce the likelihood of interethnic marriage. Premating isolating mechanisms among human populations include residential concentration, occupational specialization, distinct forms of dress and speech, separate public facilities, public rituals, prescribed and proscribed patterns of social interaction, courtship and marriage rules, folklore, and any other factor that exhibits local ethnic distinctions [Abruzzi 1982:20].

Selection theory implies that "[w]here energetic demands for the efficient exploitation of different resources favor distinct adaptive strategies within the same community, selection should produce two or more socially discrete populations to the exclusion of one uniform population" (Abruzzi 1982:19). Thus, an increase in population (including intruder pressure) or a decrease in resource availability, will lead to greater competition. Niche diversification and resource partitioning should yield a population that will develop increasingly discrete adaptive strategies within the same community as competition intensifies. The resulting populations will become more differentiated the closer they are associated with distinct adaptive strategies. If different populations are able to exploit the same resources fully, the population that can more efficiently exploit this niche will be expected to replace the less efficient population; yet if different populations exploit the same resources, but one population can better utilize marginal environments, the populations may coreside (Barth 1956:1088). Finally, the boundaries between these populations will be reinforced by isolating mechanisms and territorial signals.

The differentiation of sympatric ethnic populations depends upon an ability to communicate boundaries. This delineation can be achieved by means of overt defense and aggression or by advertising and signaling. In an effort to stipulate the conditions under which one method of mutual avoidance will be used rather than another, I suggest that where neither competing populations nor sufficient density levels occur, advertisement can afford to be general, nonspecific, and variable. However, where competing populations do coexist and/or density levels are high, nonspecific signals indicating access to critical resources may lead to conflict. Under these conditions there will be a selective premium on precision and distinctiveness of signals (Mayr 1970). Here, effective advertising will include redundancy, rhythmic repetition, bright packaging, and supernormal stimuli. These features of "symbolic" communication have been independently described for humans (Tambiah 1985:123-166) as well as for animals (Krebs and Dawkins 1984)

ADAPTIVE STRATEGIES

The Tarahumara inhabit a zone of jagged mountains and canyons, known as the Sierra Tarahumara, located in the Western Sierra Madre in the southwestern

portion of the state of Chihuahua, Mexico. Evon Vogt, in his evocative introduction to Lumholtz's pioneering classic *Unknown Mexico,* describes this
region as "one of the most rugged, most impenetrable mountain masses on the
North American continent" (Vogt 1973:vii). Climate, precipitation, topography,
and vegetation vary radically with the dramatic changes in elevation (Pennington 1963:25-38). Kennedy has summarily commented that the
Tarahumaras' "ability to preserve their cultural integrity derives chiefly from
the circumstances that their environment is among the least hospitable in the
world" (Kennedy 1978:1). The population of the Tarahumara is approximately
46,000, with 50,000 being suggested as an upper limit (Fried 1969:850; Pennington 1983:277). Relative population density is low; in general I estimate it
to be little more than several people per square kilometer. According to the 1960
census, there were also about 190,000 mestizos in the region, though this figure
has clearly increased during recent decades (Merrill 1983b:295; Pennington
1983:277). Most of this population is concentrated in the towns of the Sierra,
though occasionally mestizo families also dot the Tarahumara hinterlands as
small-scale ranchers and farmers.

Tarahumara subsistence is that of transhumant agro-pastoralism. Sheep,
goats, and occasionally oxen are the typical livestock (Bennett and Zingg
1935:9-25; Pennington 1963:137-148); maize, beans, and squash the ubiquitous
crops (Bennett and Zingg 1935:26; Pennington 1963:39-47). Families tend to
have several small plots dispersed in different locales, usually with adjacent
shelters. Residential mobility is an important aspect of Tarahumara economy,
with families migrating between summer and winter homes (Merrill
1983b:291). Livestock ranging, rules of land inheritance, and sequential utilization at different seasons of the small, widely scattered, often cliff-side fields
result in what Bennett and Zingg (1935:183-187) called the "basic pattern of
isolation." This extreme dispersion of the community therefore geographically
separates the Tarahumara not only from the mestizos but also from each other,
though pueblo meetings and maize beer drinking parties (*tesguinadas*) are
important forms of community integration (Bennett and Zingg 1935; Kennedy
1963; Merrill 1978). Fishing, hunting, and gathering are supplementary
economic activities (Pennington 1963:85-136). In contrast with other Indian
regions in Mexico, the Sierra Tarahumara lacks an aboriginal system of regional
markets to redistribute locally occurring natural resources and manufactured
goods. Tarahumara economy is therefore overwhelmingly geared towards subsistence rather than trade. In this context, economic exchanges are sporadic and,
traditionally, take place only through individualized sharing networks and
trading partnerships, especially between people in the gorges and the higher
elevations (Bennett and Zingg 1935:157-162; Kennedy 1978:91-92; Lumholtz
1902:244-245).

Tarahumara methods of pastoralism and agriculture have influenced spacing
behavior in significant ways by allowing the Tarahumara to exploit more
marginal ecological zones and thus maintain the separation from foreigners that
they so desire. The model describes how this ethnic differentiation among

sympatric populations occurs. Spaniards, and then mestizos, have tended to cluster in relatively compact settlements in the rich agricultural bottom lands of the canyons, or elsewhere in the region, where they have engaged in adjunct resource exploitation: these have tended to be mining and lumbering communities. Tarahumaras and Spaniards were not in competition for resources as long as the foreigners exploited precious minerals that were neither sought by, nor available to, the Tarahumaras with indigenous technology (though labor drafts exerted pressure on the Tarahumara population) (Dunne 1948:166-167; Sheridan and Naylor 1979:81-100). However, where Tarahumaras and mestizos (or earlier Spaniards) were farmers and/or livestock raisers in direct competition for the same resources—namely, good pasture areas and the alluvial flood plains flanking the streams and rivers—the European intruders have usually prevailed in expropriating these more fertile lands from the Tarahumaras (Pennington 1963:18-23). In response, the Tarahumara have retreated into harsher environments (Spicer 1962:35-36). Ethnic differentiation is therefore maintained, since the two groups in effect have adapted to different ecological niches. Even though the Tarahumara as a group are less numerous and organized than the mestizos, and thus politically weaker, they are better able to utilize the marginal habitats along the walls of the gorges and the rugged upland terrain due to the development of a mobile, fragmented settlement pattern and a diversified subsistence strategy. Consequently, it is possible for Tarahumaras and mestizos to reside as sympatric ethnic populations.

The Tzotzil and Tzeltal, two neighboring Maya groups that are closely related in terms of both language and culture, inhabit the Chiapas highlands—a plateau known as the Mesa Central located almost at the center of the state of Chiapas in southeastern Mexico (Vogt 1969a:134). This highland mass is characterized by stands of pine and oak, which give way to savanna and tropical broad-leaf forest as one descends towards *tierra caliente,* where sugar cane, coffee, and fruits are grown (Vogt 1969a:136-137). One of the largest valleys in the highlands is the site of the *ladino* (i.e., mestizo) city of San Cristóbal de las Casas, which is the economic and administrative hub for the region; while smaller surrounding valleys serve as the *cabeceras,* or political and ceremonial centers, for the Tzotzil and Tzeltal townships. There are fourteen Tzeltal and twenty-eight Tzotzil communities, many of which have the status of full *municipios* (Villa Rojas 1962:55).

Today there are over 120,000 Tzotzil speakers (Laughlin 1975:2). According to the 1960 Mexican census, there were some 78,000 Tzeltal, but Hunn estimates that it is "likely that Tzeltal speakers today also number well over 100,000" (1977:7). In contrast to the Sierra Tarahumara, in the Chiapas highlands Indians outnumber *ladinos*; for example, in 1960 it was reported that San Cristóbal had a population of 27,198. Population density in the highlands is relatively high—which also contrasts with the Tarahumara situation. Average population density was calculated to be 41.35 persons per square kilometer for the following predominately Tzotzil or Tzeltal *municipios*: Amatenango, Chalchihuitán, Chanal, Chenalhó, Huistán, Huitiupán, Larráinzar, Mitontic, Pantelhó,

Tenejapa, Venustiano Carranza, and Zinacantán. Two important Indian *municipios* were excluded from this sample due to their unusually high population densities; namely, Chamula (326.69 persons per square kilometer) and Oxchuc (174.70 persons per square kilometer) (VIII Censo General de Población: 1960, Estado de Chiapas, México, D.F. 1963).

There are several facets to Tzotzil-Tzeltal economy. Maize, beans, and squash are cultivated on a subsistence basis in the highlands, and some livestock are also kept (Laughlin 1969:157-161; Villa Rojas 1969:199-203). In some communities (i.e., Chamula, Zinacantán), population pressure and/or soil erosion have forced highland Indians to rent land from *ladinos* in the lowlands, especially along the Río Grijalva (Cancian 1972; G. Collier 1975; Gossen 1974:7). At times, Tzotzil and Tzeltal have also been an important source of cheap wage labor, suffering exploitation at the hands of the *ladinos,* in the lowland ranches and plantations (Pozas A. 1952; Villa Rojas 1969:213; Wasserstrom 1977).

In the Chiapas highlands, as in the Sierra Tarahumara, Indians and non-Indians are differentiated in terms of language, dress, religion, social and political organization—though here I shall only discuss differences in economics and settlement pattern. Despite the colonial policy of *reducción,* the Tzotzil and Tzeltal were never successfully concentrated into compact settlements. Instead, they have typically retained the traditional Maya settlement pattern characterized by a ceremonial center, where officials live during their term in office, and scattered outlying hamlets, where the bulk of the population resides (Vogt 1983). By contrast, *ladinos* tend to be nucleated in towns and cities "with streets in a rectilinear grid centered on the town hall, central square, market, and principal church" (G. Collier 1975:11).

Economic orientations also contrast. As land owners, merchants, craftsmen, administrators, and providers of services, *ladinos* consider manual labor and agricultural work debasing, whereas Indians regard the routine subsistence work in the milpa as the "most worthy activity for men" (Colby and van den Berghe 1961:777). In general, "Indians extract primary products, food and manpower, for consumption; Ladinos convert these into secondary products for redistribution in commerce and trade" (G. Collier 1975:12). Thus, in the Chiapas highlands, as in the Sierra Tarahumara, Indians and non-Indians are maintained as sympatric ethnic populations, with non-Indians occupying the more favorable economic niche in both regions.

However, niche diversification has proceeded further among the Tzotzil and Tzeltal than it has among the Tarahumara, as our model predicts, given the greater pressure on resources and higher population densities in the Chiapas highlands. Among the Tzotzil and Tzeltal this has resulted in the formation of a number of distinct communities—each distinguishable by its own unique dialect, dress, civil-religious organization, and economic specialization— whereas among the Tarahumara, differences between communities are far less apparent. "Considering the size of the area, the Tarahumaras present a remarkably uniform culture" (Bennett and Zingg 1935:181).

This niche diversification in the Chiapas highlands, along with the adaptive strategies associated with each niche, is reflected in the presence of a regional marketing system and sustained by the distinct local societies, the resources they control, and the commodities they trade. Although in both the Sierra Tarahumara and the Chiapas highlands there exists a highland-lowland proximity, and thus the natural distribution in a small area of both tropical and alpine products that usually give rise to markets, density-dependent factors were insufficient among the Tarahumara to produce either an indigenous regional marketing system or the socioeconomic differentiation among different Tarahumara communities that would maintain such a system (Nash 1967a).

In the Chiapas highlands, each township is characterized by its own occupational specializations which are redistributed through the market mechanism in San Cristóbal. For example, water jars and fine pottery are produced in Amatenango; maize, flowers, and salt are sold by Zinacantecos; musical instruments, firewood, charcoal, woolen fabrics, and *aguardiente* come from Chamula; fibers, cordage, eggs, poultry, and pigs are specialties of Oxchuc; peanuts and oranges are produced in Tenejapa; while ceremonial paraphernalia, tools, and manufactured goods are sold by the *ladinos* in San Cristóbal (Siverts 1969:106-107). As noted by George Collier (1975:177-181), the niche of production specialties is only partially accounted for by local physiography, since the natural resources for many products occur in numerous townships. Rather, it is the cultural differentiation in the region that protects a township's domination over particular specializations. Competition among the townships is correspondingly regulated by the stereotyped reputation of each township's specialized niche in the market. Therefore, niche diversification and resource partitioning are maintained by each township's distinct but interdependent adaptive strategy within the overall system.

CLOTHING STYLES

Differences in clothing styles can function as isolating mechanisms to the extent that they heighten ethnic visibility and thereby serve as signals or indicators differentiating sympatric ethnic populations. What is being communicated is that people who dress the same, belong to the same community and therefore have access to that community's critical resources—be they food items, local commodities, arable lands, technology, potential mates, and so forth. Differences in dress, therefore, contrast the populations that wear them by advertising differences in community membership. Throughout Mesoamerica, one of the most obvious and important ways that Indians and mestizos differentiate themselves is by marking ethnic distinctions in terms of contrasting styles of dress. This becomes even more significant when it is recalled that race or physical type is a poor indicator of ethnicity—especially in Mesoamerica, where the mestizo population represents the admixture of Hispanic and Indian populations.

Regarding clothing styles, Indians are not only differentiated from mestizos, but are further differentiated among themselves. In general, each Indian ethnic group is characterized by its own tribal costume. Greater distinctiveness is sometimes manifested even among Indians belonging to the same ethnic group or speaking the same language, as local dress styles vary from one community to another within a circumscribed area. When this happens—as it does among the Indians in the highlands of Chiapas—it is usually in combination with a stepwise increase in the complexity and distinctiveness of the textile itself; that is, more intricate weaving, more embroidery, more design elements, more parallel patterns, repetitive zonation, and brighter coloration. Yet in other circumstances—as among the Tarahumara—a relatively uniform style of dress exists for the entire group and over a wide region; the costume itself is n:arkedly plain when compared to the spectacular costumes of the former area.

In the highlands of Chiapas, each Tzotzil and Tzeltal township is characterized by its own distinctive style of dress. Consequently, on any given day in San Cristóbal de las Casas, one is likely to see members of no fewer than thirteen different townships—each immediately made recognizable by their township's own unique costume. Although there is a flamboyant variety in colors, styles, and design motifs in the region, I shall try to give some idea of the constituent parts of the "basic" Tzotzil-Tzeltal men's costume (Cordry and Cordry 1968:340-348; Laughlin 1969:162-164; Villa-Rojas 1969:208).

Men's wear usually consists of white cotton pants that may either reach to the shins (Chamula, Pantelhó) or be worn as shorts (Zinacantán, Chalchihuitán, Chenalhó, Mitontic, Cancuc, Oxchuc), the latter sometimes being heavily embroidered with red yarn (Tenejapa). In Huistán, men wear an enormous breechcloth that looks not unlike a large "diaper." Men's shirts, like their pants, are traditionally made of white homespun and loomed cotton, with long sleeves that are either white (Zinacantán), blue (Chalchihuitán), or red (Larráinzar). Sometimes these shirts may be longer in back than in the front, reaching almost to the knees, open at the sides, with two small tassels at the back of the neck (Chenalhó, Chalchihuitán); or the front and back of the knee-length shirts may be of equal length and sewn at the sides so that the garment is actually a kind of tunic (Oxchuc, Cancuc). These long shirts may, furthermore, be decorated with natural brown cotton pinstripes (Chalchihuitán) or red bands around the upper sleeves (Cancuc). In some communities, a poncho is worn over the shirt. These may be red-and-white pinstriped (Zinacantán), black or white wool with an occasional red thread (Chamula), or black wool with white wool pinstripes (Tenejapa). Men's sashes, large neckerchiefs, and hats with multicolored ribbons also vary among the townships.

The significance of dress as an indicator of community membership in the Chiapas highlands can be further illustrated by those circumstances under which individuals attempt to change their cultural identities. Thus, lower class *ladinos* or Indians who go to San Cristóbal and adopt Western-style clothing, thereby attempting to make themselves visually indistinguishable from the dominant society, are pejoratively referred to as *indios revestidos*, literally "Indians who have changed clothing" (Colby and van den Berghe 1961:781; Siverts 1969:111). Similarly, when an Indian from one township marries into another

SOCIAL ECOLOGY OF ETHNIC DIFFERENTIATION

Indian township, as sometimes happens, he or she adopts that township's style of clothing (Laughlin 1969:173).

Since costume functions as a territorial signal of ethnic visibility, the model predicts that differences in consumer density and varying levels of competition for resources will account for the observed differences in clothing. At least in theory, I am arguing that costume can function as a kind of "epideictic display," that is, "a display by which members of a population reveal their presence and allow others to assess the density of the population" (Wilson 1980:311). This concept was first postulated by Wynne-Edwards (1962:16) for nonhuman species, though Rappaport (1979:39) has adapted the idea for human groups and applied it in a compelling way to his analysis of ritual and warfare among the Maring tribes of New Guinea.

The intricate and diverse costumes typical of the Tzotzil and Tzeltal communities in the highlands of Chiapas are, in fact, correlated with a demographic environment characterized by relatively high levels of both density and competition among different communities belonging to the same Indian ethnolinguistic group. The socioeconomic features of these tightly integrated corporate communities include sedentary residence, village-based economic specializations, complex politico-religious hierarchies, intense market relations, and high rates of community endogamy. In this context, isolating mechanisms, such as contrasting clothing styles, dramatically differentiate competing communities for the obvious reason that the communities themselves are in close geographical proximity to each other. Here, Indian communities have entirely different costumes despite the fact that they all reside in the same region and are all members of either the Tzotzil or Tzeltal people. Thus, the distinctiveness of their costumes mirrors the distinctiveness the communities themselves are attempting to maintain over their microenvironments and the critical resources they contain. Since access to these resources is defined by community membership, and since community membership is signaled by wearing the community's costume, there is a selective premium favoring bright colors, intricate designs, and repetitive patterns—in short, an advertisement that is at once "loud" and "precise."

However, in areas characterized by lower population densities and/or lower levels of competition among communities belonging to the same Indian ethnic or linguistic group, the model leads us to expect there to be a corresponding simplification in costume and a relative uniformity in clothing styles over the region as a whole. This is exactly what is seen among the Tarahumara. I cannot here go into the ecological details of Tarahumara dispersal, mobile residence, nonintensive agricultural techniques, and livestock ranging that are correlated with a comparatively low man/land ratio (Levi 1987:8-24). Suffice to say that Tarahumara subsistence and settlement patterns are consistent with lower population densities. Correspondingly, there is relatively little local variation in Tarahumara costume, though the group occupies some 35,000 km^2—the most extensive tribal territory among the Indians in northern Mexico. Likewise, in comparison with the costumes of the denser Indian populations in the Chiapas highlands, Tarahumara garb appears simple in the extreme.

Tarahumara clothing is traditionally made almost exclusively of a kind of store-bought white muslin known as *manta* in Spanish or *chiní* in Tarahumara. Men's clothing consists of a white loincloth in front, a triangular white hip-cloth that hangs from the waist to just behind the knees in back, and a loose-fitting shirt with long puffy sleeves gathered tightly at the wrists. In winter, this may be complemented by a heavy, natural colored, wool blanket (predominantly black, brown, or white) worn over the shoulders or wrapped around the body. Men hold their hair in place with solid-colored headbands, usually white or red. It should be mentioned that on occasion one will see that on some part of this costume a simple design has been embroidered, but this is the exception rather than the rule and indicates a personal artistic flourish rather than a stylistic convention of the community. In general, the monotony of undecorated white or dark fabrics is broken only in areas where there is frequent trade with outsiders, brightly colored cloth and calico being in high demand. The only real evidence in indigenous Tarahumara textiles of bright colors, redundant designs, and repetitive zonation is found in the woven sashes among the upland Tarahumara and, to a lesser extent, in the narrow hair ribbons made for sale.

The important point is that among the Tarahumara there is nothing like the explosion in form and color, neither the embroidery, nor the intricate weaving, one sees in the costumes of the more densely populated Indian communities in the Chiapas highlands (or elsewhere in Mesoamerica, such as highland Guatemala, Oaxaca, or the Sierra de Puebla). In general, Tarahumara make little use of sartorial codes among themselves. They do not need to separate themselves symbolically in costume, since demographic and economic factors allow them to be already physically separated in space. The regionally generalized rather than locally specialized patterns of settlement and subsistence are reflected in the use of a costume that is both simple and relatively uniform throughout the entire Sierra Tarahumara. Subtle distinctions among the Tarahumara—for example, pueblo differences in the way the headband or hip-cloth is worn or the use of one of several types of white muslin overgarments—are barely recognizable in comparison with the dramatic distinctions in clothing among the Indian townships in the Chiapas highlands. Therefore, the Tarahumara's ethological responses exhibited by low economic defendability and a pattern of withdrawal from contacts with foreigners is associated with little territorial signaling. The Tarahumara can "afford" this nonspecificity in sartorial spacing signals and the lack of distinctiveness in local costume because, relative to other indigenous groups in Mesoamerica, they are neither densely settled nor competing among themselves.

Unlike the Tzotzil-Tzeltal, the Tarahumara are not especially preoccupied with symbolizing through clothing codes the precise dimensions of fine internal boundaries among themselves, but like the Tzotzil-Tzetal they are very interested in maintaining a well-defined external boundary between themselves and the mestizos. Hence, in both regions Indian costume is in marked contrast to mestizo clothing—the latter being rural "Western" dress: slacks, shirt, boots, cowboy hat, and so forth. If costume is associated with community, then mestizo clothing signals that the wearer is a member of a "national" community and, at least in theory, has access to the organizations and resources of the dominant society.

PUBLIC RITUAL

Due to the importance of the Indian/non-Indian divide in both the Chiapas highlands and the Sierra Tarahumara, the isolating mechanisms that maintain this ethnic differentiation not only include differences in adaptive strategies and clothing codes, but extend beyond them to include other spacing devices—such as public ritual—that, among other things, reinforce local endogamy and thus both cultural and genetic separation from non-Indians.

The portrayal of "Judas" in the Tarahumara Holy Week ceremonial serves as a graphic example of isolating mechanisms involving ritualized aggression and supernormal stimuli. The Holy Week rites are long and complex, but here I shall analyze only the most striking ritual mechanism of ethnic boundary maintenance; namely, the depiction and meaning of an effigy representing Judas (Kennedy and Lopez 1981; Merrill 1983a; Velasco Rivero 1983:189-233).

During Holy Week in most Tarahumara communities, one of two competing groups of ritual participants construct a grass or wooden dummy that is called the "Judas." Judas is said to be a *chabochi,* literally a "whiskered one," which is the Tarahumara term for mestizos or non-Indians. According to Tarahumara, some of the characteristics most typical of the *chabochi* are their greed and lust—for power, land, money, and sex. They are held to be inherently aggressive, both sexually and politically, and this, say the Tarahumara, explains why the *chabochi* persist in violating Indian customs, raping Indian lands, and stealing Indian women. The mestizos have in fact encroached on the best lands and generally hold Tarahumara culture in low esteem.

On Holy Saturday, the Judas figure is paraded around the pueblo center, while Tarahumara celebrants, and sometimes mestizo onlookers, gather near the church. The following activities take place: Since the Judas is a *chabochi,* he must look like one. Thus he is dressed in discarded Western-style long pants, shirt, cowboy hat, boots and is given a goat-hair beard and mustache. He is also portrayed with outstretched arms and large hands and fingers and is supplied with a prominent, erect phallus. Since the Judas is a *chabochi,* he must act like one. Therefore, he is carried though the pueblo, where, amidst much ribald laughter and joking, he ridicules the way that the *chabochi* intrude on the Indians. Consequently, he is made to say that he has come searching for gold and silver, desires a Tarahumara woman, and demands exorbitant quantities of Tarahumara property, such as land, livestock, and maize. Finally, since Judas represents a *chabochi,* he deserves to be treated like one—or at least how the Tarahumara must at times feel like they would want to treat the mestizos, were they able to. Thus, the Judas is insulted, and people hurl rocks, dung, or clods of dirt at the effigy. Next, the dummy is ritually "killed": he is shot with rifles, riddled with arrows, or stabbed with lances—depending on community custom.

In the end, the effigy is set on fire and burned to ashes.

From a historical perspective, what we see here is a transference from actual to *ritual* killing of enemies. According to ecological theories of nonverbal communication, ritualization in animals also involves a "process of evolution of signals from non-signal movements" (Krebs and Dawkins 1984:382). The message of danger, and consequently mutual avoidance, resulting from non-prescribed patterns of interethnic contact is conveyed to both Tarahumara (who make and attend the ceremonies) and mestizos (who know about the rituals but attend only sporadically). As supernormal stimuli meant to communicate spacing between Tarahumara and *chabochi,* there are the effigy's exaggerated "grasping" arms and hands as well as its oversized phallus, all of which suggests threat and aggression.

Phallic displays may themselves be boundary markers: "In vervet monkeys, baboons and others, some males sit at the periphery of the group 'on guard': with their backs to the group they display their genitals, which are often conspicuously colored. This display is addressed to members of other groups and serves to aid in spacing" (Eibl-Eibesfeldt 1972:306). Furthermore, it is noted "that guards, scaredevils, and gargoyles in very different cultures are shown in phallic display. We find such figures in Europe, Japan, Africa, New Guinea, Polynesia, Indonesia, and ancient South America, to mention just a few examples. . . . These similarities indicate that a perceptual structure, probably of subhuman primate origin, guides man, when he produces such guards" (Eibl-Eibesfeldt 1972:307). These data suggest that the Tarahumara may also be constructing the phallic display of Judas as an aggressive territorial signal meant to communicate distance between themselves and the mestizos.

Interethnic conflict—typified by the stereotyped ridicule of non-Indians—is also a feature of public ritual among the Tzotzil and Tzeltal. In the ceremonies of the Indians of the Chiapas highlands, as among the Tarahumara, non-Indians are often parodied in ritual as being sexually licentious, cruel, and conspicuous consumers of great wealth. The ritual burlesque of *ladinos* is evidenced in many forms and in many ceremonies in the Chiapas highlands—here I can mention only a few of them.

During Easter Week, the Tzeltal of Amatenango construct an effigy representing Judas. Like his Tarahumara counterpart, the Judas of Amatenango is unequivocally identified as a non-Indian and thus is dressed as a *ladino* (Nash 1968:320). The similarities with the Tarahumara ritual are striking: "The Judas figure, which was the church's symbol of the hated semite, is subverted by the Indians to appear as their enemy, the Ladino. In the acts in which he figures he symbolizes the sexual license of Ladinos with Indian women, the oppression of Indians, and the killer of Christ. In retaliation, the Indians symbolically castrate and hang him, and finally burn his body, thus dramatically vanquishing the alien in their midst" (Nash 1968:321).

Among the Tzotzil, an important form of ethnic criticism is manifested in the role of ritual actors known as *j'ik'aletik,* or Blackmen, who are prominent ritual entertainers during the festival of Carnival. As among the Tarahumara, the passion of Christ has been reinterpreted in terms of contemporary ethnic conflict, such that the purported "enemies" of Christ become the enemies of the Indians. Thus, in addition to symbolizing demons and Jews, the Blackmen also represent *ladinos*. In Zinacantán, an indefinite number of young men act as Blackmen by dressing as *ladinos* (Vogt 1970b:87). The Blackmen also recite *bombas*, short humorous verses often with sexual overtones, that caricature Indian perceptions of *ladinos* and, significantly, are sung in Spanish, the language of non-Indians (Bricker 1973a:68-83). Finally, it is decided that the Blackmen must be jailed for their "crimes," and though they are pursued by Zinacanteco policemen, they escape—fighting their way through the crowds—until they are recaptured. Bricker theorizes that this struggle between men dressed as *ladinos* and men dressed as Indians actually represents the historical battles between these ethnic groups in the Caste War of 1867-1870 (1973a:82).

In Chenalhó the *ladinos* are portrayed by six Blackmen, four of whom impersonate dogs. Among the many myths told in the neighboring community of Chalchihuitán (Levi 1988) is the story of how *ladinos* originated from the union of two white dogs, who copulated in public in order to show the first Indians how they were to reproduce. Indians attribute certain animal-like qualities to non-Indians, among these viciousness and promiscuity. Thus, "the dog impersonations of the Blackmen of Chenalhó serve two purposes. On the one hand they symbolize uncontrolled sexuality; on the other hand, they dramatize the cruelty of Ladinos, who hunt down their enemies with bloodhounds" (Bricker 1973a:162).

Another set of ritual actors who ridicule *ladinos* are the *jkaxlanetik* (Spanish Gentlemen) and *jxinulanetik* (Spanish Ladies), dressed as Indian interpretations of colonial Spaniards, who perform during the festival of San Sebastián in Zinacantán. During one episode, two Spanish Ladies pretend to comb lice out of a woman's hair, while the musicians tease them in song about their "whoring" activities. "The Spanish Lady's preoccupation with finding lice in the hair of Indian women satirizes the commonly held ladino belief that Indians are slovenly, dirty, and inattentive to matters of personal health; the 'fastidious' Spanish Ladies are portrayed not only as vain and self-important but also—another common Zinacantecan conception—as promiscuous" (Vogt 1976:169). Likewise, the Spanish Gentleman parodies the behavior of *ladino* men. For example, "When the Spanish Gentleman brags of his wealth, he mentions cattle and ranches rather than the cornfields valued by Indians" (Bricker 1973a:164).

Given the interdigitation of Indian and non-Indian populations in the Chiapas highlands and the Sierra Tarahumara, our model leads us to expect that isolating mechanisms ethnically differentiating these populations would be present in the public rituals of these two regions. The Tarahumara and Tzeltal portrayal of Judas and the Tzotzil depiction of Blackmen, Spanish Ladies, and Spanish Gentlemen supports the predictions. In both regions, non-Indians are ritually criticized for their unrestrained sexual, political, and financial appetites. The obvious intent of this caricature is to negatively sanction interethnic marriage and limit interaction to prescribed modes of behavior.

Another important mechanism of ethnic boundary maintenance involving public ritual in the Chiapas highlands is the *cargo* system—the politico-religious hierarchies in which Indian men assume sponsorship for costly fiestas in exchange for prestige (Cancian 1965). Because wealth is channelled into traditional fiestas rather than being invested in the *ladino* world, the *cargo* system functions to promote community integration in the Indian township, while at the same time insulating it from the *ladino* sphere. Thus, at least for men, participation in the *cargo* system is an important means for defining one's membership and relative position in an Indian community in the Chiapas highlands.

However, among the Tarahumara, fiesta sponsorship does not result in the complex politico-religious hierarchies or convert into prestige in the same ways as the *cargo* systems in the Chiapas highlands. Although the Tarahumara do have ranked civil-religious offices, the organization appears to be structurally simpler and in general less competitive than the relatively more baroque *cargo* systems of the Tzotzil and Tzeltal. Broadly speaking, this difference is in concert with the fact that Tarahumara culture is ideally egalitarian, whereas the Tzotzil and Tzeltal evidence more social stratification. Moreover, it does not really seem to define ethnic boundaries, since I have recorded cases of mestizos assuming sponsorship of Tarahumara religious festivals.

According to our ecological model, patterns of conflict should vary with group size, consumer density, and level of internal differentiation. Since the potential for conflict frequently increases exponentially as group size increases, the size of groups is often limited by conflict thresholds (Hayden 1981:360-374). To the extent that stratification implies increased control of subordinates, larger aggregates may become economical where dominance hierarchies tend to structure or otherwise mediate the probable outcomes of conflicts. Given the different levels of consumer density among the Tarahumara, on the one hand, and the Tzotzil and Tzeltal, on the other, it is therefore expected that complex politico-religious hierarchies would be relatively more pronounced in the Chiapas highlands than in the Sierra Tarahumara.

CONCLUSION

Employing a behavioral ecological framework that has utilized arguments based on ecological analogy, habitat adaptation, and intergroup processes, I have outlined an ecological model of ethnic differentiation and applied it to the Sierra Tarahumara and the Chiapas highlands. The model predicts that if different niches are allocated to a population, the development of distinct adaptive strategies will yield resulting populations associated with each niche. These populations are expected to be ethnically differentiated. This differentiation will be reinforced by ethological barriers, known as premating isolating mechanisms, that inhibit random interbreeding between the populations, heighten ethnic visibility, and regulate interaction. Increasing levels of population density and/or competition will select for greater precision in isolating mechanisms; that is, it will heighten the distinctiveness of the signals of ethnic differentiation.

The information on adaptive strategies, clothing styles, and public ritual in the Sierra Tarahumara and the Chiapas highlands supports this model. These data suggest that there has taken place significant niche diversification between Indians and non-Indians, with Indians occupying more marginal niches in both regions. But whereas additional niche diversification has occurred among the Tzotzil-Tzeltal townships, reflected in the distinctiveness of each township's costume and economic specialization, competitive exclusion has not reached this level among the Tarahumara, as is shown by the use of a costume that is comparatively uniform throughout the entire region and the absence of a regional marketing system associated with community specializations. As a premating isolating mechanism, public ritual among the Tarahumara, as well as among the Indians of the Chiapas highlands, has emphasized the aggressiveness, hypersexuality, and acquisitiveness of non-Indians. Spatial organization, textile complexity, and politico-religious hierarchies were also predicted by the model, given the different levels of consumer density in the two regions.

Moreover, this paper has built upon at least two of Evon Vogt's enduring contributions to anthropology. First, the discussion of ethnic differentiation in the Chiapas highlands and the Sierra Tarahumara has extended the range of comparative ethnographic research—the comparative study of American Indian cultures being a research program that Vogt has stressed in his studies over the past forty years (Vogt n.d.). Second, this essay has applied selection theory to Vogt's (1964d) notion of adaptive radiation. But whereas he explained how groups diverged culturally from a proto-stock as they dispersed from a central area and occupied new ecological niches, I have sought to analyze how populations within a circumscribed area are differentiated relative to resource competition and density dependent factors.

Of course, in southern Mexico, "the highlands of Chiapas would appear to have great research potentiality as a region for eventually untangling the processes of change that have taken place in the differentiation of the varieties of local communities from a proto-stock" (Vogt 1969a:143). However, northwest Mexico is also an especially rich region for the researcher interested in the processes differentiating related indigenous ethnic groups. Here I have only discussed the Tarahumara, but the bases (ecological and otherwise) for similarities and differences among other groups—such as the Cora and Huichol (Nahmad Sitton 1981; Vogt 1955c), the Yaqui and Mayo (Crumrine 1981; Spicer 1969), the Southern Tepehuan and Tepecano (Riley 1969), and the Yuman-speaking groups of northern Baja California (Levi 1978; Owen 1969)—still provide much fertile terrain for future research.

ACKNOWLEDGMENTS. I would like to express my gratitude to the Department of Anthropology, Harvard University, for supporting my research among the Tzotzil in San Pablo Chalchihuitán, Chiapas (1978-1979), and to the Teschemacher Fund, the Tinker Foundation, the ITT International Fellowship

Program—Institute for International Education, and the Fulbright-Hays Doctoral Dissertation Research Abroad Program for supporting my fieldwork among the Tarahumara in the barrancas surrounding Batopilas, Chihuahua (1985, 1986, 1988-1989). I would also like to thank Evon Z. Vogt for his insights and assistance during both of these field projects. I am also indebted to Robert W. Levi, without whose word processor this essay would never have been brought to completion.

CUMULATIVE BIBLIOGRAPHY OF EVON ZARTMAN VOGT, JR.

Vogt, Evon Z.

1922   El Morro National Monument. *El Palacio* 12:161-168

1924   The Ice Caves and Vagaries of Volcanoes. *El Palacio* 16:35-39.

1925   Inscriptions at El Morro. *El Palacio* 18:194.

1926   Inscription Rock (with Charles Fletcher Lummis). *El Palacio* 21:232-237.

1927   El Morro National Monument. *El Palacio* 23:46.

1947   Social Stratification in the Rural Middlewest: A Structural Analysis. *Rural Sociology* 12(4):364-375.

1949   Between Two Worlds: A Case Study of a Navaho Veteran. *American Indian* 5(1):13-21.

1949   Town and Country: The Structure of Rural Life. In *Democracy in Jonesville: A Study in Equality and Inequality,* edited by W. Lloyd Warner, pp. 236-265. Harpers and Brothers, New York.

1949   Navaho and Zuni Veterans: A Study of Contrasting Modes of Culture Change (with John Adair). *American Anthropologist* 51(4):547-561.

1950   Review of *The Stars in Our Heavens* by Peter Lum and *Starlore among the Navaho* by Berard Haile. *Journal of American Folklore* 63(248):254-255.

1950   Review of *The Desert People: A Study of the Papago Indians* by Alice Joseph, Rosamond Spicer, and Jane Chesky. *Journal of American Folklore* 63(250):488-489.

1951   Comments on Hatt's review of *Democracy in Jonesville: A Study in Equality and Inequality. American Sociological Review* 16(1):194-195.

1951   *Navaho Veterans: A Study of Changing Values.* Peabody Museum Papers 41(1). Harvard University, Cambridge.

1951   *Navaho Means People* (with Leonard McCombe and Clyde Kluckhohn). Harvard University Press, Cambridge.

1952   Water-Witching: An Interpretation of a Ritual Pattern in a Rural American Community. *Scientific Monthly* 75(3):175-186.

1953   Review of *New Mexico: A Pageant of Three Peoples* by Erna Fergusson. *The American Indian* 6(4):39-40.

1953   A Comparative Study of the Role of Values in Social Action in Two Southwestern Communities (with Thomas F. O'Dea). *American Sociological Review* 18(6):645-654.

1953   Review of *Innovation: The Basis of Cultural Change* by H.G. Barnett. *American Anthropologist* 55(5):721-722.

1954   Review of *Notes and Queries on Anthropology,* 6th ed., edited by Committee of the Royal Anthropological Institute, London. *American Anthropologist* 56(6):1154-1156.

1954   Methods for Collecting and Processing Ethnological Data. Review of papers in *Anthropology Today,* edited by A.L. Kroeber, Sol Tax, Loren C. Eiseley, Irving Rouse, and Carl F. Voegelin. *American Anthropologist* 56(3):483-487.

1954 Review of *Class, Status, and Power: A Reader in Social Stratification,* edited by Reinhard Bendix and Seymour Martin Lipset. *American Anthropologist* 56(6):1147-1149.

1954 Acculturation: An Exploratory Formulation (with L. Broom, B.J. Siegel, and J.B. Watson). *American Anthropologist* 56(6):973-1002.

1955 The Son of Many Beads, 1866-1954 (with Clyde Kluckhohn). *American Anthropologist* 57(5):1036-1037.

1955 Review of *Shadows in the Sun* by Chad Oliver. *American Anthroplogist* 57(5):1109-1110.

1955 Review of *America's Resources of Specialized Talent: A Current Appraisal and a Look Ahead* by Dael Wolfle. *American Anthropologist* 57(5):1106-1107.

1955 A Study of the Southwestern Fiesta System as Exemplified by the Laguna Fiesta. *American Anthropologist* 57(4):820-839.

1955 *Modern Homesteaders: The Life of a Twentieth Century Frontier Community.* Belknap Press of Harvard, University Press, Cambridge.

1955 American Subcultural Continua as Exemplified by the Mormons and Texans. *American Anthropologist* 57(6):1163-1172.

1955 Some Aspects of Cora-Huichol Acculturation. *América Indígena* 15(4):249-263.

1955 Anthropology in the Public Consciousness. In *Yearbook of Anthropology-1955,* edited by William L. Thomas, Jr., pp. 357-374. Wenner-Gren Foundation for Anthropological Research, New York.

1956 An Appraisal of Prehistoric Settlement Patterns in the New World. In *Prehistoric Settlement Patterns in the New World,* edited by Gordon R. Willey, pp. 173-182. Viking Fund Publications in Anthropology 23.

1956 Interviewing Water Dowsers. *American Journal of Sociology* 62:198.

1956 Review of *America's Concentration Camps: The Facts About Our Indian Reservations Today* by Carlos K. Embry. *American Sociological Review* 21(5):665-666.

1956 Review of *Sociocultural and Psychological Processes of Menomini Acculturation* by George D. Spindler. *American Anthropologist* 58(2):390-392.

1956 A Study of Values (with John M. Roberts). *Scientific American* 195(1):24-31.

1957 Review of *Some Uses of Anthropology: Theoretical and Applied,* edited by Joseph B. Casagrande and Thomas Gladwin. *American Sociological Review* 20(2):266-267.

1957 Review of *Acculturation: Critical Abstracts, North America,* edited by Bernard J. Siegel. *Ethnohistory* 4:105-109.

1957 Review of *The Pollen Path: A Collection of Navaho Myths* by

Margaret Schevill Link. *American Anthropologist* 59(2):386-388.

1957 The Acculturation of the American Indians. *Annals of the American Academy of Political and Social Science* 311:137-146.

1957 A Comparative Study of the Role of Values in Social Action in Two Southwestern Communities (with Thomas F. O'Dea). 1953 article reprinted in *Religion, Society, and the Individual,* edited by J. Milton Yinger, pp. 563-577. MacMillan, New York.

1958 Diversas formas de aculturación de los indígenas norteamericanos. *Boletín indigenista* 18(1):42-48.

1958 Some Facts and Theories on Water Witching in the United States (with Ray Hyman). *GeoTimes* 2(9):6-15.

1958 Rabdomancia, o advinación de aguas, en los Estados Unidos (with Ray Hyman). Reprinted from *Notas y Communicaciones* del Instituto Geológico y Minero de España 51.

1958 *Middle American Anthropology, A Special Symposium of the American Anthropological Association* (edited with Gordon R. Willey and Angel Palerm). Social Science Monographs 5. Pan American Union, Washington, D.C.

1958 Review of *Beautyway: A Navaho Ceremonial* by Leland C. Wyman. *The Personalist* 39(4):439-440.

1958 Review of *Indian Shakers: A Messianic Cult of the Pacific Northwest* by H.G. Barnett. *American Sociological Review* 23(3):346-347.

1958 Review of *Mushrooms, Russia, and History* by Valentina Pavlovna Wasson and R. Gordon Wasson. *American Antiquity* 24(1):85-86.

1958 Review of *Primitive Man as Philosopher* and *Primitive Religion* by Paul Radin. *American Anthropologist* 60(5):947-949.

1958 *Reader in Comparative Religion: An Anthropological Approach* (edited with William A. Lessa). Row, Peterson, Evanston, Illinois.

1958 Some Aspects of Water Witching in the United States (with Peggy Golde). *Journal of American Folklore* 71(282):519-531.

1959 The Truth about Dowsing. *Yankee* 23(9):38-41, 102-108.

1959 *Water Witching U.S.A.* (with Ray Hyman). University of Chicago Press, Chicago.

1960 The Automobile in Contemporary Navaho Culture. In *Men and Cultures: Selected Papers of the Fifth International Congress of Anthropological and Ethnological Sciences,* pp. 359-363. University of Pennsylvania Press, Philadelphia.

1960 Review of *Chamula: un pueblo indio de los altos de Chiapas* by Ricardo Pozas A. *American Anthropologist* 62(4):707-708.

1960 On the Concepts of Structure and Process in Cultural Anthropology. *American Anthropologist* 62(1):18-33.

1961 Clyde Kay Maben Kluckhohn (1905-1960). In *Biographical Memoirs, American Philosophical Society Year Book,* pp. 133-137. George H. Buchanan, Philadelphia.

1961 Some Aspects of Zinacantán Settlement Patterns and Ceremonial

Organization. *Estudios de Cultura Maya* 1:131-145.

1961 Review of *Basic Values of Western Civilization* by Shepard B. Clough. *Science* 132(3443):1883.

1961 Review of *Now We Are Civilized* by Charles M. Leslie. *Journal of American Folklore* 74(292):172-173.

1961 Review of *The Virgin's Children: Life in an Aztec Village Today* by William Madsen. *Science* 134(3471):43.

1961 Navaho. In *Perspectives in American Indian Culture Change*, edited by Edward H. Spicer, pp. 278-336. University of Chicago Press, Chicago.

1962 Clyde Kay Maben Kluckhohn, 1905-1960 (with Talcott Parsons). *American Anthropologist* 64(1):140-161.

1962 A Biographical Introduction (with Talcott Parsons). Obituary article on Clyde Kluckhohn. In *Navaho Witchcraft,* by Clyde Kluckhohn, pp. ix-xx. Beacon Press, Boston.

1962 Review of *Perils of the Soul: The World View of a Tzotzil Indian* by Calixta Guiteras Holmes. *American Anthropologist* 64(4):649-651.

1962 Review of *Indians of North America* by Harold E. Driver. *American Anthropologist* 64(5):1109-1111.

1963 Courses of Regional Scope. In *The Teaching of Anthropology*, edited by David G. Mandelbaum, Gabriel W. Lasker, and Ethel M. Albert, pp. 183-190. American Anthropological Association Memoir 94.

1964 Ancient Maya Concepts in Contemporary Zinacantán Religion. *VIe Congres International des Sciences Anthropologiques et Ethnologiques* 2(2):497-502.

1964 Some Implications of Zinacantán Social Structure for the Study of the Ancient Maya. *Actas y Memorias del XXXV Congreso Internacional de Americanistas* 1:307-319.

1964 *Desarrollo cultural de los Mayas* (edited with Alberto Ruz L.). Universidad Nacional Autónoma de México, México, D.F..

1964 The Genetic Model and Maya Cultural Development. In *Desarrollo cultural de los Mayas*, edited by Evon Z. Vogt and Alberto Ruz L., pp. 9-48. Universidad Nacional Autónoma de México, México, D.F.

1964 Summary and Appraisal. In *Desarrollo cultural de los Mayas*, edited by Evon Z. Vogt and Alberto Ruz L., pp. 385-403. Universidad Nacional Autónoma de México, México, D.F.

1964 Cosmología maya antigua y tzotzil contemporánea: Comentario sobre algunos problemas metodológicos. *América Indígena* 24(3):211-219.

1964 Ancient Maya and Contemporary Tzotzil Cosmology: A Comment on Some Methodological Problems. *American Antiquity* 30(2):192-195.

1965 *Reader in Comparative Religion: An Anthropological Approach* (edited with William A. Lessa). 2nd ed. Harper and Row, New York.

1965 Ceremonial Organization in Zinacantán. *Ethnology* 4(1):39-52.

1965 Structural and Conceptual Replication in Zinacantán Culture. *American Anthropologist* 67(2):342-353.

1965 Zinacanteco 'Souls.' *Man* 29:33-35.

1965 Foreword to *Economics and Prestige in a Maya Community: The Religious Cargo System in Zinacantán* by Frank Cancian, pp. vii-ix. Stanford University Press, Stanford.

1965 Review of *Medicina maya en los altos de Chiapas: un estudio del cambio sociocultural* by William R. Holland. *American Anthropologist* 67(2):524-526.

1965 Review of *Other Cultures* by John Beattie. *American Anthropologist* 67(2):554-555.

1966 Ancestor Worship in Zinacantán Religion. *Actas y Memorias del XXXVI Congreso Internacional de Americanistas* 3:281-285.

1966 *The People of Rimrock: A Study of Values in Five Cultures* (edited with Ethel M. Albert). Harvard University Press, Cambridge.

1966 The "Comparative Study of Values in Five Cultures" Project (with Ethel M. Albert). In *The People of Rimrock: A Study of Values in Five Cultures*, edited by Evon Z. Vogt and Ethel M. Albert, pp. 1-33. Harvard University Press, Cambridge.

1966 H'iloletik: The Organization and Function of Shamanism in Zinacantán. In *Summa antropológica en homenaje a Roberto J. Weitlaner*, edited by Antonio Pompa y Pompa, pp. 359-369. Instituto Nacional de Antropología e Historia.

1966 Some Implications of Weather Modification for the Cultural Patterns of Tribal Societies. In *Human Dimensions of Weather Modification*, edited by W.R. Derrick Sewell, pp. 373-392. University of Chicago Department of Geography Series, Paper 105.

1966 (editor) *Los zinacantecos: un pueblo tzotzil de los altos de Chiapas*. Instituto Nacional Indigenista, Colección de Antropología Social 7. México, D.F.

1966 Algunos aspectos de patrones de poblamiento y de la organización ceremonial de Zinacantán. In *Los zinacantecos: un pueblo tzotzil de los altos de Chiapas,* edited by Evon Z. Vogt, pp. 63-87. Instituto Nacional Indigenista, Colección de Antropología Social 7. México, D.F.

1966 Algunas implicaciones de la estructura social de Zinacantán en el estudio de los antiguos mayas. In *Los zinacantecos: un pueblo tzotzil de los altos de Chiapas,* edited by Evon Z. Vogt, pp. 97-112. Instituto Nacional Indigenista, Colección de Antropología Social 7. México, D.F.

1966 Conceptos de los antiguos mayas en la religión contemporánea. In *Los zinacantecos: un pueblo tzotzil de los altos de Chiapas,* edited by Evon Z. Vogt, pp. 88-96. Instituto Nacional Indigenista, Colección de Antropología Social 7. México, D.F.

1967 Tendencia del cambio cultural en las tierras altas de Chiapas. *América Indígena* 27(2):199-222.

1967 Water Witching: Magical Ritual in Contemporary United States (with Ray Hyman). *Psychology Today* 1(1):34-42.

1968 Culture Change. *Encyclopedia of the Social Sciencs* 3:554-558.

1968   Penny Capitalists or Tribal Ritualists?—The Relationship of Market Behavior to Ceremonial Life in a Modern Maya Community. *Proceedings, VIII International Congress of Anthropological and Ethnological Sciences* 2:243-244.

1968   People of the Bat Country. *Harvard Alumni Bulletin* 70:12-25.

1968   Recurrent and Directional Processes in Zinacantán. *Actas y Memorias del XXXVII Congreso Internacional de Americanistas* 1:441-447.

1968   Cosmología maya antigua y tzotzil contemporánea: Comentario sobre algunos problemas metodológicas. 1964 article reprinted in *Nicaragua Indígena* 46:31-41.

1969   (editor) *Handbook of Middle American Indians,* vols. 7-8. Robert Wauchope, general editor. University of Texas Press, Austin.

1969   Introduction. In *Ethnology, part 1,* edited by Evon Z. Vogt, pp. 3-17. Handbook of Middle American Indians, vol. 7, Robert Wauchope, general editor. University of Texas Press, Austin.

1969   The Maya: Introduction. In *Ethnology, part 1,* edited by Evon Z. Vogt, pp. 21-29. Handbook of Middle American Indians, vol. 7, Robert Wauchope, general editor. University of Texas Press, Austin.

1969   Chiapas Highlands. In *Ethnology, part 1,* edited by Evon Z. Vogt, pp. 133-151. Handbook of Middle American Indians, vol. 7, Robert Wauchope, general editor. University of Texas Press, Austin.

1969   Review of *Tiempo y realidad en el pensamiento Maya* by Miguel León-Portilla. *Anales de Antropología* 6:282-286.

1969   *Zinacantán: A Maya Community in the Highlands of Chiapas.* Belknap Press of Harvard, University Press, Cambridge.

1969   The Urban American Dowser (with Linda K. Barrett). *Journal of American Folklore* 82(325):195-213.

1970   Human Souls and Animal Spirits in Zinacantán. In *Echanges et communications, mèlanges offerts á Claude Lévi-Strauss á l'occasion de son 60ème anniversaire,* edited by Pierre Maranda and Jean Pouillon, pp. 1148-1167. Mouton, The Hague.

1970   *The Zinacantecos of Mexico: A Modern Maya Way of Life.* Holt, Rinehart, and Winston, New York.

1970   Social Integration and the Classic Maya: Some Problems in Haviland's Argument (with Frank Cancian). *American Antiquity* 35(1):101-102.

1970   Lévi-Strauss among the Maya (with Catherine Vogt). *Man* 5(3):379-392.

1970   *The People of Rimrock: A Study of Values in Five Cultures* (edited with Ethel M. Albert). 1966 book reprinted. Atheneum, New York.

1971   *Desarrollo cultural de los Mayas* (edited with Alberto Ruz L.). Rev. ed. Universidad Nacional Autónoma de México, México, D.F.

1971   The Use of Aerial Photographic Techniques in Maya Ethnography (with A. Kimball Romney). *Papers of the VII Congres International des*

Sciences Anthropologiques et Ethnologiques 11:156-171.

1971 Review of *Oxchuc: una tribu Maya de México* by Henning Siverts. *American Anthropologist* 73(3):336-338.

1972 *Reader in Comparative Religion: An Anthropological Approach* (edited with William A. Lessa). 3rd. ed. rev. Harper and Row, New York.

1972 Algunos aspectos de aculturación cora-huichol (translated by Corine Joseph de Hernandez). In *Coras, Huicholes, y Tepehuanes*, edited by Thomas B. Hinton, pp. 119-126. Instituto Nacional Indigenista, México, D.F.

1973 *Culture and Life: Essays in Memory of Clyde Kluckhohn* (edited with Walter W. Taylor and John L. Fischer). Southern Illinois University Press, Carbondale.

1973 Clyde Kluckhohn as Ethnographer and Student of Navaho Ceremonialism (with Louise Lamphere). In *Culture and Life: Essays in Memory of Clyde Kluckhohn*, edited by Walter W. Taylor, John L. Fischer, and Evon Z. Vogt, pp. 94-135. Southern Illinois University Press, Carbondale.

1973 Gods and Politics in Zinacantán and Chamula. *Ethnology* 12(2):99-114.

1973 Introduction to *Unknown Mexico* by Carl Lumholtz, pp.vii-x. Reprinted. A.M.S. Press,New York.

1973 *Los Zinacantecos: un grupo maya en el siglo XX* [Translation of *The Zinacantecos of Mexico: A Modern Way of Life*]. Sep Setentas 69. Secretaría de Educación Pública, México, D.F.

1974 (editor) *Aerial Photography in Anthropological Field Research*. Harvard University Press, Cambridge.

1974 Aerial Photography in Highland Chiapas Ethnography. In *Aerial Photography in Anthropological Field Research*, edited by Evon Z. Vogt, pp. 57-77. Harvard University Press, Cambridge.

1974 Zinacanteco Divination. In *Homenaje a Gonzalo Aguirre Beltrán*, vol. 2., edited by Gonzalo Rubio Orbe and Roberto Bravo Garzón, pp. 195-208. Instituto Indigenista Interamericano, México, D.F.

1975 El simbolismo en las ceremonias de curación en Zinacantán (with Suzanne Abel). *Plural* 4(9):36-41.

1975 Alfred Marston Tozzer and Maya Social Anthropology. In *The Maya and Their Neighbors*, edited by Gordon R. Willey with Jeremy A. Sabloff, Frank P. Saul, and Evon Z. Vogt, pp. 22-33. Peabaody Museum, Harvard University, Cambridge.

1976 Rituals of Reversal as a Means of Rewiring Social Structure. In *The Realm of the Extra-Human: Ideas and Actions*, edited by Agehananda Bharati, pp. 201-211. Mouton, The Hague.

1976 *Tortillas for the Gods: A Symbolic Analysis of Zinacanteco Rituals*. Harvard University Press, Cambridge.

1977 On Political Rituals in Contemporary Mexico (with Suzanne Abel). In *Secular Ritual*, edited by Sally F. Moore and Barbara G. Myerhoff, pp.

173-188. Royal Van Gorcum Press, Amsterdam.

1977   On the Symbolic Meaning of Percussion in Zinacanteco Ritual. *Journal of Anthropological Research* 33(3):231-244.

1978   Town (Cabecera) Planning in the Chiapas Highlands. In *Codex Wauchope: A Tribute Roll,* edited by Marco Giardino, Barbara Edmonson, and Winifred Creamer, pp. 65-72. Human Mosaic, vol. 12. Tulane University, New Orleans.

1978   *Bibliography of the Harvard Chiapas Project: The First Twenty Years 1957-1977.* Peabody Museum, Harvard University, Cambridge.

1979   *Reader in Comparative Religion: An Anthropological Approach* (edited with William A. Lessa and with the assistence of John M. Watanabe). 4th ed. Harper and Row, New York.

1979   The Harvard Chiapas Project: 1957-1975. In *Long-Term Field Research in Social Anthropology,* edited by George M. Foster, Thayer Scudder, Elizabeth Colson, and Robert V. Kemper, pp. 279-303. Academic Press, New York.

1979   *Ofrendas para los dioses,* [Translation of *Tortillas for the Gods*]. Fondo de Cultura Económica, México, D.F.

1980   Pre-Columbian Mayan and Mexican Symbols in Zinacanteco Ritual (with Catherine C. Vogt). In *La Antropología Americanista en la Actualidad,* Homenaje a Raphael Girard, vol. 1, pp. 499-524. Editores Mexicanos Unidos, México, D.F.

1981   Some Aspects of the Sacred Geography of Highland Chiapas. In *Mesoamerican Sites and World-Views,* edited by Elizabeth B. Benson, pp. 119-142. Dumbarton Oaks, Washington, D.C.

1982   Tendencias de cambio social y cultural en los altos de Chiapas. *América Indígena* 42(1):85-98.

1982   Forward to *Compadrazgo en Apas* by Elena Uribe Wood. *Investigaciones Sociales* 11:5-7.

1983   *Prehistoric Settlement Patterns: Essays in Honor of Gordon R. Willey* (edited with Richard M. Leventhal). University of New Mexico Press, Albuquerque.

1983   Ancient and Contemporary Maya Settlement Patterns: A New Look from the Chiapas Highlands. In *Prehistoric Settlement Patterns: Essays in Honor of Gordon R. Willey,* edited by Evon Z. Vogt and Richard M. Leventhal, pp. 89-114. University of New Mexico Press, Albuquerque.

1983   Some New Themes in Settlement Pattern Research. In *Prehistoric Settlement Patterns: Essays in Honor of Gordon R. Willey,* edited by Evon Z. Vogt and Richard M. Leventhal, pp. 3-20. University of New Mexico Press, Albuquerque.

1983   Review of *Margaret Mead and Samoa: The Making and Unmaking of an Anthropological Myth* by Derek Freeman. *Boston Globe,* Sunday, April 10, 1983, pp. A10-A11.

1985   The Chiapas Writer's Cooperative. *Cultural Survival Quarterly* 9(3):46-48.

1985   Cardinal Directions and Ceremonial Circuits in Mayan and South-western Cosmology. *National Geographic Society Research Reports* 21:487-496.

1986   How the Yucatec Survived the Spanish Conquest. Review of *Maya Society Under Colonial Rule: The Collective Enterprise of Survival* by Nancy M. Farriss. *Reviews in Anthropology* 13(1):37-45.

1987   Comment on *History, Phylogeny, and Evolution in Polynesia* by Patrick V. Kirch and Roger C. Green. *Current Anthropology* 28(4):431-456.

1988   Some Contours of Class in a Southern Mexican Town (with Cynthia McVay). *Ethnology* 27(1):27-44.

1988   Staffs of Office as Symbols of Authority among the Maya. *Bulgarian Folklore* 14(2):30-40.

1989   Review of *Power and Persuasion: Fiestas and Social Control in Rural Mexico* by Stanley Brandes. *American Anthropologist* 91.

n.d.   Cardinal Directions in Mayan and Southwestern Indian Cosmology. *Homenaje for Alfonso Villa Rojas.* Universidad Autónoma de Chiapas, México.

n.d.   On the Application of the Phylogenetic Model to the Maya. In *The Social Anthropology and Ethnohistory of American Tribes: Essays in Honor of Fred Eggan.* Festchrift for Fred Eggan, edited by Raymond J. DeMallie and Alfonso Ortiz. University of Oklahoma Press, Norman.

n.d.   Indian Crosses and Scepters: The Results of Circumscribed Spanish-Indian Interactions in Mesoamerica. In *Word and Deed: Interethnic Images and Responses in the New World,* edited by Manuel Gutiérrez Estévez. Universidad Complutense, Madrid.

REFERENCES CITED

Abruzzi, William S.
  1982 Ecological Theory and Ethnic Differentiation among Human Populations. *Current Anthropology* 23:13-21.
Agar, Michael H., and Jerry Hobbs
  1985 How to Grow Schemas out of Interviews. In *Directions in Cognitive Anthropology,* edited by Janet W.D. Dougherty, pp. 413-431. University of Illinois Press, Urbana.
Alpers, Svetlana
  1983 *The Art of Describing: Dutch Art in the Seventeenth Century.* University of Chicago Press, Chicago.
Als, Heidi, Edward Tronick, Laurie Adamson, and T. Berry Brazelton
  1976 The Behavior of the Full-Term Yet Underweight Newborn Infant. *Developmental Medicine and Child Neurology* 18:590-602.
Anschuetz, Mary
  1966 To be Born in Zinacantán. MS on file, Harvard Chiapas Project, Department of Anthropology, Harvard University, Cambridge.
Antonovsky, Aaron
  1987 *Unraveling the Mystery of Health: How People Manage Stress and Stay Well.* Jossey-Bass, San Francisco.
Ardrey, Robert
  1966 *The Territorial Imperative: A Personal Inquiry into the Animal Origins of Property and Nations.* Atheneum, New York.
Barkun, Michael
  1968 *Law without Sanctions.* Yale University Press, New Haven.
Barrera Rubio, Alfredo
  1979 Las pinturas murales del área Maya del Norte. In *Enciclopedia Yucatanese,* vol. 10, pp. 189-222. Gobierno de Yucatán, Mérida.
Barth, Fredrick
  1956 Ecological Relationships of Ethnic Groups in Swat, North Pakistan. *American Anthropologist* 58:1079-1089.
Barth, Fredrick (editor)
  1969 *Ethnic Groups and Boundaries: The Social Organization of Culture Difference.* Little, Brown, Boston.
Baum, Richard
  1983 Chinese Science after Mao. *The Wilson Quarterly* 7(2):156-167.
Bayley, Nancy
  1961 *Bayley Scales of Mental and Motor Development: Collaborative Perinatal Research Project.* National Institute of Neurological Diseases and Blindness, Bethesda, Maryland.
Bazant, J.
  1971 *The Alienation of Church Wealth in Mexico.* Cambridge University Press, Cambridge.

REFERENCES CITED

Beaugrande, Robert de
   1980   *Text, Discourse, and Process: Toward a Multidisciplinary Science of Texts.* Ablex Publishing, Norwood, New Jersey.
Bell, Clive
   1913   *Art.* Frederick A. Stokes, New York.
Bennett, Wendell C., and Robert M. Zingg
   1935   *The Tarahumara: An Indian Tribe of Northern Mexico.* University of Chicago Press, Chicago.
Blanco, Marida H., and Nancy J. Chodorow
   1964   Children's Work and Obedience in Zinacantán. MS on file, Harvard Chiapas Project, Department of Anthropology, Harvard University, Cambridge.
Blom, Frans F.
   1956   Vida precortesiana de indio chiapaneco de hoy, In *Estudios antropológicos publicados en homenaje al Doctor Manuel Gamio,* pp. 277-285. Universidad Nacional Autónoma de México, México, D.F.
Bolles, John S.
   1977   *Las Monjas: A Major Pre-Mexican Complex at Chichén Itzá.* University of Oklahoma Press, Norman.
Bornstein, Marc, and Marian Sigman
   1984   Continuity in Mental Development from Infancy. *Child Development* 57:251-274.
Brazelton, T. Berry
   1972   Implications of Infant Development among the Mayan Indians of Mexico. *Human Development* 15:90-111
   1973   *Neonatal Behavioral Assessment Scale.* Clinics in Developmental Medicine 5. Lippincott, Philadelphia.
   1984   *Neonatal Behavioral Assessment Scale.* Rev. ed. Clinics in Developmental Medicine 88. Spastics International Medical Publications, London
Brazelton, T. Berry, Barbara Kosiowaki, and Edward Tronick
   1976   Neonatal Behavior among Urban Zambians and Americans. *Journal of Child Psychiatry* 15:97-107.
Brazelton, T. Berry, John S. Robey, and George Collier
   1969   Infant Development in the Zinacanteco Indians of Southern Mexico. *Pediatrics* 44:274-283.
Brazelton, T. Berry, John S. Robey, and Mary Scholl
   1966   Visual Responses in the Newborn. *Pediatrics* 37:289-290.
Breton, Adela C.
   1917   Preliminary Study of the North Building (Chamber C), Great Ball Court, Chichén Itzá, Yucatán. In *19th International Congress of Americanists (1915),* pp. 187-194. Washington, D.C.
Bricker, Victoria R.
   1973a   *Ritual Humor in Highland Chiapas.* University of Texas Press, Austin.
   1973b   Three Genres of Tzotzil Insult. In *Meaning in Mayan Languages,*

edited by Munro S. Edmonson, pp. 183-203. Mouton Press, The Hague.

1981   *The Indian Christ, the Indian King: The Historical Substrate of Maya Myth and Ritual*. University of Texas Press, Austin

Bunzel, Ruth

1952   *Chichicastenango: A Guatemalan Village*. Publications of the American Ethnological Society 12. J.S. Augustin, Locust Valley, New York.

Burguess, Robert L., Jeffrey Kurland, and Emily E. Pensky

1988   Ultimate and Proximate Determinants of Child Maltreatment: Natural Selection, Ecological Instability, and Coercive Interpersonal Contingences. In *Sociobiological Perspectives on Human Development*, edited by K.B. MacDonald, pp. 293-319. Springer-Verlag, New York.

Caldeyro-Barcia, R.

1979   The Influence of Maternal Position on Time Spontaneus Rupture of the Membranes, Progress of Labor, and Fetal Head Compression. *Birth and Family Journal* 6:7-15.

Cancian, Francesca M.

1963   *Family Interaction in Zinacantán*. Unpublished Ph.D. dissertation, Harvard University, Cambridge.

1964   Interaction Patterns in Zinacanteco Families. *American Sociological Review* 29:540-550.

1971a   Affection and Dominance in Cambridge and Zinacanteco Families. *Journal of Marriage and the Family* 33:207-213.

1971b   New Methods for Describing What People Think. *Sociological Inquiry* 41:85-93.

Cancian, Frank

1965   *Economics and Prestige in a Maya Community: The Religious Cargo System in Zinacantán*. Stanford University Press, Stanford.

1972   *Change and Uncertainty in a Peasant Economy: The Maya Corn Farmers of Zinacantán*. Stanford University Press, Stanford.

1974   New Patterns of Stratification in the Zinacantán Cargo System. *Journal of Anthropological Research* 30:164-173.

1983   Changing Patterns of Social Stratification in Zinacantán. MS in author's possession. University of California, Irvine.

1985   The Zinacanteco Cargo Waiting Lists as Reflection of Social, Political, and Economic Changes, 1952-1980. MS on file, Harvard Chiapas Project, Department of Anthropology, Harvard University, Cambridge.

1987   Proletarianization in Zinacantán, 1960-1983. In *Household Economies and Their Transformations*, edited by Morgan D. Maclachlan, pp. 131-142. University Press of America, Lanham, New York.

Carneiro, Robert L.

1973   The Four Faces of Evolution. In *Handbook of Social and Cultural Anthropology*, edited by John J. Honigmann, pp. 89-110. Rand McNally, Chicago.

Cassidy, C.M.

REFERENCES CITED

1980   *Being Neglect and Toddler Malnutrition: Social and Biological Predictors of Nutrituional States, Physical Growth and Neurological Development.* Academic Draper, Patricia and Henry Harpending, New York.

1988   A Sociobiological Perspective on the Development of Human Reproductive Strategies. In *Sociobiological Perspectives on Human Development,* edited by K.B. MacDonald, pp. 340-372. Springer-Verlag, New York.

Castañeda, Jorge G.
1988   The Silver Lining in Mexico's Election. *New York Times,* July 13.

Cecil, Lord D.
1954   *Lord M.* Collins, London.

Chávez, A., C. Martínez, and T. Yashine
1974   The Importance of Nutrition and Stimuli on Child Mental and Social Development. In *Early Malnutrition and Mental Development,* edited by J. Cravioto, L. Hambreus, and B. Vahlquist, pp. 211-225. Almquest and Wiksell, Uppsala, Sweden.

Childs, Carla
1968   Unpublished field notes. Harvard Chiapas Project, Department of Anthropology, Harvard University, Cambridge.

Childs, Carla P., and Patricia M. Greenfield
1980   Informal Modes of Learning and Teaching: The Case of Zinacanteco Weaving. In *Studies in Cross-Cultural Psychology,* vol. 2, edited by Neil Warren, pp. 269-316. Academic Press, London.

Chock, Phyllis P.
1986   The Outsider Wife and the Divided Self: The Geneses of Ethnic Identities. In *Discourse and the Social Life of Meaning,* edited by Phyllis P. Chock and June R. Wyman, pp. 185-204. Smithsonian Institution Press, Washington, D.C.

Clancy, Flora
1980   *A Formal Analysis of the Relief Carved Monuments at Tikal, Guatemala.* Ph.D. dissertation, Yale University. University Microfilms, Ann Arbor.

Coe, Michael D.
1973   *The Maya Scribe and His World.* Golier Club, New York.
1978   *The Lords of the Underworld.* Princeton University Press, Princeton.

Coggins, Clemency C., and Orrin Shane III (editors)
1984   *Cenote of Sacrifice: Maya Treasures from the Sacred Well at Chichén Itzá.* University of Texas Press, Austin.

Cohen, Erik
1976   Environmental Orientations: A Multidimensional Approach to Social Ecology. *Current Anthropology* 17:49-70.

Cohodas, Marvin
1978   *The Great Ball Court at Chichén Itzá, Yucatán, México.* Garland, New York.

Colby, Benjamin N.
   1976   The Anomalous Ixil—Bypassed by the Postclassic? *American Antiquity* 41(1):74-80.
   1985   Towards an Encyclopedic Ethnography for Use in Intelligent Computer Programs. In *Directions in Cognitive Anthropology,* edited by Janet W.D. Dougherty, pp. 269-290. University of Illinois Press, Urbana.
Colby, Benjamin N., and Lore M. Colby
   1981   *The Daykeeper: The Life and Discourse of an Ixil Diviner.* Harvard University Press, Cambridge.
Colby, Benjamin N., and Rodger Knaus
   1974   Men, Grammars, and Machines: A New Direction for the Study of Man. In *On Language, Culture, and Religion: In Honor of Eugene A. Nida,* edited by Matthew Black and William A. Smalley, pp. 187-197. Mouton, The Hague.
Colby, Benjamin N., and Pierre L. van den Berghe
   1961   Ethnic Relations in Southeastern Mexico. *American Anthropologist* 63:772-792.
   1969   *Ixil Country: A Plural Society in the Highlands of Guatemala.* University of California Press, Berkeley.
Cole, Michael, and Jerome S. Bruner
   1971   Cultural Differences and Inferences about Psychological Processes. *American Psychologist* 26:867-876.
Collier, George A.
   1975   *Fields of the Tzotzil: The Ecological Bases of Tradition in Highland Chiapas.* University of Texas Press, Austin.
   1987   Peasant Politics and the Mexican State. *Mexican Studies/ Estudios Mexicanos* 3:71-98.
   n.d.   Culture and History in Highland Chiapas: Zinacantán Reconsidered, 1900-1980. MS in author's possession.
Collier, George A., and Daniel C. Mountjoy
   1987   Adaptándose a la crisis de los ochenta: cambios socio-económicos en Apás, Zinacantán. Doc. 035-II/88, Serie: *Documentos de trabajo sobre cambio en el campo chiapaneco.* Instituto de Asesoría Antropológica para la Región Maya, A.C., San Cristóbal de las Casas.
Collier, Jane F.
   1968   *Courtship and Marriage in Zinacantán, Chiapas, Mexico.* Middle American Research Institute Publication 25. Tulane University, New Orleans.
   1969   Changing Kinship Terminology in a Tzotzil Maya Community. MS in author's possession.
   1973   *Law and Social Change in Zinacantán.* Stanford University Press, Stanford.
   1974   Women in Politics. In *Woman, Culture, and Society,* edited by M.Z. Rosaldo and L. Lamphere, pp 89-96. Stanford University Press, Stanford.
   1975   Legal Processes. *Annual Review of Anthropology* 4:121-144.

REFERENCES CITED

1980   Responsibility for Conflict. Paper presented at the annual meeting of the American Anthropological Association, Washington, D.C.

1988   *Marriage and Inequality in Classless Societies.* Stanford University Press, Stanford.

Comaroff, John L., and Simon Roberts

1981   *Rules and Processes: The Culture of Dispute in an African Context.* University of Chicago, Chicago.

Cordry, Donald, and Dorothy Cordry

1968   *Mexican Indian Costumes.* University of Texas Press, Austin.

Crump, T.

1976   *Boundaries in the Function of Money: Internal and External Debt in Selected Mexican Communities.* Unpublished Ph.D. dissertation, University of London, London.

1981   *The Phenomenon of Money.* Routledge and Kegan Paul, London.

1987   The Alternative Economy of Alcohol in the Chiapas Highlands. In *Constructive Drinking,* edited by Mary Douglas, pp. 239-49. Cambridge University Press, Cambridge.

Crumrine, N. Ross

1981   The Mayo of Southern Sonora: Socio-economic Assimilation and Ritual-Symbolic Syncretism—Split Acculturation. In *Themes of Indigenous Acculturation in Northwest Mexico,* edited by Thomas B. Hinton and Phil C. Weigand, pp. 22-35. University of Arizona Press, Tucson.

Dasen, Pierre R.

1984   The Cross-Cultural Study of Intelligence: Piaget and the Baole. In Changing Conceptions of Intelligence and Intellectual Functioning: Current Theory and Reseach, edited by Prem M. Fry. *International Journal of Psychology* 19:108-134.

Dasen, Pierre R., Dembele Barthelemy, Ettien Kan, Kabran Kouame, Kamagate Daouda, Koffi Kouakou Adjei, and N'guessan Assande.

1985   N'glouele, L'intelligence chez les Baole. *Archives de Psychologie* 53:293-324.

De la Fuente, Julio

1967   Ethnic Relationships. In *Social Anthropology,* edited by Manning Nash, pp. 432-448. Handbook of Middle American Indians, vol. 6, Robert Wauchope, general editor. University of Texas Press, Austin.

Douglas, Mary

1967   Primitive Rationing: A Study in Controlled Exchange. In *Themes in Economic Anthropology,* edited by Mary Douglas, pp. 239-249. Cambridge University Press, Cambridge.

Draper, Patricia, and Henry Harpending

1988   A Sociobiological Perspective on the Development of Human Reproductive Strategies. In *Sociobiological Perspectives on Human Development,* edited by K.B. MacDonald, pp.340-372. Springer-Verlag, New York.

Dumont, Louis

1986   *Essays on Individualism: Modern Ideology in Anthropological Perspective*. University of Chicago Press, Chicago.

Dunne, Peter M.
1948   *Early Jesuit Missions in Tarahumara*. University of California Press, Berkeley.

Durham, William H.
1981   Optimal Foraging Analysis in Human Ecology. In *Hunter-Gatherer Foraging Strategies: Ethnographic and Archaeological Analyses,* edited by Eric A. Smith and Bruce Winterhalder, pp. 218-231. University of Chicago Press, Chicago.

Dyson-Hudson, R., and E.A. Smith
1978   Human Territoriality: An Ecological Reassessment. *American Anthropologist* 8:21-41.

Edmonson, Munro S.
1976   The Mayan Calendar Reform of 11.16.0.0.0. *Current Anthropology* 17:713-717

Eggan, Frederick R.
1954   Social Anthropology and the Method of Controlled Comparison. *American Anthropologist* 56:743-763.

Eggan, Frederick R. (editor)
1955   *Social Anthropology of North American Tribes*. University of Chicago Press, Chicago.

Eibl-Eibesfeldt, I.
1972   Similarities and Differences Between Cultures in Expressive Movements. In *Non-Verbal Communication,* edited by Robert A. Hinde, pp. 297-314. Cambridge University Press, Cambridge.

Engel, David M.
1984   The Oven-Bird's Song: Insiders, Outsiders and Personal Injuries in an American Community. *Law and Society Review* 18:549.
1987   Law, Time, and Community. *Law and Society Review* 21(4):605-637.

England, Nora C.
1983   *A Grammar of Mam Mayan Language*. University of Texas Press, Austin.

Erikson, Erik E.
1963   *Childhood and Society*. Norton, New York. Originally published 1950.

Errington, Frederick
1987   Reflexivity Deflected: The Festival of Nations as an American Cultural Performance. *American Ethnologist* 14(4):654-667.

Fernández, James
1972   Persuasions and Performances: Of the Beast in Every Body . . . And the Metaphors of Everyman. *Daedalus* 101:39-60.
1974   The Mission of Metaphor in Expressive Culture. *Current Anthropology* 15(2):119-144.

REFERENCES CITED

Flaceliere, Robert
    1965   *Greek Oracles.* Translated by Douglas Garman. W.W. Norton, New York.
Folan, William J.
    1968   El Chichan Chob y la Casta del Venado, Chichén Itzá, Yucatán. *Instituto Nacional de Antropología e Historia Anales* 19:49-61.
Fontenrose, Joseph E.
    1978   *The Delphic Oracle: Its Responses and Operations with a Catalogue of Responses.* University of California Press, Berkeley.
Foster, George M.
    1944   Nagualism in Mexico and Guatemala. *Acta Americana* 2:85-103.
Freed, Stanley A., Ruth S. Freed, and Laila Williamson
    1988   Capitalism, Philanthropy, and Russian Revolutionaries: The Jesup North Pacific Expedition (1897-1902). *American Anthropologist* 90(1):7-24.
Freedman, Daniel G.
    1979   Ethnic Differences in Babies. *Human Nature* 2:36-43.
Freedman, Daniel G., and Nina Freedman
    1969   Behavioral Differences Between Chinese-American and European-American Newborns. *Nature* 224:1127.
Freidel, David A.
    1986   Terminal Classic Lowland Maya: Successes, Failures and Aftermaths. In *Late Lowland Maya Civilization: Classic to Postclassic,* edited by Jeremy A. Sabloff and E. Wyllys Andrews V, pp. 409-432. University of New Mexico Press, Albuquerque.
Freidel, David A., and Linda Schele
    1985   Knot-Skull the Shining Seed: Death, Rebirth, and Heroic Amplification in the Lowland Maya Ballgame. Paper presented at the International Symposium on the Mesoamerican Ballgame and Ballcourts, Tucson.
Freud, Sigmund
    1905   Three Essays on the Theory of Sexuality. In *The Standard Edition of the Complete Psychological Works of Sigmund Freud,* vol. 7, edited and translated by J. Strachey, pp 125-245. Hogarth Press, London.
    1949   *An Outline of Psychoanalysis.* Translated by J. Strachey. Norton, New York. Originally published 1940.
Fried, Jacob
    1969   The Tarahumara. In *Ethnology, part 2,* edited by Evon Z. Vogt, pp 846-870. Handbook of Middle American Indians, vol. 8, Robert Wauchope, general editor. University of Texas Press, Austin.
Friedlander, Judith
    1975   *Being Indian in Hueyapán: A Study in Forced Identity in Contemporary Mexico.* St. Martins Press, New York.
Fry, Roger E.
    1920   *Vision and Design.* Chatto and Windus, London.
Geertz, Clifford

1963   *Agricultural Involution: The Process of Ecological Change in Indonesia.* University of California Press, Berkeley.

Giddens, Anthony
1979   *Central Problems in Social Theory.* Macmillan, London.

Gillin, John
1948   Magical Fright. *Psychiatry* 11:387-400.
1951   *The Culture of Security in San Carlos: A Study of a Guatemalan Community of Indians and Ladinos.* Middle American Research Institute Publication 16. Tulane University, New Orleans.

Goldschmidt, Walter
1959   *Man's Way: A Preface to the Understanding of Society.* Holt, Rinehart, and Winston, New York.

Goody, J.
1986   *The Logic of Writing and the Organization of Society.* Cambridge University Press, Cambridge.

Gorer, Geoffrey
1964   *The American People: A Study in National Character.* Rev. ed. W.W. Norton and Company, New York.

Gossen, Gary H.
1974   *Chamulas in the World of the Sun: Time and Space in a Maya Oral Tradition.* Harvard University Press, Cambridge.
1975   Animal Souls and Human Destiny in Chamula. *Man* 10(3):448-461.
1979   *Los Chamulas en el mundo del sol: tiempo y espacio en una tradición oral maya.* Instituto Nacional Indigenista, Colección de Antropología Social 58. México, D.F.

Graham, Ian S.
1979   *Corpus of Maya Hierogliphic Inscriptions, vol. 3, part 2: Yaxchilán.* Peabody Museum of Archaeology and Ethnology, Harvard University, Cambridge
1982   *Corpus of Maya Hieroglyphic Inscriptions, vol. 3, part 3: Yaxchilán.* Peabody Museum of Archaeology and Ethnology, Harvard University, Cambridge.

Graham Ian S., and Eric von Euw
1977   *Corpus of Maya Hieroglyphic Inscriptions, vol. 3, part 1: Yaxchilán.* Peabody Museum of Archaeology and Ethnology, Harvard University, Cambridge.

Greenfield, Patricia M.
1966   On Culture and Conservation. In *Studies in Cognitive Growth,* edited by Jerome S. Bruner, Rose R. Olver, Patricia M. Greenfield, et al., pp. 225-256. Wiley, New York.
1972a   Oral or Written Language: The Consequences for Cognitive Development in Africa, the United States, and England. *Language and Speech* 15:169-178.
1972b   Studies in Mother-Infant Interaction: Towards a Structural-Functional Approach. *Human Development* 15:131-138.

340

REFERENCES CITED

1974   Comparing Dimensional Categorization in Natural and Artificial Contexts: A Developmental Study among the Zinacantecos of Mexico. *Journal of Social Psychology* 93:157-171.

1983   Ontogenesis, Use, and Representation of Cultural Categories: A Pyschological Perspective. In *The Sociogenesis of Language and Human Conduct,* edited by Bruce Bain, pp. 109-130. Plenum, New York.

1984   A Theory of the Teacher in the Learning Activities of Everyday Life. In *Everyday Cognition: Its Development in Social Context,* edited by Barbara Rogoff and Jean Lave, pp. 117-138. Harvard University Press, Cambridge.

Greenfield, Patricia M., and Jerome S. Bruner

1969   Culture and Cognitive Growth. In *Handbook of Socialization Theory,* edited by David Goslin, pp. 653-657. Rand McNally, Chicago.

Greenfield, Patricia M., and Carla Childs

1977   Weaving, Color Terms, and Pattern Representation: Cultural Influences and Cognitive Development among the Zinacantecos of Southern Mexico. *Interamerican Journal of Psychology* 11:23-48.

1978   Understanding Sibling Concepts: A Developmental Study of Kin Terms in Zinacantán. In *Piagetian Psychology: Cross-Cultural Contributions,* edited by Pierre Dasen, pp. 337-358. Gardner Press, New York.

Greenfield, Patricia M., and Jean Lave

1982   Cognitive Aspects of Informal Education. In *Cultural Perspectives on Child Development,* edited by Daniel Wagner and Harold Stevenson, pp. 181-207. Freeman, San Francisco.

Greenfield, Patricia M., Lee Reich, and Rose R. Olver

1966   On Culture and Equivalence-II. In *Studies in Cognitive Growth,* edited by Jerome S. Bruner, Rose R. Olver, Patricia M. Greenfield, et al., pp. 270-318. Wiley, New York.

Greenhouse, Carol J.

1986   *Praying for Justice: Faith, Order, and Community in an American Town.* Cornell University Press, Ithaca.

1988   Courting Difference: Issues of Comparison and Interpretation in the Ideology of Law. *Law and Society Review* 22(4):687-707.

Groenewegen-Frankfort, Henrietta

1972   *Arrest and Movement.* Hacker Art Books, New York.

Guiteras Holmes, Calixta

1961   *Perils of the Soul: The World View of a Tzotzil Indian.* Free Press, Glencoe, Illinois.

1974   *Los Peligros del Alma.* Fondo de Cultura Económica. México, D.F.

Harkness, Sara, and Charles Super

1982   The Development of Affect in Infancy and Early Childhood. In *Cultural Perspectives on Child Development,* edited by Daniel Wagner and Harold Stevenson, pp. 1-19. Freeman, San Francisco.

Harpending, Henry, and Herbert Davis

1977   Some Implications for Hunter-Gatherer Ecology Derived from the

Spatial Structure of Resources. *World Archeology* 8:275-283.
Haviland, John Beard
1977   *Gossip, Reputation, and Knowledge in Zinacantán.* University of Chicago Press, Chicago.
Haviland, Leslie K.M.
1978   *The Social Relations of Work in a Peasant Community.* Unpublished Ph.D. dissertation, Harvard University, Cambridge.
Haviland, Susan E., and Eve V. Clark
1974   "This Man's Father is My Father's Son": A Study of the Acquisition of English Kin Terms. *Journal of Child Language* 1:23-47.
Hawkins, John
1984   *Inverse Images: The Meaning of Culture, Ethnicity, and Family in Postcolonial Guatemala.* University of New Mexico Press, Alburquerque.
Hayden, B.
1981   Subsistence and Ecological Adaptations of Modern Hunter-Gatherers. In *Omnivorous Primates: Gathering and Hunting in Human Evolution,* edited by Robert S.O. Harding and Geza Teleki, pp. 344-421. Columbia University Press, New York.
Herzfeld, Michael
1986   Of Definitions and Boundaries: The Status of Culture in the Culture of the State. In *Discourse and the Social Life of Meaning,* edited by Phyllis Pease Chock and June R. Wyman, pp. 75-93. Smithsonian Institution Press, Washington, D.C.
Hewitt de Alcántara, Cynthia
1984   *Anthropological Perspectives on Rural Mexico.* Routledge and Kegan Paul, London.
Hinz, Eike
1979   *Analyse aztekischer Gedankensysteme. Wahrsageglaube und Erziehungsnormen als Alltagstheorie sozialen Handelns. Auf Grund des 4. und 6. Buches der "Historia general" Fray Bernardino de Sahagúns aus der Mitte des 16. Jahrhunderts.* Acta Humboldtiana, series Geographica et Ethnographica 6. Franz Steiner Verlag GMBH, Weisbaden.
Hirschfeld, Lawrence A.
n.d.   Rethinking the Acquisition of Kin Terms. *International Journal of Behavioral Development,* in press.
Hobsbawm, Eric
1983   Mass-Producing Traditions: Europe, 1870-1914. In *The Invention of Tradition,* edited by Eric Hobsbawm and Terence Ranger, pp. 263-307. Cambridge University Press, Cambridge.
Holland, William R.
1961   El tonalismo y nagualismo entre los indios tzotziles de Larráinzar, Chiapas, México. *Estudios de Cultura Maya* 1:167-181.
1978   *Medicina maya en los altos de Chiapas: un estudio del cambio sociocultural.* Instituto Nacional Indigenista, Colección de Antropología

REFERENCES CITED

Social 2. México, D.F.

Hunn, Eugene S.
1977 *Tzeltal Folk Zoology: The Classification of Discontinuities in Nature.* Academic Press, New York.

Hutchins, Edwin
1980 *Culture and Inference: A Trobriand Case Study.* Harvard University Press, Cambridge.

James, Mark, and Benjamin N. Colby
1979 *Discourse Research System Instruction Manual.* School of Social Sciences, Scientiarum Ancillae 1. University of California, Irvine.

Jones, Christopher
1977 Inauguration Dates of Three Late Classic Rulers of Tikal, Guatemala. *American Antiquity* 42(1):28-60

Kampen, Michael E.
1972 *The Sculptures of El Tajin.* University of Florida Press, Gainesville.

Kaye, Kenneth
1977 Infants' Effects upon Their Mothers' Teaching Strategies. In *The Social Context of Learning and Development,* edited by J. Glidewell, pp. 173-206. Gardner Press, New York.

Keffer, C.S., S. Dixen, Edward Tronick, and T. Berry Brazelton.
1982 Specific Differences in Motor Perfomance Between Gusii and American Newborns and a Modification of the Neonatal Behavioural Assessment Scale. *Child Development* 53:754-759

Keil, Charles
1966 *Urban Blues.* University of Chicago Press, Chicago.

Kennedy, John G.
1963 Tesguino Complex: The Role of Beer in Tarahumara Culture. *American Anthropologist* 65:620-640.
1978 *Tarahumara of the Sierra Madre: Beer, Ecology, and Social Organization.* AMH Publishing, Arlington Heights, Illinois.

Kennedy, John G., and Raul A. Lopez
1981 *Semana Santa in the Sierra Tarahumara: A Comparative Study in Three Communities.* Occasional Papers of the Museum of Cultural History, University of California, Los Angeles.

Knobloch, H., B. Pasamanick, and E.S. Sherard
1966 A Developmental Screening Inventory for Infants. *Pediatric Supplement* 38:1095-1099.

Kokot, Waltraud
1982 *Perceived Control and the Origins of Misfortune: A Case Study in Cognitive Anthropology.* Dietrich Reimer Verlag, Berlin.

Krebs, John R., and Richard Dawkins
1984 Animal Signals: Mind-reading and Manipulation. In *Behavioural Ecology: An Evolutionay Approach,* edited by J.R. Krebs and N.B. Davies, pp. 380-402. Blackwell Scientific Publication, Oxford.

Lappe, Francis Moore

1971 *Diet for a Small Planet.* Ballantine Books, New York.

Laughlin, Robert M.

1969 The Tzotzil. In *Ethnology, part 1,* edited by Evon Z. Vogt, pp. 152-194. Handbook of Middle American Indians, vol. 7, Robert Wauchope, general editor. University of Texas Press, Austin.

1975 *The Great Tzotzil Dictionary of San Lorenzo Zinacantán.* Smithsonian Contributions to Anthropology 19. Smithsonian Institution Press, Washington, D.C.

1976 *Of Wonders Wild and New: Dreams from Zinacantán.* Smithsonian Contributions to Anthropology 22. Smithsonian Institution Press, Washington, D.C.

1977 *Of Cabbages and Kings: Tales from Zinacantán.* Smithsonian Contributions to Anthropology 23. Smithsonian Institution Press, Washington, D.C.

1980 *Of Shoes and Ships and Sealing Wax: Sundries from Zinacantán.* Smithsonian Contributions to Anthropology 25. Smithsonian Institution Press, Washington, D.C.

Lazarus, R.S., and S. Folkman

1984 *Stress, Appraisal, and Coping.* Springer, New York.

Leach, Edmund R.

1954 *Political Systems of Highland Burma: A Study of Kachin Social Structure.* London School of Economics and Political Science, London.

1961 *Pul Eliya: A Study of and Tenure and Kinship.* Cambridge University Press, Cambridge.

Lee, Richard B.

1979 *The Ikung San: Men, Women, and Work in a Foraging Society.* Cambridge University Press, Cambridge.

Lessa, W.A., and E.Z. Vogt (editors)

1958 *Reader in Comparative Religion: An Anthropological Approach.* Row, Peterson, Evanston, Ilinois.

Lester, Barry M., and T. Berry Brazelton

1982 Cross-Cultural Assessment of Neonatal Behavior. In *Cultural Perpective on Child Development,* edited by Daniel Wagner and Harold Stevenson, pp. 20-53. Freeman, San Francisco.

Levi, Jerome M.

1978 Wii'ipay: The Living Rocks—Ethnographic Notes on Crystal Magic among Some California Yumans. *Journal of California Anthropology* 5:42-52.

1987 The Social Ecology of Spacing Behaviour among the Tarahumara Indian of Northwest Mexico: A Preliminary Model of the Functions of Dispersal. MS on file, Department of Anthropology, Harvard University, Cambridge.

1988 Myth and History Reconsidered: Archaeological Implications of Tzotzil-Maya Mythology. *American Antiquity* 53(3):605-619.

LeVine, Robert

REFERENCES CITED

    1977   Child Rearing as Cultural Adaptation. In *Culture and Infancy: Variations in the Human Experience,* edited by P. Leiderman, S. Tulkin, and A. Rosenfeld, pp. 15-28. Academic Press, New York.

Lincoln, Charles
    1986   The Chronology of Chichén Itzá: A Review of the Literature. In *Late Lowland Maya Civilization: Classic to Postclassic,* edited by Jeremy A. Sabloff and E. Wyllys Andrews V, pp. 141-196. University of New Mexico Press, Albuquerque.

Linn, Priscilla Rachun
    1970-1972   Unpublished field notes. Harvard Chiapas Project, Department of Anthropology, Harvard University, Cambridge.
    1975   Unpublished field notes. Harvard Chiapas Project, Department of Anthropology, Harvard University, Cambridge.
    1976   *The Religious Office Holders in Chamula: A Study of Gods, Rituals, and Sacrifice.* 2 vols. Unpublished Ph.D. dissertation, University of Oxford, England.
    1982   Chamula Carnival: The "Soul" of Celebration. In *Celebration: Studies in Festivity and Ritual,* edited by Victor Turner, pp. 190-198. Smithsonian Institution Press, Washington, D.C.

Littleton, C. Scott
    1986   The Pneuma Enthusiastikon: On the Possibility of Hallucinogenic "Vapors" at Delphi and Dodona. *Ethos* 14(1):76-91.

Lizardi Ramos, Cesar
    1936   Los Secretos de Chichén Itzá. *Excelsior,* December 21, Mexico City.
    1937 New Discoveries of Maya Culture at Chichén Itzá. *Illustrated London News,* July 3, London.

Llewellyn, Karl, and E.A. Hoebel
    1941   *The Cheyenne Way.* University of Oklahoma Press, Norman.

Lothrop, Samuel K.
    1952   *Metals from the Cenote of Sacrifice, Chichén Itzá, Yucatán.* Peabody Museum Memoir 10(2). Harvard University, Cambridge.

Lowie, Robert
    1920   *Primitive Society.* Boni and Liveright, New York.

Lubchenco, L.O.
    1970   Assessment of Gestational Age and Development at Birth. *Pediatric Clinics of North America* 17:125-145.

Lumholtz, Carl S.
    1902   *Unknown Mexico.* 2 vols. Charles Scribner's Sons, New York.

Lynd, Robert S., and Helen Merrell Lynd
    1929   *Middletown: A Study in Modern American Culture.* Harcourt, Brace, and World, New York.

Mahler, M.S., F. Pine, and A. Bergman
    1975   *The Psychological Birth of the Human Infant: Symbiosis and Individuation.* Basic Books, New York.

Maldonado, Juan, Juan Ordoñez, and Juan Ortiz

REFERENCES CITED

1986   *Diccionario Mam de San Ildefonso Ixtahuacán, Mam-español.*
Proyecto Lingüístico Francisco Marroquín, Antigua, Guatemala.

Marcus, George E., and Michael M.J. Fischer
1986   *Anthropology as Cultural Critique: An Experimental Moment in the Human Sciences.* University of Chicago Press, Chicago.

Marcus, Joyce
1976   *Emblem and State in the Classic Maya Lowlands: An Epigraphic Approach to Territorial Organization.* Dumbarton Oaks, Washington, D.C.

Marquina, Ignacio
1951   *Arquitectura prehispánica.* Instituto Nacional de Antropología e Historia Memorias 1. México, D.F.

Mathews. Peter
1980   Notes of the Dynastic Sequence of Bonampak, part I. In *Third Palenque Round Table, 1978, part 2,* edited by Merle Greene Robertson, pp. 60-73. Universty of Texas Press, Austin.

Maudslay, Alfred P.
1889-1902   Archaeology. In *Biologia Centrali-Americana.* 5 vols. R.H. Porter and Dulau, London.

Mauss, M.
1954   *The Gift.* Translated by I. Cunnison. Cohen and West, London.

Mayr, Ernst
1963   *Animal Species and Evolution.* Belknap Press of Harvard, University Press, Cambridge.
1970   *Population Species: Evolution An Abridgement of Animal Species and Evolution.* Belknap Press of Harvard, University Press, Cambridge.

McLuhan, H. Marshall
1964   *Understanding Media: The Extensions of Man.* McGraw-Hill, New York.

Mead, Margaret
1943   *And Keep Your Powder Dry: An Anthropologist Looks at America.* William Morrow, New York.

Meillassoux, Claude
1972   From Reproduction to Production: A Marxist Approach to Economic Anthropology. *Economy and Society* 1(1):93-105.

Merrill, William L.
1978   Thinking and Drinking: A Raramuri Interpretation. In *The Nature and Status of Ethnobotany,* edited by Richard I. Ford, pp. 101-117. Museum of Anthropology, Anthropological Papers 67. University of Michigan, Ann Arbor.
1983a   God's Saviours in the Sierra Madre. *Natural History* 92:58-67.
1983b   Tarahumara Social Organization, Political Organization, and Religion. In *Southwest,* edited by Alfonso Ortiz, pp. 290-305. Handbook of North American Indians, vol. 10, William C. Sturtevant, general editor. Smithsonian Institution, Washington, D.C.

REFERENCES CITED

Metzger, Duane, and Gerald Williams
1963a   Tenejapa Medicine. I: The Curer. *Southwestern Journal of Anthropology* 19:216-234.
1963b   *Procedures and Results in the Study of Native Categories: Tzeltal Firewood.* Anthropology Research Projects 12. Stanford University Press, Stanford.

Miller, Frank C.
1965   Cultural Change as Decision-Making: A Tzotzil Example. *Ethnology* 4:53-65.

Miller, Virginia G.
1984   *Izapa Relief Carving: Form, Content, Rules for Design, and Role in Mesoamerican Art History and Archeology.* Studies in Pre-Columbian Art and Archeology 27. Dumbarton Oaks, Washington, D.C.
1985   Eclectism in the Northern Maya Lowlands. Paper presented at the 74th annual meeting of the College Art Association, Los Angeles.

Miyamoto, John
1969   Cognitive Equivalence in Zinacantán: A Developmental Study. Unpublished honors thesis, Harvard University. MS on file, Harvard Chiapas Project, Department of Anthropology, Harvard University, Cambridge.

Moffatt, Michael
1986   The Discourse of the Dorm: Race, Friendship, and 'Culture' among College Youth. In *Symbolizing America,* edited by Herve Varenne, pp. 159-177. University of Nebraska Press, Lincoln.

Moore, Sally Falk
1986   *Social Facts and Fabrications: "Customary" Law on Kilimanjaro, 1880-1980.* Cambridge University Press, Cambridge.

Morris, Earl, Jean Charlot, and Ann Morris
1931   *The Temple of the Warriors at Chichén Itzá, Yucatán.* 2 vols. Carnegie Institution of Washington Publication 406. Washington, D.C.

Mueller, Edward C., and Deborah Cohen
1986   Peer Therapies and the Little Latency: A Clinical Perspective. In *Process and Outcome in Peer Relations,* edited by E.C. Muller and C.R. Cooper, pp. 161-183. Academic Press, New York.

Mullings, Leith (editor)
1987   *Cities of the United States.* Columbia University Press, New York.

Nahmad Sitton, Salomon
1981   Some Considerations of the Indirect and Controlled Acculturation in the Cora-Huichol Area. In *Themes of Indigenous Acculturation in Northwest Mexico,* edited by Thomas B. Hinton and Phil C. Weigand, pp. 4-8. University of Arizona Press, Tucson.

Nash, June
1964   The Structuring of Social Relations: An Activity Analysis. *Estudios de Cultura Maya* 4:335-359.
1968   The Passion Play in Maya Indian Communities. *Comparative Studies in Society and History* 10:318-327.

1970   *In the Eyes of the Ancestors: Belief and Behavior in a Mayan Community.* Yale University Press, New Haven.

Nash, Manning
1967a   Indian Economies. In *Social Anthropology,* edited by Manning Nash, pp. 87-102. Handbook of Middle American Indians, vol. 6, Robert Wauchope, general editor. University of Texas Press, Austin.
1967b   Witchcraft as Social Process in a Tzeltal Community. In *Magic, Witchcraft, and Curing,* edited by John Middleton, pp. 127-133. Natural History Press, Garden City, New York.

Nash, Roderick
1973   *Wilderness and the American Mind.* Rev. ed. Yale University Press, New Haven.

Needham, Joseph
1956   *Science and Civilisation in China.* History of Scientific Thought, vol. 2. Cambridge University Press, Cambridge.

Neville, Gwen Kennedy
1987   *Kinship and Pilgrimage: Rituals of Reunion in American Protestant Culture.* Oxford University Press, New York.

O'Barr, William, and John Conley
1985   Litigant Satisfaction versus Legal Adequacy in Small Claims Court Narratives. *Law and Society Review* 19(4):661-701.

Ochs, Elinor, and Bambi B. Schieffelin
1984   Language Acquisition and Socialization: Three Developmental Stories and Their Implications. In *Culture Theory: Essays on Mind, Self, and Emotion,* edited by Richard Shweder and Robert LeVine, pp. 276-320. Cambridge University Press, Cambridge.

O'Neale, Lila Morris
1945   *Textiles of Highland Guatemala.* Carnegie Institution of Washington Publication 567. Washington, D.C.

Owen, Roger C.
1969   Contemporary Ethnography of Baja California, Mexico. In *Ethnology, part 2,* edited by Evon Z. Vogt, pp. 871-878. Handbook of Middle American Indians, vol. 8, Robert Wauchope, general editor. University of Texas Press, Austin.

Pennington, Cambell W.
1963   *The Tarahumara of Mexico: Their Environment and Material Culture.* University of Utah Press, Salt Lake City.
1983   Tarahumara. In *Southwest,* edited by Alfonso Ortiz, pp. 276-289. Handbook of North American Indians, vol. 10, William C. Sturtevant, general editor. Smithsonian Institution, Washington, D.C.

Perin, Constance
1977   *Everything in Its Place.* Princeton University Press, Princeton.
1986   A Biology of Meaning and Conduct. In *Discourse and the Social Life of Meaning,* edited by Phyllis Pease Chock and June R. Wyman, pp. 95-125. Smithsonian Institution Press, Washington, D.C.

REFERENCES CITED

Piaget, Jean
  1928   *Judgment and Reasoning in the Child.* Harcourt, Brace, New York.
Pitt-Rivers, Julian A.
  1970   Spiritual Power in Central America: The Naguals of Chiapas. In *Witchcraft Accusations and Confessions,* edited by Mary Douglas, pp. 183-206. A.S.A. Monographs 9. Tavistock, London.
Pomerantz, Anita
  1978   Attributions of Responsibility: Blamings. *Sociology* 12:115-121.
Pozas A., Ricardo
  1952   El trabajo en las plantaciones de café y el cambio socio-cultural del indio. *Revista Mexicana de Estudios Antropológicos* 13:31-48.
  1959   *Chamula: un pueblo indio de los altos de Chiapas.* Memorias del Instituto Nacional Indigenista 8, México. Nueva Edición 1977, Colección Clásicos de la antropología mexicana. 2 vols. Instituto Nacional Indigenista, México, D.F.
  1962   *Juan the Chamula: An Ethnological Re-creation of the Life of a Mexican Indian.* Translated by Lysander Kemp. University of California Press, Berkeley.
Price, Richard
  1968   Land Use in a Maya Community. *International Archives of Ethnography* 51:1-19.
  1974   Aerial Photography in the Study of Land Use: A Maya Example. In *Aerial Photography in Anthropological Research,* edited by Evon Z. Vogt, pp. 94-111. Harvard University Press, Cambridge.
Price, Richard, and Sally H. Price
  1965   Preliminary Field Report Muktahok. MS on file, Harvard Chiapas Project, Department of Anthropology, Harvard University, Cambridge.
  1970   Aspects of Social Organization in a Maya Hamlet. *Estudios de Cultura Maya* 8:297-318.
Price, Sally H.
  1966   I Was Pashku and My Husband Was Telesh. *Radcliffe Quarterly* 50:4-8.
Proskouriakoff, Tatiana
  1950   *A Study of Classic Maya Sculpture.* Carnegie Institution of Washington Publication 593. Washington, D.C.
  1970   On Two Inscriptions at Chichén Itzá. In *Monographs and Papers in Maya Archeology,* edited by W. R. Bullard, Jr., pp. 457-467. Papers of the Peabody Museum 61.
Rappaport, Roy A.
  1968   *Pigs for the Ancestors: Ritual in the Ecology of a New Guinea People.* Yale University Press, New Haven.
  1979   Sanctity and Lies in Evolution. In *Ecology, Meaning, and Religion,* pp. 223-246. North Atlantic Books, Berkeley.
Rebelsky, Freda
  1972   First Discussant's Comments: Cross-Cultural Studies of Mother-In-

fant Interaction. *Human Development* 15:128-130.

Redfield, Robert, and Alfonso Villa Rojas
1934   *Chan Kom, a Maya Village.* Carnegie Institution of Washington Publication 448. Washington, D.C.

Reynolds, V.
1966   Open Groups in Hominid Evolution. *Men* 1:441-452.

Rheingold, Harriet L.
1960   The Measurement of Maternal Care. *Child Development* 31:565-570.

Riley, Carroll L.
1969   The Southern Tepehuan and Tepecano. In *Ethnology, part 2,* edited by Evon Z, Vogt, pp. 814-821. Handbook of Middle American Indians, vol. 8, Robert Wauchope, general editor. University of Texas Press, Austin.

Robertson, John S., John P. Hawkins, and Andres Maldonado.
n.d.   *Mam Basic Course.* 2 vols. U.S. Peace Corps, Guatemala.

Robertson, Merle Greene
1986   Some Observations on the X'Tehlu Panels at Yaxcaba, Yucatán. In *Research and Reflections in Archaeology and History,* edited by E. Wyllys Andrews V, pp. 87-111. Tulane University Press, New Orleans.

Robertson, Merle Greene, Edward Kujack, and Ruben Maldonado C.
1985   Ball Courts of the Nothern Maya Lowlands. Paper presented at the International Symposium on the Mesoamerican Ballgame and Ballcourts, Tucson.

Romney, Kimball, and Romaine Romney
1966   *The Mixtecans of Juxtlahuaca, Mexico.* Six Cultures Series, vol. 4, Beatrice B. Whiting, general editor. John Wiley, New York.

Roof, Stephen L.
1980   *Cultural Brokers, Factionalism, and Modernization in Zinacantán.* B.A. thesis, Harvard College.

Rubel, Arthur J., Carl W. O'Nell, and Rolando Collado-Ardon
1984   *Susto, A Folk Illness.* University of California Press, Berkeley.

Ruppert, Karl
1931   *The Temple of the Wall Panels, Chichén Itzá.* Carnegie Institution of Washington Publication 403, Contribution 3. Washington, D.C.
1943   *The Mercado, Chichén Itzá, Yucatán.* Carnegie Institution of Washington Publication 546, Contribution 43. Washington, D.C.

Rus, J., and Wasserstrom, R.
1980   Civil-Religious Hierarchies in Central Chiapas: A Critical Perspective. *American Ethnologist* 7(3):466-478.

Rush, Timothy
1971   *Navenchauk Disputes: The Social Basis of Factions in a Mexican Indian Village.* B.A. thesis, Harvard College.

Russell, J.G.B.
1969   Molding of the Pelvic Outlet. *Obstetrics and Gynecology of the*

REFERENCES CITED

British Commonwealth 76:818-828.

Saler, Benson
   1964   Nagual, Witch, and Sorcerer in a Quiché Village. *Ethnology* 3:305-328.
   1967   Nagual, Witch and Sorcerer in a Quiché Village. In *Magic, Witchcraft, and Curing,* edited by John Middleton, pp. 69-99. Natural History, Garden City, New York.

Satterthwaite, Linton
   1965   Calendrics of the Maya Lowlands. In *Archaeology of Southern Mesoamerica, part 2,* edited by Robert Wauchope and Gordon R. Willey, pp. 603-631. Handbook of Middle American Indians, vol. 3, Robert Wauchope, general editor. University of Texas Press, Austin.

Schama, Simon
   1988   *The Embarrassment of Riches: An Interpretation of Dutch Culture in the Golden Age.* Fontana, London.

Schele, Linda, and Mary Miller
   1986   *The Blood of Kings: Dynasty and Ritual in Maya Art.* George Braziller, New York.

Sheridan, Thomas E., and Thomas H. Naylor (editors)
   1979   *Raramuri: A Tarahumara Colonial Chronicle, 1607-1791.* Northland Press, Flagstaff.

Silver, Daniel B.
   1966   Enfermedad y Curación en Zinancantán: Esquema provisional. In *Los zinacantecos: un pueblo tzotzil de los altos de Chiapas,* edited by Evon Z. Vogt. pp. 455-473. Instituto Nacional Indigenista, Colección de Antropología Social 7. México, D.F.

Simpson, John E.
   1976   The New York Relief Panel—and Some Associations With Reliefs at Palenque and Elsewhere, part 1. In *Segunda Mesa Redonda de Palenque,* edited by Merle Greene Robertson, pp. 95-106. Herald Printers, Monterey, California.

Singer, Milton
   1984   *Man's Glassy Essence: Explorations in Semiotic Anthropology.* University of Indiana Press, Bloomington.

Siverts, Henning
   1969   Ethnic Stability and Boundary Dynamics in Southern Mexico. In *Ethnic Groups and Boundaries: The Social Organization of Culture Difference,* edited by Fredrick Barth, pp.101-116. Little, Brown, Boston.

Smith, Eric A.
   1981   The Application of Optimal Foraging Theory to the Analysis of Hunter-Gatherer Group Size. In *Hunter-Gatherer Foraging Strategies: Ethnographic and Archaeological Analyses,* edited by Eric A. Smith and Bruce Winterholder, pp. 66-98. University of Chicago Press, Chicago.

Spicer, Edward H.
   1962   *Cycles of Conquest: The Impact of Spain, Mexico, and the United*

States on the Indians of the Southwest 1533-1960. University of Arizona Press, Tucson.

1969   The Yaqui and Maya. In *Ethnology, part 2,* edited by Evon Z. Vogt, pp. 830-845. Handbook of Middle American Indians, vol. 8, Robert Wauchope, general editor. University of Texas Press, Austin.

Stern, Theodore

1948   *The Rubber-Ball Games of the Americas.* American Ethnological Society Monograph 17. American Ethnological Society, New York.

Steven, Hugh

1976   *They Dared to be Different.* Harvest House Publishers, Irvine, California.

Steward, Julian H.

1955   *Theory of Culture Change: The Methodology of Multilinear Evolution.* University of Ilinois Press, Urbana.

Strathern, Marilyn

1980   No Nature, No Culture: The Hagen Case. In *Nature, Culture, and Gender,* edited by Carol MacCormack and Marilyn Strathern, pp. 174-222. Cambridge University Press, Cambridge.

Tambiah, Stanley J.

1985   *Culture, Thought, and Social Action.* Harvard University Press, Cambridge.

Tax, Susan

1964   Displacement Activity in Zinacantán. *América Indígena* 24:111-121.

Tedlock, Dennis (translator)

1985   *Popol Vuh: The Definitive Edition of the Mayan Book of the Daan Life and the Glories of Gods and Kings.* Simon and Schuster, New York.

Terray, Emmanuel

1972   Historical Materialism and Segmentary Lineage-Based Societies. In *Marxism and Primitive Societies,* pp. 93-186. Monthly Review Press, New York.

Thoits, Peggy A.

1983   Dimensions of Life Events That Influence Psychological Distress: An Evaluation and Synthesis of the Literature. In *Psychosocial Stress: Trends in Theory and Research,* edited by H.B. Kaplan, pp. 33-103. Academic Press, New York.

Thomas, Cyrus H.

1882   A Study of the Manuscript Troano. *U.S. Department of Interior Contribution to North American Ethnology* 5:1-27. Washington, D.C.

Thomas, Keith

1983   *Man and the Natural World.* Pantheon, New York.

Thompson, J. Eric S.

1937   *A New Method of Deciphering Yucatecan Dates, with Special Reference to Chichén Itzá.* Carnegie Institution of Washington Publication 483, Contribution 22. Washington, D.C.

1970   *Maya History and Religion.* University of Oklahoma Press, Norman.

REFERENCES CITED

1972 *A Commentary on the Dresden Codex: A Maya Hieroglyphic Book.* Memoirs of the American Philosophical Society 93. American Philosophical Society, Philadelphia.

Tocqueville, Alexis de
1945 *Democracy in America.* 2 vols. Revised by Francis Bowen, edited by Phillips Bradley. Vintage, New York.

Tozzer, Alfred M.
1930 Maya and Toltec Figures at Chichén Itzá. In *23rd International Congress of Americanist Proceedings*, pp. 155-164. New York.
1941 *Landa's Relación de las cosas de Yucatán.* Papers of the Peabody Museum of American Archaeology and Ethnology 18. Harvard University Press, Cambridge.
1957 *Chichén Itzá and Its Cenote of Sacrifice.* 2 vols. Peabody Museum Memoirs 11-12. Harvard University Press, Cambridge.

Trosper, Ronald L.
1967 Schools and Schooling in Zinacantán. MS on file, Harvard Chiapas Project, Department of Anthropology, Harvard University, Cambridge.

Turok, Marta
1972 Handicrafts: A Case Study on Weaving in the Highlands. MS on file, Harvard Chiapas Project, Department of Anthropology, Harvard University, Cambridge.

Varenne, Herve
1977 *Americans Together: Structured Diversity in a Midwestern Town.* Teachers College Press, New York.
1986 Drop in Anytime: Community and Authenticity in American Everyday Life. In *Symbolizing America,* edited by Herve Varenne, pp. 209-228. University of Nebraska Press, Lincoln.

Velasco Rivero, Pedro de
1983 *Danzar o morir: religión y resistencia a la dominación en la cultura Tarahumara.* Centro de Reflexión Teológica, México, D.F.

Villacorta C., J.A., J. Antonio, and Carlos A. Villacorta
1976 *Codices Mayas.* 2nd ed. Tip Nacional, Guatemala City.

Villa Rojas, Alfonso
1962 El Centro Coordinador Tzeltal-Tzotzil. In *Los centros coordinadores indigenistas,* pp. 51-68. Edición conmemorativa en ocasión del XXXV Congreso Internacional de Americanistas, Instituto Nacional Indigenista, México, D.F.
1969 The Tzeltzal. In *Ethnology, part 1,* edited by Evon Z. Vogt, pp.195-225. Handbook of Middle American Indians, vol. 7, Robert Wauchope, general editor. University of Texas Press, Austin.

Vogt, Evon Z.
1948 *Navaho Veterans: A Study of Acculturation.* Ph.D. dissertation, University of Chicago.
1951 *Navajo Veterans: A Study of Changing Values.* Peabody Museum Papers 41(1). Harvard University, Cambridge.

1955a *Modern Homesteaders: The Life of a Twentieth Century Frontier Community.* Belknap Press of Harvard, University Press, Cambridge.

1955b American Subcultural Continua as Exemplified by the Mormons and Texans. *American Anthropologist* 57(6):1163-1172.

1955c Some Aspects of Cora-Huichol Acculturation. *América Indígena* 15(4):249-263.

1956 An Appraisal of Prehistoric Settlement Patterns in the New World. In *Prehistoric Settlement Patterns in the New World,* edited by Gordon R. Willey, pp. 173-182. Viking Fund Publications in Anthropology 23.

1961 Some Aspects of Zinacantán Settlement Patterns and Ceremonial Organization. *Estudios de Cultura Maya* 1:131-145.

1964a Ancient Maya Concepts in Contemporary Zinacantán Religion. *VIe Congres International des Sciences Anthropologiques et Ethnologiques* 2(2):497-502.

1964b Cosmología maya antigua y tzotzil contemporánea: Comentario sobre algunos problemas metodológicos. *América Indígena* 24(3):211-219.

1964c Some Implications of Zinacantán Social Structure for the Study of the Ancient Maya. *Actas y Memorias del XXXV Congreso Internacional de Americanistas* 1:307-319.

1964d The Genetic Model and Maya Cultural Development. In *Desarollo cultural de los Mayas,* edited by Evon Z. Vogt and Alberto Ruz L., pp. 9-48. Universidad Nacional Autónoma de México, México, D.F.

1965a Structural and Conceptual Replication in Zinacantán Culture. *American Anthropologist* 67(2):342-353.

1965b Zinacanteco 'Souls.' *Man* 29:33-35

1969a Chiapas Highlands. In *Ethnology, part 1,* edited by Evon Z. Vogt, pp. 133-151. Handbook of Middle American Indians, vol. 7, Robert Wauchope, general editor. University of Texas Press, Austin.

1969b *Zinacantán: A Maya Community in the Highlands of Chiapas.* Belknap Press of Harvard, University Press, Cambridge.

1970a Human Souls and Animal Spirits in Zinancantán. In *Echanges et communications, mèlanges offerts á Claude Lévi-Strauss á l'occasion de son 60ème anniversaire,* edited by Pierre Maranda and Jean Poullon, pp. 1148-1167. Mouton, The Hague.

1970b *The Zinacantecos of Mexico: A Modern Maya Way of Life.* Holt, Rinehart, and Winston, New York.

1973 Introduction to *Unknown Mexico* by Carl Lumhotz. Reprinted. AMS Press, New York. Originally published 1902, Charles Scribner's Sons, New York.

1976 *Tortillas for the Gods: A Symbolic Analysis of Zinancanteco Rituals.* Harvard University Press, Cambridge.

1978 *Bibliography of the Harvard Chiapas Project: The First Twenty Years 1957-1977.* Peabody Museum, Harvard University, Cambridge.

1979 The Harvard Chiapas Project: 1957-1975. In *Long-Term Field Re-*

REFERENCES CITED

search in Social Anthropology, edited by George M. Foster, Thayer Scudder, Elizabeth Colson, and Robert V. Kemper, pp. 279-303. Academic Press, New York.

1983　Ancient and Contemporary Maya Settlement Patterns: A New Look from the Chiapas Highlands. In *Prehistoric Settlement Patterns: Essays in Honor of Gordon R. Willey,* edited by Evon Z. Vogt and Richard M. Leventhal, pp. 89-114. University of New Mexico Press, Alburquerque.

n.d.　On the Application of the Phylogenetic Model to the Maya. In *The Social Anthropology and Ethnohistory of American Tribes: Essays in Honor of Fred Eggan.* Festchrift for Fred Eggan, edited by Raymond J. DeMallie and Alfonso Ortiz. University of Oklahoma Press, Norman. In press.

Vogt, Evon Z., and Ethel M. Albert
1966　*The People of Rimrock: A Study of Values in Five Cultures.* Harvard University Press, Cambridge.

Vogt, Evon Z., and Ray Hyman
1959　*Water Witching U.S.A.* University of Chicago Press, Chicago.

Vogt, Evon Z., and T.F. O'Dea
1953　A Comparative Study of the Role of Values in Social Action in Two Southwestern Communities. *American Sociological Review* 18(6):645-654.

Vogt, Evon Z., and J.M. Roberts
1956　A Study of Values. *Scientific American* 195(1):24-31.

Vogt, Evon Z., and Alberto Ruz L., (editors)
1964　*Desarrollo cultural de los Mayas.* Universidad Nacional Autónoma de México, México, D.F.

1971　*Desarrollo cultural de los Mayas.* Rev. ed. Universidad Nacional Autónoma de México, México, D.F.

Vogt, Evon Z., and Catherine C. Vogt
1970　Lévi-Strauss among the Maya. *Man* 5(3):379-392.

Wagley, Charles
1941　*Economics of a Guatemalan Village.* Memoirs of the American Anthropological Association 58. Menasha, Wisconsin.

1949　*The Social and Religious Life of a Guatemalan Village.* Memoirs of the American Anthropological Association 71. Menasha, Wisconsin.

Wagner, Roy
1981　*The Invention of Culture.* Rev. and expanded ed. University of Chicago Press, Chicago.

Warman, Arturo
1976　*. . . Y Venimos a contradecir.* Ediciones de la Casa Chata, México, D.F.

1980　*We Come to Object.* Translated by Stephen K. Ault. Johns Hopkins University Press, Baltimore.

Warner, W. Lloyd
1949　*Democracy in Jonesville: A Study in Equality and Inequality.* Har-

pers and Brothers, New York.

1959   *The Living and the Dead.* Yale University Press, New Haven.

1962   *American Life: Dream and Reality.* Rev. ed. University of Chicago Press, Chicago.

Warner, W. Lloyd, and P.S. Lunt

1941   *The Social Life of a Modern Community.* The Yankee City Series 1. Yale University Press, New Haven.

Warren, Kay B.

1978   *The Symbolism of Subordination: Indian Identity in a Guatemalan Town.* University of Texas Press, Austin.

Wasserstrom, Robert

1977   Land and Labor in Central Chiapas: A Regional Analysis. *Development and Change* 9:441-463.

1983   *Class and Society in Central Chiapas.* University of California Press, Berkeley.

Watanabe, John M.

1981   Cambios económicos en Santiago, Chimaltenango, Guatemala. *Mesoamérica* 2:20-41.

1984   *"We Who Are Here": The Cultural Conventions of Ethnic Identity in a Guatemalan Indian Village, 1937-1980.* Ph.D. dissertation, Harvard University. University Microfilms, Ann Arbor.

1988   Enduring Yet Ineffable Community in the Western Periphery of Guatemala. Paper presented at the 14th International Congress of the Latin American Studies Association, New Orleans.

Wauchope, Robert (general editor)

1964-1975   *Handbook of Middle American Indians,* vols. 1-15. University of Texas Press, Austin.

Wauchope, Robert, and E.Z. Vogt (editors)

1969   *Handbook of Middle American Indians,* vols. 7-8. Robert Wauchope, general editor. University of Texas Press, Austin.

Werner, Heinz

1948   *Comparative Psychology of Mental Development.* Science Editions, New York.

Werner, Oswald

1978   The Synthetic Informant Model on the Simulation of Large Lexical/Semantic Fields. In *Discourse and Inference in Cognitive Anthropology,* edited by Marvin D. Loflin and James Silverberg, pp. 45-82. Mouton, The Hague.

Wertsch, James, N. Minick, and F. Arns

1984   The Creation of Context in Joint Problem-Solving. In *Everyday Cognition: Its Development in Social Context,* edited by Barbara Rogoff and Jean Lave, pp. 115-171. Harvard Universilty Press, Cambridge.

Whiting, Beatrice B., and Caroline P. Edwards

1988   *Children of Different Worlds: The Formation of Social Behavior.* Harvard University Press, Cambridge.

REFERENCES CITED

Whiting, John W.M., and Irving L. Child
  1953   *Child Training and Personality.* Yale University Press, New Haven.
Wilhelm, Richard (translator)
  1967   *The I Ching or Book of Changes.* Princeton University Press, Princeton.
Willey, Gordon R.
  1956   The Structure of Ancient Maya Society: Evidence from the Southern Lowlands. *American Anthropologist* 58(5):777-782.
  1981   Lowland Maya Settlement Patterns: A Summary Review. In *Lowland Maya Settlement Patterns,* edited by Wendy Ashmore, pp. 385-415. University of New Mexico Press, Albuquerque
Willey, Gordon R. (editor)
  1956   *Prehistoric Settlement Patterns in the New World.* Viking Fund Publications in Anthropology 23.
Wilson, Edward O.
  1980   *Sociobiology: The Abridged Edition.* Belknap Press of Harvard, University Press, Cambridge.
Winter, Irene
  1985   After the Battle is Over: The Stele of the Vultures and the Beginning of Historical Narrative in the Art of the Ancient Near East. *Studies in the History of Art* 16:11-32.
Wober, Mallory
  1974   Towards an Understanding on the Kiganda Concept of Intelligence. In *Culture and Cognition Readings in Cross-Cultural Psychology*, edited by John W. Berry and Pierre R. Dasen, pp. 26-280. Methuen, London.
Wren, Linnéa
  1986   The Great Ball Court Stone. Paper delivered at the Sexta Mesa Redonda de Palenque, Palenque, Chiapas, México.
Wren, Linnéa, and Peter Schmidt
  1986   Elite Interaction during the Terminal Classic Period of the Nothern Maya Lowlands: Evidence from the Reliefs of the North Temple of the Great Ball Court at Chichén Itzá. Paper deliverd at the Advanced Seminar of the School of American Research, Santa Fe.
Wynne-Edwards, V.C.
  1962   *Animal Dispersion in Relation to Social Behaviour.* Oliver and Boyd, Edinburgh.
Yourcenor, M.
  1971   *Denier du Reve.* Gallinard, Paris.
Yngvesson, Barbara
  1988   Making Law at the Doorway: The Clerk, the Court, and the Construction of Order in a New England Town. *Law and Society Review* 22(3):411-448.